The Trial(s) of Psychoanalysis

The
Trial(s)
of
Psychoanalysis

Edited by
Françoise Meltzer

The University of Chicago Press
Chicago and London

Most of the essays in this volume originally appeared in CRITICAL INQUIRY, Winter 1987 (volume 13, number 2).

The University of Chicago Press, Chicago 60637
The University of Chicago Press, Ltd., London
© 1987, 1988 by The University of Chicago
All rights reserved. Published 1988
Printed in the United States of America
95 94 93 92 91 90 89 88   5 4 3 2 1

Library of Congress Cataloging-in-Publication Data

The Trial(s) of psychoanalysis/edited by Françoise Meltzer.

    p.   cm.
    "Most of the essays in this volume originally appeared in Critical inquiry, Winter 1987 (volume 13, number 2)"—T.p. verso.
    Includes bibliographical references and index.
    ISBN 0-226-51969-4 (alk. paper): $25.00 (est.).
    ISBN 0-226-51970-8 (alk. paper): $15.00 (est.)
    1. Psychoanalysis.   2. Freud, Sigmund, 1856–1939.   I. Meltzer,
Françoise.   II. Critical inquiry.   III. Title: Trial(s) of psychoanalysis
BF175.T737 1988
150.19′5—dc19   87-34687
                                                CIP

The paper used in this publication meets the minimum requirements of American National Standard for Information Sciences—Permanence of Paper for Printed Library Materials, ANSI Z39.48-1984.

Cover illustration by James Elkins.

Contents

Introduction: Partitive Plays, Pipe Dreams

Françoise Meltzer

> There is no means of knowing whether the unconscious exists outside of psychoanalysis.
>
> —LACAN

> The use of analysis as a weapon of controversy can clearly lead to no decision.
>
> —FREUD

There is the famous anecdote about Freud: upon being reminded by a disciple that to smoke cigars is clearly a phallic activity, Freud, cigar in hand, is said to have responded, "Sometimes a good cigar is just a good cigar." The anecdote demonstrates, it seems to me, a problematic central to psychoanalysis: the discipline which insists on transference and, perhaps even more significantly, on displacement as fundamental principles, ultimately must insist in turn on seeing everything as being "really" something else. Such an ideology of metamorphosis is so much taken for granted that unlike the rest of the world, which generally has difficulty in being convinced that a pipe, for example, is not necessarily a pipe at all, psychoanalysis needs at times to remind itself, in a type of return to an *adaequatio*, that it is possible for a cigar really to *be* a cigar. Psychoanalysis, in other words, has not only an economy which is hydraulic (mirroring the nineteenth-century physics from which it springs), but has as well an economy of seepage: each apparent object, whether in dream, literature, or psychic narrative, splashes over onto at least one "something else." Not only is there always a remainder, but the remainder generally proliferates, multiplies, from more than one quotient, such that the original "thing" in question becomes merely the agent for production. Its status as thing-in-the-world is easily lost.

Such seepage has, of course, appeared almost everywhere. Psychoanalysis has infiltrated such diverse areas as literature (to which it owes its myths), linguistics, philosophy, anthropology, history, feminism, psychology, archeology, neurology, to name some. And it is in the notion of "some," perhaps, that lies the crux of the problem. For there is in psychoanalysis an overt conviction that it exists as the ultimate totality, of which everything else is a part. Not content to see itself as one in a number of enterprises, the psychoanalytic project has at its foundation a vision of itself as the meaning which will always lie in wait; the truth which lies covered by "the rest." Jacques Derrida has, of course, pointed to this tendency. Psychoanalysis, he noted, wishes a peculiar logic for itself, one in which "the species would include the genus."[1] Moreover, says Derrida in the same essay, once psychoanalysis has discovered itself, what it then again proceeds to discover around it is always itself.[2] What happens, then, is that psychoanalysis becomes a ubiquitous subject, assimilating every object into itself. But it is also a Subject which sees itself as omnipresent, omniscient, and without a center—precisely the terms in which God has been described. It is not then by chance that the unconscious is likened to a divinity: always present but revealing itself only obliquely and at privileged moments, the unconscious takes the place of the Judeo-Christian God. It is within every being, but inaccessible unless it "chooses" to manifest itself. And in a peculiar reversal of the notion of the partitive, psychoanalysis would have the unconscious reveal itself in fleeting moments and fragments, thereby suggesting its fullness and totality; and it would have "other" intellectual enterprises be only apparent totalities which are revealed through psychoanalysis alone to be "really" incomplete because they exist without recognizing the unconscious and its mother, psychoanalysis itself.

Ten years ago, a collection of essays appeared entitled *Literature and Psychoanalysis: The Question of Reading: Otherwise.* In her introduction to this volume, Shoshana Felman articulated an attempt to understand the "and" between these two fields: literature was no longer to play the role of slave to psychoanalysis' master; nor always to be the object to which psychoanalysis was subject.

> In the literary critic's perspective, literature is a subject, not an object; it is therefore not simply a body of knowledge with which

---

1. Jacques Derrida, "Graphesis," "The Purveyor of Truth," trans. Willis Domingo et al., *Yale French Studies* 52 (1975): 32.

2. See the syllogism with which Derrida opens his "Purveyor of Truth," p. 31. Part of what I am calling the "syllogism" appears at the beginning of Stephen Melville's article in the present volume.

to interpret, since psychoanalysis itself is equally a body of language, and literature also a body of knowledge, even though the mode of that knowledge may be different from that of psychoanalysis.[3]

Felman suggested a "real *dialogue*" between literature and psychoanalysis, "as between two different bodies of language and between two different modes of knowledge." That dialogue, she argued, would have to take place outside of the (Hegelian) master-slave dialectic or we would fall back into "a unilateral monologue of psychoanalysis *about* literature." And yet the "dialogue" that Felman ultimately suggests does *not* in fact fall "outside" of the master-slave dialectic: "In an attempt to disrupt this monologic, master-slave structure, we would like to reverse the usual perspective, and to consider the relationship between psychoanalysis and literature *from the literary point of view*." Felman notes that such a reversal does not intend "to simply reverse the positions of master and slave," but rather "to deconstruct the very structure of the *opposition*, mastery/ slavery."[4]

What Felman is running up against here, it seems to me, is once again the totalizing teleology of psychoanalysis. If we read her unspoken argument closely, we note that the logic is something like this: since literature always stands in the passive, slavish mode vis-à-vis psychoanalysis, and the latter always stands in the active, master role, then the only way radically to undo such a relation is by reversing it. But because the usual relation is so *natural* for psychoanalysis, and so natural even (significantly) to the slave, reversing the perspective does not simply reinstate the same relation with switched players, as one would normally expect. No. So unnatural is it for literature to play subject to psychoanalysis' object that the very dialectic is abolished. The slave is freed only because, when he assumes the role of master, he is so ludicrous that he destroys the concept of mastery altogether. Similarly, the original master is such an unconvincing slave that he too annihilates the place of slavery. But this is only a temporary state of affairs: once the role-playing is over, the players ineluctably return to their "rightful" positions. At best, in other words, literature can be imagined as the momentary equal of psychoanalysis, and this only when both are in disguise.

Literature is not alone in its uneasy status with respect to psycho-analysis—quite the contrary. To all of the other disciplines psychoanalysis has visited, invaded, and (at times) colonized, it assigns the same "place" as it does to literature. In what Hegel called the "fight for recognition," they too, like literature, are already slaves—the ones who recognize rather than are recognized; the ones interpreted, not the active interpreter. It is not just that they go unrecognized in the discourse of the master;

3. Shoshana Felman, "To Open the Question," *Yale French Studies* 55/56 (1977): 6.
4. Ibid., pp. 6, 7.

in the fight for recognition which is already lost by whatever chooses to do battle with psychoanalysis, that which is "outside" will not only be reduced to other, not only be ultimately unrecognized. It will also rarely recognize *itself* in the way it is articulated by psychoanalysis.

For example, how is literature recognized and how is it to recognize itself in Freud's reading of Sophocles' *Oedipus Rex*? Or in Freud's interpretation of "Der Sandmann" by E. T. A. Hoffmann, which Freud will read according to his own, already established notion of castration anxiety and displacement, which in turn stems from his Oedipal model? Or Lacan's brief bow to Edgar Allan Poe in the "Seminar on 'The Purloined Letter,'" which openly announces that Poe's story is to be a cover for the psychoanalytic truth, namely that "the symbolic order . . . is constitutive for the subject." It is such a truth, moreover, "which makes the very existence of fiction possible."[5] Lacan continues,

> And in that case, a fable is as appropriate as any other narrative for bringing it [the truth] to light—at the risk of having the fable's coherence put to the test in the process. Aside from that reservation, a fictive tale even has the advantage of manifesting symbolic necessity more purely to the extent that we may believe its conception arbitrary.[6]

Literature here exists for the purpose of manifesting, almost in spite of itself, a psychoanalytic truth. Since fiction is made possible by the constitution of the subject, and since it is the role of psychoanalysis to demonstrate how that constitution occurs, then it follows, psychoanalysis would have it, that fiction becomes truth and thus useful only when decoded by psychoanalysis. Otherwise, it remains merely fable. Literature is then "recognized" by psychoanalysis only as the producer of *Stoff* for interpretation and consumption—precisely the position of the slave in the Hegelian model. In this position, literature cannot afford to recognize itself. Even if literature is mystified, as it often is in Freud or Lacan, it is so because it appears to have an arbitrary conception, which psychoanalysis will unravel as the ineluctable and incessant unfolding of the unconscious—nothing accidental, finally, at all. Except that literature does not know this. Its coherence, further, will be destroyed by the psychoanalytic reading; but it is only a surface coherence—the deeper one, the one of which literature itself is ignorant, will be revealed by psychoanalysis.

If literature cannot—indeed must not—recognize itself here, it is because it is made to play the role not only of slave, but of an eternally

---

5. Jacques Lacan, "Seminar on 'The Purloined Letter,'" trans. Jeffrey Mehlman, *Yale French Studies* 48 (1972): 40. See, of course, Derrida's response to this seminar, "The Purveyor of Truth."

6. Ibid.

ignorant slave as well. It is psychoanalysis which "knows" and will tell literature what it is "really" about. From psychoanalysis literature is supposed to learn what it itself "means." Literature is then forever unacknowledged as a "body of knowledge"; it is, like dreams, unknowing until interpreted. Beautiful at times, even "poetic," literature remains essentially useless, unconscious without psychoanalysis. Or, to return to my earlier model, literature is partitive in the perspective of psychoanalysis.

But so is everything else. Everything I have said thus far could be applied to all of the other disciplines from a psychoanalytic point of view. Linguistics, philosophy, anthropology, history, feminism, "humanism" could all be said to remain incomplete and ultimately less than meaningful without the overarching vision offered by psychoanalysis, at least as far as the latter is concerned. And that, clearly, demarcates the problem: psychoanalysis, in considering all aspects of the "human sciences" as aspects of itself, can be said not only to be narcissistic (at best a weak, uninteresting criticism), but therefore to *erase difference*—difference not only between the intellectual disciplines, but between *modes of thinking*. And this is the charge for which psychoanalysis, which has tried itself upon many things, is now to be brought to trial.

Psychoanalysis is on trial not in order to be attacked, but in order to be put back into its place—or, at least, into *a* place. In order to make psychoanalysis the object, not the all-consuming master subject, of inquiry. To make it that which is interpreted. To find, again, a place; to shrink it back to size. But also to try as in "attempt."

Finding a place for psychoanalysis is in part so difficult because it often shifts the rules of the game and, like a child, pretends that the other had agreed upon them from the outset. For example, imagine the following scenario—one which actually took place at a psychoanalytic institute in a major American city (I will change the names and authors to protect the guilty and probably as well to protect myself): We are at a seminar, for analysts only, with a few spouses and friends sprinkled in. Dr. Smith, a very important training analyst, gives a paper in which he argues that Baudelaire wrote his *Fleurs du mal* because he struggled with a "negative maternal introject." Such a problem explains, he continues, the thrust of the entire work. When it is the literary critic's turn to respond, however, she points out that Dr. Smith is translating (metamorphosing) Baudelaire into a series of pathologies of which his text serves as symptoms. Such an approach is reductive, says Professor X. She further points out that lots of people have trouble with their mothers but do not produce *Les Fleurs du mal;* that the assumption is that art is a disease which, once the author is cured, disappears. Dr. Smith retorts that analysis has always admired—indeed idealized—literary authors. Professor X replies that it seems to her that what is being worshiped is the psychoanalytic symptom, of which the art is seen as concrete proof. Here Dr. Smith (sensing himself to be trapped, perhaps?) changes the rules of the game. Turning suddenly to Professor X, rather than to the audience where his gaze had previously rested, he announces to her, "From your reaction to my paper, I am afraid that I must inform you that you too seem to have an unresolved conflict with your mother. Since you are a woman, this conflict has blocked your normal Oedipal development, and thus makes your relationship to your father problematic. As I am the paternal figure here—male, older—I must conclude that you are resisting my interpretation of Baudelaire because you are personally defensive with me and what I represent." To which Professor X responds, "I am not thinking about *you* at all; I am thinking about Baudelaire's text." Dr. Smith: "That is overt denial." Total silence ensues.

This little story demonstrates, I think, the problem. Of course, not all analysts (or, for that matter, literary critics) behave in this way.[7] But the fact that analysis provides tools which can be used in this fashion at all is more our concern here (the police do not always kill people; but they *can*—their position in society allows for it in certain circumstances).

If I have concentrated on the way literature is often shrunken by psychoanalysis, it is only because literary criticism is the field with which I am most familiar. One wonders similarly, however, how linguistics is to recognize itself in, for example, Lacan's use of Benveniste; his reliance upon Saussure's model of the sign (and inversion of the same); his use of Roman Jakobson; his conviction that had Freud possessed modern linguistic theory, he would have been Lacan. Or how does etymology respond when it reads Freud's essay on the antithetical meaning of primal words, or his play, in the essay on the uncanny, with the root of *Unheimlich*? Or, one can again wonder, how does history recognize itself with such notions as repetition automatism and the "political unconscious"? Or feminism, when it reads Freud's struggle to establish, and then abolish, a "symmetry" between the male and female child; female orgasm as a battle between the clitoris and the vagina; motherhood as ultimately always otherness. Or logic, when it confronts Lacan's symbols and mathemes. Or philosophy, when Freud "rejects" it and Lacan embraces it. Or psychology, when it is told (by psychoanalysis) that it is not a "science." Are we to reduce everything to phantom gestures, in Nicolas Abraham's sense? Hamlet's father revealed to be Freud?

---

7. For a debate which produces precisely the problems of reductionism (on all sides) which I have been describing, and the territorial stakes, see Erich Heller's "The Dismantling of a Marionette Theater; or, Psychology and the Misinterpretation of Literature" and Heinz Kohut's response, "Psychoanalysis and the Interpretation of Literature: A Correspondence with Erich Heller," *Critical Inquiry* 4 (Spring 1978). See also Margaret Schaefer's response to Heller's attack on her article about Kleist: "Psychoanalysis and the Marionette Theater: Interpretation Is Not Depreciation," *Critical Inquiry* 5 (Autumn 1978). And again, Kohut's "A Reply to Margaret Schaefer" in the same issue.

To be actively reductive with psychoanalysis, to shrink—that is what is attempted here. And while psychoanalysis is far from being the only discipline guilty of such empire-building, I have chosen it to put on trial because of its peculiar presence and insistence in our century, in our own intellectual trials. Of course, this trial of psychoanalysis must finally be a hopeless one. Psychoanalysis can always shift the rules again—always respond that a desire to reduce it is itself a symptom. Perhaps. But, more important, perhaps not. By forcing psychoanalysis to be "outside," and by having various disciplines view it from their own notion of "inside," we will perhaps be better able to see what the lure has been, the attraction to, the fear of, this idea that Freud once had.

Of course, we may never know when a cigar is "really" just a cigar— Kant saw to that. But there is a nostalgia here for the right to say *this* cigar is a cigar, and there is nothing "just" about it.

Françoise Meltzer

I would like to thank my coeditors for their advice and assistance with this volume, W. J. T. Mitchell in particular. The editorial staff and research assistants—Susan Olin, Margaret Berg, James W. Williams, Ellen Feldman, and Michael Sittenfeld—were patient and tireless. I am very grateful to them, and I cannot imagine better editors. Finally, I wish to thank the contributors to this volume, who agreed with me that this subject was of sufficient importance to warrant their time and effort. The results, I think, speak for themselves.—F. M.

History and Psychoanalysis

Dominick LaCapra

> It may thus be said that the theory of psycho-analysis is an attempt to account for two striking and unexpected facts of observation which emerge whenever an attempt is made to trace the symptoms of a neurotic back to their sources in past life: the facts of transference and of resistance. Any line of investigation which recognizes these two facts and takes them as the starting point of its work has a right to call itself psycho-analysis, even though it arrives at results other than my own.
> —FREUD, "On the History of the Psycho-analytic Movement"

> Le transfert c'est le concept même de l'analyse, parce que c'est le temps de l'analyse.
> —JACQUES LACAN, Le Séminaire I

The focus of this essay will be on Freud, although my approach is informed by certain aspects of "post-Freudian" analysis. In the works of Freud, however, history in the ordinary sense often seems lost in the shuffle between ontogeny and phylogeny. When Freud, in the latter part of his life, turned to cultural history, he was primarily concerned with showing how the evolution of civilization on a macrological level might be understood through—or even seen as an enactment of—psychoanalytic principles and processes. And he openly acknowledged the speculative nature of his inquiry into prehistory, "archaic" society, and their putative relation to the civilizing process.

One might nonetheless argue that throughout Freud's work there are theoretical bases and fruitful leads for a more delimited investigation of specific historical processes for which documentation is, to a greater or lesser extent, available. This kind of investigation is, moreover, required to test the pertinence of Freud's speculative and at times quasi-mythological initiatives. At present one can perhaps do little more than tentatively suggest how such an investigation might proceed and the sorts of issues it might conceivably illuminate. For its elaboration has been relatively underdeveloped in the research of those who look to Freud for guidance.

In psychoanalysis itself, there has been a widespread concern for the refinement of theory and its application to individual case histories. Distinctive in the recent French initiative is a textual focus, often with only an allegorical sense of the relation of textual to other historical processes. The succinct editorial introduction to an issue of *Diacritics* on "The Tropology of Freud" provides a lucid epitome of the assumptions of those looking to the "French Freud":

> Tropology: 1. "A speaking by tropes" (Blount, 1656); the use of metaphor in speech or writing; figurative discourse. 2. A moral discourse. 3. A treatise on tropes or figures of speech. OED.
>
> In these essays the writing of Freud is considered from the triple perspective of tropology. Freud's topics and descriptions are taken to constitute a new rhetoric or treatise on tropes—versions of the mind which are themselves new figures for classifying and describing the structure and movement of texts, according to what Nicolas Abraham and others here call an 'anasemic' transcription of the very concept of figure under the influence of the 'radical anasemic change that psychoanalysis has introduced into language' (Abraham, "The Shell and the Kernel"). At the same time Freud's scientific project is itself an example of figurative writing, examined here in several of these essays as if it were a literary text, a piece of poetic language, or a narrative fiction. Finally, since psychoanalysis is not merely a rhetorical exercise but an instrument of ethical and therefore eventually political power, these essays in turn raise questions about the ethics and politics of rhetoric.[1]

This program guides much valuable work in the wake of Freud. One of its incentives is a "Freud-on-Freud" rereading of Freud's own

---

1. *Diacritics* 9 (Spring 1979), p. 1 (special issue conceived by Richard Klein).

Dominick LaCapra is Goldwin Smith Professor of European Intellectual History at Cornell University. His most recent books are *"Madame Bovary" on Trial* (1982), *Rethinking Intellectual History* (1983), and *History and Criticism* (1985). He has just completed a book-length manuscript entitled "History, Politics, and the Novel."

texts, oriented toward the disclosure of how those texts both "act out" and try to account for (or "work through") processes, such as those of "dream-work," that Freud investigated. This program is enhanced and, to some extent, redirected when history and its representation are seen as a crucial mediation (if not the "missing link") between "rhetoric" and ethicopolitical concerns. The difficulty is to take the understanding of history beyond the point of allegorical implication, or at least to inquire more closely into the nature and workings of that implication.

Existing research and reflection among professional historians are, unfortunately, of only limited value in confronting that difficulty. "Psychohistory" has won its way as a subdiscipline in the historical profession, although it is still able to raise the hackles of some traditionalists.[2] Yet the typical procedure of psychohistorians has been to make more or less selective use of psychoanalytic concepts as they proceed to put individuals or groups from the past "on the couch." Whatever may be their interest, studies of John Stuart Mill's or Max Weber's Oedipus complex, the phantasms of the Nazi youth cohort, the phobias of the other Victorians, or even the discreet sexual charms of the Victorian bourgeoisie tend to remain on the level of the application of psychoanalytic concepts to historical objects. History as applied psychoanalysis does not confront the broader problem of how psychoanalysis can lead to a basic reconceptualization of historical self-understanding and practice or even to a mutual rearticulation of both history and psychoanalysis as implicated in a reciprocally provocative exchange. (It is, after all, this kind of "dedefinition" and rearticulation of concepts that motivates the notion of "anasemia.")

A second approach to Freud prevalent among historians is, in certain respects, even further from the perspective I want to explore. It is the straightforward contextual "explanation" of Freud as symptomatic of his own circumscribed society and culture. Here Freud is seen as more or less blindly effecting a self-deceived "escape" from reality, politics, society, history, and so forth, into the egocentric and phantasmatic labyrinths of the isolated self.[3] Freud's thought does have significant "symptomatic" aspects in its less examined relations to culture and ideology—a point certain recent feminist critics have developed in an especially forceful way. But the danger in the interpretation of Freud as symptom (or as disease posing as cure, in the phrase of Karl Kraus) is the propensity to

2. For a defense of psychohistory, see Peter Loewenberg, "Psychohistory," in *The Past Before Us: Contemporary Historical Writing in the United States,* ed. Michael Kammen (Ithaca, N.Y., 1980), pp. 408–32. See also the disparaging comments dispersed throughout John Lukacs, *Historical Consciousness, or, The Remembered Past* (New York, 1985).

3. See, for example, the influential interpretation in Carl Schorske, *Fin-de-siècle Vienna: Politics and Culture* (New York, 1980). I shall return to the recent rendition of the "escape from reality" view of Freud in Jeffrey Moussaieff Masson, *The Assault on Truth: Freud's Suppression of the Seduction Theory* (New York, 1984).

abstract one reductionist (or "vulgar Freudian") dimension from Freud's own texts and then to apply it to the interpretation of those texts without countering or at least qualifying it with other tendencies also active in Freud. The very understanding of "reality," "politics," "society," and "history" operative in such "critiques" is often precritical. In any event, this type of approach may not question the extent to which Freud's texts intimate how these concepts may be reworked in ways that at least resist symptomatic replication of some of the most dubious and destructive forces in modern history. To make these points is not to eliminate the complex problem of determining a text's relation to hegemonic or dominant discourses. Nor is it to subscribe to an indiscriminate pluralism or a displaced, "talk-show" variant of "dialogism" ("equal time for all 'voices'"). It is rather to insist upon a careful and self-critical investigation of both the possibly divided movements in certain texts and the question of their specific relation to larger discourses and practices. It is also to raise the question of the implications of psychoanalysis for one's own protocols of inquiry and criticism.

One may begin an inquiry into the exchange between psychoanalysis and history with the issue of the relation between history and historiography—or, to change the terms somewhat, between the historical process and its representation in the historian's account of it. This relation is complicated by two factors: one finds repetition on both sides of the equation, and the relation is mediated by various traces of the past (memories, documents, texts, monuments, icons, and so forth) through which the historian reconstructs the historical process in his or her account.

The historian repeats an already repetitive historical process—a process that variably combines repetition with change. I shall later try to indicate how psychoanalysis construes temporality as a process of repetition with change on all levels, from the drives to the attempt of the analyst to control repetition (both through its limited enactment in the analytic situation and through the effort to "work through" repetition in transference). Historians have traditionally accepted the Aristotelian stabilization of repetition/change by confiding in the binary opposition between the universal and the particular, between intemporal "synchrony" and changing "diachrony." In this decisive gesture, repetition is idealized and fixated on an ahistorical level while "history" is identified with a dissociated, equally idealized and fixated concept of change. This binary allows for a neat separation, if not isolation, of philosophy and history (with "poetry" as a rather unstable mediator or supplement between the two).

The reductive stabilization of potentially uncontrollable repetitive processes is necessary and inevitable. But it may be both contested and effected through more problematic distinctions that themselves hold out the possibility of a different articulation of relations allowing for a significant measure of responsible control. In Freud temporality is understood both in stabilizing terms (the quest for a primal origin or scene, the elaboration of stages of development, the construction of linear narratives) and in more disconcerting ways. The mechanisms of dream-work—particularly displacement, condensation, and staging (or considerations of representability)—indicate the role of nonlinear, repetitive temporality. (Secondary revision is itself a stabilizing form closer to processes prevalent in waking life, notably in the daydream, but dream-work itself cannot be entirely confined to literal states of sleep.) "Deferred action" (*Nachträglichkeit*) is of course the most patent form of repetitive temporality, and while its significance is heightened in Freud's later work through his insistence upon the repetition compulsion, it plays an important role throughout his career. For Freud a traumatic influx of excitation—an overwhelming rupture which the subject cannot effectively bind—is brought about not through an original event in isolation but through repetition: an event becomes traumatic retrospectively when it is recalled by a later event. In the trauma one thus has a conjunction of repetition and change. As Freud put it as early as the *Project for a Scientific Psychology* (1895): "Here we have the case of a memory arousing an affect which it did not arouse as an experience, because in the meantime the changes [brought about] by puberty had made possible a different understanding of what was remembered. . . . We invariably find that a memory is repressed which has only become a trauma by *deferred action* [*nachträglich*]."[4] The later event, seemingly trivial in itself, may recall the earlier one in only the most indirect manner. (Here the event that triggers a trauma through "deferred action" resembles the insignificant event in the "forward repetition" of displacement,[5] and the often remote linkage between significant and insignificant events signals the difficulties of tracking figurative processes in a "new rhetoric.")

Jacques Lacan has referred displacement to the trope of metonymy (understood as the mechanism of desire), and he has correlated condensation with metaphor. This initial step in the development of a new rhetoric (whose end is not yet in sight) provides valuable insight into temporal processes as well as into the attempt to represent them. Metonymy constitutes a time line of different, serial events which one tries to integrate through a metaphoric concordance of beginning and end. For Lacan this effort can never fully succeed, for desire (unlike need) cannot be satisfied, although the quest for satisfaction (the prototypical *quête de l'absolu*) motivates utopian yearning (including the yearning for full narrative closure and theoretical totalization). The further implication for

4. Sigmund Freud, *Project for a Scientific Psychology, The Standard Edition of the Complete Psychological Works of Sigmund Freud*, ed. and trans. James Strachey, 24 vols. (London, 1953–74), 1:356.
5. I here of course adapt a term from Kierkegaard.

rhetoric in a different key comes with the elusive "dialogic" dimension of transference, which for both Freud and Lacan is an axial aspect of the analytic relation.

The tendency of psychoanalysis to emphasize the importance of transference in the relation between analyst and analysand has often had the unfortunate consequence of diverting attention from its role elsewhere. The restriction of transference to the analytic situation may even be seen as an unwarranted domestication of the notion. As Freud noted: "It must not be supposed . . . that transference is created by analysis and does not occur apart from it. Transference is merely uncovered and isolated by analysis. It is a universal phenomenon of the human mind, it decides the success of all medical influence, and in fact dominates the whole of each person's relations to his human environment."[6] Historiography is no exception to this bold generalization.

It may be argued that the historian is implicated in a twofold "dialogic" relation that involves transference in somewhat different ways. The closest analogue to the analytic situation (with its displaced repetition of the Oedipal scene) is found in the historian's relation to other students of the past whose renditions of it must be taken into account in his or her own work. Indeed the very delimitation of inquirers whose views are deemed pertinent for historians—those whose influence is sufficiently proximate to cause anxiety—is a vital constituent of the discipline. The turn toward currently avoided or marginalized interlocutors (such as philosophers, literary critics, or novelists) is part and parcel of an attempt to reorient priorities or alter the horizons of the discipline, which has been drawn toward a certain kind of social science in the recent past. A questionable feature of professionalization is the attempt to establish clear-cut if not unbreachable boundaries separating history from other disciplines, thus giving the historian an unequivocal identity, and even historians more than one generation back may become not vital inter-locutors but only objects of innocuous ritual invocation. Hence one has the oft-noted divide that marks the distance between "methodology" and "research" seminars. (To put the point simply: in methodology seminars, one reads past historians and theorists; in research seminars, one proceeds as if one had never read them.)

The most easily located instance of transferential relations in his-toriography (and in academics more generally) is probably to be found in the nexus between teachers and students. These relations are most intense in graduate study, particularly in the initial period: the teacher (who may, for the student, initially be an imago projected from written texts) is often intent on establishing a "presence," and the student, in a particularly vulnerable or even "regressive" position, confronts for the

6. Freud, *An Autobiographical Study,* trans. Strachey (New York, 1963), pp. 79–80; all further references to this work, abbreviated *AS,* will be included in the text.

first time the problem of a near total (and often phantasmatic) identity between his or her professional and personal self. Peter Loewenberg has discussed this dimension of transference, and, despite certain overstated aspects of his account, his thought-provoking initiative deserves to be followed up and extended in other directions.[7]

Instead of pursuing this route, I would like to stress an equally important but often unnoticed sense in which transference is at play in history, that is, in the very relation of the historian to the "object" of study. Transference in this somewhat more indirect and attenuated sense refers to the manner in which the problems at issue in the object of study reappear (or are repeated with variations) in the work of the historian. "Transference" offers a better way of understanding a "dialogic" relation to the past than do standard, round-robin debates about objectivity or subjectivity, truth or relativism. It may even provide perspective on aspects of those debates that cannot be entirely transcended but perhaps can be rethought in a less compulsively predictable fashion.

In one important sense, objectivity refers to criteria of meticulous research in the accurate reconstitution of events through the critical examination of all relevant sources. Formulated another way, objectivity implies an injunction to face facts that may prove embarrassing for the theses one would like to propound or the patterns one is striving to elicit. It is reciprocally related to a "coefficient of resistance" in both the "textual" material one is interpreting and in the modes of empirical reality one is inferring from that material or its cognates. Whatever the problematic nature of reconstituting events, given available documentation, or the necessary interaction between the construal of events and one's theoretical assumptions, the notion of objectivity is valuable even for approaches that stress the mediating and supplementary role of texts (including documents) in all historiography. Freud tried to maintain this notion of objectivity, and it underwent one of its greatest trials (as we shall see) with respect to the so-called seduction theory.

In Freud's work, moreover, objectivity might be correlated with what he called *gleichschwebende Aufmerksamkeit*—"evenly suspended" or "poised" attention. In accordance with this rule—which was the analyst's counterpart to the analysand's "fundamental rule" of reporting everything that came into his or her mind—the analyst should try to be attentive to all material,

---

7. See Peter Loewenberg, *Decoding the Past: The Psychohistorical Approach* (New York, 1983), pp. 45–80. Bruce Mazlish writes in his review of this book: "As for educating psychohistorians (and historians), I fully applaud Loewenberg's call for a greater diffusion of knowledge of psychoanalysis, but I wonder about his compulsive attention to the infantilizing pressures in history graduate students, exacerbated by unacknowledged sadism, hostility, and so forth on the part of their mentors (surely this was not Loewenberg's experience with his teacher, Carl Schorske)" (*American Historical Review* 89 [1984]: 94). One may, however, note that the actual nature of an authority figure does not determine all aspects of transference.

including any that upset expectations or had no place in preexisting theoretical assumptions, even material that seemed to contradict them. "Poised" attention might enable access to phenomena that themselves would have a meaning only *nachträglich* if at all, and it also allowed for the play of the analyst's unconscious in responding to that of the analysand. The very poise of the analyst might be upset by what he or she was led to notice through an attentiveness that might rub against the grain of method without ever simply eliminating the need for it. As J. Laplanche and J.-B. Pontalis put it, *gleichschwebende Aufmerksamkeit* is the rule "which in Freud's view allows the analyst to discover the unconscious connections in what the patient says. Thanks to it the analyst is able to keep in mind a multitude of apparently insignificant elements whose correlations are only to emerge later on"; "suspended attention is the only truly objective attitude in that it is suited to an essentially distorted object."[8]

Objectivity in this sense clearly does not obviate the role of transference. Indeed it challenges the simple idea of recounting the past purely in its own terms and for its own sake—the historicist dream that (like its complement, presentism, or the dream of total liberation from the "burden" of history) rests on a disavowal of transference. Objectivity as "suspended" or "poised" attention would also jeopardize the overriding desire (prone to give rise to "secondary revision") that leads the historian to "find order in chaos." It would instead imply the need to investigate the interaction between order and challenges to it in the more or less "distorted" objects of the past as well as in one's own discourse about them. Transference in this sense would highlight the issue of the historian's voice in narration and analysis—an issue prematurely foreclosed when one assumes full unity not only of narrative but of narrative and authorial voice. It would attune one to modulations of voice, both in specifically marked hypothetical forms and in more subtle, often unconscious, movements. It would simultaneously raise the question of the extent to which the historian's voice does or should reveal significant parallels with experiments that have been more pronounced in other genres, such as the modern novel.

Freud himself encountered the tension between "objectivity" and the temptation to impose a convincing, coherent interpretation on the experience of the suggestible patient. A recurrent problem for him was whether (or to what extent) his theories informed the patient's experience or actively formed, indeed constrained, it by imposing compulsive schemata that functioned as surrogate myths. (One of course has here the problem of the status of the Oedipus complex.) Freud moved from hypnosis to free association and the "fundamental rule" in order to mitigate the effects of suggestibility and decrease the incidence of short-lived, deceptive solutions to problems brought about by "cathartic" abreaction. But he

---

8. J. Laplanche and J.-B. Pontalis, *The Language of Psycho-analysis,* trans. Donald Nicholson-Smith (New York, 1973), p. 43.

never fully achieved the "liberation" from hypnosis that he somewhat histrionically announces at the beginning of chapter 3 of *An Autobiographical Study*.[9] Indeed the ensuing textual movement not only qualifies but threatens to retract the force of his statement, for aspects of what Freud earlier recognized to be problematic in hypnosis were regenerated in transference.[10] Transference was thus a "substitute" for hypnotism which at most enabled one to "exclude," or "at all events, to isolate" "the mysterious element that was at work behind hypnotism" (*AS*, p. 50). Transference, however, was explicitly recognized by Freud to be inherently ambivalent, for in replacing the original neurosis it might also generate new resistances, and it could both impede the work of analysis and indicate the direction that work had to take to be effective.

> This *transference*—to give it its shortened name—soon replaces in the patient's mind the desire to be cured, and, so long as it is affectionate and moderate, becomes the agent of the physician's influence and neither more nor less than the mainspring of the joint work of analysis. Later on, when it has become passionate or has been converted into hostility, it becomes the principal tool of the resistance. It may then happen that it will paralyse the patient's powers of associating and endanger the success of the treatment. Yet it would be senseless to try to evade it; for an analysis without transference is an impossibility.

> It is perfectly true that psychoanalysis, like other psychother-apeutic methods, employs the instrument of suggestion (or trans-ference). But the difference is this: that in analysis it is not allowed to play the decisive part in determining the therapeutic results. It is used instead to induce the patient to perform a piece of mental work—the overcoming of his transference-resistances—which in-volves a permanent alteration in his mental economy. The trans-ference is made conscious to the patient by the analyst, and it is resolved by convincing him that in his transference-attitude, he is *re-experiencing* emotional relations which had their origin in his earliest object-attachments during the repressed period of his child-hood. In this way the transference is changed from the strongest weapon of the resistance into the best instrument of the analytic treatment. Nevertheless its handling remains the most difficult as well as the most important part of the technique of analysis. [*AS*, pp. 79–81]

9. "My expectations were fulfilled; I was set free from hypnotism" (*AS*, p. 52).

10. "Even the most brilliant results were liable to be suddenly wiped away if my personal relation with the patient became disturbed. It was true that they would be re-established if a reconciliation could be effected; but such an occurrence proved that the personal emotional relation between doctor and patient was after all stronger than the whole cathartic process, and it was precisely that factor which escaped every effort at control" (*AS*, p. 49).

The relation of transference to the process of "remembering, repeating, and working through" may well constitute "the most difficult as well as the most important" problem for any attempt to articulate the relation of psychoanalysis to other disciplines or critical theories. The above-quoted passage provides some insight into this problem. "Working through" allows for limited abreaction in the "acting out" or reenactment of earlier experience in ways both continuous and discontinuous with the former cathartic method. "Acting out" is to some extent "bound" by its restriction to the analytic situation itself, while it is discouraged in other areas of life. It is further restricted in that it is counteracted by the role of memory. "Acting out" is phantasmatic: it repeats an earlier experience as though it were a fully present reality. In this sense it is, in Jacques Derrida's term, "logocentric." Freud was at times not sufficiently sensitive to the possibility that memory, in its fully speculative form of "Hegelian" in-teriorization, also involved a quest for full presence (or totality) on a higher, "sublimated" level and thus was prey to its own phantasmatic investments, notably in the guise of complete self-possession.[11] It too might entail a disavowal of transference—indeed might become a the-oretical analogue of psychosis or "narcissistic neurosis"—instead of creating the possibility of "working through" a transferential relation. In an other than totalizing sense, however, memory provided critical distance on the past, allowed for the distinction between mnemic trace and phantasm, and posed the question of the role of judgment in relating past and present. In this sense, remembrance was a counterweight to the compulsive repetition of "acting out," and it opened the prospect of a more reciprocal relation between analyst and analysand (one definition of cure). Through it, "acting out" was staged on a larger scene that was not entirely dominated by the repetition compulsion, and there arose a greater chance of re-sponding critically to that "mysterious element" that held blind sway in hypnosis.

The recent debate about Freud's "abandonment" of the so-called seduction theory has an obvious interest for anyone trying to relate psychoanalysis and history. What is striking in *The Assault on Truth* is Jeffrey Masson's compulsiveness in asserting both the reality of scenes of seduction in the genesis of severe disorders and Freud's failure of courage in "abandoning" the seduction theory and with it the "reality" of his patients. (A subplot in the book, which threatens to short-circuit its story line, is of course Masson's own sense of abandonment by the founding father and his legitimate heirs in the psychoanalytic profession.) Equally striking is the lack of a psychoanalytic treatment of the relation between mnemic traces of real events and phantasmatic investments, although this relation is "acted out" in Masson's own passionately Oedipal reactions to the avatars of psychoanalysis. At least mildly surprising,

11. See esp. Samuel Weber, *The Legend of Freud* (Minneapolis, 1982).

moreover, is the fact that, given his insistence on a certain conception of reality, Masson provides no new evidence—in the form of case histories, for instance—for the seduction theory. He bases his reaffirmation on, at best, a rereading of texts (often an extremely reductionist rereading) and, at worst, on inadequately documented and poorly argued assertions (for example, the assertion, on the basis of "some notes by Ruth Mack Brunswick for a paper she never published" that "as a child [the Wolf-Man] had been anally seduced by a member of his family—and that Freud did not know this"[12]). "Reality"—textual, procedural, and empirical—thus suffers a few assaults at Masson's own hands. But the concerns agitating Masson are important ones. And his book does have the merit of insisting that Freud's own reasons for questioning the seduction theory were not always cogent and that they have often been repeated without further testing by later analysts. (He also brings out the extent of Freud's own strongly transferential relation to Wilhelm Fliess, which at times prompted behavior that was inexcusable, notably in the case of Emma Eckstein.)

The seduction theory might perhaps be better termed the child-abuse theory, and evidence of the prevalence of child abuse makes certain hypotheses less implausible than they might have seemed to Freud. (Freud's own case histories do contain evidence of child abuse in one form or another, and Freud does not do enough with this evidence.) The abuse of a more or less helpless child might even be taken as a paradigm of an event whose reality is not purely psychic. And it is a real event of the sort that attests to the element of enduring validity in certain "naive" responses—an event that makes one uncomfortable, indeed impatient, with the notion of Reality as an asymptote of the detours of the Imaginary and the Symbolic. However difficult it may be to gather evidence in certain cases, one would certainly like to know how prevalent the abuse of children is, what role it plays in the etiology of pathological conditions, and what it means for the nature of a society and a culture. Indeed it is curious that Freud seemed to be staunchly attached to the "reality" of the primal crime, for which no evidence was available, in contrast to his views on the actual seduction or abuse of children, where gathering evidence was at least theoretically possible. The degree of his attachment to the "reality" of the primal crime might even be interpreted as an overcompensation for his residual doubts about the seduction theory.

Yet the formula stating that Freud simply "abandoned" or "suppressed" the seduction theory is itself far from adequate. As Laplanche and Pontalis point out (in a work that predates Masson's book), "right up to the end of his life, Freud continued to assert the existence, prevalence and patho-

---

12. Masson, *The Assault on Truth*, p. xxvii.

genic force of scenes of seduction actually experienced by children."[13] In addition, Freud continued to insist on the importance of deferred action, the traumatizing role of memories that are phantasmatically invested, and the need to "ground" fantasy in reality. Indeed Laplanche and Pontalis argue that the seduction theory is not an alternative to the Oedipus complex but an adumbration of it.

It is nonetheless true that Freud's emphasis shifted after 1897 and that he at times formulated the relation between the seduction theory on the one hand and the Oedipus complex, infantile sexuality, screen memories, and psychic reality on the other as pointing different directions, if not incompatible alternatives, in the elaboration of psychoanalytic theory. One need not go to letters to find rather explicit statements of Freud's change in attitude toward his "neurotica." As Freud put it in "On the History of the Psycho-Analytic Movement":

> Influenced by Charcot's view of the traumatic origin of hysteria, one was readily inclined to accept as true and aetiologically significant the statements made by patients in which they ascribed their symptoms to passive sexual experiences in the first years of childhood—to put it bluntly, to seduction. When this aetiology broke down under the weight of its own improbability and contradiction in definitely ascertainable circumstances, the result at first was helpless bewilderment. Analysis had led back to these infantile sexual traumas by the right path, and yet they were not true.... At last came the reflection that, after all, one had no right to despair because one has been deceived in one's expectations; one must revise those expectations. If hysterical subjects trace back their symptoms to traumas that are fictitious, then the new fact which emerges is precisely that they create such scenes in *phantasy*, and this psychical reality requires to be taken into account alongside practical reality. This reflection was soon followed by the discovery that these phantasies were intended to cover up the auto-erotic activity of the first years of childhood, to embellish it and raise it to a higher plane. And now, from behind the phantasies, the whole range of a child's sexual life came to light.[14]

There is a similar account in *An Autobiographical Study* where Freud refers to his belief that the seduction theory "might well have had fatal consequences for the whole of my work" and states that, after his recognition

---

13. Laplanche and Pontalis, *The Language of Psycho-analysis*, p. 406. Laplanche and Pontalis refer to such works as *Three Essays in the Theory of Sexuality* (1905) and *An Outline of Psycho-Analysis* (1940).

14. Freud, "On the History of the Psycho-analytic Movement," *Standard Edition*, 14: 17–18; all further references to this essay, abbreviated "HPM," will be included in the text.

that scenes of seduction were "only phantasies," he was "for some time completely at a loss" (*AS*, pp. 62, 63). Freud's apparent disorientation when his belief in seduction was shaken—something which he describes as putting him in a helpless, traumatizing position analogous to that of the "seduced" child in the seduction theory itself—attests to the strength of his earlier investment in its reality. It also indicates that he may have been overreacting to a sense of loss when he suggested a break in psychoanalytic theory itself or at least put forth conflicting views about the role of seduction in the etiology of pathology. In any event, Freud did try to maintain that whether or not actual seduction took place, the result would be the same for the patient in light of the "psychic reality" of fantasy.

Masson finds the latter view entirely implausible. Whether or to what extent it is accurate is moot but quite important for our self-understanding, and it certainly deserves further investigation. Masson, as I have already noted, does not offer new evidence but rests his case on a restricted rereading of Freud's texts (including his letters). A more far-ranging if controversial rereading, undertaken from a very different theoretical perspective from Masson's but converging in circumscribed ways with certain of his concerns, is Nicolas Abraham and Maria Torok's *Cryptonymie: Le Verbier de l'Homme aux loups.*

Freud in his study of the Wolf-Man is undecided about the reality of the primal scene as witnessed by the patient as a child of one-and-a-half. He concludes with a *non liquet,* commenting that the child may have seen dogs copulating and projected this scene back onto the earlier one. But the primal scene Freud has in mind is not child abuse but coitus *a tergo* between the parents. In his own account, Freud has evidence that he either leaves uninterpreted or interprets only in a certain direction. The sister of the Wolf-Man, who was a few years older than the boy, showed "precocious" sexual activity, not only in trying to seduce her little brother but in attempting to take a cousin's member. Freud does not ask the seemingly obvious question: Where could a little girl of five or so have learned such specific behavior? Freud knew that the Wolf-Man's father was "manic-depressive" and that he entered a sanitarium when the Wolf-Man was only six. Freud also knew that the sister committed suicide later. But the most Freud admits is the "suspicion that the father of our present patient used himself to indulge in 'affectionate abuse,' and may have played at wolf or dog with the little boy and have threatened as a joke to gobble him up."[15]

15. Freud, "From the History of an Infantile Neurosis" (1918), *Three Case Histories,* ed. Philip Rieff (New York, 1963), p. 300; all further references to this work, abbreviated "IN," will be included in the text. On Freud's hypothesis, the Wolf-Man would have shown a phobic response to carnivalesque behavior on the part of his father.

For Abraham and Torok, "affectionate abuse" is not the issue, and the relation is other than a joking one. The plausibility of an infant witnessing coitus between parents pales in the face of the scene Freud did not entertain. Abraham and Torok arrive at another scene on the basis of multilingual analysis which is both close and at times seemingly outlandish—but with an outlandishness that presumably parallels the "new rhetoric" of the unconscious itself. They argue that the Wolf-Man believed his father had abused his sister and that he himself had witnessed the scene and reported it to his nurse, only to see it suppressed by his mother in defense of the family's honor. Abraham and Torok leave it undecided whether this belief corresponded to an actual event, and they even indicate the possibly fictional nature of their own analysis. But for the reader the event may seem to acquire the weight of reality or at least of extreme plausibility by the end of their account.[16]

What is less moot than the role of a real event of child abuse (or "seduction") is another point which emerges from the *Cryptonymie:* even an actual event must be the object of phantasmatic investment to become pathogenic. This point returns in a more qualified way to Freud's insistence on the importance of "psychic reality," and it in no sense implies either a disavowal of the significance of actual events of "seduction" or their incompatibility with the theories of infantile sexuality, the Oedipus complex, screen memories, or the role of "psychic reality" itself. Indeed the intervention of "deferred action" implies that in the time between the unassimilated event of early childhood and the later event that somehow recalls it, the "original" event is transformed through the work of fantasy. The phantasmatic position of the father as a grandiose object of love and hate may itself foster denial of, or resistance to, the possibility of certain actions on his part. The Wolf-Man himself, for Abraham and Torok, incorporated his sister as well as his father in his split or divided self. And they stress the general importance of incorporation (contrasted with introjection) as a phantasmatic activity that "encrypts" others in the split self in a manner that creates a symbolic cyst in the psyche. The power of these phantomlike revenants may require a more complex notion of the unconscious and the "rhetorical" workings of language both in the self and in the discourse of psychoanalysis that tracks it.

While the initiatives of figures such as Abraham and Torok go in directions that at times might have seemed as strange to Freud as his own work did to many contemporaries, it is nonetheless significant that Freud's case histories are complex combinations of narrative and analysis in which a quest for unified theory is recurrently rendered problematic. His account of the Wolf-Man, for example, is in no sense a simple linear narrative—indeed a straightforward chronology is supplied, almost as

16. See Nicolas Abraham and Maria Torok, *Cryptonymie: Le Verbier de l'Homme aux loups* (Paris, 1976).

an afterthought, in a footnote at the very end of the text.[17] In the case history, as in an analytic session, "interrelated material makes its appearance at different times and at different points in the treatment" (*AS*, p. 78). In fact the very interweaving of linear and nonlinear narrative in Freud's accounts, as well as of narrative and theoretical analysis, is emblematic of larger problems concerning the psyche and its relation to society and culture—and of any discursive attempt to come to terms with these problems, including psychoanalysis itself.

A story becomes followable, linear, and satisfactory in its attempt to integrate "metonymic" desire and "metaphoric" recognition through the structuring role of plots.[18] Freud's own preferred plot or schema was of course Oedipal, with the Oedipus complex grounded in an original or primal crime that actually played it out at the dawn of history. And a crucial question one may raise is whether the Oedipus complex is the key to transference or too one-dimensional and compulsive an interpretation of it. In his study of the Wolf-Man, Freud both invoked his idea of the inheritance of acquired characteristics in culture and (without remarking upon the possibly recursive and self-referential nature of his gesture) used it to explain the phantasmatic potential of compulsive schemata. (His point would of course apply more plausibly to social transmission or tradition than to an unmediated movement from psychology to biology.)

> Phylogenetically inherited schemata . . . like the categories of philosophy, are concerned with the business of "placing" the impressions derived from actual experience. I am inclined to take the view that they are precipitates from the history of human civilization. The Oedipus complex, which comprises a child's relation to its parents, is one of them—is, in fact, the best known member of the class. Whenever experiences fail to fit in with the hereditary schema, they become remodelled in the imagination—a process which might very profitably be followed out in detail. It is precisely such cases that are calculated to convince us of the independent existence of the schema. We are often able to see the schema triumphing over the experience of the individual. ["IN," pp. 314–15]

Much recent criticism has been devoted to showing, in often brilliant detail, how the very plots and structures Freud seemed to take "straight"

---

17. Juliet Mitchell observes in a more general vein, "Freud's case-histories show that there is little justification for treating the 'stages' either as absolutes or as even separate and sequential" (Mitchell, *Psychoanalysis and Feminism* [New York, 1974], p. 27).

18. See, for example, Peter Brooks, "Freud's Masterplot: Questions of Narrative," *Yale French Studies* 55/56 (1977): 280–300, and "Fictions of the Wolfman: Freud and Narrative Understanding," *Diacritics* 9 (Spring 1979): 72–81.

theoretically and thematically were nonetheless contested or even radically disoriented by the very movements of his own stories and accounts. (Paradigmatic here is the essay on "The 'Uncanny'" in which the repetitive "return of the repressed" is reduced to castration anxiety and used to "explain" E. T. A. Hoffmann's "The Sandman," only to return in less clear-cut and familiarized form in the intricate and at times uncanny tropisms of Freud's own text.) Instead of venturing to offer another "Freud-on-Freud" reading of a Freudian text, I shall—at the risk of courting reduction—confine myself to a few observations that may perhaps indicate how this proliferating series of readings, while not simply reducible to a single thematic, may nonetheless be seen to point in certain directions.

Freud of course looked to Sophocles' *Oedipus Rex* for a rendition of the Oedipus complex, but he explicitly read the play from Oedipus' perspective and reduced it to a vehicle for a compulsive myth without asking how the play critically staged the myth or situated Oedipus. Yet the way the play enacted its compulsive schema may be argued to disclose a telling relation among myth, narrative closure, and the scapegoat mechanism. Myth (at least in one important narrativist sense of the term) collapses levels of intelligibility by attempting to account for structural relations or possibilities (the passage from nature to culture, incest, guilt, and so forth) in terms applicable to particular events (an act of incest or of parricide, for example). Myth tries to "explain" structures through events that enact them. It thus fixates and "totalizes" repetition through a story of events, and it seeks a point of undivided origin in a first event which begins the story. Narrative closure is achieved when repetitive processes are reduced to *peripeteia* between beginning and end, and the original event is ultimately redeemed or "lifted to a higher level." Freud was closest to myth in his story of the primal crime as well as in his tendency to present the drives (from below) in terms of a biologistic fantasia or (from above) as titans engaged in combat for the destiny of man. The original event in Sophocles' play would seem to be the pollution of Thebes with the ensuing effort to find the origin of pollution in a guilty act.

Oedipus himself emerges in the play as a master sleuth who, in one gesture, reduces the drama to a detective story (perhaps the most compulsively reductive of narrative forms). He seeks, through a schema that offers blinding closure, to localize guilt and to impute it to a given agent, if need be by assuming the dual role of scapegoat and victim himself. Never explicitly pertinent in Freud's Oedipal reading of *Oedipus Rex,* however, is the way the play stages rather than simply acts out Oedipus' gesture. For it provides evidence that Oedipus may be no more or no less guilty than anyone else—indeed that the kind of guilt Oedipus seeks may be misplaced.

The play never resolves the issue of whether the murderers of Laius were one or many. The witness who is summoned to give testimony on this issue never addresses it. Instead the inquiry shifts to a question of origins: the origins of Oedipus. The displaced witness is of course the very herdsman who had been charged by Laius and Jocasta to expose the child whose ankles they had pierced and so to avert the oracle's Oedipal prophecy.[19] (It is interesting that the protagonists invoke the parents' mistreatment of the child only as evidence in the attempt to establish the guilt of the adult for other putative crimes. Oedipus is driven to take upon himself the particular guilt of the parents as well as the pollution of the city.) Thus the play does indeed present the Oedipal scenario, complete with the symbolic castration of the child, but it does so in conjunction with a scapegoating scenario that is itself linked to a certain kind of narrative and dramatic intelligibility. *Oedipus Rex* also includes unresolved elements through which one may contest these scenarios and proceed to the possibility of different readings of both their dubious reductivism and the larger sociopolitical situation in which it operates (for example, a reading that stresses the ideologically stabilizing function of reacting to anxiety through a scapegoat mechanism).

Freud never recognized the extent to which Sophocles' play cast doubt upon the Oedipal scenario, perhaps because the way it questioned that scenario was arguably more explicit than anything to be found in Freud's work. It is nonetheless noteworthy that Freud, in recounting the story of his own life and thought, showed resistance to assuming the Oedipal position. Freud was reluctant to avow a symbolic slaying of his actual or intellectual fathers, and he even shied away from acknowledging the problem of succession. In his well-known reference to his own father, Jacob, in *The Interpretation of Dreams,* Freud has his father undergo "castration" at the hands of an anti-Semitic stranger, and the father's passive acceptance of the insult serves to repeat his castration in the eyes of his son. One might perhaps entitle this scene, reminiscent of one in *The Brothers Karamazov,* "A Father Is Being Beaten":

> I may have been ten or twelve years old, when my father began to take me with him on his walks and reveal to me in his talk his views upon things in the world we live in. Thus it was, on one such occasion, that he told me a story to show me how much better things were now than they had been in his days. "When I was a young man," he said, "I went for a walk one Saturday in the streets of your birthplace; I was well dressed, and had a new fur cap on my head. A Christian came up to me and with a single blow knocked off my cap into the mud and shouted: 'Jew! Get off the pavement!'" "And what did you do?" I asked. "I went into the roadway and picked up my cap," was his quiet reply. This struck me as unheroic conduct on the part of the big, strong man who

19. See Cynthia Chase, "Oedipal Textuality: Reading Freud's Reading of Oedipus," *Diacritics* 9 (Spring 1979): 54–68.

was holding the little boy by the hand. I contrasted this situation with another which fitted my feelings better: the scene in which Hannibal's father, Hamilcar Barca, made the boy swear before the household altar to take vengeance on the Romans. Ever since that time Hannibal had had a place in my phantasies.[20]

It is unclear from this passage whether the progressivist reason for the story (so blatantly enmeshed in displacement that its little object lesson is rendered abject) was actually given by Freud's father or was imputed to him by Freud himself. One might also see the story as de-mythologizing the role of the father in a manner Freud refused to acknowledge. Indeed Freud seems to reverse roles by having the father undergo symbolic castration and to localize in his "bad" example an infantile threat of powerlessness that recurs throughout life. In any event, Freud's affirmed identification with figures such as Hannibal and Moses furnished him with more potent role models and symbolic fathers. In the case of Moses, one had, on Freud's own interpretation, a markedly liminal figure—an Egyptian who became a Jew, and therefore someone who deliberately chose the fate Freud inherited as destiny from his parents. In his *Autobiographical Study* Freud will implicitly differentiate himself from his father by stating that he "refused absolutely" to feel inferior because he was a Jew and that through his acceptance of an alien, oppositional status "the foundations were . . . laid for a certain degree of independence of judgment" (*AS*, pp. 14, 15).

Part of the allure of autobiographical writing is the opportunity it offers to become one's own symbolic genitor. Freud never mentions his mother in his *Autobiographical Study*, and his only overt reference to his father is limited to the remarkably "unpsychoanalytic" statement: "Although we lived in very limited circumstances, my father insisted that, in my choice of a profession, I should follow my own inclinations" (*AS*, p. 13). Yet his autobiography is, after all, intellectual and professional, and in recounting the story of his thought he confirms the impression of self-genesis rather than of Oedipal anxiety—although the two may of course be interpreted as having a compensatory relation to one another. Freud provides little "ancestry" for his ideas and highlights the image of the lonely discoverer by stressing his isolation for ten years as the first psychoanalyst. (This image is duly replicated in the "filiopious" biography of Ernest Jones.) Freud avoided reading thinkers, such as Nietzsche, who might undercut his sense of creativity, and he even saw his position as founding father as authorizing him in maintaining that "no one can know better than I do what psycho-analysis is, how it differs from other ways of investigating the life of the mind, and precisely what should be called psycho-analysis and what would better be described by some other

20. Freud, *The Interpretation of Dreams* (New York, 1965), p. 230.

name" ("HPM," p. 7).[21] When he did acknowledge the role of three powerful fathers—Josef Breuer, Jean Martin Charcot, and Rudolf Chrobak (the latter being "perhaps the most eminent of all our Vienna physicians")—it was to indicate how they had blinded themselves by not seeing what was plainly before them (the importance of sexuality in the etiology of neurosis). Freud did not have to rise up against them; he had only to complement their blindness with his insight by noticing or paying attention to what they unknowingly transmitted to him. And he did so in a manner that confirmed his theory of *Nachträglichkeit* (thereby managing to qualify the thesis of absolute originality in a rather original way).

> These three men had all communicated to me a piece of knowledge which, strictly speaking, they themselves did not possess. Two of them later denied having done so when I reminded them of the fact; the third (the great Charcot) would probably have done the same if it had been granted me to see him again. But these three identical opinions, which I had heard without understanding, had lain dormant in my mind for years, until one day they awoke in the form of an apparently original discovery. ["HPM," p. 13]

A final instance of Freud's resistance to assuming the Oedipal position, being faced with the threat of castration and having to work through it to "maturity," is provided by *Civilization and Its Discontents* (1930). I shall later quote the famous passage concerning the possibility of pathological states of society. Here I would simply note that the repeated detours in his argument—which Freud himself remarks upon—as well as the suspicious demurrers intimating that he is merely stating the obvious may be related to his reluctance in taking up the position of social critic. Such a step would cast him in the Oedipal role writ large: that of someone challenging the collective superego of society. As a psychoanalyst, Freud always experienced a perhaps necessary role tension between the status of the practitioner dealing with people on a one-to-one basis (a professional status) and that of the social critic addressing structural problems (a nonprofessional status).[22] And there were good reasons for hesitancy and self-doubt in making sweeping judgments about the state of society or the course of civilization. But, on Freud's own "authority," one might argue that his hesitations concerning social criticism were overdetermined and that the Oedipal scenario was at play—notably in a resistance to

---

21. The claim of course prefaced an attack upon the apostasies of Jung and Adler.

22. This tension is eliminated by the adamantly collectivist and revolutionary position taken by Herbert Marcuse in *Eros and Civilization: A Philosophical Inquiry into Freud* (Boston, 1955). The role tension in Freud had an "economic" dimension: the individual practitioner did not engage basic social problems but had a greater chance of success, if only in returning people from "hysterical misery" to "everyday unhappiness"; the social critic probably had less chance of success but directed attention to structural causes of "discontent."

having it set fully into motion, a resistance that need not be taken in a simply negative sense but in one that may help generate questions about the "imperial" scope of the scenario itself. Especially in his own narrative practice, there may on some level have been—however problematically—a bit of the *Anti-Oedipe*.

In Freud's theoretical rendition of the Oedipus complex and in his thematic application of it in the explicit interpretation of other narratives, however, the Oedipus complex tends to be portrayed as an unproblematic discovery, and castration anxiety tends to function as an ultimate sanction—the penal confirmation of the law of the father and the closure of one crucial stage of the life cycle. The boy in accepting the threat of castration undergoes a *Bildungsreise* cum *Biedermeier* saga in which he learns that a deferral of gratification will in time enable him to assume the role of the father and find a substitute for the mother. He will thus enter into a legitimate heritage wherein he will be like (but not too incestuously like) the father and be rewarded for giving up union with the mother. In its more general function as a structure of closure, castration anxiety seems to provide a definitive reduction of the anxiety of ambivalence, divided origins, and repetition (as it seems to do in the essay on the uncanny). It furnishes a clear-cut answer to the possibly uncertain origins of anxiety and converts a potentially intractable problem into a puzzle which detective work may solve. (It thus operates as a good, orthodox historian presumably does.) With it, we know what the boy wants in his *Heimweh;* we know why he cannot fulfill his primal wish to return to the womb (the once familiar place later defamiliarized through repression); and we know how the boy may achieve a modified, domesticated happy ending in founding a family of his own (the existential and hermeneutic pot of gold at the end of the psychoanalytic rainbow).

But castration anxiety also opens another story and unfolds other narrative sequences with consequences that may themselves generate anxiety over the status of the entire theory. The girl cannot resolve problems as readily as the boy, and for her castration anxiety is a point of entry to, rather than exit from, the Oedipus complex: it presumably inhibits the formation of her superego and threatens to underwrite her position of sociocultural inferiority. One also has the genesis of what might be called a castration narrative that may impede the boy's own *Bildung* through its phantasmatic snares.

The bizarre narrative of castration anxiety tells the story of fetishism. It begins with a nonevent, a disavowal of perception, a refusal to see what is there. For "in the beginning" the vagina is foreclosed—a derealized reality. It is replaced by another reality which is "perceived" as absent—something one "knows" should be there: the penis. This "knowledge" is of course based upon an invidious comparison with a privileged object. But the even more decisive step is the conversion of what is absent into what is missing. This is perhaps the true *coup d'Oedipe*, for at this point the narrative becomes blatantly phantasmatic. (There is a crucial relation between the conversion of absence into loss and the genesis of the phantasm.) What is missing is the very phallus which the woman (the phantasmatic phallic mother) had "in the beginning" but lost through some misdeed—an obvious lesson for the boy himself. The fetish for Freud is itself the narcissistically invested surrogate for the phantasmatic lost totality—a totality that never existed and whose imaginary constitution requires a conversion of absence into loss on the basis of a nonperception. Yet with the appearance of the imaginary totality, the castration narrative becomes a variant of (or perhaps the prototype for) the greatest story ever told—the classical "apocalyptic" narrative (as well as the displaced narrative of speculative dialectics) in which a totality fully present at the origin is lost through a sinful fall only to be regained in a utopian future.[23]

In the remainder of this essay, I shall more or less speculatively attempt to specify ways in which my discussion bears not only on the history of psychoanalysis but on history and criticism in general. An obvious question is the extent to which the ideal of providing comprehensive accounts or global theories that "bring order to chaos" entails phantasmatic investments—notably when this ideal prompts questionable methodological solutions, for example, in the form of classical narratives and noncommittal analyses of situations in which one is transferentially implicated. The "archive" itself may become a fetish when it is seen not as a repository of traces in the inferential reconstruction of historical processes but as a surrogate for the missing thing itself—*l'histoire totale*. But a more general approach to the problem of articulating history and psychoanalysis would, I think, have to begin with the contention that it is inadequate to rest content (as Freud sometimes did) with the *analogy* between ontogeny and phylogeny or between the individual and society. Instead one must actively recognize that the analogy itself conceals the more basic interaction of psychoanalytic and sociocultural processes involving social individuals. This interaction calls for an investigation of specific historical processes that cannot be treated as simple derivatives of a totalizing, macrological schema of the civilizing process or the evolution of the species.

---

23. For sympathetic portrayals of the "apocalyptic" narrative, see Frank Kermode, *The Sense of an Ending: Studies in the Theory of Fiction* (New York, 1967), and M. H. Abrams, *Natural Supernaturalism: Tradition and Revolution in Romantic Literature* (New York, 1971). Marx's understanding of "commodity fetishism" is itself indentured to the "castration narrative" insofar as it assumes a human essence or social totality from which one is "alienated" under capitalism. To this extent, what certain Marxists oppose to alienation may be part of the same complex as their object of criticism. The further question, however, is whether there are in Marx other dimensions of the critique of commodity fetishism and alienation as well as other possible bases for alternatives to them. On this question, see my "Marxism and Intellectual History," *Rethinking Intellectual History: Texts, Contexts, Language* (Ithaca, N.Y., 1983), pp. 325–46.

Freud's very understanding of temporality as repetition/change, bringing with it deferred action and transference, itself implied the importance of displacement over (or as) time. Freud's own second topology (ego–id–superego) did not simply supersede but displaced his first topology (conscious–unconscious–preconscious) in a complex network of continuities and discontinuities. It required an attempt to resituate the earlier concepts, with portions of the ego and the superego placed in the unconscious and the earlier notion of the "censor" expanded into a larger understanding of sociocultural norms (prohibitions and prescriptions). It also signaled the mutual articulation of the psyche and society. However one further explicates the notions of the superego and the ego, it is evident that they are constitutively implicated in sociocultural and historical processes. But what is less apparent is that a similar point may be made about the id and the drives. Freud called the drives the myths of psychoanalysis—its sometimes substantialized postulates that could never be directly perceived but could be inferred on the basis of their effects, traces, or "representatives." They may also be called the myths of historicity. When Freud asserted that the unconscious was intemporal and knew no contradiction, he relied for the contrast on a classical notion of history as chronological change and on an equally classical notion of the law of noncontradiction. In terms of his own notion of "contradictory" temporality as repetition with change (at times traumatically disruptive change), the drives themselves became historicized. They were not purely static or intemporal entities, and they could not be defined according to the law of noncontradiction. They mutually marked or supplemented one another, and they shared predicates in a complex exchange of continuity and discontinuity. Freud's own flexible, if not labile, determination of the drives (first, sexuality and self-preservative or ego drives, then "life" and "death" drives) is itself emblematic of their historicity. The drives were internally divided ("life" involving both free-flowing energy and binding into higher unities, with a tendency toward constancy or lowest possible tension, "death" involving both aggression and unbinding, with a tendency toward nirvana or absolute discharge), and their relation to one another was not that of simple binary opposition but rather of "chiasmatic" pairing.[24] In this sense, it is more accurate to speak not of the dualism of Freud's basic concepts but of their duality—a duality allowing for contradiction as well as for more undecidable modes of exchange. The historicity of the drives was further compounded by their interaction with the ego and superego in a subject that was decentered both "internally" and socioculturally but was also in quest of unity—phantasmatic unity and unity in more viable forms of "binding."

24. See Laplanche, *Life and Death in Psychoanalysis*, trans. Jeffrey Mehlman (Baltimore, 1976).

The entire question of psychoanalysis and history might be posed with respect to the notions of "binding" and "unbinding" as they bear upon sociocultural processes. Institutions (in the largest sense) are normative modes of "binding" with variable relations to more ecstatic, sublime, or uncanny modes of "unbinding." They require repetitive performance that may become compulsive but may also facilitate exchanges. Freud often referred to "mental work" in its *Wechselwirkung* with free-flowing, "primary-process" energy, and his thought in this regard opens onto the problem of institutions as loci of work that interacts with more or less "unbound" play. And it directs attention to the modalities of displacement in the history of society and culture.

Freud himself was preoccupied with secularization as a displacement of religious onto secular phenomena, including psychoanalysis itself. Indeed Freud's own "Enlightenment" hostility to religion may have been exacerbated by similarities that were too close for comfort. Not only did psychopathological symptoms seem like religious rituals or beliefs that had lost their collective institutional moorings to reestablish themselves in markedly self-punitive forms in the "private" psyche. (As Freud wrote to Fliess: "By the way, what have you to say to the suggestion that the whole of my brand-new theory of the primary origins of hysteria is already familiar and has been published a hundred times over, though several centuries ago? Do you remember my always saying that the mediaeval theory of possession, that held by the ecclesiastical courts, was identical with our theory of a foreign body and the splitting of consciousness?"[25]) But the psychoanalyst might himself bear an uncanny resemblance to the exorcist—a similitude that was anticipated as early as the sixteenth century when ecclesiastical authorities preemptively attacked attempts to construe demonic possession in terms of madness as the ultimate ruse of the devil himself.[26]

In *The Future of an Illusion*, Freud both disarmingly invokes "our God *logos*" and tries to distinguish between religious "delusions" and his own "illusions" on the grounds that the latter are open to correction and would be given up if experience were to contradict the expectations they fostered.[27] Weighting continuities and discontinuities in historical displacements in order to arrive at specific delineations that are neither identities nor simple differences is an extremely difficult, perhaps in-

---

25. Freud, *The Origins of Psycho-analysis: Letters, Drafts, and Notes to Wilhelm Fliess, 1887–1902*, ed. Marie Bonaparte, Anna Freud, Ernst Kris (Garden City, N.Y., 1957), p. 90.

26. See Mary R. O'Neill, "*Sacerdote overro strione:* Ecclesiastical and Superstitious Remedies in 16th Century Italy," in *Understanding Popular Culture,* ed. Steven L. Kaplan (Berlin, 1984), pp. 53–83.

27. See Freud, *The Future of an Illusion* (Garden City, N.Y., 1964), pp. 86 and 89. This text would repay an extended reading, particularly in view of its explicitly dialogic format in which Freud at times gives voice to the *advocatus diaboli* yet softly affirms the abiding power of reason and experience.

tractable, problem.[28] And it is a problem that is not limited to the already vast ramifications of the process of secularization. Indeed it raises the general question of the extent to which what is repressed or suppressed historically and socioculturally tends to return as the repressed in psychology.

One issue here is the formation of levels of culture in the modern period. The distinction among popular, mass, and elite (or high) culture seems to parallel and in certain respects may shape Freud's topology of id, ego, superego. Particularly in the late sixteenth and seventeenth centuries in Europe, elite culture (in the sense of artifacts of creative elites) became, to a significant extent, aligned with official state culture in a hegemonic formation that (notably in a country like France) tried to establish a shared superego (or what Emile Durkheim would call a *conscience collective*) extending to other sections of society and culture. Language was normalized according to elite standards. And the very definition of what constituted popular religion was the work of ecclesiastical elites concerned with circumscribing and controlling "superstition" and heterodoxy.[29] More generally, religious reform, the development of capitalism, and the rise of state bureaucracies combined to create more disciplined forms of social life in which priority was given to the delay of gratification and the minute surveillance of activity, including the role of "spiritual" exercises. As Michel Foucault has argued with some exaggeration in *Discipline and Punish,* the nineteenth century witnessed an expansion of technologies and mechanisms of surveillance and control, with Jeremy Bentham's Panopticon serving as a normative model for all bureaucratic institutions in which close and constant regulation of personnel was at a premium. Punishment itself was displaced from the physical to the psychical with the decline of torture and the generalization of incarceration as the homogeneous response to a wide variety of crimes.

For Foucault, the psychoanalytic session is the heir of the confessional in its scrutiny of the interior life and sexual desire of the individual. One might add that Freud's all-seeing superego is the internalized counterpart of the techniques of surveillance and control that were being disseminated

28. It is too simple to argue, as Hans Blumenberg does, that the displacement in secularization is functional, not substantive—that is, it constitutes a different answer to similar questions as were posed in religion. That the similarities and differences, continuities and discontinuities cannot be isolated or so sharply separated is intimated in Blumenberg's own attempt to ground the so-called legitimacy of the modern age on self-assertive will—what Heidegger took as the modern displacement par excellence of the traditional metaphysical quest for an ultimate ground. See Blumenberg, *The Legitimacy of the Modern Age,* trans. Robert M. Wallace (Cambridge, Mass., 1983).

29. My generalizations barely scratch the surface of an inordinately intricate and differentiated series of problems. See, for example, Roger Chartier, "Culture as Appropriation: Popular Cultural Uses in Early Modern France," and Jacques Revel, "Forms of Expertise: Intellectuals and 'Popular' Culture in France (1650–1800)," in *Understanding Popular Culture.* See also my comments in *History and Criticism* (Ithaca, N.Y., 1985).

in public life. The very opposition between public and private opened the public sphere to regulatory agencies while the private sphere was to be kept inviolate from "external" control only to be subjected to extremely demanding "internal" strictures. (This division of labor is evident in the thought of both Mill and Herbert Spencer.) Civil rights and freedom of speech in public life were thus offset by internal norms and mechanisms which set up "private" parameters to freedom of "inner" life and thought. For figures such as Mill and Spencer, it went without saying that sexual life would be subject to the strictest of inner controls. (One may note in passing the need for a general genealogy of the concepts of the public and the private.)

For a multiplicity of reasons, elites in the modern period tended to withdraw from earlier participation in certain "popular" forms, including carnivalesque activities, which were severely regulated and even repressed. Especially for the rising middle classes, the carnivalesque became the object of equivocal fascination and phobic investment. The very idea of either a communally festive consumption of an economic surplus or an exchange that did not seem determined by the profit motive might appear as the height of irrationality itself. The carnivalesque was domesticated and made to serve either the state in nationalistic celebrations or the family in both the situation comedies of daily life and the private observances of special occasions ("there's no place like home for the holidays"). Older and now suspect popular forms became something like a collective id, and they were relegated, at times in vestigial form, to the "folkloric" if not opaque world of the peasantry, the dangerous subculture of the urban proletariat, and the shocking antics of *la bohème*. Yet these forms might also threaten to return in distorted, indeed sadomasochistic variants. (In this sense there may be no contradiction between the interpretations of the Wolf-Man's father offered by Freud and by Abraham and Torok. Indeed a crucial problem in the modern period—ignored in the work of Norbert Elias and only intimated in Foucault's critique of the "repressive hypothesis"—is the conjunction of extremely "civilized," if not "repressive," control and at times "neobarbaric" excess, including sadomasochistic variants of the carnivalesque.)

The rise of mass or commodified culture, particularly in the pervasive modes it has taken in the recent past, added another dimension to this complex of forces. Mass culture was distributed to various levels of society but of course consumed differently by different groups. It nonetheless acted as a "relay" system that might threaten to reprocess older popular forms in more acceptably commodified and marketable packages. It "liberated" artists and intellectuals from aristocratic patronage, but by the nineteenth century it also came to define a culture from which artistic and intellectual elites often felt "alienated." Elite culture itself became inward-turning and often inaccessible not only to popular but to many middle-class groups—when it made use, for example, of older popular forms (such as the carnivalesque) in difficult, hermetic guises. It also became internally fragmented in ways which the so-called two cultures thesis vastly oversimplifies. Its artifacts entertained (and continue to entertain) a complex, internally divided relation to society and culture at large, involving both a reinforcement of newer forms of hegemony and contestation of them.

This brief, overly selective, and inadequate sketch of cultural processes in modern history, made with reference to certain psychoanalytic concepts, at least suggests areas for the articulation of psychoanalytic and historical research. The very definition of levels of culture raises the question of processes of boundary formation (with its inclusions, exclusions, isolations, and so forth) that psychoanalysis has explored in terms of the psyche. More pointedly, Freud looked to all types of signifying practice with specific concern for the role of the body as an organizing trope. (As he puts it with tragicomic, perversely carnivalesque force in his study of the Wolf-Man, "his bowel began, like a hysterically affected organ, to 'join in the conversation'" ["IN," p. 265].) The paradigm of the trauma was the rupture of the skin, and the body provided a reference point for divisions between an "inside" and an "outside." The body might well serve as tropaic matrix in the investigation of sociocultural processes, including the opposition between public and private spheres as well as the formation of disciplines on both discursive and institutional levels. What is good to "ingest" in a given group or discipline, what should be "expelled" as indigestible, and what metabolism is considered "normal" in the rhythm of social life are only some of the most pressing questions in this respect.

On a more directly institutional plane, the network formed by family, educational system, state, organized religion, and commodified economy has complex connections with levels of culture and psychic processes. Freud focused on the family as the "relay" between the child and the larger society and culture. Yet the family itself might of course seek closure as a proverbial haven in a heartless world. Freud himself seemed symptomatically to underwrite this closure in his restricted ability to thematize the problem of the relation of the family to other institutions and discursive practices. But he also introduced considerations of authority and power into the seeming haven of the family itself, intimating one direction for an analysis of the politics of everyday life. His own accounts of the family, moreover, included, however equivocally, the presence of interrupters of familial closure and uneasy participants in the family romance. This was notably the case of the maid or nurse as a liminal figure between the family and the larger society—an "other" from a lower social class who partially shared the intimacy and even the secrets of the family without being a full-fledged member of its charmed circle. (It is significant that the embarrassing scene between Freud and a woman patient, which he employs in his *Autobiographical Study* to introduce transference as a displacement of familial relations, is itself interrupted by a maid whose "unexpected entrance" relieved the psychoanalytic couple from a "painful discussion."[30]) In contemporary society, the mediating and supplementary function of the maid in the family is to a large extent taken by the peer group and the media—two "interrupters" of familial closure given scant attention in Louis Althusser's discussion of so-called Ideological State Appartuses.[31]

The apparent problem is how to extend further Freud's analysis of the relation of the family to other institutions and to join it with sociocultural criticism. (This is of course a problem that has bedeviled intellectuals, especially on the left, since Freud's own time, and a prominent form it has taken is the attempt to "build a bridge" between Marx and Freud, often with assistance from other classical social theorists such as Durkheim and Weber.) The *locus classicus* of Freud's own confrontation with the issue is the following passage from *Civilization and Its Discontents:*

> I hasten to come to a close. But there is one question which I can hardly evade. If the development of civilization has such a far-reaching similarity to the development of the individual and if it employs the same methods, may we not be justified in reaching the diagnosis that, under the influence of cultural urges, some civilizations, or some epochs of civilization—possibly the whole of mankind—have become "neurotic"? An analytic dissection of such neuroses might lead to therapeutic recommendations which could lay claim to great practical interest. I would not say that an attempt of this kind to carry psycho-analysis over to the cultural community was absurd or doomed to be fruitless. But we should have to be very cautious and not forget that, after all, we are only dealing with analogies and that it is dangerous, not only with men but also with concepts, to tear them from the sphere in which they have originated and been evolved. Moreover, the diagnosis of communal

30. See *AS,* p. 49. On the role of the nurse, see, for example, Jane Gallop, *The Daughter's Seduction: Feminism and Psychoanalysis* (Ithaca, N.Y., 1982), pp. 141–48.

31. See Louis Althusser, "Ideology and Ideological State Apparatuses," *Lenin and Philosophy and Other Essays,* trans. Ben Brewster (New York, 1971), pp. 127–86. Althusser of course tries to link Marxism and Lacanian psychoanalysis in a theory of institutions and ideology in modern society. His important effort is limited in a number of ways. He attempts to position Lacan in relation to Freud on the analogy of his own relation to Marx, as he conceives it. This results in a rather misleading image of Lacan as providing a "science" of a new "object": the Freudian unconscious. Althusser's definition of ideology as centered on the subject, moreover, both occludes the problem of the subject in the constitution of science and obviates the possibility of an objectivist or scientistic ideology (toward which Althusser himself at times veers). The notion of Ideological State Apparatuses itself begs the question of the relation of the state and official culture to other institutions and levels of culture, and the overdrawn conception of hegemony tends to respond to the deficiencies of economic determinism with an equally one-sided and deceptively generalized construction of the political and sociocultural order.

neuroses is faced with a special difficulty. In an individual neurosis we take as our starting-point the contrast that distinguishes the patient from his environment, which is assumed to be "normal". For a group all of whose members are affected by one and the same disorder no such background could exist; it would have to be found elsewhere. And as regards the therapeutic application of our knowledge, what would be the use of the most correct analysis of social neuroses, since no one possesses authority to impose such a therapy upon the group? But in spite of all these difficulties, we may expect that one day someone will venture to embark upon a pathology of cultural communities.[32]

Recently Jürgen Habermas has found his own reasons for backing away from the earlier effort of the Frankfurt school to answer Freud's expectation by converting psychoanalysis itself into a paradigm for critical theory, and he has turned to his own version of macrological evolutionary theory and "universal pragmatics." Martin Jay provides this lucid summary of Habermas' position:

> Whereas the patient and analyst shared an a priori interest in relieving the patient's neurotic symptoms, in society no such consensus could be assumed. Indeed, insofar as certain men or classes benefited from the maintenance of ideological distortion and exploitative power relations, there was no reason to assume they would willingly enter the process of dialogic enlightenment suggested by the psychoanalytic model. Nor would their improved understanding of reality necessarily generate a desire to transform it. Symmetrical relations in a truly democratic public sphere could not be seen as a condition for social change, when in fact they were one of its goals.[33]

Here one may call into question not the insistence on impediments to discursive enlightenment or dialogic reciprocity in existing societies but the basis of the contrast with the psychoanalytic model. It is not true that the analyst and the patient simply share the goal of relieving symptoms or of "entering the process of dialogic enlightenment." Habermas' own understanding of analysis is overly predetermined by an "ego-psychological" perspective. The difficulties in working through transference, countertransference, and resistances pose severe obstacles to consensus, as does the difference in authority (or relative helplessness) between analyst and analysand. Freud, moreover, stressed the secondary benefits from illness that create major blocks to the dissolution of symptoms; he also recognized the danger that even more severe symptoms might replace

---

32. Freud, *Civilization and Its Discontents* (New York, 1961), pp. 102–3.
33. Martin Jay, *Marxism and Totality: The Adventures of a Concept from Lukács to Habermas* (Berkeley and Los Angeles, 1984), pp. 480–81.

those that were eliminated. There are of course analogues of these problems in social life. The most obvious is the risk of radical change, especially when there is little idea of viable alternatives or even the tendency to confide in blank utopianism and apocalyptic euphoria. But one may also mention the way established regimes institute (as Foucault has argued) systematic and at times flagrant discrepancies between affirmed norms and actual performance. In this manner, "pathology" is "normalized": normative expectations are continually frustrated but in a way that evokes recurrent attempts at reform, sustained by rhetorical appeals to a founding program, constitution, or charter.

One may also argue that Freud's own "analogy" is both better and worse than he thought. It is better because psychoanalysis and social theory face similar problems. These problems tend to be obscured by the assumptions active in Freud's passage: the enabling idea that someone (presumably the analyst supported by social forces) has the authority to impose therapy on the patient (which Freud elsewhere questioned) and the initial postulate that existing society is normal (which takes psychoanalysis in the direction of uncritically adaptive therapy). Yet Freud's analogy is also worse than he thought. It reverts to the macrological parallel of ontogeny and phylogeny. More important, it takes as an analogy between entities presumed to be discrete and to have autonomous origins and evolutionary paths what is both more and other than an analogy— what in fact involves the interaction of social individuals and the mutual articulation of psychoanalytic and social categories. As we have noted, Freud sometimes emphasized the fact that, in elaborating psychoanalytic concepts and theories, he was already working on and transforming existing sociocultural material.

The very concept of normality is normative and implicated in sociocultural judgments, and for this very reason it calls for critical reflection. Yet it often functions as a residual category in Freud—a category on which he relies but which he defines largely in terms of its implicit contrast with pathology. (It is also noteworthy that there is no entry for "normality" in Laplanche and Pontalis' *Language of Psycho-analysis*.) In this sense, "normality" functions as the absent center of Freud's thought.

It must, however, be added that one of the most forceful incentives in Freud is to question the simple binary opposition between normality and pathology and instead to see these concepts in terms of interacting differences of degree problematically related to judgments of kind. He will refer at most to the "approximately normal person" (his self-designation in *The Interpretation of Dreams*), and he will show how pathogenic forces are not only active to different degrees in all people but ambivalently related to the most "positive" forces in life. Transference itself is a bridge between normality and pathology (both within and between selves)—a sign that movements in both directions are possible, short of irremediable psychosis (if indeed there is such a state beyond transference). But the absence of critical reflection about the category of normality facilitates its identification with conformity or adaptation in the existing sociocultural state of affairs.

The concepts of social normality and pathology are both highly problematic and probably necessary. Their status in this respect is no more and no less questionable than their psychoanalytic counterparts. Indeed the task (as Durkheim saw) was how to articulate the relations between the two sets of concepts. The active recognition that this task is itself normative and ethicopolitical and that it cannot be neatly disjoined from research and analysis is the *sine qua non* of any attempt to work through it toward that "elsewhere" which, Freud noted, had to be found for social criticism to be possible. In that attempt transference is at its most intense, yet the chances of acquiring critical perspective may also be greatest.

How to Do the History of Psychoanalysis:
A Reading of Freud's *Three Essays on the Theory of Sexuality*

Arnold I. Davidson

I have two primary aims in the following paper, aims that are inextricably intertwined. First, I want to raise some historiographical and epistemological issues about how to write the history of psychoanalysis. Although they arise quite generally in the history of science, these issues have a special status and urgency when the domain is the history of psychoanalysis. Second, in light of the epistemological and methodological orientation that I am going to advocate, I want to begin a reading of Freud's *Three Essays on the Theory of Sexuality,* one whose specificity is a function of my attachment to this orientation, to a particular way of doing the history of psychoanalysis. Despite the enormous number of pages that have been written on Freud's *Three Essays,* it is very easy to underestimate the density of this book, a density at once historical, rhetorical, and conceptual. This underestimation stems in part from historiographical presumptions that quite quickly misdirect us away from the fundamental issues.

In raising questions about the historiography of the history of science, I obviously cannot begin at the beginning. So let me begin much further along, with the writings of Michel Foucault. I think of the work of Foucault, in conjunction with that of Gaston Bachelard and Georges Canguilhem, as exemplifying a very distinctive perspective about how to write the

Discussions, both recent and ancient, with Dan Brudney, Nancy Cartwright, Peter Galison, Erin Kelly, and David Wellbery have greatly benefited this paper. Conversations with Stanley Cavell about how to approach the texts of Freud were enormously helpful. A version of this paper was given as a talk to the Institute for Psychoanalytic Training and Research in New York, and I am grateful for the discussion that followed my presentation.

history of science. In the English-speaking world, perhaps only the work of Ian Hacking both shares this perspective and ranks with its French counterparts in terms of originality and quality. No brief summary can avoid eliding the differences between Bachelard, Canguilhem, Hacking, and Foucault; indeed, the summary I am going to produce does not even fully capture Foucault's perspective, which he called "archaeology."[1] But this sketch will have to do for the purposes I have in mind here, whose ultimate aim is to reorient our approach to the history of psychoanalysis.

In a 1977 interview, Foucault gave what we might take to be a one-sentence summary of his archaeological method: " 'Truth' is to be understood as a system of ordered procedures for the production, regulation, distribution, circulation and operation of statements."[2] Given this characterization of his standpoint, we should think of Foucault as having undertaken in his archaeological works to write a history of statements that claim the status of truth, a history of these systems of ordered procedures. The attempt to write such a history involves isolating certain kinds of discursive practices—practices for the production of statements—which will be "characterized by the delimitation of a field of objects, the definition of a legitimate perspective for the agent of knowledge, and the fixing of norms for the elaboration of concepts and theories. Thus, each discursive practice implies a play of prescriptions that designate its exclusions and choices."[3] Foucault's project, announced in the foreword to the English edition of *The Order of Things*, was to write the history of what Hacking has called the *immature sciences*—those sciences that, in Foucault's words, are "considered too tinged with empirical thought, too exposed to the vagaries of chance or imagery, to age-old traditions and external events, for it to be supposed that their history could be anything

1. The sketch that follows reproduces, with some omissions and additions, the beginning of my "Archeology, Genealogy, Ethics," in *Michel Foucault: A Critical Reader,* ed. David Hoy (London, 1986), pp. 221–34.

2. Michel Foucault, "Truth and Power," *Power/Knowledge: Selected Interviews and Other Writings, 1972–1977,* ed. Colin Gordon, trans. Gordon, Leo Marshall, John Mepham, and Kate Soper (New York, 1980), p. 133.

3. Foucault, "History of Systems of Thought," *Language, Counter-Memory, Practice: Selected Essays and Interviews,* ed. Donald F. Bouchard, trans. Bouchard and Sherry Simon (Ithaca, N.Y., 1970), p. 199.

Arnold I. Davidson is assistant professor in the department of philosophy, the Committee on the Conceptual Foundations of Science, and the Committee on General Studies in the Humanities at the University of Chicago. He is currently writing a book on the history and epistemology of nineteenth-century psychiatric theories of sexuality.

other than irregular"[4]—from the standpoint of an archaeology of discursive practices.[5] Foucault made the claim, perhaps commonplace now, but bold and even radical when he first wrote, that this kind of knowledge possesses a well-defined regularity, that a history of this knowledge can exhibit systems of rules, and their transformations, which make different kinds of statements possible. These rules are, however, never formulated by the participants in the discursive practice; they are not available to their consciousness but constitute what Foucault once called the "positive unconscious of knowledge."[6]

If these rules are both relatively autonomous and anonymous, if they make it possible for individuals to make the claims they do when they do, then the history of such rules and such knowledge will not look like the sort of history with which we are most familiar. It will not, for example, necessarily group sets of regularities around individual works and authors; nor will it rest content with the ordinary boundaries of what we think of as a science or a discipline. It will rather force regroupings of statements and practices into a "a new and occasionally unexpected unity."[7] Because Foucault wanted to describe discursive practices from the standpoint of archaeology, the theme of discontinuity was prominent in some of his major works. The unearthing of discontinuities between systems of knowledge is not an assumption of his method but a consequence of it. If one sets out to describe the historical trajectories of the sciences in terms of anonymous rules for the formation and production of statements, then what looked continuous from some other perspective now may very well appear radically discontinuous. Problems of periodization and of the unity of a domain may be almost entirely transformed: one will find, for example, that new kinds of statements which seem to be mere incremental additions to scientific knowledge are in fact made possible only because underlying rules for the production of discourse have significantly altered. However, the method of archaeology also makes possible the discovery of new continuities, overlooked because of a surface appearance of discontinuity. Archaeology makes no presumption about the predominance of discontinuity over continuity in the history of knowledge; but it does make it extremely likely that what had been taken to be natural groupings of thought will turn out, at this new level of analysis, to be quite unnatural indeed.

In other writings, I have tried to adopt and adapt Foucault's archaeological perspective, using it to write a history of nineteenth-century

4. Foucault, *The Order of Things: An Archaeology of the Human Sciences* (New York, 1970), p. ix.

5. See Ian Hacking, "Michel Foucault's Immature Science," *Noûs* 13 (Mar. 1979): 39–51.

6. Foucault, *The Order of Things*, p. xi.

7. Foucault, "History of Systems of Thought," p. 200.

psychiatric theories of sexuality.[8] I have argued that starting around 1870 a new psychiatric style of reasoning about diseases emerges, one that makes possible, among other things, statements about sexual perversion—about homosexuality, fetishism, sadism, and masochism—that then quickly become commonplaces in discussions of sexuality. The appearance and proliferation of these statements were a direct consequence of this new style of reasoning, which we can think of, in Foucault's terms, as the birth of a new discursive practice. An epistemologically central constituent of a style of reasoning, as I interpret it, is a set of concepts linked together by specifiable rules that determine what statements can and cannot be made with the concepts.[9] So to write a history of nineteenth-century psychiatry by way of this notion requires writing a history of the emergence of a new system of concepts and showing how these concepts are internally related by a set of rules to form what we might think of as a determinate conceptual space. We want to see what concepts, connected in what particular ways, allowed statements about sexual perversions that had never been made before; allowed the creation of a new object of medical discourse—sexuality. Thus, I have urged that we need a conceptual history of sexuality, without which we cannot know what was being talked about when the domain of psychiatric discourse became fixated on sexuality.

This same kind of method was employed by Heinrich Wölfflin in his *Principles of Art History: The Problem of the Development of Style in Later Art*. Wölfflin characterized the differences between classic and baroque art in terms of two distinct systems of determining concepts. He tried to show the way in which the features of classic art were linked together to form a specific classic visual space, while opposing features were linked together to form a distinctive baroque visual space.[10] It is no surprise that Paul Veyne, in his inaugural lecture at the Collège de France, has conjoined the names of Wölfflin and Foucault; nor is it a surprise, remembering the derivative role that great men in the history of science play in Foucault's work, that Arnold Hauser has referred to Wölfflin's art history as "art history without names."[11]

Whatever the plausibility of an art history without names, and whatever the general applicability of this methodological perspective in the history

8. See my "Closing Up the Corpses: Diseases of Sexuality and the Emergence of the Psychiatric Style of Reasoning," in *Handbook for the History of Psychiatry*, ed. J. Gach and E. Wallace, forthcoming; and my "Sex and the Emergence of Sexuality," forthcoming.

9. I discuss this notion at length in an unpublished paper, "Styles of Reasoning, Conceptual History, and the Emergence of Psychiatry."

10. See Heinrich Wölfflin, *Principles of Art History: The Problem of the Development of Style in Later Art*, trans. M. D. Hottinger (New York, 1950).

11. See Paul Veyne, *L'Inventaire des différences: leçon inaugurale au Collège de France* (Paris, 1976); see Arnold Hauser, *The Philosophy of Art History* (Evanston, Ill., 1985). Hauser is referring to Wölfflin's own phrase, "Kuntsgeschichte ohne Namen," which appears in the foreword to the first edition of *Principles of Art History*. This foreword was omitted from later editions, and from the English translation of Wölfflin's book.

of science, a thoroughgoing skepticism about its usefulness for writing the history of psychoanalysis might well persist. Since psychoanalysis is so completely intertwined with the name of Sigmund Freud, it is natural to object that writing its history without his name would not be to write its history at all. It is, no doubt, a peculiar feature of psychoanalysis, a feature that requires a more detailed account than I can provide here, that no matter what one takes as the last word of psychoanalysis, its first and second words are always the words of Freud. And this is not merely because Freud was the originator of psychoanalysis but primarily because the central concepts, claims, and problems of psychoanalysis have not received deeper specification beyond their congealment in his texts. So there is an obvious sense in which any history of psychoanalysis must continuously invoke the name of Freud. This fact, however, does not, and should not, settle the question of what form this invocation should take. Wölfflin was not reluctant to discuss the great works of classic and baroque art; he wanted to demonstrate that this greatness was not incompatible with their artists being subject to specifiable constraints. "Not everything is possible at all times," Wölfflin famously remarked, and his art history, without names, was meant to conceptualize the limits of the artistically possible in a given historical period and to show how a change in constraints could lead to a reorganization of the limits of the possible.[12] To do this successfully, Wölfflin had to operate at a level distinct from individual biography and psychology. In writing the history of psychoanalysis, I want to preserve this level, one whose articulation requires a history of a structurally related system of concepts, a conceptual space, that lies below, or behind, the work of any particular author, even great works of great authors.

Two competing myths about Freud have gradually developed. The first myth, that of official psychoanalysis, depicts Freud as a lonely genius, isolated and ostracized by his colleagues, fashioning psychoanalysis single-handedly and in perpetual struggle with the world at large. The history of psychoanalysis under the sway of this myth has become the story of Freud as triumphant revolutionary. The second, opposing myth pictures Freud as getting all of his ideas from someone else—usually Wilhelm Fliess, although the names of Jean Martin Charcot, Havelock Ellis, and Albert Moll, among many others, are also mentioned frequently—and taking credit for what were in fact no more than minor modifications in previously developed theories. This is the myth of the career discontents, and the history of psychoanalysis dominated by it has become the story of Freud as demagogue, usurper, and megalomaniac. To the first myth, one can reply *ex nihilo nihil fit,* which is as appropriate a slogan in the history of science as in theology. The second myth derives its strength from an impoverished reading of Freud and an equally impoverished

12. Wölfflin, *Principles,* p. ix.

notion of how to read Freud. When applied to the *Three Essays on the Theory of Sexuality*, this myth proceeds by showing that, for example, Richard von Krafft-Ebing employed the idea of libido and Ellis the idea of autoerotism, that Fliess made central use of the notion of bisexuality, that Moll discovered infantile sexuality years before Freud, that Iwan Bloch talked about erotogenic zones, and so on, ad infinitum. Since Freud was fully aware of these writings, the story continues, how could he be anything other than a usurper, with a kingdom made of stolen materials?

Both of these myths, mirror images of one another, depend on the same kind of historiographical presumptions, unacknowledged, prejudicial, and, in my opinion, misguided. Whether Freud did or did not discover infantile sexuality, whatever his own changing assessment of his indebtedness to Fliess, whether he was the first, second, or third to use the word *Trieb* when speaking of sexuality, all of these claims, both pro and con, are radically inadequate if we want to understand his place in the history of psychiatry. Both myths rely on an inappropriate invocation of his name, both misplace the role that such invocation should have in writing the history of psychoanalysis. Freud's biography, his personal drama, and whom he read in what year are all topics that, of course, are interesting and important. But they will not allow us accurately to ground the question whether he was an originator of thought or merely a conserver, and sometimes extender, of other people's ideas.

How we characterize Freud's place in the history of psychiatry ought to depend not on who said what first, but on whether the structure of concepts associated with Freud's writings continues, extends, diverges from, or undermines the conceptual space of nineteenth-century psychiatry. What we need, as I have indicated, is a history of the concepts used in psychoanalysis, an account of their historical origins and transformations, their rules of combination, and their employment in a mode of reasoning.[13] This task presumes, first, that we can isolate the distinctive concepts of nineteenth-century psychiatry, articulate their rules of combination, and thereby discern their limits of the possible. We must then undertake the very same enterprise for Freud's work, which, with sufficient detail, should enable us to see more clearly whether Freud's conceptual space continues or breaks with that of his predecessors. Although Freud may use much the same terminology as many of the people we know he read, the structure of concepts he employs, what I have been calling his conceptual space, may nevertheless deviate to greater or lesser extent from theirs.

These methodological remarks, however brief and abstract, should stand or fall depending on whether or not they enable us to produce a philosophically enlightening, historically plausible account of the issues at hand. If they do not directly guide us toward a more adequate reading

---

13. I have discussed some of these issues in relation to hysteria in my "Assault on Freud," *London Review of Books*, 5–19 July 1984, pp. 9–11.

of Freud, then their interest will remain but brief and abstract. So I now want to turn to some of the historical questions that this archaeological method dictates. This is the place to acknowledge the somewhat misleading implications of the title of this essay. I will not even attempt anything like a complete reading of the *Three Essays*. I want to focus exclusively on the problems encountered in reading the first essay, "Sexual Aberrations." Given the structure of Freud's book, I will obviously have to look at passages in the other essays as well, but I will discuss these only when, and insofar as, they are relevant to excavating Freud's conceptualization of the sexual perversions. The scope of my task is limited here by my desire to approximate to a comprehensive reading only of this first essay. In order to do even that, I will have to start before Freud, with the prevailing concept of sexual perversion in the literature of nineteenth-century psychiatry. So let me try to demarcate the conceptual space of which perversion was an element that dominated European psychiatry at the time Freud was writing the *Three Essays*.[14]

During the second half of the nineteenth century there was a virtual explosion of medical discussions about the sexual perversions, what Foucault has called an incitement to discourse, an immense verbosity.[15] These discussions saturated European and, eventually, American psychiatric concerns, resulting in an epidemic of perversion that seemed to rival the recent cholera outbreaks. Despite many differences between these loquacious psychiatrists, differences both theoretical and clinical, all shared the concept of perversion that underpinned these discussions—the perversions were a *shared object* of psychiatric discourse about which there were commonly recognized and fully standardized forms of reasoning. The best way to begin to understand the nineteenth-century conceptual space encircling perversion is to examine the notion of the sexual instinct, for the conception of perversion underlying clinical thought was that of a functional disease of this instinct. That is to say, the class of diseases that affected the sexual instinct was precisely the sexual perversions. A functional understanding of the instinct allowed one to isolate a set of disorders or diseases that were disturbances of its special functions. Moreau (de Tours), in a book that influenced the first edition of Krafft-Ebing's *Psychopathia Sexualis*, argued that the clinical facts forced one to accept as absolutely demonstrated the psychic existence of a sixth sense, which he called the genital sense.[16] Although the notion of a genital sense may appear ludicrous, Moreau's characterization was adopted by subsequent

14. In what follows, I recount, with some additional quotations, parts of my article, "Closing Up the Corpses." More detailed historical documentation for my claims can be found in that paper.

15. See Foucault, *The History of Sexuality, Vol. 1: An Introduction*, trans. Robert Hurley (New York, 1978).

16. See Paul Moreau (de Tours), *Des Aberrations du sens génésique*, 2d ed. (Paris, 1880), p. 2.

French clinicians, and his phrase "sens genital" was preserved, by Charcot among others, as a translation of our "sexual instinct." The genital sense is just the sexual instinct, masquerading in different words. Its characterization as a sixth sense was a useful analogy. Just as one could become blind, or have acute vision, or be able to discriminate only a part of the color spectrum, and just as one might go deaf, or have abnormally sensitive hearing, or be able to hear only certain pitches, so too this sixth sense might be diminished, augmented, or perverted. What Moreau hoped to demonstrate was that this genital sense had special functions distinct from those served by other organs and that, just as with the other senses, this sixth sense could be psychically disturbed without the proper working of other mental functions, either affective or intellectual, being harmed.[17] A demonstration such as Moreau's was essential in isolating diseases of sexuality as distinct morbid entities.

The *Oxford English Dictionary* reports that the first modern medical use in English of the concept of perversion occurred in 1842 in Dunglison's *Medical Lexicon: "Perversion,* one of the four modifications of function in disease: the three others being augmentation, diminution, and abolition."[18] The notions of perversion and function are inextricably connected. Once one offers a functional characterization of the sexual instinct, perversions become a natural class of diseases; without this characterization there is really no conceptual room for this kind of disease. It is clear, for instance, that Krafft-Ebing understood the sexual instinct in a functional way. In his *Text-book of Insanity* Krafft-Ebing is unequivocal in his claim that life presents two instincts, those of self-preservation and sexuality; he insists that abnormal life presents no new instincts, although the instincts of self-preservation and sexuality "may be lessened, increased, or manifested with perversion."[19] The sexual instinct was often compared with the instinct of self-preservation, which manifested itself in appetite. In his section on "Disturbances of the Instincts," Krafft-Ebing first discusses the anomalies of the appetites, which he divides into three different kinds. There are increases of the appetite ("hyperorexia"), lessening of the appetite ("anorexia"), and perversions of the appetite, such as a "true impulse to eat spiders, toads, worms, human blood, etc." (*TI*, p. 80; see also pp. 77–81). Such a classification is exactly what one should expect on a functional understanding of the instinct. Anomalies of the sexual instinct are similarly classified as lessened or entirely wanting ("anesthesia"), abnormally increased ("hyperesthesia"), and perversely expressed ("paresthesia"); in addition there is a fourth class of anomalies of the sexual

17. See ibid., p. 3.
18. *Oxford English Dictionary*, s.v. "perversion."
19. Richard von Krafft-Ebing, *Text-book of Insanity Based on Clinical Observations*, trans. Charles Gilbert Chaddock (Philadelphia, 1904), p. 79; further references to this work, abbreviated *TI*, will be included in the text. Krafft-Ebing considers abolition to be the extreme case of diminution.

instinct which consists in its manifestation outside of the period of anatomical and physiological processes in the reproductive organs ("paradoxia") (see *TI*, p. 81).[20] In both his *Text-book of Insanity* and *Psychopathia Sexualis*, Krafft-Ebing further divides the perversions into sadism, masochism, fetishism, and contrary sexual instinct (see *TI*, pp. 83–86 and *PS*, pp. 34–36).

To be able to determine precisely what phenomena are functional disturbances or diseases of the sexual instinct, one must also, of course, specify in what the normal or natural function of this instinct consists. Without knowing the normal function of the instinct, everything and nothing could count as a functional disturbance. There would be no principled criterion to include or exclude any behavior from the disease category of perversion. So one must first believe that there is a natural function of the sexual instinct and then believe that this function is quite determinate. We might think that questions as momentous as these would have received extensive discussion during the heyday of perversion in the nineteenth century. But, remarkably enough, no such discussion appears. There is virtually *unargued unanimity* both on the fact that this instinct does have a natural function and on what that function is. Krafft-Ebing's view is representative here:

> During the time of the maturation of physiological processes in the reproductive glands, desires arise in the consciousness of the individual, which have for their purpose the perpetuation of the species (sexual instinct). . . .
>
> With opportunity for the natural satisfaction of the sexual instinct, every expression of it that does not correspond with the purpose of nature—i.e., propagation—must be regarded as perverse. [*PS*, pp. 16, 52–53][21]

Should anyone doubt the representativeness of Krafft-Ebing's conception, let me cite a long passage from Moll's *Perversions of the Sex Instinct* (1891), since Moll is considered by Frank Sulloway, among others, to be a direct anticipator of Freud.[22] Although Moll disputed many of Krafft-Ebing's specific claims, the degree of unspoken agreement on the appropriate conception of perversion is remarkable. Moll believed that many of the theories of homosexuality with which he was familiar (homosexuality being the most clinically well documented of the sexual

---

20. This same classification is given in Krafft-Ebing, *Psychopathia Sexualis, with Especial Reference to the Antipathic Sexual Instinct: A Medico-Forensic Study*, trans. Franklin S. Klaf (New York, 1965), p. 34; all further references to this work, abbreviated *PS*, will be included in the text.

21. See also *TI*, p. 81.

22. See Frank J. Sulloway, *Freud, Biologist of the Mind* (New York, 1979), esp. chap. 8.

perversions) did not sufficiently take into account the analogy between the sexual instinct and other functions:

> To understand the homosexual urge we should consider the genital instinct not as a phenomenon apart from the other functions but rather as a psychic function. The morbid modifications of the genital instinct would appear to be less incomprehensible if we were to admit that almost all the other functions whether physical or psychic may be susceptible to similar modifications. The sexual anomalies strike us as singular because most individuals who possess the attributes of the masculine sex have a sexual urge for women. But one must not be led astray by the frequence and regularity of this phenomenon. From a teleological point of view, that is from the point of view of the reproduction of the species, we consider *natural* the urge that the normal man feels for woman. Still in certain pathological conditions the organs do not meet the end assigned to them. The teeth are meant to grind food yet there are men who have no teeth or who have very few of them. The function of the liver is to secrete bile which is diverted into the intestine, and in certain disorders of the liver or of the bile ducts the bile is not secreted and does not reach the intestine. The function of hunger is to remind the organism that it needs food. However, there are pathological states in which the sensation of hunger is absent, although the stomach continues to function normally. It is the same with the absence of the sexual urge for women in a man possessing normal genital organs. We can hardly establish a connection between man's genital organs and his urge for women except from a teleological point of view. Otherwise, one does not see why men should be urged to have connections with women since ejaculation of the sperm may be brought about in quite other ways. It would be rather surprising to see the genital instinct not presenting the same morbid anomalies as the other functions.[23]

Like that of other late nineteenth-century psychiatrists, Moll's teleological *façon de parler* was mixed with, and presumably grounded in, evolutionary considerations. But my concern is not with why Moll said what he did but rather with exactly what he said. In this respect, his conception and Krafft-Ebing's are quite literally interchangeable.

Nineteenth-century psychiatry silently adopted this conception of the function of the sexual instinct. It was often taken as so natural as not to need explicit statement[24] since it was the only conception that

23. Albert Moll, *Perversions of the Sex Instinct: A Study of Sexual Inversion*, trans. Maurice Popkin (Newark, N.J., 1931), pp. 171–72; my emphasis.

24. For some French examples of this understanding, see Maurice Paul Legrain, *Des Anomalies de l'instinct sexuel et en particulier des inversions du sense génital* (Paris, 1896), and Dr. Laupts (pseudonym of Georges Saint-Paul), *L'Homosexualité et les types homosexuels: Nouvelle édition de perversion et perversité sexuelles* (Paris, 1910).

made sense of psychiatric practice. It is not at all obvious why sadism, masochism, fetishism, and homosexuality should be treated as species of the same disease, for they appear to have no essential features in common. However, if one takes the natural function of the sexual instinct to be propagation, and if one takes the corresponding natural, psychological satisfaction of this instinct to consist in the satisfaction derived from heterosexual, genital intercourse, then it becomes possible to see why they were all classified together as perversions. Sadism, masochism, fetishism, and homosexuality all exhibit the same kind of perverse expression of the sexual instinct, the same basic kind of functional deviation, which manifests itself in the fact that psychological satisfaction is obtained primarily through activities disconnected from the natural function of the instinct. As Moll succinctly states it, emphasizing the psychological constituent of this natural function, "we ought to consider the absence of heterosexual desires morbid even when the possibility of practicing normal coition exists."[25] This understanding of the instinct permits a unified treatment of perversion, allowing one to place an apparently heterogeneous group of phenomena under the same natural disease-kind. Had anyone denied either that the sexual instinct has a natural function or that this function is procreation, diseases of perversion, as they were actually understood, would not have entered psychiatric nosology.

With this conceptual and historical background, we can place the opening two paragraphs of Freud's first essay in proper perspective:

> The fact of the existence of sexual needs in human beings and animals is expressed in biology by the assumption of a 'sexual instinct', on the analogy of the instinct of nutrition, that is of hunger. Everyday language possesses no counterpart to the word 'hunger', but science makes use of the word 'libido' for that purpose.
>
> Popular opinion has quite definite ideas about the nature and characteristics of this sexual instinct. It is generally understood to be absent in childhood, to set in at the time of puberty in connection with the process of coming to maturity and to be revealed in the manifestations of an irresistible attraction exercised by one sex upon the other; while its aim is supposed to be sexual union, or at all events actions leading in that direction. We have every reason to believe, however, that these views give a very false picture of the true situation. If we look into them more closely we shall find that they contain a number of errors, inaccuracies and hasty conclusions.[26]

25. Moll, *Perversions of the Sex Instinct*, p. 180.

26. Sigmund Freud, *Three Essays on the Theory of Sexuality, The Standard Edition of the Complete Psychological Works of Sigmund Freud*, ed. and trans. James Strachey, 24 vols. (London, 1953–74), 7:135; further references to this work, abbreviated *T*, will be included in the text.

In describing popular opinion about the sexual instinct, Freud's use of the analogy of hunger indicates, as it did throughout the nineteenth century, the functional conception of this instinct. Moreover, just as we should expect, the natural function of the sexual instinct is expressed by an irresistible attraction of the sexes toward one another, an attraction whose ultimate aim is sexual union. Freud's use of the phrase "popular opinion" can easily mislead a reader to think that this conception of the sexual instinct defines popular as opposed to learned opinion. But however popular this opinion was, it was exactly the view of those psychiatrists, listed in the first footnote of this first essay, from whom Freud says his information has been derived.[27] If the argument of Freud's first essay is that these views "give a very false picture of the true situation," then we can expect Freud's conclusions to place him in opposition to both popular and, more importantly, medical opinion. The problem is how precisely to characterize this opposition.

In the last paragraph of this preliminary section of the first essay, Freud introduces what he calls "two technical terms." The *sexual object* is "the person from whom sexual attraction proceeds," while the *sexual aim* is "the act towards which the instinct tends" (*T*, pp. 135–36). Freud's motivation for introducing these terms is not merely, as he explicitly states it, that scientific observation uncovers many deviations in respect of both sexual object and sexual aim. More significantly, these are precisely the two conceptually basic kinds of deviations we should expect of those writers who subscribed to the popular conception of the sexual instinct. Deviations with respect to sexual object are deviations from the natural attraction exercised by one sex upon the other; deviations with respect to sexual aim are deviations from the natural goal of sexual union. The remainder of the first essay is structured around this distinction between sexual object and sexual aim, and the central role of this distinction is itself firmly dependent on the view of the sexual instinct that Freud will argue is false. I emphasize this point because one must recognize that Freud's opposition to the shared opinion concerning the sexual instinct is an opposition from within, that his argument unfolds while taking this shared opinion as given. Freud's opposition, let me say in anticipation, participates in the mentality that it criticizes. This decisive starting point, Freud's immanent criticism, will show itself in his final formulations and conclusions, specifically in their ambiguities and hesitations.

I want to proceed by reminding you of the general outlines of the next two sections of the first essay, in many ways the core of this essay. The next section discusses deviations in respect of the sexual object. Under this category Freud includes the choice of children and animals

27. In my discussion, I shall leave aside Freud's comments about popular opinion concerning the absence of infantile sexuality. The question of the relationship between popular and learned opinion on this issue is too complex to take up here.

as sexual objects, but his most detailed discussion is of inversion, the deviation to which nineteenth-century psychiatrists had themselves devoted the most attention. After describing different degrees of inversion, Freud argues that inversion should not be regarded as an innate indication of nervous degeneracy—an assessment which was widespread, even if not universal, in the nineteenth century. The overturning of the theory of degeneracy as the explanation of nervous disorders was of central importance in the history of nineteenth- and early twentieth-century psychiatry, and Freud played a role here, as did many others.[28] Indeed, Freud insisted that the choice between claiming inversion to be innate and claiming it to be acquired is a false one, since neither hypothesis by itself gives an adequate explanation of the nature of inversion. Freud immediately turns, in a section both complicated and problematic, to the role of bisexuality in explaining inversion, and I shall not even attempt to discuss this section now. Despite the recent attention that has been given to the notion of bisexuality in the development of Freud's early psychoanalytic thought, his remarks in this section become more and more puzzling the more carefully they are studied.

Freud next describes the characteristics of the sexual object and sexual aims of inverts and ends this whole section on deviations in respect of the sexual object with an extraordinary conclusion, a conclusion more innovative, even revolutionary, than I suspect he was able to recognize.

> It has been brought to our notice that we have been in the habit of regarding the connection between the sexual instinct and the sexual object as more intimate than it in fact is. Experience of the cases that are considered abnormal has shown us that in them the sexual instinct and the sexual object are merely soldered together —a fact which we have been in danger of overlooking in consequence of the uniformity of the normal picture, where the object appears to form part and parcel of the instinct. We are thus warned to loosen the bond that exists in our thought between instinct and object. It seems probable that the sexual instinct is in the first instance independent of its object; nor is its origin likely to be due to its object's attractions. [*T,* pp. 147–48]

In the nineteenth-century psychiatric theories that preceded Freud, both a specific object and a specific aim formed part and parcel of the instinct. The nature of the sexual instinct manifested itself, as I have said, in an attraction to members of the opposite sex and in a desire for genital intercourse with them. Thus, inversion was one unnatural functional deviation of the sexual instinct, a deviation in which the natural object of this instinct did not exert its proper attraction. By claiming, in effect, that there is no natural object of the sexual instinct, that the sexual object

---

28. For a useful overview, see Sulloway, *Freud, Biologist of the Mind.*

and sexual instinct are merely soldered together, Freud dealt a conceptually devastating blow to the entire structure of nineteenth-century theories of sexual psychopathology. In order to show that inversion was a real functional deviation and not merely a statistical abnormality without genuine pathological significance, one had to conceive of the "normal" object of the instinct as part of the very content of the instinct itself. If the object is not internal to the instinct, then there can be no instrinsic clinico-pathological meaning to the fact that the instinct can become attached to an inverted object. The distinction between normal and inverted object will not then coincide with the division between the natural and the unnatural, itself a division between the normal and the pathological. Since the nature of the instinct, according to Freud, has no special bond with any particular kind of object, we seem forced to conclude that the supposed deviation of inversion is no more than a mere difference. Indeed, Freud's very language is indicative of the force of this conclusion. He says, "Experience of the cases that are *considered* abnormal," thus qualifying "abnormal" in a rhetorically revealing manner.[29] These cases of inversion are *considered* abnormal because of a certain conception of the sexual instinct in which one kind of object is a natural part of the instinct itself. Unhinged from this conception, these cases cannot be considered pathological, cannot instantiate the concept of abnormality employed by Krafft-Ebing, Moll, and others. I think that what we ought to conclude, given the logic of Freud's argument and his radically new conceptualization in this paragraph, is precisely that cases of inversion can no longer be considered pathologically abnormal.

In light of these remarks, I think that we can conclude further that Freud operates with a concept of the sexual instinct different from that of his contemporaries, or, better yet, that he does not employ the concept of the sexual instinct in his theory of sexuality. What is at issue here is not Freud's choice of words. Commentators are forever remarking that English-reading readers of Freud are led astray by the translation of *Trieb* as "instinct," since *Trieb* is better translated by "drive," reserving "instinct" for *Instinkt*.[30] However, since many of Freud's contemporaries, among them, Krafft-Ebing, used *Trieb*, Freud's terminology did not constitute a break with previously established terminology. It is not the introduction of a new word that signals Freud's originality but rather the fact that *Sexualtrieb* is not the same concept as that of the sexual instinct. We can see this, to reiterate my main point, by recognizing that Freud's conclusion is explicitly and directly opposed to any conclusion that could be drawn

29. The German is "Die Erfahrung an den für abnorm gehaltenen Fällen lehrt uns . . . " (Freud, *Gesammelte Schriften* [Vienna, 1924], 5:20).

30. For one recent example, see Bruno Bettelheim, *Freud and Man's Soul* (New York, 1982). I have criticized Bettelheim's claims in "On the Englishing of Freud," *London Review of Books*, 3–16 Nov. 1983.

by using the concept of the sexual instinct. The relationship between the concepts of *sexual instinct* and *sexual object* found in nineteenth-century texts, a rule of combination partially constitutive of the concept of the sexual instinct, was completely undermined by Freud, and as a consequence of this cutting away of old foundations, inversion could not be thought of as an unnatural functional deviation of the sexual instinct. That *Sexualtrieb* is not the same as sexual instinct is shown by the fact that the concept of sexual instinct played a very specific role in a highly structured, rule-governed, conceptual space, a space within which psychiatric theories of sexuality had operated since about 1870.

If Freud's conclusions are as radical as I have made them out to be, if his conclusions really do overturn the conceptual structure of nineteenth-century theories of sexual psychopathology, then we might well wonder what prepared the way for these conclusions. I think that we can point to an *attitude* that prepared the way for Freud, even though there is a very large gap between this attitude and the new conclusions Freud drew. Freud himself tells us in a footnote the source of his attitude, and the fact that he mentions it only in passing should not lead us to underestimate the depth of its significance: "The pathological approach to the study of inversion has been displaced by the anthropological. The merit for bringing about this change is due to Bloch" (*T*, p. 139 n. 2). In 1902–3, Iwan Bloch published a two-volume book, *Beiträge zur Aetiologie der Psychopathia Sexualis,* which was central in establishing the inadequacy of the degeneracy explanation of perversion. This work is exhaustive in cataloging the utter pervasiveness of sexual aberrations, which, according to Bloch, have appeared in all historical periods, all races, and all cultures. His attitude toward these facts is surprising and, one might say, potentially revolutionary, although his work lacks the conceptual rearticulation that was a precondition of any radical conclusions.

In the introduction to the first volume of his work, Bloch announces that he intends to show that "the purely medical view of the sexual anomalies, which has been stated so well by Casper, von Krafft-Ebing, A. Eulenburg, A. Moll, von Schrenck-Notzing, [and] Havelock Ellis, . . . [does not suffice] for a fundamental explanation of the phenomena in this field," and he then opposes to the "clinico-pathological theory" of the sexual aberrations his own "anthropologic-ethnologic concept of the facts of so-called *'psychopathia sexualis.'* "[31] He claims that he will show that "this general concept of the sexual anomalies as universal human, ubiquitous phenomena makes it necessary to recognize as physiologic

---

31. Iwan Bloch, *Anthropological Studies on the Strange Sexual Practises of All Races and All Ages* (New York, 1933), pp. 5, 6; all further references to this work, abbreviated *AS*, will be included in the text. This is a translation of vol. 1 of Bloch's *Beiträge zur Aetiologie der Psychopathia Sexualis* (Dresden, 1902–3). I believe that Sulloway does not adequately see the role of Bloch's work in Freud's *Three Essays.*

much that previously has been regarded as pathologic" (*AS*, p. 6). (Bloch follows a standard nineteenth-century medical convention of often using the contrast physiologic/pathologic instead of normal/pathologic.) Given his "anthropologic" attitude, Bloch finds no difficulty in making statements such as the following:

> We find minor deviations from the norm of *vita sexualis* quite general. There are few persons who have not somewhere touched the narrow boundary between normal and pathological indulgence. [*AS*, pp. 165–66]

> There can be no doubt that a normal individual can accustom himself to the various sexual aberrations so that these come to be "perversions," which deviations appear in the same form in sound persons as well as in diseased.[32]

The narrow boundary between the normal and the pathological, the fact that sexual aberrations are a universal human phenomenon, was the primary evidence for Bloch that nervous degeneracy was not an accurate explanatory or diagnostic rubric under which perversion could be placed. And his attitude about sexual aberrations was distinctively different— less unequivocal, less psychiatric—from that of the authors with whom he was engaged in debate. But this attitude toward inversion and toward the other perversions, however different it was from the purely medical view and however unstable it often seemed, never led Bloch to throw into doubt the concept of the sexual instinct that made possible the classification of these phenomena as deviant (and that therefore required some alternative explanation of their status as pathological). Freud might have taken Bloch's anthropological observations, in conjunction with the other clinical evidence he cites, to show merely that inversion, if only in a rudimentary or shadow form, was much more widespread than many psychiatrists had believed. This claim would still have allowed a conceptual priority to the "uniformity of the normal picture." Freud might then have advanced with this conclusion to blur the boundary between the normal and the pathological even further, thereby providing yet one more attack on the idea that a distinctive class of degenerate individuals suffered from inversion. But rather than drawing this limited, though significant, conclusion, Freud went to the core of the matter and decisively replaced the concept of the sexual instinct with that of a sexual drive "in the first instance independent of its object." This was a conceptual in- novation worthy of the name of genius—although genius need not be

---

32. Bloch, *Anthropological and Ethnological Studies in the Strangest Sex Acts in Modes of Love of All Races Illustrated* (New York, 1935), pt. 2, p. 4. This is a translation of vol. 2 of Bloch's *Beiträge zur Aetiologie der Psychopathia Sexualis.*

conscious of itself as such, as we shall see if we turn to the next section of the first essay, entitled "Deviations in Respect of the Sexual Aim."
  Freud defines perversions as

> sexual activities which either (*a*) extend, in an anatomical sense, beyond the regions of the body that are designed for sexual union, or (*b*) linger over the intermediate relations to the sexual object which should normally be traversed rapidly on the path towards the final sexual aim. [*T*, p. 150]

This definition of perversion is explained by the fact that, as Freud puts it,

> The normal sexual aim is regarded as being the union of the genitals in the act known as copulation, which leads to a release of the sexual tension and a temporary extinction of the sexual instinct—a satisfaction analogous to the sating of hunger. [*T*, p. 149]

So since the normal sexual aim is copulation and the anatomical region appropriate to this aim is the genitals, two main kinds of perverse deviations in respect of the sexual aim are possible. Under the heading of anatomical extensions, Freud discusses oral-genital sexual activities, anal-genital sexual activities, kissing, and fetishism, recognizing that the latter might also have been classified as a deviation in respect of the sexual object. Under fixations of preliminary sexual aims, Freud discusses touching and looking, and sadism and masochism. Since I cannot discuss each of these examples here, let me focus on a few representative ones.
  Sexual use of the mucous membrane of the lips and mouths of two persons, otherwise known as kissing, is, strictly speaking, a perversion, since, as Freud says, "the parts of the body involved do not form part of the sexual apparatus but constitute the entrance to the digestive tract" (*T*, p. 150). But when the mucous membranes of the lips of two persons come together, we are not in the habit of classifying the anatomical extension or resulting aim as a perversion. Indeed, Freud notes that we hold kissing in "high sexual esteem" and he goes on to claim that kissing is "the point of contact with what is normal" (*T*, pp. 150–51). So given kissing's technical status as a perversion and our refusal to classify it as such, those who claim oral-genital and anal-genital activities are perversions must be "giving way to an unmistakable feeling of *disgust,* which protects them from accepting sexual aims of this kind" (*T*, p. 151). Freud immediately adds that "the limits of such disgust are, however, often *purely conventional*" (*T*, p. 151; my emphasis).[33]

33. The German is "Die Grenze dieses Ekels ist aber häufig rein konventionell" (*Gesammelte Schriften*, 5:25).

In discussing the kind of looking that has a sexual tinge to it, Freud acknowledges that most normal people linger to some extent over this form of pleasure, so he gives a number of conditions under which this pleasure in looking, usually called scopophilia, becomes a perversion. The most important of these conditions is when "instead of being *preparatory* to the normal sexual aim, it [pleasure in looking] supplants it." And Freud goes on to remark that "the force which opposes scopophilia, but which may be overridden by it (in a manner parallel to what we have previously seen in the case of disgust), is *shame*" (*T*, p. 157). Similarly, when the aggressive component of the sexual instinct "has usurped the leading position" so that sexual satisfaction "is entirely conditional on the humiliation and maltreatment of the object," we are faced with the perversion of sadism (*T*, p. 158). Shame and disgust are the two "most prominent" forces that keep the sexual instinct "within the limits that are regarded as normal" (*T*, p. 162), but Freud also lists pain, horror, and aesthetic and moral ideals as other normalizing restraints.[34]

In the conclusion to the third section, after mentioning the importance of such restraints, Freud insists that since these perversions admit of analysis, that is, since they "can be taken to pieces," they must be of a "composite nature":

> This gives us a hint that perhaps the sexual instinct itself may be no simple thing, but put together from components which have come apart again in the perversions. If this is so, the clinical observation of these abnormalities will have drawn our attention to amalgamations which have been lost to view in the uniform behaviour of normal people. [*T*, p. 162]

This passage introduces the concept of component instincts, a notion that will assume its full role in Freud's conception of sexuality only when he later connects it with the further idea of pregenital libidinal organizations. Some of these component instincts are specified by their source in an erotogenic zone, a zone of the body capable of sexual excitation—examples are oral and anal component instincts (see esp. *T*, pp. 167–69).[35] Other component instincts are specified by their aim, independent of any erotogenic zone—examples are the component instincts of scopophilia and cruelty (see *T*, pp. 191–93).

In the 1905 edition, the first edition, of the *Three Essays*, the component instincts are thought to function anarchically until the primacy of the genital zone is established. In his 1913 article, "The Disposition to Ob-

---

34. Pain and horror are mentioned, respectively, on pp. 159 and 161; aesthetic and moral ideals are listed on p. 177.

35. Freud uses the term "erotogenic instincts" once on p. 193. The German is "erogenen Trieben" (*Gesammelte Schriften*, 5:68).

sessional Neurosis," Freud introduces the concept of pregenital organization, recognizing that there is an anal organization of the libido. In
the 1915 edition of the *Three Essays*, Freud recognizes an oral organization
of the libido, and, finally, in his 1923 article, "The Infantile Genital
Organization," he describes a phallic organization of it. All of these pregenital organizations are theoretically incorporated into the 1924 edition
of the *Three Essays* in the section of the second essay entitled "The Phases
of Development of the Sexual Organization." Though we should not
undervalue the importance of the notion of pregenital organizations of
the libido, it was Freud's articulation of the concept of component instincts
that constituted another one of his major conceptual innovations (without
which the notion of pregenital organizations would have made no sense).
The concept of component instincts made it possible for Freud to say,
to quote from his concluding summary of the *Three Essays*, that "the
sexual instinct itself must be something put together from various factors,
and that in the perversions it falls apart, as it were, into its components"
(*T*, p. 231).

The idea that the sexual instinct is made up of components, that it
so combines a multiplicity of erotogenic zones and aims, is a further
radical break with the nineteenth-century medical conceptualization of
the sexual instinct. Freud's argument, his structure of concepts, leads to
the claim that neither the erotogenic zone of the genitals nor the aim of
copulation bear any privileged connection to the sexual instinct. The
"normal" aim of the sexual instinct, genital intercourse, is not part of
the content of the instinct; or, to put it another way, recurring to Freud's
previous conclusions about the sexual object, the sexual instinct and
sexual aim are merely soldered together. If there is no natural aim to
the sexual instinct, no given aim internal to this instinct, then deviations
from the aim of genital intercourse appear to lose their status as genuine
perversions, as pathological aberrations whose status outstrips any supposed
statistical abnormality. If the structure of Freud's argument here, in
conjunction with his argument in the previous section, is to show that
neither a specific aim nor a specific object has any constitutive bond with
the sexual instinct, and if the previously shared concept of the sexual
instinct is thus effectively dismantled, then it is difficult to see how any
conceptual foothold could remain for the concept of unnatural functional
deviations of this instinct. In the case of both sexual aim and sexual
object, it is only the apparent uniformity of normal behavior that directs
us to think otherwise. But this apparently well-entrenched uniformity
actually masks the operations of the sexual instinct, operations which,
when conceptualized by Freud, show us that the idea of the natural function
of the instinct has no basis whatsoever.[36] We ought to conclude from

---

36. Freud uses this notion of uniformity in two crucial passages. See *T*, pp. 148 and
162. For the German uses of "gleichförmig," see *Gesammelte Schriften*, 5:21 and 36.

what Freud says here that there are no true perversions. The conceptual space within which the concept of perversion functions and has a stable role has been thoroughly displaced—and displaced in a way that requires a new set of concepts for understanding sexuality and a new mode of reasoning about it.

This is the place, obviously enough, at which someone might retreat to Freud's discussion of disgust and shame, claiming that these reactions can provide an independent criterion for classifying certain sexual phenomena as perversions. But however we are to understand the role of these reactions, it is absolutely clear from Freud's remarks that even though he believes that some of these phenomena are such that "we cannot avoid pronouncing them 'pathological'" (*T,* p. 161), these pronouncements, our shame, disgust, and moral and aesthetic ideals, cannot provide an appropriate criterion of perversion. The tone of his example that we may be disgusted at the idea of using someone else's toothbrush, which follows his claim that these reactions are "often purely conventional," permits no other intelligible reading (see *T,* pp. 151–52). And, of course, it almost goes without saying that such a last-ditch attempt to save the concept of perversion would be at odds with the structure of the *Three Essays* as a whole and would make most of its content completely beside the point.

Even if Freud's conclusions in effect overturn the conceptual apparatus of perversion, it is well known that he did not embrace these conclusions unambiguously or unhesitatingly. The language of Freud's discussion sometimes reads as if he is unaware of the conceptual innovations he has wrought, as if nineteenth-century theories of sexual psychopathology can remain secure in their conceptual underpinnings. In the section of the third essay entitled "The Primacy of the Genital Zones and Fore-Pleasure," Freud can be found referring to "the appropriate [*geeignete*] stimulation of an erotogenic zone (the genital zone itself, in the glans penis) by the appropriate [*geeignetste*] object (the mucous membrane of the vagina)" (*T,* p. 161). But the whole point of Freud's argument in the first essay has been that no particular zone of the body and no particular object is specially suitable to, or qualified for, stimulation. The notion of appropriateness has lost all of its conceptual plausibility because the concept of the sexual drive is detached from that of a natural object and aim. And whatever transformations of puberty Freud may want to sketch in the third essay, these transformations cannot reinstate the old concept of the sexual instinct, the concept which gives a place to the notions of appropriate object and stimulation. The uneasy attitude of Freud's discussion is highlighted again in the next section of the third essay, "Dangers of Fore-Pleasure" (*Gefahren der Vorlust*), where Freud talks of the "normal sexual aim" as being "endangered by the mechanism in which fore-pleasure is involved." The danger in question consists in the fact that one may become fixated on the pleasure of the preparatory acts of the sexual process, and these acts may then take the place of the normal sexual aim. Such displacement, Freud tells us, is the "mechanism of many perversions" (*T,* p. 211). But again this is dangerous, in the sense of pathogenic, only if it exhibits some kind of unnatural deviation from the normal aim of the sexual instinct;[37] and given Freud's previous argument, he cannot maintain this latter claim. He dimly indicates his awareness of this fact when he introduces the distinction between forepleasure and endpleasure. The first is the "kind of pleasure due to the excitation of erotogenic zones," while the second is the kind of pleasure "due to discharge of the sexual substances" (*T,* p. 210). Since no conceptual space remains for the distinction between, as it were, natural and unnatural pleasure, or normal and abnormal pleasure, Freud is left merely with the difference between two kinds or degrees of pleasure, shorn of any pathological implications. This is not the only place where Freud hesitates to believe what he has said.

Let me focus on just a few more passages that will reinforce still further the complexity of this problem. The first passage comes from Freud's discussion of "The Perversions in General" in the first essay, and I want to notice especially the attitude embodied in this passage.

> If a perversion, instead of appearing merely *alongside* the normal sexual aim and object, and only when circumstances are unfavorable to *them,* and favorable to *it*—if, instead of this, it ousts them completely and takes their place in all circumstances—if, in short, a perversion has the characteristics of exclusiveness and fixation—then we shall usually be justified in regarding it as a pathological symptom. [*T,* p. 161][38]

The phrase "we shall usually be justified in regarding it as a pathological symptom" shows that we find here the attitude of, let us say, a pathologist, apparently the very same kind of medical attitude found in Krafft-Ebing, Moll, and their fellow-travelers. The rhetoric of this passage emphasizes the characteristics of exclusiveness and fixation, as though perversions are harmless until they become exclusive and fixed, as though this is the real criterion of pathology. But it is clear enough that the tendency toward exclusiveness and fixation on genital activity is not only non-pathological but a central component of Freud's conception of normal, healthy sexuality. It is only when sexual activity is divorced from the normal sexual aim and object that it can become a perversion and so qualify for pathological status. The moment the concept of perversion is introduced, with its corresponding concepts of normal aim and object, we are prepared for the attitude that treats perversion as pathological.

---

37. Freud uses the word pathogenic (*pathogene*) in this context.
38. The German passage appears in *Gesammelte Schriften,* 5:34–35.

The crucial move, the moment that makes the medicalizing attitude inevitable, is not the explicit listing of characteristics that make perversions pathological, but the use of the concept in the first place.

Freud's problemization of perversion is shown by the fact that in the first essay the words "normal," "pathological," and "perversion" often appear in scare quotes or qualified by a phrase like "what we would describe as"; as we move through the other essays, the scare quotes become scarcer and the qualifications less emphatic, until, in the concluding summary of the book, these terms appear *simpliciter*. Indeed, in the paragraph preceding the one I have just quoted, "pathological" does appear in scare quotes, but by the end of the next paragraph the fact that we regard perversions as pathological is something which is unqualified and justified.

Although I could discuss the only later, detailed passage of the *Three Essays* in which Freud returns to inversion, as opposed to perversion, a passage where the same questions of attitude arise (see *T*, pp. 229–30), it will be more useful, I think, to concentrate on a remarkable passage in the concluding summary to the book. The passage appears during Freud's discussion of the various factors that can interfere with the development of a normal sexual instinct.

> Writers on the subject, for instance, have asserted that the necessary precondition of a whole number of perverse fixations lies in an innate weakness of the sexual instinct. In this form the view seems to me untenable. It makes sense, however, if what is meant is a constitutional weakness of one particular factor in the sexual instinct, namely the genital zone—a zone which takes over the function of combining the separate sexual activities for the purposes of reproduction. For if the genital zone is weak, this combination, which is required to take place at puberty, is bound to fail, and the strongest of the other components of sexuality will continue its activity as a perversion. [*T*, p. 237][39]

We find in the writings of both Moll and Ellis the claim that an innate weakness of the sexual instinct is often responsible for the failure of normal heterosexual development, with perversion being the manifest result. In fact many writers before Freud used the terms "sexual instinct" and "genital instinct" interchangeably, as if the latter were simply a more precise name for the former. This identification was not in the least bit arbitrary, since the sexual instinct was conceived of as psychically expressing itself in an attraction for members of the opposite sex, with genital intercourse as the ultimate aim of this attraction. And since these features specified the natural operation of the sexual instinct, the common use

39. The corresponding German passage appears in *Gesammelte Schriften*, 5:113.

of the alternative phrase "genital instinct" was not conceptually misplaced. But once Freud reconceived the sexual instinct as having no natural operation, once any specific aim and object of the drive were thought to be merely soldered to it, the genital zone lost the conceptual primacy that was a precondition of its principled identification with the instinct itself. When the sexual instinct is conceived of as an amalgamation of components, the genital zone being one such component but without any natural privilege, then to single out this zone as Freud does in this passage, to claim that a constitutional weakness of it is responsible for the perversion, is to maintain an attitude toward genitality that is no longer appropriate. Freud in effect reintroduces, behind his own back, an identification that he has shown to be untenable. His claim that these writers are mistaken in asserting that an innate weakness of the sexual instinct is responsible for perversion, but that their assertions would make sense "if what is meant is a constitutional weakness of one particular factor in the sexual instinct, namely the genital zone," is astonishing, since this is, of course, exactly what they meant, and had to mean, given their conception of the sexual instinct. It is Freud who cannot mean to say that the absence of this particular factor, the primacy of the genital zone, is a condition of perversion. The last sentence of this paragraph reads, "For if the genital zone is weak, this combination, which is required to take place at puberty, is bound to fail, and the strongest of the other components of sexuality will continue its activity as a perversion." But the system of concepts Freud has been working with in the first essay requires a slightly different conclusion, one whose subtle modulation from Freud's actual conclusion must be emphasized. The appropriate formulation of the conclusion should read, "For if the genital zone is weak, this combination, which often takes place at puberty, will fail, and the strongest of the other components of sexuality will continue its activity." The differences between these two formulations represent what I have been calling Freud's attitude.

Although it is a central feature of commentary that it can go on indefinitely, I want to stop and return in conclusion to issues of historiographical orientation. I should perhaps first describe the sense in which I think that my reading of the *Three Essays* is a history of psychoanalysis without names. It is not, of course, that I have refused to invoke Freud's name, or the names of Bloch, Moll, and others. It is rather that I have treated their names as, so to speak, place-holders for certain sets of concepts and the way these concepts fit together to constitute a conceptual space. We see that the concept of perversion in nineteenth-century psychiatry was part of a conceptual space in which, for example, the concept of the sexual instinct combined, according to definite rules, with those of sexual object, sexual aim, unnatural functional deviation, and so on. It was this conceptual space, itself a nineteenth-century invention, that made it possible for psychiatrists to make the statements about perversion that so dominated the period. These statements were thus set within a shared discursive practice. Freud's *Three Essays on the Theory of Sexuality* provided the resources to overturn this conceptual space by fundamentally altering the rules of combination for concepts such as sexual instinct, sexual object, sexual aim—with the consequence that these shared concepts, among others, were destroyed. The conclusion forced upon us is that perversion is no longer a legitimate concept, that the conceptual preconditions for its employment no longer exist in Freud's text. So that if Freud, despite himself, said that such and such phenomena were perversions, he could not have meant what Krafft-Ebing, or Moll, or Charcot had meant. We will not be able to arrive at this conclusion if we focus simply on whom Freud read, on who before him used what words in which contexts. We must turn rather to the issue of conceptual articulation, to reconstructing nineteenth-century and Freudian concepts of sexuality and determining their points of contact and dissociation. Many writers before Freud possessed bits and pieces of his terminology and exhibited an inchoate, unself-possessed grappling with the problems brought to light by the *Three Essays*. But it was Freud who ascended to the level of concepts, who systematically and lucidly thought what had previously remained in a kind of precognitive blockage, who turned what had been, at most, a creeping anxiety into a conceptual mutation.

Yet we know that Freud continued to use the idea of perversion, as if he failed to grasp the real import of his own work. And so now we must directly invoke Freud's name, and wonder about the accessibility of his achievement to Freud himself. I have said that what prepared the way for Freud's achievement was a certain attitude, one that was most clearly appropriated from the writings of Bloch but that could no doubt be found in other authors as well. This attitude allowed a sort of opening so that perversions might no longer be treated as unambiguously pathological. This notion of attitude, which I cannot elaborate theoretically here, is one component of the concept of *mentalité*, a concept that has been put to extraordinarily fertile use by recent historians, especially in France.[40] A mentality includes, among other constituents, a set of mental habits or automatisms that characterize the collective understanding and representations of a population. Bloch's *Beiträge zur Aetiologie der Psychopathia Sexualis* exhibit the tremors of a shift in mentality in which what was taken for granted begins to become dislodged. But this displacement

40. Useful introductions to the history of mentalities can be found in Jacques LeGoff, "Les mentalités: Une histoire ambigue," in *Faire de l'histoire: Nouveaux objets,* ed. LeGoff and Pierre Nora (Paris, 1974), and Roger Chartier, "Intellectual History or Sociocultural History? The French Trajectories," in *Modern European Intellectual History: Reappraisals and New Perspectives,* ed. Dominick LaCapra and Steven L. Kaplan (Ithaca, N.Y., 1982), pp. 13–46. The notion of mentality is invoked for the history of science in some of the essays in *Occult and Scientific Mentalities in the Renaissance,* ed. Brian Vickers (London, 1984).

could only be partial, and one was always in danger of falling back into the old mentality, precisely because there was no conceptual backing for this change of attitude. That Bloch never pushed this attitude into conceptual innovation starts to explain why his attitude was inherently unstable, why his work often reads like a kind of unsteady bridge between the old and new mentalities, a bridge always ready to collapse because still in need of completion.

Freud's genius consisted not simply in appropriating this attitude but in seizing and exploiting it. He provided a conceptual foundation for the newly emerging mentality that made it possible, once and for all, for us to change decisively our old mental habits. So why, one wonders, did Freud himself not so change his own mental habits, why did he exhibit an attitude virtually no less ambiguous and unstable than Bloch's? Any answer to this question is bound to be complicated, so in lieu of an answer let me provide the structure for what I take this answer to consist in. Automatisms of attitude have a durability, a slow temporality, which does not match the sometimes rapid change of conceptual mutation. Mental habits have a tendency toward inertia, and these habits resist change that, in retrospect, seems conceptually required. Such resistance can take place not only in a scientific community but even in the individual who is most responsible for the conceptual innovation. Freud was a product of the old mentality that regarded perversions as pathological, a mentality whose first real signs of disintegration can be found at the beginning of the twentieth century. Freud's *Three Essays* ought to have stabilized the new mentality, speeding up its entrenchment by providing it with a conceptual authorization. But given the divergent temporality of the emergence of new concepts and the formation of new mentalities, it is no surprise that Freud's mental habits never quite caught up with his conceptual articulations. The attitudes that comprise a mentality are sufficiently impervious to recognition, so much like natural dispositions, that many decades may intervene before habit and concept are aligned. However, without some appropriate conceptual backdrop, it is very unlikely that a new scientific mentality can genuinely displace an old one, since concepts, especially in science, are one fundamental habit-forming force, one force which, even if over a long span of time, makes possible a stable set of firm mental habits. Although social, cultural, institutional, and psychological factors may all delay the definitive formation of these new habits, it is conceptual innovation of the kind Freud produced that marks one place of genius. But we must remember that genius too has its habits, its inert tendencies, that create a form of friction between what could be said and what is said, so that genius is always ahead even of itself.

The hesitations and ambiguities of Freud's *Three Essays on the Theory of Sexuality* are not the result of some deconstructive indeterminacy or undecidability of the text but are rather the consequence of the dynamics of fundamental change. Mentality and concept are two different aspects of systems of thought, and we should not expect them to be coherently connected all at once, as if forms of experience could be dissolved and reconstituted overnight. Sidney Morgenbesser is said to have asked the following question on an exam at Columbia University: "Some people argue that Freud and Marx went too far. How far would you go?" Whether Freud went too far or not far enough, this is exactly the right range of question. How far can you go? How far will you go?

The Secret of Psychoanalysis:
History Reads Theory

Nicholas Rand and Maria Torok

All disciplines have their histories in addition to their theories. In general, the history of a set of problems is treated separately from the nature of the problems themselves. The axioms of a given discipline may be the object of external inquiry but are not usually subject to historical examination. In this way, psychoanalysis has been investigated, even challenged, by a variety of other disciplines: biology, linguistics, history, philosophy, literature, and so forth. One may ask whether psychoanalysis can also become its own object, effectively distancing itself from itself. Will historical scrutiny provide criticism from within and thereby alter the nature of psychoanalysis?

It has been our observation that the history of the creation of psychoanalysis and of the psychoanalytic movement suggests deficiencies and omissions within psychoanalytic theory. This implies something far beyond the simple idea that no serious examination of theoretical problems can occur without an understanding of their history. Not only the past but the future of psychoanalysis, both as a theory and as a clinical practice, may well depend on the conscious assessment and assimilation of its own history. "The Secret of Psychoanalysis: History Reads Theory" is intended in part as an introduction to Nicolas Abraham's "Notes on the Phantom" which will, in turn, illuminate the theoretical and practical scope of this essay.

A history of Freudian psychoanalysis could be written based on the voices of dissenting insiders, without including schismatics such as Carl Jung, Alfred Adler, Wilhelm Stekel, and others who eventually developed independent systems of thought. The detailed interpretation of such rifts is already a consecrated approach to psychoanalytic history. But much remains to be learned from the internal criticism of those who have participated in Freud's movement or have sought sympathetically to understand the birth and progress of Freudian psychoanalysis. Most of the disagreements concern theoretical and clinical issues or the blocked access to documents that are essential to the historical assessment of psychoanalysis. This is Ludwig Marcuse's case as he writes to Ernest Jones on 10 October 1957.[1]

> Still it is incomprehensible to me why Freud's major correspondence [to Fliess] is not being made available to the public in its entirety so that those who would draw Freud's picture should not be limited to expurgated selections. You will most certainly understand that some people, despite their veneration of your book on Freud, wish to see all the materials. . . . The desire to arrive at an independent opinion is quite great, at least as far as I am concerned.[2]

Marcuse is responding here to a letter Jones had written to him on 14 September 1957:

> I have just been reading with great interest your book on Freud the greater part of which I admire very much for its fascinating exposition and good understanding. . . .
> Unfortunately in writing about Freud's personality in the first chapter you have suffered the same fate of the many other approaches to the subject. It seems always to stir some unconscious

---

1. Ludwig Marcuse is the author of *Freud und sein Bild vom Menschen* [Freud and his image of man] (Frankfurt, 1956).
2. Marcuse to Ernest Jones, 10 Oct. 1957, *Briefe von und an Ludwig Marcuse* (Zurich, 1975), pp. 148–49; our translation.

Nicholas Rand, assistant professor of French at the University of Wisconsin–Madison, is completing a book on the notion of hiding in literature, philosophy, and psychoanalysis. **Maria Torok** is the author (with Nicolas Abraham) of *The Wolf Man's Magic Word (Le Verbier de L'Homme aux loups),* recently published in translation. "The Secret of Psychoanalysis" is part of a book-length study Rand and Torok are writing on Freud and psychoanalytic theory.

conflicts which lead to serious misinterpretations and incorrect hypotheses which only add to the distorted legends of that personality which are so frequent. It even affects the capacity to quote correctly simple facts even when they are perfectly clear in my Biography.

> You are entirely mistaken in supposing that the family employed me as a censor or that I myself suppressed any material. They gave me carte blanche with the result that reviewers have praised me for the extreme frankness with which I dealt with Freud's intimate life. Where you find data missing in the book you may be sure that they do not exist. . . . The same applies to the publication of the Fliess correspondence. I have of course read all the unpublished letters. In a few cases I found a couple of sentences of sufficient interest to be worth publishing and Anna Freud promptly did so in the English translation. The rest were entirely uninteresting talks about the weather of a holiday, each other's children, and the date of his resuming work.[3]

Now that *The Complete Letters of Sigmund Freud to Wilhelm Fliess* are in the public domain, we know that the "couple of sentences of sufficient interest to be worth publishing" have swollen to over one hundred letters, omitted in their entirety from the original English-language edition. The claimed triviality of the omitted passages is refuted in a letter Anna Freud wrote to Jones himself in 1953. The importance of the material to which Anna Freud referred can be appreciated in light of Jeffrey Masson's *Assault on Truth*, which is partially devoted to Emma Eckstein's case. Masson quotes Anna Freud's letter:

> Emma Eckstein was an early patient of my father's and there are many letters concerning her in the Fliess correspondence which were left out, since the story would have been incomplete and rather bewildering to the reader.[4]

What we see here is censorship—a key concept in Freud's early metapsychology and a correlative to the notions of repression and superego—applied to the primary materials of psychoanalysis. In the historical metapsychology that the fabric of psychoanalysis thus inevitably becomes, who, we may ask, assumes the role of censor? The circumstances leading to the "creation of a *secret* committee for the supervision of the

3. Jones to Marcuse, 14 Sept. 1957, ibid., pp. 144–46.
4. Anna Freud to Jones, 19 Nov. 1953, quoted in Jeffrey Moussaieff Masson, *The Assault on Truth: Freud's Suppression of the Seduction Theory* (New York, 1984), p. 55.

development of psychoanalysis" provide an answer.[5] In July 1912 Jones proposes to Sándor Ferenczi that an "Old Guard" or secret society of sorts be set up to protect against potential dissensions which might betray the growing body of Freud's basic tenets (such as the primacy of infantile sexuality, the unconscious, and dream interpretation, among others). Quite enthusiastic about an idea that had been conjured up in Jones by "stories of Charlemagne's paladins from boyhood, and many secret societies from literature," Freud responds to Jones' proposal in a letter dated 1 August 1912:[6]

> What took hold of my imagination immediately is your idea of a secret council composed of the best and most trustworthy among our men to take care of the further development of psycho-analysis and defend the cause against personalities and accidents when I am no more ... I know there is a boyish and perhaps romantic element too in this conception, but perhaps it could be adapted to meet the necessities of reality. I will give my fancy free play and leave to you the part of censor.
>
> I daresay it would make living and dying easier for me if I knew of such an association existing to watch over my creation.
>
> First of all: The committee would have to be *strictly secret* in its existence and its actions. It could be composed of you, Ferenczi and [Otto] *Rank* among whom the idea was generated. [Hanns] Sachs, in whom my confidence is unlimited in spite of the shortness of our acquaintance—and [Karl] *Abraham* could be called next, but only under the condition of all of you consenting. I had better be left outside of your conditions and pledges: to be sure I will keep the utmost secrecy and be thankful for all you communicate to me. [*LW* 2:153–54; ellipsis in original]

The role of censor Freud bestowed on Jones in 1912 and the censoring the loyal paladin performed in 1957 are contrary to the concept of censorship in psychoanalytic theory. Identified as the agency responsible for the distortion of dream thoughts, censorship can be overcome through interpretation. Even the underlying silence dreams and symptoms symbolize may ultimately be opened to scrutiny. The paladin, on the other hand, must never betray the trust placed in him as a guardian censor: permitting the restoration of any deleted material would constitute a betrayal. In Jones' letter to Marcuse we can see something like a censor's

---

5. "Bildung eines *geheimen* Comitees zur Uberwachung der Entwicklung der PA [Psychoanalyse]" (Sigmund Freud to Sándor Ferenczi, 12 Aug. 1912). This unpublished letter is quoted here through the generosity of Judith Dupont.

6. Jones, *The Life and Work of Sigmund Freud*, 3 vols. (New York, 1981), 2:152; all further references to this work, abbreviated *LW*, will be included in the text.

credo: first, my being a censor is itself a secret ("You are entirely mistaken in supposing that the family employed me as a censor"); second, whatever is missing does not exist ("When you find data missing . . . you may be sure that they do not exist"), or, alternatively, what does exist is entirely trivial ("The rest were entirely uninteresting talks about the weather").[7]

Freud's apprehensions for the safety of his psychoanalytic system in 1912–13 may seem perfectly reasonable. But historical documents were being suppressed in 1957—a time when, at least in the West, all threats to eradicate the psychoanalytic movement had vanished. How can we explain the discrepancy between the psychoanalytic concept and the historical fact of censorship? In principle, all of psychoanalysis is based on the theoretical and therapeutic objective of detecting the work of censorship in order to overcome it. This is not true in the case of censored documents. Unlike a patient who can overcome the effects of censorship, Marcuse is totally powerless to do so. If the purpose of psychoanalysis is to interpret and dispel all forms of censorship, Jones' censorship of historical documents is inherently contradictory.

The paradox of "censorship" in Freudian theory and in the history of the psychoanalytic movement will emerge more clearly if we turn to an early clinical work in which Freud assumes the unusual role of a "censor" who deletes traumas. The case of Emmy von N., the first Freud records in *Studies on Hysteria*, may be considered the forerunner of the tension between lifting and imposing censorship.

Emmy von N. represented Freud's first attempt at applying the hypnotic-cathartic method of treatment he had acquired from Josef Breuer. "On May 1, 1889, I took on the case of a lady of about forty years of age. . . . She was a hysteric and could be put into a state of somnambulism with the greatest ease; . . . I decided that I would make use of Breuer's technique of investigation under hypnosis. . . . This was my first attempt at handling that therapeutic method."[8] Freud does in fact use hypnosis to help his patient recall and describe traumatic events from her past. At the same time, however, the "therapeutic method" he employed shows features that have little, if anything, to do with catharsis' (the abreaction of traumatic affects through talking and outbursts of psychic tension). Contrary to the objectives of catharsis and to the subsequent development of Freudian psychoanalysis—toward the conscious working out of traumas and conflicts in the transferential relationship between patient and analyst—we see in "Frau Emmy von N." the singular workings of a series

7. Censorship of the Freud–Fliess letters often concerns the unstable aspects of early psychoanalytic theory. See Maria Torok, "Unpublished by Freud to Fliess," *Critical Inquiry* 12 (Winter 1986): 391–98.

8. Josef Breuer and Freud, *Studies on Hysteria*, ed. and trans. James Strachey (New York, 1982), p. 48; all further references to this work, abbreviated *S*, will be included in the text.

of deletions. The aim of both catharsis and psychoanalysis is to provide therapeutic tools for coming in contact with oneself. And yet, Freud's description of his first case reveals a process of suppression.

> Under hypnosis I asked her what event in her life had produced the most lasting effect on her and came up most often in her memory. Her husband's death, she said. I got her to describe this event to me in full detail, and this she did with every sign of the deepest emotion. . . . I made it impossible for her to see any of these melancholy things again, not only by wiping out her memories of them in their *plastic* form but by removing her whole recollection of them, as though they had never been present in her mind. [*S*, pp. 60–61]

> My therapy consists in wiping away these pictures, so that she is no longer able to see them before her. [*S*, p. 53]

> I remembered that she had already mentioned this experience this morning, and, as an experiment, I asked her on what other occasions this "seizing hold" had happened. To my agreeable surprise she made a long pause this time before answering and then asked doubtfully, "My little girl?" She was quite unable to recall the other two occasions. My prohibition—my expunging of her memories —had therefore been effective. [*S*, pp. 58–59]

Freud's procedure of deletion leads to a unique relationship between patient and therapist.

> When, as much as eighteen months later, I saw Frau Emmy again in a relatively good state of health, she complained that there were a number of most important moments in her life of which she had only the vaguest memory. She regarded this as evidence of a weakening of her memory, and I had to be careful not to tell her the cause of this particular instance of amnesia. [*S*, p. 61 n.1]

Entirely without the consent of the primary party—the patient—and therefore in a way quite different from that implied by a pact of professional secrecy, Freud becomes the sole depository of Emmy von N.'s life and expunged memories.

As far as Emmy herself is concerned, she too is far from thinking of professional secrets when the following incident occurs:

> Another time, when she was feeling in good health, she told me of a visit she had paid to the Roman Catacombs, but could not recall two technical terms; nor could I help her with them. Immediately afterwards I asked her under hypnosis which words she

had in mind. But she did not know them in hypnosis either. So I said to her: "Don't bother about them any more now, but when you are in the garden to-morrow between five and six in the afternoon—nearer six than five—they will suddenly occur to you." Next evening, while we were talking about something which had no connection with catacombs, she suddenly burst out:" 'Crypt', doctor, and 'Columbarium'." [*S*, p. 98]

For Emmy von N. the words "crypt" and "columbarium" refer to Rome. She will never know that in these words she described her therapist as *Herr Doktor Krypte*, as the place where the burial of her past had secretly occurred.

The conclusion that Freud has become Emmy von N.'s crypt or secret reliquary must either represent a metaphorical abuse of language or identify a mystery. And if there is a mystery, it will seem all the more obscure once we uncover a structural analogy between Freud, the secret warden of his patient's deleted memories, and Jones, the secret guardian of those censored documents whose very existence he denied to Marcuse.

While it is true that the particular approach taken in Emmy von N.'s case remains without parallel in Freud's clinical writings, the procedure of removal by deletion employed in this case history must be understood as central to psychoanalytic theory. No matter how unimportant the "therapeutic method" of "wiping out" may seem given the treatment's early data, the case of deletion epitomized by "Frau Emmy von N." remains an integral part of the development of psychoanalysis.

The secret committee, established to supervise the development of psychoanalysis, is a direct corollary to the secret depository Freud created during Emmy von N.'s therapy. In Emmy's case Freud had performed the twofold action of wiping out her memories and then depositing them in a secret storehouse (that is, in Freud himself). The Committee established some twenty years later represents the creation of a secret enclave within the larger boundaries of a publicly proclaimed psychoanalytic association (founded in 1910). The Committee had to be "strictly secret in its existence" while at the same time it was called upon to guarantee the existence and coherence of psychoanalysis. It follows that in 1913 psychoanalysis itself becomes a secret as it is withdrawn—under the seal of absolute secrecy pledged by the members of its most powerful body—into the Committee.

Rather curiously, but certainly not without reason, the seven rings owned by the members of the Committee allegorize the same structure:

On May 25, 1913, Freud celebrated the event [the creation of the Committee] by presenting us each with an antique Greek intaglio from his collection which we then got mounted in a gold ring. Freud himself had long carried such a ring, a Greek-Roman intaglio with the head of Jupiter, and when some seven years later [Max]

> Eitingon was also given one there were the "Seven Rings" of the chapter heading in Sachs' book. [*LW* 2:154]

Each intaglio Freud presented to his paladins was recessed in a ring as the Committee was set within the Association.

The case of Emmy von N., the creation of a secret committee, and the censorship of the Freud–Fliess letters mark a hitherto unnoted thread of continuity in the development of psychoanalysis. The nature of such developments does not fall within the province of psychoanalytic theory as it was known in 1957, the year of Marcuse's exchange with Jones. In light of the secret committee and Freud's early case of deletion, Jones' censorship cannot be construed as merely performing the function of superego in the historical topography of Freud's system of thought. Neither the secret existence of the Committee nor Emmy von N.'s expunged memories can be understood in terms of dynamic repression since they were not subject to a return of the repressed. Furthermore, none of Freud's celebrated concepts—prohibition of desire, family romance, the polarity of instincts and their vicissitudes—can account for the creation and fostering of secrets or for their repercussions within the psychoanalytic movement.

The secrets which permeate the history of psychoanalysis will yield up their meaning once we posit the continuous presence of a secret in Freud himself.[9] Whatever its content or cause, the structure of this secret must be related to the basic contradiction that separates psychoanalytic theory from its history: that between the construction of clinical and theoretical tools for the recovery of dynamic repression and the creation of areas of absolute silence, a *preservative* repression that defies all attempts at discovery.

Once noted, the contradiction between the theoretical aims and the historical development of psychoanalysis may point toward a moment of contact. An encounter, not a confrontation, between history and theory would offer the possibility of generating internal criticism within psychoanalysis itself. The critique of Freudian psychoanalysis emerges from a consideration of the psychoanalysis and its most fundamental theoretical concerns. The theory itself cannot be considered comprehensive unless it includes the history of its creation and of its dissemination. Consequently, the history of psychoanalysis finds itself in the role of reader and analyst: history reads theory and in so doing forces the latter to modify its framework. The originality of this analysis resides precisely in the methodological

---

9. See in this connection the afterword, "What Is Occult in Occultism," in Nicolas Abraham and Torok, *The Wolf Man's Magic Word: A Cryptonymy*, trans. Nicholas Rand (Minneapolis, 1986).

proposition that the theoretical future of our field of inquiry cannot be divorced from the study and conceptual integration of its history.

While future research may produce results different from those presented here, the fact remains that the history of psychoanalysis points to the problem of secret depositories. Strange though this may seem, the concept of the secret is a theoretical and clinical contribution of the history of psychoanalysis. The metapsychological theory of the phantom furnishes, in its turn, the necessary means for detecting the work of secrets that—no matter how faint their marks may be—pervade the entire field of psychoanalysis.

Notes on the Phantom:
A Complement to Freud's Metapsychology

Nicolas Abraham

Translated by Nicholas Rand

The belief that the spirits of the dead can return to haunt the living exists either as a tenet or as a marginal conviction in all civilizations, whether ancient or modern. More often than not, the dead do not return to reunite the living with their loved ones but rather to lead them into some dreadful snare, entrapping them with disastrous consequences. To be sure, all the departed may return, but some are predestined to haunt: the dead who have been shamed during their lifetime or those who took unspeakable secrets to the grave. From the brucolacs, the errant spirits of outcasts in ancient Greece, to the ghost of Hamlet's vengeful father, and on down to the rapping spirits of modern times, the theme of the dead—who, having suffered repression by their family or society, cannot enjoy, even in death, a state of authenticity—appears to be omnipresent (whether overtly expressed or disguised) on the fringes of religions and, failing that, in rational systems. It is a fact that the "phantom," whatever its form, is nothing but an invention of the living. Yes, an invention in the sense that the phantom is meant to objectify, even if under the guise of individual or collective hallucinations, the gap that the concealment of some part of a loved one's life produced in us. The phantom is, therefore, also a metapsychological fact. Consequently, what haunts are not the dead, but the gaps left within us by the secrets of others.

This essay first appeared in French in 1975 and was collected in the author's *L'écorce et le noyau* (Paris, 1978). The subtitle is added here to indicate the status of this study within that collection. [Translator's note]

Because the phantom is not related to the loss of a loved one, it cannot be considered the effect of unsuccessful mourning, as is the case of melancholics or of all those who carry a tomb within themselves. It is the children's or descendants' lot to objectify these buried tombs through diverse species of ghosts. What comes back to haunt are the tombs of others. The phantoms of folklore merely objectify a metaphor active within the unconscious: the burial of an unspeakable fact *within the loved one.*

Here we are in the midst of clinical psychoanalysis and still shrouded in obscurity, an obscurity, however, that the nocturnal being of phantoms (if only in the metapsychological sense) can, paradoxically, be called upon to clarify.

A resourceful and enthusiastic young scientist is filled with energy for his work, the comparative study of the morphology and microchemistry of human spermatozoids. During his lengthy analysis with a woman, he discovers a new hobby for his free time: studying the genealogy of the high- and middle-rank nobility in Europe and its heraldic expression. Given the identity of illegitimate children, he can trace on request anyone's origins to prestigious forebears. When I receive him after a break in his long years of analysis, he immediately insults me in a fit of persecution: I am of low birth, despise aristocrats and the nobility. Not religious, I am a liberal conspiring against everything on which the nobility prides itself. I do not care about my origins; neither do I insist that his be known and publicized. Instead, I do everything I can to destroy him since he lays claim to a world other than my own. A moment's hesitation. Then, he apologizes for his lack of decorum. He does not really mean what he just said so vehemently. His father is quite a liberal. He hates genealogical inquiries. A man is worth what he is on his own. Why delve into the past? This, however, did not stop his father from marrying an aristocrat. And his grandfather? Well, he died long before the First World War when my father was still quite small. Grandmother had always stayed with us. She had had many children after my father who was the eldest. How much older than the others? I don't even know. Must have been twelve years or more. They were mostly boys; all of them became important people. Do I know them? No, I never knew them; (confused) oh, you

The most recently published book of essays by **Nicolas Abraham** (1919–75) is *Rythmes de l'oeuvre, de la traduction et de la psychanalyse* (1985). "Notes on the Phantom" is the preliminary statement of his theory of transgenerational haunting. **Nicholas Rand,** assistant professor of French at the University of Wisconsin–Madison, is the English-language editor of Abraham's works.

know, it was all on account of my father's beliefs. . . . The family on his side deserted us. I am also the eldest and my name is the same as my father's middle name. In fact, it is also one of the Christian names of an uncle who must be the youngest of the boys. My first analysis? It was a wonderful analysis, very successful, except for the end. From time to time I would speak about myself with another very well known analyst, a man. He made a crucial remark which I instantly reported to my analyst. After that everything went along beautifully, except for the one thing which makes me seem worthless and ridiculous to everybody: *my analyst refuses to admit that I am the child she had with her prestigious colleague.* Then I became very anxious and left her. My parents? They are very fond of each other, they never fight. They help each other. My father is very busy in his plant. He puts herbal teas into airtight packages bearing the names of various eighteenth-century courtesans. He has been awarded several medals at exhibitions.

Who would have failed to grasp in this speech what our subject does not know, what must be covered with the veil of modesty: the fact that his father is a bastard who bears the name of his own mother. An insignificant fact in itself, had it not led to a secret pain in the father and to his constructing an entire family romance about his aristocratic origins along with some efficiently repressed ill feelings toward his "whore" mother. The father's unconscious is focused on one thought: if my mother had not hidden the name of the illustrious lover whose son I am, I would not have to hide the degrading fact that I am an illegitimate child. How could this thought, alive in the father's unconscious, become transferred into the unconscious of his eldest son, everybody's favorite, and remain so active there as to provoke fits? In all respects and by all accounts, the patient appears possessed not by his own unconscious but by someone else's. The father's family romance was a repressed fantasy: the initially restrained and finally delirious preoccupation of the patient seems to be the effect of being haunted by a phantom, itself due to the tomb enclosed within the psyche of the father. The patient's delirium embodies this phantom and stages the verbal stirrings of a secret buried alive in the father's unconscious.

This is one case among several dozen others I am fortunate enough to know. Can I begin to theorize? I am jotting down ideas as they come. The grand synthesis, if it is called for, will have to wait. . . . Perhaps I can say this much in the meantime:

The phantom is a formation of the unconscious that has never been conscious—for good reason. It passes—in a way yet to be determined—from the parent's unconscious into the child's. Clearly, the phantom has a function different from dynamic repression. The phantom's periodic and compulsive return lies beyond the scope of symptom-formation in the sense of a return of the repressed; it works like a ventriloquist, like a stranger within the subject's own mental topography. The imaginings coming from the presence of a stranger have nothing to do with fantasy strictly speaking. They neither preserve a topographical status quo nor announce a shift in it. Instead, by their gratuitousness in relation to the subject, they create the impression of surrealistic flights of fancy or of *oulipo*-like verbal feats.[1]

Thus, the phantom cannot even be recognized by the subject as evident in an "aha" experience. And during analysis it can only give rise to constructions with all their attendant uncertainties. It may nevertheless be deconstructed by analytic construction, though only by fostering the impression that the patient has in fact not been the subject of the analysis. It is understandable that, in contrast to other cases, this type of work requires a genuine partnership between patient and analyst: all the more so since the construction arrived at in this way bears no direct relation to the patient's own topography but concerns someone else's. The special difficulty of these analyses lies in the patient's horror at violating a parent's or a family's guarded secrets, even though the secret's text and content are inscribed within the unconscious. The horror of transgressing, in the strict sense of the term, is compounded by the risk of undermining the fictitious yet necessary integrity of the parental figure in question.

Let me offer, among others, one idea to explain the birth of a phantom. The phantom counteracts libidinal introjection; that is, it obstructs our perception of words as implicitly referring to their unconscious portion. In point of fact, the words which the phantom uses to carry out its return (and which the child sensed in the parent) do not refer to a source of speech in the parent. Instead, they point to a gap, that is, to the unspeakable. In the parent's topography, these words play the crucial role of having to some extent stripped speech of its libidinal grounding. Summoning the phantom occurs, therefore, as the recognition at the opportune moment of the gap transmitted to the subject with the result of barring him from specific introjections he seeks at present.

The difference between *the stranger incorporated* through suggestion and *the dead returning to haunt* does not necessarily come to the fore at first, precisely because both act as foreign bodies lodged within the subject. In classical analysis an attempt is made to uncover the roots in a parental

1. OuLiPo (Ouvroir de Littérature Potentielle = Workshop for Potential Literature) is a research group of experimental writing founded in 1960 by Raymond Queneau and François de Lionnais. The aim of the group is to invent "artificial" formal constraints (not unlike the traditional sonnet form or acrostics, for example) and to demonstrate that by applying them systematically, the potential scope of linguistic creation can be expanded. As in Queneau's *Cent Mille Milliards de Poèmes*, semantic coherence is virtually never pursued. [Translator's note]

wish. Now, while incorporation, which behaves like a posthypnotic suggestion, recedes before appropriate forms of classical analysis, the phantom
remains beyond the reach of traditional analysis. It will only vanish once
we recognize its radically heterogeneous nature with respect to the
subject—to whom it at no time bears any direct reference. In no way
can the subject relate to it as his own repressed experience, not even as
an experience by incorporation. *The phantom which returns to haunt bears
witness to the existence of the dead buried within the other.*

A surprising fact gradually emerges: the work of the phantom coincides
in every respect with Freud's description of the death instinct. First of
all, it has no energy of its own; it cannot be "abreacted," merely designated.
Second, it pursues in silence its work of disarray. Let us add that the
phantom is sustained by secreted words, invisible gnomes whose aim is
to wreak havoc, from within the unconscious, in the coherence of logical
progression. Finally, it gives rise to endless repetition and, more often
than not, eludes rationalization.

At best, words of this kind can be invested with libido and can
determine the choice of hobbies or leisure activities. Thus, one carrier
of a phantom became a nature lover on weekends, acting out the fate
of his mother's beloved. The loved one had been denounced by the
grandmother (an unspeakable and secret fact) and, having been sent to
"break rocks" (*casser les cailloux* = do forced labor), he died in the gas
chamber. What does our man do on weekends? A lover of geology, he
"breaks rocks," then catches butterflies which he proceeds to kill in a can
of cyanide.

Cases like this rarely provide sufficient material to "construct" the
phantom purely on the basis of information gleaned from the patient.
At times, the patient's surroundings quite accidentally reveal the nature
of the missing pieces. As soon as we lend an ear to the possibility of
detecting a phantom, and after having eliminated other explanations, it
is usually possible to formulate some likely, if general, hypothesis. To
take the example above, even without knowledge of the antecedents, one
ends up noticing that the subject is possessed by a question of "forced
labor." And though the story is entirely foreign to the subject himself,
it does influence his habits and actions while, at the same time, running
counter to his own desires. Often enough, patients need only feel that
the analytic construction does not endanger their own topography; they
need only sense, apart from any form of transference, an alliance with
the analyst in order to eject a *bizarre foreign body*—and not the content
of a repression Freud had termed a *familiar stranger*. In this way, "the
phantom effect" (in the form of acting out as well as other specific symptoms) will gradually fade. When the analyst offers a comment like "*Somebody
is breaking rocks,*" the patient no doubt notices his analyst's frame of

mind and the fact that the latter refrains from implicating the subject himself: the analyst implicitly signals the emergence of the stranger and thereby masters it.

Only in such cases can one reject the analytic stance that is characteristically, albeit here incongruously, bent on tracing the information received to instincts or to the Oedipus complex. This would result in the patient's displaced acceptance of the phantom as part of his own libidinal life which could, in turn, lead to bizarre and even delirious acts.

In general, "phantomogenic" words become travesties and can be acted out or expressed in phobias of all kinds (such as impulse phobia), obsessions, restricted phantasmagorias or ones that take over the entire field of the subject's mental activities. In all cases, these words undo the system of relationships that, in an Oedipal fashion, the libido is trying in vain to establish. The Oedipal conflict is rather more acute in these cases than in others and can lead to the complacent use of the phantom as a guard against the Oedipus complex. This occurs sometimes at the close of the treatment when the phantom has already been successfully exorcised.

It is crucial to emphasize that the words giving sustenance to the phantom return to haunt from the unconscious. These are often the very words that rule an entire family's history and function as the tokens of its pitiable articulations.

Taking the idea of the phantom somewhat further, it is reasonable to maintain that the "phantom effect" progessively fades during its transmission from one generation to the next and that, finally, it disappears. Yet, this is not at all the case when shared or complementary phantoms find a way to be established as social practices along the lines of *staged words* (see above). We must not lose sight of the fact that to stage a word—whether metaphorically, as an alloseme or as a cryptonym—constitutes an attempt at exorcism, that is, an attempt to relieve the unconscious by placing the effects of the phantom in the social realm.

Descartes' Dreams and Freud's Failure, or The Politics of Originality

Françoise Meltzer

> Que ce qui est passion au regard d'un subjet est toujours action à quelque autre égard.
>
> —Descartes, *Les Passions de l'âme*

On 10 November 1619, Descartes was twenty-three years old and in Germany. He had a few months earlier witnessed the crowning of the emperor Ferdinand and signed up for the Duke of Bavaria's army. As early as 23 April in the same year, Descartes was writing to Isaac Beeckman of tremendous mental activity: "My mind," he wrote, "is already travelling." The day of 10 November is spent with his brain "on fire." The goal is to "distinguish the true from the false, to cast aside all prejudice."[1] It is a day of great joy, during which no mention is apparently made of God. What followed is well known: the three consecutive dreams Descartes has in the night, which were to become the foundation of his philosophy. For the dreams revealed an "admirable science" to Descartes. They were

An earlier version of this paper was given as a lecture at The University of California, Berkeley, and I benefited greatly from the discussion which followed. I am also grateful to Arnold Davidson, Bernard Rubin, Michael Salda, and Jayne Walker for their help in the development of the ideas put forward here.

1. All three quotations are cited by Georges Poulet in his "Le Songe de Descartes," *Etudes sur le temps humain*, 4 vols. (Paris, 1949–68), 1:65–66; my translation. The reader is referred here and throughout the discussion on Descartes to a "narration" of the dreams which forms an appendix to this paper. I have taken this "narration" from Lewis S. Feuer's unswerving psychoanalytic reading, "The Dreams of Descartes," *American Imago* 20 (Spring 1963): 3–26. For a complete text of the dreams in English, see Norman Kemp Smith, *New Studies in the Philosophy of Descartes: Descartes as Pioneer* (London, 1952), pp. 33–39. The French text is in *Oeuvres de Descartes*, ed. Charles Adam and Paul Tannery, 13 vols. (Paris, 1908–13), 10:180–88.

important, moreover, not only intellectually and spiritually: only after those dreams, Descartes was to write his friend Balzac twelve years later, in sleep "I experience all the pleasures imagined in the Fables, I mix insensibly my reveries of the day with those of the night."[2] And whereas until the three dreams, Descartes' nights were filled with phantoms, after the dreams he claimed never to have had a nightmare again.

In terms of the Western metaphysical "Tradition," of course, these dreams are equally astonishing: they are the *cause* of what Hegel (in his famous text on Descartes) called a revolution of the mind which marks the beginning of modern Western philosophy—a revolution born of three dreams. In terms of Descartes' own psychic life, further, these dreams mark a birth into health and productivity; they usher in the confident, mature Descartes. Not only do they allow him to sleep henceforth, and to sleep peacefully, they also, according to their author, rid him of the pallor and dry cough which he claimed he received from his mother who had died of a lung ailment. The dreams, then, free him from the mother's lingering legacy: her disease, imposed phantomlike, upon the son.[3]

An entire philosophy inspired by dreams; a self-cure which emerges as the unexpected side effect; a revolution in thought—surely such an event prefigures, almost as if in resonant preparation, Freud's own finding. Freud, who himself calls his psychoanalysis a "discovery," also dubs it a philosophy—this despite his protestations against philosophers and their works. Moreover, Freud claims that, whereas his "discovery" of repression bore a striking resemblance to Schopenhauer's idea on insanity, Freud himself had not read that philosopher: "The theory of repression," he writes firmly, "quite certainly came to me independently of any other

2. "Le sommeil . . . où j'éprouve tous les plaisirs qui sont imaginés dans les fables, je mêle insensiblement mes rêveries du jour avec celles de la nuit" (*Descartes: Oeuvres et lettres,* ed. André Bridoux [Paris, 1953], p. 941). The English translation is cited by Feuer, "The Dreams of Descartes," p. 22.

3. In a letter to Princess Elizabeth, Descartes says: "For, having been born of a mother who died a few days after my birth of a lung ailment, caused by unhappiness, I had inherited from her a dry cough and a pale complexion which I kept until I was over twenty years of age" ("Car, étant né d'une mère qui mourut, peu de jours apres ma naissance, d'un mal de poumon, causé par quelques désplaisirs, j'avais hérité d'elle une toux sèche, et une couleur pâle, que j'ai gardée jusques à l'âge de plus de vingt ans." [Descartes, *Oeuvres et lettres,* p. 1188; my translation]). Thus, as Feuer notes, the end of bad health and the occurrence of the dreams essentially coincide (Feuer, "The Dreams of Descartes," p. 12). When I say that her disease was "imposed phantomlike, upon the son," I am using the notion of the phantom particularly in Nicolas Abraham's sense—that of transgenerational haunting. See his essay, "Notes on the Phantom" (pp. 75–80), in this volume.

Françoise Meltzer teaches literary theory at the University of Chicago, where she is professor of comparative literature. Her most recent book is *Salome and the Dance of Writing: Portraits of Mimesis in Literature.*

source; I know of no outside impression which might have suggested it to me." For a long time, he continues, he had thought this idea to be "entirely original," but upon being shown a passage from *The World as Will and Idea*, Freud concluded "once again I owe the chance of making a discovery to my not being well-read. Yet others have read the passage and passed it by without making this discovery." Therefore, says Freud, in a less-than-convincing manner, "[I] forgo all claims to priority in the many instances in which laborious psychoanalytic investigation can merely confirm the truths which the philosopher recognized by intuition."[4] (Note that analysis "labors" to attain a truth, while philosophy essentially stumbles upon it.) The concern with priority in relation to philosophy seems particularly problematic with Freud. It should come as no surprise, further, that the situation becomes even more delicate when it concerns a "discovery" by one Descartes who is called, after all, "the father of modern philosophy." Freud has no wish to inherit or be derivative. His wish is to create—to be the origin; the father, not the son.

Consider, in this light, the fantasy plaque Freud imagines on the house where he had the dream of Irma's injection (as with Descartes, a type of "specimen" dream): "In This House, on July 24th, 1895, the Secret of Dreams was Revealed to Dr. Sigm. Freud."[5] By the time Freud

---

4. Sigmund Freud, *On the History of the Psycho-Analytic Movement, The Standard Edition of the Complete Psychological Works of Sigmund Freud,* ed. and trans. James Strachey, 24 vols. (London, 1953–74), 14:15–16. The extent to which priority (and thus originality) are troublesome issues for Freud here is clear from the vocabulary choice: "discovery" and "came to me independently" rather seriously clash with the modest promise to forgo "all claims to priority." The defensive assurance that the notion of "repression" is his own discovery, caused by "no *outside* impression" (and thus emerging from *inside* Freud alone) is clearly at odds with the bow to philosophy, a bow with which Freud professes to collaborate, as it were, in exploring the unknown. This second statement of relinquishing "all claims to priority" has already been rendered meaningless, then, by the previous ones which insist upon Freud's priority. So, too, when in the same passage Freud informs us that he has "denied" himself "the very great pleasure of reading the work of Nietzsche," so as to avoid "being hampered" by any sort of "anticipatory ideas," we need no rhetorician to recognize the innate contradiction in both these statements.

For a thoroughly convincing argument which demonstrates that Freud's disinterest in philosophy "protest[s] too much," see Stanley Cavell's piece, "Psychoanalysis and Cinema: The Melodrama of the Unknown Woman" (pp. 227–58), in this volume. Cavell cites a passage from *The Interpretation of Dreams* which is particularly apt for our discussion here: "These considerations," wrote Freud, "may lead us to feel that the interpretation of dreams may enable us to draw conclusions as to the structure of our mental apparatus which we have hoped for in vain from philosophy" (p. 239).

5. Freud, *The Interpretation of Dreams, Standard Edition,* 4:121 n. 1; further references to *Interpretation,* abbreviated *ID,* will be included in the text. The passage is from a letter to Fliess of 12 June 1900. Descartes himself frequently uses a house metaphor to describe his philosophy, which he says calls for the demolition of the old house of thought in order to permit the building of a new house, complete with a new foundation. See, for example, the second part of the *Discourse* in *Oeuvres et lettres,* p. 134. See, too, the opening to the *Meditations* (ibid., p. 267).

writes this wish to Wilhelm Fliess, the history of Western philosophy has long since hung a plaque on its own house, and it reads something like this: "In this place, on November 11, 1619, the secret of three dreams was revealed to René Descartes." And yet Freud, as will be shown later, expressed no real interest in these "specimen" dreams of Descartes— none at all. Such a lack of interest is by far the most curious aspect of the entire sequence; and yet few critics have remarked on it. It is as if Freud's feigned indifference to Descartes' dreams had been donned, like so many green glasses, by everybody else. Freud insists upon the word "discovery"—revealing, as we have noted, his well-documented obsession with originality, with possession. The same holds true for Descartes, who equally struggles with the problem of the original, of discovery.[6] But if Descartes has nagging doubts, like Freud, about the political implications of his stance, for the French philosopher those doubts turn on the possibility of recantation, and on the Church.[7]

Before we get further entangled in Freud's struggles, let us take a look at Descartes' famous dreams. First, a few remarks about the manuscript: the three consecutive dreams were written down by Descartes in his own words, in Latin. Adrien Baillet, Descartes' highly deferential biographer, possessed this Latin manuscript, the "Olympica," which has since been lost. Thus we cannot compare Baillet's paraphrasing of Descartes' descriptions to the original. We have only Baillet's summary and translation into French.[8] Occasionally, Baillet gives us the original Latin, but these instances are rare. Since we are here working from an English text, we have the translation of a translation to the third power: the translation of the dreams into language; the translation of the Latin into French, and further transmuted by paraphrase; and the French put into English, with the text again abridged.

6. After I had finished writing this essay, Michael André Bernstein drew my attention to a helpful and penetrating article by Ben-Ami Scharfstein, which raises several of the same points as I do here, but to a different end. In particular, Scharfstein notes, as I have, the recurring image in the *Discourse* of following the right path and the kinship of this image with the first dream. Scharfstein adds that Descartes had his own problems with originality and an obsession with authorship, particularly in his relation to Beeckman, and characterizes Descartes as a man who feared losing things, including "losing his ideas to others." However, Scharfstein makes no link to the rivalry with Galileo which I am suggesting here, nor does his article address itself to the issue of Freud's "reading" of these dreams. See Scharfstein, "Descartes' Dreams," *Philosophical Forum* 1 (Spring 1969): 293–317.

7. For some (especially Jeffrey Moussaieff Masson), the problem of recantation would extend to Freud as well, thus continuing the "mirroring" between Freud and Descartes which I am suggesting. I am thinking here, of course, of Masson's interpretation of why Freud abandoned the seduction theory and the former's conclusion concerning such abandonment, giving him the title to his book. See Masson, *The Assault on the Truth: Freud's Suppression of the Seduction Theory* (New York, 1984).

8. We also have Leibnitz's notes taken from the "Olympica"; he had no interest in the dreams but was rather concerned with mathematical proofs.

On the day of the dreams, Baillet tells us, Descartes had "decided to put aside all prejudice, to render the mind naked." A spiritual ardor left him only with "a great love for the truth." The past was severed. Let us retain the notion of the mind rendered naked ("son imagination lui présentât son esprit tout nud");[9] for now, however, let us turn to the severance with the past. Baillet's vocabulary describing this day of intense intellectual joy and frenzy is one of light: he uses words such as fever, ardor, light, fire, enthusiasm. These words prepare the way for the contrast of the dark and frightening night. The severance with the past is in a sense prefigured by the severance from the joyous day brought by the night and its dark dreams.

There is insufficient room here to go into these dreams with the full consideration they deserve, but a few of the most important points must be mentioned. The first dream, having to do with the difficulty of walking upright, gives Descartes a metaphor for the second part of his *Discourse on Method:* to walk with assurance in darkness, the philosopher tells us, one must walk slowly to avoid falling.[10] This first dream is traditionally read as an attempt to return to the past: the college on the road, with its retreat and remedy for sickness, is the desire to return to the college of La Flèche, where Descartes had spent happy years. The dream, like the *Discourse,* uses the metaphor of walking. Again in the third part of the *Discourse,* Descartes notes that his thought will not imitate "travellers lost in a wood [who] wander about." It will rather learn to walk in a straight line, to go to the end of a given path before giving it up.[11] The motif of walking in circles, of failing to walk upright in a straight line, becomes the metaphor in the philosophical works for the difficulty of maintaining a logical, linear progression of thought; for the ever-present lure of prejudice which leads thought in circles, like lost travellers in the forest.

But walking on one side also becomes a metaphor for the division of body and mind—the new and the old Descartes, the one who likes his life of debauchery, as he was later to call it, and the one who is demanding an existence dedicated to a life of the mind. But this now-famous cleavage between body and mind, which the dream seems to inaugurate, also suggests a different split: that of the subject from itself: "It does not follow," Descartes was later to write, "that I must now be that which I have been before." As Georges Poulet notes, this is a dream which says that only the present exists; the past (the phantoms, the

9. Adrien Baillet, *La Vie de monsieur Des-Cartes,* 2 vols. (Paris, 1691), 1:80.

10. "Mais, comme un homme qui marche seul et dans les ténèbres, je me résolus d'aller si lentement et d'user de tant de circonspection en toutes choses, que si je n'avançais que fort peu, je me garderais bien au moins de tomber" (Decartes, *Discourse, Oeuvres et lettres,* p. 136).

11. Descartes, *Discourse, Philosophical Writings,* ed. and trans. Elizabeth Anscombe and Peter Thomas Geach (1954; London, 1969), p. 25; see *Oeuvres et lettres,* p. 142.

college) and the future (the inability to walk forward, in a straight line) are closed.[12]

The whirlwind, of course, is a traditional way for God to speak to man (in Job, God speaks "out of the tempest"). And the wind acts, in this tradition, as the breath and spirit of God. It is impetuous: *ventus spiritum significat*, said the "Olympica" (Descartes' Latin manuscript), as Leibnitz notes. But it is also an evil genius, pushing Descartes violently against the Church. Here again, we have the Latin: *a malo spiritu ad Templum propellebar. Malo spiritu*—the evil wind which, as Baillet later says, is forcing Descartes "into a place he had voluntarily planned to go." Namely, church.

The Monsieur N. who appears in this dream is probably the dream's abbreviation for Marin Mersenne, Descartes' friend and mentor, eight years older than he, and the teacher associated with the happy days at La Flèche. The melon from a foreign land is first a repetition in assonance of M. N. Its meaning is, to put it mildly, obscure.[13] And yet we may try to push the meaning here. The dream ends, and the waking Descartes decides (for Descartes "analyzes" his dreams) that an "evil genius" (echoing *malo spiritu*) had tried to seduce him. The seduction here is one of intellectual pride (so the deferential Baillet will note). Such a reading makes some sense if we remember that Descartes confesses that the day of 10 November, spent as it was in mental exaltation, was without any mention or thought of God (the second dream will in fact make explicit what this first dream fears but represses: the wrath of God at this intellectual pride). Whereas the day is described as one of great joy, with Descartes' brain "on fire," the first dream is ushered in by exhaustion, burnout, and marks the place

12. See Poulet, "Le Songe de Descartes," pp. 72–73. One can already sense the beginnings of the problem which Freud was to take up himself, in the manner of Descartes: in Freud's statement "Wo Es war, soll Ich werden" there is first the assumption of the *cogito's dédoublement de l'être*, as Poulet calls it.

13. Scharfstein sheds some interesting light on the melon problem, suggesting that its appearance in the dream is stimulated by Saint-Amant's poem, "Le melon," coupled with another called "Ode à la solitude." This information seems to me to be helpful in suggesting what the day residue might have been for this dream image. Scharfstein also notes a possible connection between the melon and Descartes' passion for anatomy (and dissection). See Scharfstein, "Descartes' Dreams," pp. 304–5. I might add that the melon also suggests the dissection of the human eye, which Descartes was frequently undertaking in his study of optics. Such an association will take on greater significance in the section on Freud of this essay. Gregor Sebba is equally industrious with this mystery, discovering that a fellow student of Descartes' at La Flèche was important enough to be mentioned in a 1641 letter of Descartes'. This student, a certain Chauveau, was from the town of Melun. "A memory arose," writes Sebba, "and was quickly defused by a verbal pun: *Melun* becomes *melon*. Freud would have loved that." Except that he didn't. (Sebba, *The Dream of Descartes*, ed. Richard A. Watson [Carbondale and Edwardsville, Ill., 1987], p. 14). Interestingly, Descartes' melon does not appear in the definitive (and sole?) study of literary melons. See Rolf Norrmann and Jon Haarberg, *Nature and Language: A Semiotic Study of Cucurbits in Literature* (London, 1980).

of a *tristis casus,* as the "Olympica" put it. But to return to the melon: Baillet will later tell us that the melon signifies the "charms of solitude" for Descartes, charms "presented as human sollicitudes"—a silly, obviously wrong reading, whether it be Descartes' or Baillet's. I would suggest that the melon (an exotic, rare fruit in seventeenth-century France) represents first a displacement of the forbidden fruit of knowledge—the fruit which Descartes' night dreams fear has been arrogantly plucked in the day's exalted reverie. The dream shows the fear that there has been a transgression of the divine order—too much has been learned which is perhaps not man's to know. As the result of eating from the tree of knowledge is separation (from Eden, from innocence, from unity of mind and body), so the great discovery which the dreams reveal announces itself as a *tota simul,* a fundamental unity. The discovery is of a unity which necessitates first and foremost a split, a separation, an inability of the mind to walk in step with its own body, a loss of innocence in the movement of the limbs in response to the commands of the brain. This path of life which the third dream highlights and the first dream problematizes already forks in several ways: backward (past) and forward (future), left and right, back and forth. We do not know yet as we read the first dream that left and right signify science versus philosophy, which will combine into the *mathesis universalis.* The first dream is the dream of separation, of eating the forbidden fruit. (Descartes even turns over to his right side after this dream.) Later, after the *tota simul* and *mathesis universalis* are harmonized into the *mirabilis scientia*—the foundation of a miraculous science—the same image of transgression, the forbidden fruit, will become a happier metaphor: Descartes' own Tree of Knowledge. This tree will demonstrate the necessity of separation and division as the grounding for unity: the roots of this tree, as Descartes draws it, are metaphysics; the trunk is physics; the three main branches are mechanics, medicine, and morals—the application of knowledge to the external world. Thus the continuity of metaphysics and science, in spite of their apparent split, is the secret to be revealed in the progression of the three dreams.[14]

And this discovery, of the necessity of division as the grounding for an ultimate unity, occurs on 10 November, the Eve of Saint Martin. Baillet reminds us that this is a day of debauchery but hastily assures us that Descartes was not drunk when he had his three dreams. But Saint Martin is significant not only as an excuse for revelling: he is the patron saint of the poor and is famous for having once torn his coat in two pieces in order to give one half of it to a pauper. Saint Martin's Day is celebrated even now in many parts of Europe by a figure riding on

14. For recent literature on the important connection between Descartes' scientific thought and his philosophy, see the essays in Stephen Gaukroger, *Descartes: Philosophy, Mathematics and Physics,* Harvester Readings in the History of Science and Philosophy 1 (Totowa, N.J., 1980).

horseback, playing the role of the saint with his cape torn in two, one half resting on his shoulder. The torn cape will serve for two—one for the poor man and one for the saint, united in a brotherhood of charity. Is it possible that Descartes unconsciously identifies with the saint of the divided coat? Or with the actor who plays the saint, displaying but half of his cloak as his emblem? Descartes, it will be remembered, felt that he had inherited his pallor and ill health from his mother—a mask of a kind. In the same year as the dreams (in January), Descartes writes that he sees himself as playing a part:

> As an actor puts on a mask in order that the color of his visage may not be seen, so I who am about to mount upon the stage of that world of which I have as yet been a spectator only: I appear masked upon the scene.[15]

The actor who plays Saint Martin, his cloak torn in half, is as if symbolic of division, the second step of the *méthode:* "to divide each problem I examined into as many parts as feasible, and as was requisite for its better solution."[16]

The second dream takes place after two hours of meditation and consists in a clap of thunder followed by sparks. Initially, Descartes took this to be the common manifestation of the wrath of God (for the sin of intellectual pride: Descartes had spent a day believing that he had penetrated the heart of science). Baillet tells us that Descartes later decided that the thunder (with its lightning) was the spirit of truth, descending upon him in order to possess him. In any case, this minidream, which begins by instilling terror, ends in relative calm—mirroring perhaps the two interpretations just mentioned: the wrath of God followed by the spirit of truth. The absolute reality of God is conceived of as simple and spontaneous fact, like the lightning, like truth.

It is the third dream which is the most famous and the most quoted. Descartes first finds a dictionary and then a collection of poetry. He will himself analyze this: the dictionary is science, and the book of poetry is "Philosophy and Wisdom joined together." The book contains two poems by Ausonius: the first is "Est et Non" (the yes and no of Pythagoras, as

15. This is taken from Descartes' private notes or *Pensées*. The translation here is in Feuer's "The Dreams of Descartes," p. 26. For the Latin original, see *Oeuvres de Descartes,* 10:213.

16. Descartes, *Discourse, Philosophical Writings,* ed. and trans. Anscombe and Geach, p. 20 ("de diviser chacune des difficultés que j'examinerais en autant de parcelles qu'il se pourrait et qu'il serait requis pour les mieux résoudre" [*Oeuvres et lettres,* p. 138]). Francis Barker has another, sociohistorical notion of the Cartesian notion of division, linking it to the moment when the ego "divides itself from itself to become both the subject and the object of its fabular narration." The bourgeois individual is thus seen as "a split narration isolated within a censored discourse" (Barker, *The Tremulous Body: Essays on Subjection* [New York, 1984], pp. 55, 57).

Baillet tells us, and the "Truth and Falsehood in human knowledge and the secular sciences"). Now the thunderclap as spirit of truth becomes that which ushers in the "treasures of all the sciences," so there is a return of sorts to the intellectual arrogance which the thunder seemed initially to chastise.

The second of Ausonius' poems is "Quod vitae sectabor iter?" ("What path of life shall I pursue?"). Here is a poem suggesting the problem of freedom and necessity, but also echoing the question of the first dream: should our philosopher continue his life of carefree pleasure, or must he devote himself to God and mind? What path of life to pursue, and how to walk upon it? While the first poem raises the question of science and existence, this second poem raises the question of the *cogito,* the answer to which will eventually be: I will always necessarily choose God.

There are many other wonderful aspects to this dream (the books, in good dreamlike fashion, keep appearing and disappearing, and so on), but for our present purposes, it seems to me that three things should be noted: the first is that Descartes loses both poems when he is leafing through another book. This book contains "several small portraits engraved in copperplate," leading Descartes to declare that the "book was very beautiful, but that it was not of the same printing as the one he had known." So the second thing to be noted is that this book is not the same as the first, but it is beautifully illlustrated with portraits of copperplate. The third point of significance is the character of the poet in question, Ausonius. He was a Latin poet of the fourth century and the governor of Gaul. He converted to Christianity for the sake of convenience—it made his life easier. To turn to Christianity for the sake of convenience does not seem unrelated to the unspoken problem of the dreams: the search for the truth at any cost versus the very real and severe power and rules of the Church. Which path of life does Descartes pursue? The path which is straight and narrow—in other words, the path which adheres to the Church's views. The famous 1910 edition of the *Encyclopaedia Britannica* puts it rather neatly, I think: "Descartes was not disposed to be a martyr; he had a sincere respect for the church, and had no wish to begin an open conflict with established doctrines."[17] This third dream is generally read, for obvious reasons, to be a dream about the future: the first dream is about Descartes' relation to the past; the second is the spontaneous—alethic—presence of God; and the third is the contemplation of Descartes' future course in life. All this is clear enough. But I think that this last dream is more about the future than first appears: it prefigures, and even puts into place, what we may call the recantation Descartes will set into motion after he learns of what happened to Galileo.

The third dream is the one in which Descartes chooses what path of life to follow; it is a path which is already marked out by Ausonius.

17. *Encyclopaedia Britannica,* 11th ed., s.v. "Descartes."

The half-sleeping Descartes will interpret the "Quod vitae" poem to "mark the sound advice of a wise person, or even of Moral Theology." And yet it is rather Ausonius who will have already cut out the path which Descartes will take fourteen years later, when he will shelve *Le Monde*, his work on cosmology, because he learns of Galileo's fate at the hands of the Church authorities. Like Galileo, Descartes had intended to adhere to a Copernican notion of the universe. But in 1633, near the end of that year, Descartes writes to Mersenne that *Le Monde* will not be sent to him:

> I had intended sending you my *World* . . . but I have just been at Leyden and Amsterdam to ask after Galileo's cosmical system as I imagined I had heard of its being printed last year in Italy. I was told that it had been printed, but that every copy had been at the same time burnt at Rome, and that Galileo had been himself condemned to some penalty.[18]

Is then the evil wind which throws Descartes against the church door—where he wanted to go anyway, he complains—none other than Descartes himself, whose mind is at odds with his faith, and whose politics are in collision with his discovery? Is Descartes walking out of step with himself?

I am not chastising Descartes for cowardice: no good would have been served had his *Monde* received the same fate as Galileo's works. I am pointing out, however, that the presence of Ausonius in this text is not coincidental and that the third dream resolves the question of what path is to be taken in the light of Descartes' dangerous views. Moreover,

18. Ibid. ("je m'étais proposé de vous envoyer mon *Monde* . . . mais m'étant fait enquérir ces jours à Leyde et à Amsterdam, si le *Système du Monde* de Galilée n'y était point, à cause qu'il me semblait avoir appris qu'il avait été imprimé en Italie l'année passée, on m'a mandé qu'il était vrai qu'il avait été imprimé, mais que tous les exemplaires en avaient été brûlés à Rome au même temps, et lui condamné à quelque amende" [Descartes to Mersenne, Nov. 1633, *Oeuvres et lettres*, p. 947]). To be fair to Descartes, it should also be said that he was as worried about truncating his work on cosmology as he was about getting into trouble with the Church: "But, since for nothing in the world would I wish to produce a discourse in which the Church could find a single word with which to disagree, I prefer to suppress it, rather than to have it appear in crippled form" ("Mais comme je ne voudrais pour rien du monde qu'il sortit de moi un discours, où il se trouvât le moindre mot qui fût désapprouvé de l'Eglise, aussi aimé-je mieux le supprimer, que de le faire paraître estropié" [ibid., p. 948; my translation]). Moreover, Descartes began to feel, a few months later, that someday the world would be ready for his *Mondo*. Nevertheless, it should be remembered that the first moral law drawn from the *méthode* (in the third part of the *Discourse*) is obedience: "to obey the laws and customs of my country; faithfully keeping to the religion in which by God's favour I was brought up from childhood" ("d'obéir aux lois et aux coutumes de mon pays, retenant constamment la religion en laquelle Dieu m'a fait la grâce d'être instruit dès mon enfance" [ibid., p. 141; translated in *Discourse*, ed. and trans. Anscombe and Geach, p. 24]).

let us consider the odd copperplates. Baillet tells us that Descartes was at a loss to explain them until "an Italian painter visited him the next day." Such a statement makes no sense at all, even on the most superficial level, unless we remember that dreams were considered to be prophetic at times—and prophetic, often, of banal events. I think that when the Italian painter visits, Descartes decides that the dream simply forsaw such an event—for copperplates were best executed in Italy, by Italian artists.

And yet Italy is first and above all for Descartes the land of Galileo, already in trouble for his views at the time of the dreams. It is to be noted that in this last dream, the copperplates appear in a book which is beautiful, but "not of the same printing as the one he had known." The dream is then about censorship—and recantation. It is about a book which is lost, and found again—but altered: an alteration which even the pretty copperplates cannot mask. We have another split here, then: the stranger who disappears with the books is like the part of Descartes which wants to have the "original" book, the one he remembers. And then there is the Descartes who holds in his hands the revised book, with the plates. Is Galileo sending a message to Descartes in the form of a melon (itself reminiscent of a cosmos, a world)?[19] Galileo's work was also, it should be remembered, in optics—a field again shared by Descartes. The cutting of lenses is not unrelated to the cutting of copperplates; similar tools and techniques are used. Moreover, it is with copperplates that Descartes himself will illustrate his work on optics, which was begun in 1613 in Paris when Descartes met Claude Mydorge, the great lense maker. And optics for Descartes are also tied to the *Est et Non*—it is by opening and closing his eyes (as in the second dream, and as at the end of the third) that Descartes ascertains whether something exists or not, whether it is imagined or real. The eye is both a physical mechanism to be explained and metaphorically (as represented by the mind) the primary organ of knowledge for Descartes. So too with Galileo, for whom his telescope was to prove his cosmology. The violent censorship visited upon Galileo will become a self-imposed censorship in Descartes.

Such censorship is mirrored by Baillet himself. The first biography was published in 1691 in two volumes and contains the text of the three dreams. Baillet, a priest, prided himself on working all but five hours out of every twenty-four-hour day. He was not pleased when, in 1692, there appeared a vicious attack on his biography. Entitled *Réflexions d'un academicien sur la vie de M. Descartes envoyées à un de ses amis en Hollande*,

19. Mersenne (Monsieur N. in the dream?) was in communication with Galileo as early as 1610. Mersenne himself was viewed as a link between philosophers and scientists in Europe, the two realms of knowledge which the dreams try to fuse. Mersenne's gift is in a sense this link—a Galileo, to which Descartes will add philosophy. See, too, Feuer's reading, which raises many of the same points and reaches entirely different conclusions (Feuer, "The Dreams of Descartes," p. 22).

the work was anonymous but generally attributed to Gilles Ménage, the famous literary critic. It consists of two "letters," one dated 15 November 1691, and the other 22 November, from Paris. These letters attack Baillet on every level: his knowledge of classical works, of contemporary works, of history, historical method, logic, and so on. They also attack Baillet's conclusion to the dream sequence. Out of context, Baillet appears foolish (as he sometimes does in context) and Descartes, drunk. Baillet's answer to the *Réflexions* was the greatly abridged edition of 1692, in which the dream sequence disappears entirely, replaced by a paragraph which summarizes the dreams' importance. Since the original document, the "Olympica," is now inaccessible as well, Baillet's skill as an interpreter is conveniently unimpeachable and beyond attack. In the introduction to the 1693 (abridged) text, Baillet says that this new edition represents the original of 1691 "comme une miniature représente un portrait" ("as a miniature represents a portrait"). So—as the copperplate portraits were the moment in the third dream marking the place of censorship, here Baillet actually labels his own censorship a "portrait." In any case, the two later editions, considerably smaller than the two-volume first one, are cheaper as well as smaller, suggesting the great popularity of Baillet's work in, as he would have wished it, the abridged form. (Indeed, the abridgement was reprinted as late as the 1950s.) So the father of modern philosophy, as Descartes is called, has three dreams which in turn father his thought; and these dreams are expunged from the "official" biography by the obsequious Baillet who, it should be noted, once got into trouble for his *Saints' Lives* because he was skeptical of the miracles attributed to his subjects. With Descartes, however, Baillet was more than willing to believe the miracle of the dreams—until the attack, at which point the dreams, and their context, promptly disappear. In this text, then, we have the triad structure, not only of the three dreams, but of the three censors or recanters as well: Ausonius, Descartes, and Baillet.

But there is, of course, a fourth: Freud will enter this hierarchy by inscribing his own censorship of the dreams. To contextualize such censorship, let us pause to remember that Descartes is the philosopher who declares awareness to be one and the same as the mind: "By the term *conscious experience* (*cogitationis*), I understand everything that takes place within ourselves so that we are aware of it."[20] The notion that all mental activity is conscious is diametrically opposed, of course, to the stance which will be taken by psychoanalysis: that there is an Other in the Subject itself, unreachable and largely unknowable, and that this Other is the unconscious. For Descartes, as Hegel remarks, "being and thought are in themselves the same."[21] And yet, before we dismiss Cartesianism al-

20. Descartes, *Principles of Philosophy, Philosophical Writings*, ed. and trans. Anscombe and Geach, p. 183 ("Par le mot de penser, j'entends tout ce qui se fait en nous de telle sorte que nous l'apercevons immédiatement par nous-mêmes" [*Oeuvres et lettres*, p. 574]).

21. G. W. F. Hegel, *Phenomenology of Spirit*, trans. A. V. Miller (Oxford, 1977), pp. 351–52.

together from psychoanalysis, let us remember that Descartes' famous dualism—the split between body and mind—is a bipartite structure appropriated by psychoanalysis as the dialectical construct of conscious and unconscious; subject and other; eros and the death instinct. The inherent unity in all things which Descartes presents rests first in division, both in the initial steps of the *méthode* and in the famous body/mind cleavage: *una est in rebus*, the *tota simul*, and the *mathesis universalis*, are grounded in duality and division. The transparency between being and thought to which Hegel points in Descartes is possible only by division, by complete enumeration, and by the implied *ergo* which acts as the pivot between *cogito* and *sum*. And yet the mind, Descartes maintains, is indivisible. "We must," he writes, "occupy ourselves only with those objects that our intellectual powers appear competent to know certainly and indubitably."[22] Surely this formula is against all that Freud believes in, for his psychoanalysis concentrates itself on the unconscious—precisely that which remains uncertain and doubtful as an object of knowledge for the mind. And yet, as we shall see, Freud's response to Descartes' dreams adheres, surprisingly enough, to Descartes' principle here: Freud will claim that he cannot concern himself with dreams that can only remain uncertain to him. One can accuse Freud here of a certain epistemologically oriented imitative fallacy.

Freud was asked in 1929 by Maxime Leroy to take a look at Descartes' dreams. Leroy was working on his book, *Descartes: le philosophe au masque*. As usual, Freud did his homework. Although Leroy paraphrased Baillet's own paraphrasing of the dreams (and I might add here that Leroy's summary is inaccurate and bizarre), Freud studied Baillet's full text.[23] In his response to Leroy, Freud stresses that first he felt dismay, since he could not ask Descartes himself to free associate; then his task "turned out to be easier than I anticipated." But he adds, "the fruit of my investigations will no doubt seem to you much less important than you had a right to expect" ("SD," p. 203). As usual, Freud's opening remarks are cautious and apologetic, but one wonders here whether he is apologizing for the paucity of his own remarks on the dreams, or for Descartes himself.

Freud first says that these dreams are "dreams from above" (*Traüme von oben*). This assertion is remarkable because it is identical to the one used by Baillet to describe the dreams: as Baillet leads into the dreams,

---

22. Descartes, *Rules for the Direction of the Mind, Philosophical Writings*, ed. and trans. Anscombe and Geach, p. 153 ("Il ne faut s'occuper que des objets dont notre esprit paraît capable d'acquérir une connaissance certaine et indubitable" [*Oeuvres et lettres*, p. 39]).

23. As Strachey points out in his note to Freud's response to Leroy, Freud must have consulted Baillet. While Leroy mentions only a "melon," it is Baillet who says that it comes from "a foreign land," and Freud refers to it in those terms as well. See Freud, "Some Dreams of Descartes': A Letter to Maxime Leroy," *Standard Edition*, 21:199–204; further references to this letter, abbreviated "SD," will be included in the text.

he tells us that Descartes believed that they could only have come "from above"—"Il s'imagina ne pouvoir être venus que d'enhaut."[24] But whereas Descartes means that the dreams were from heaven (and not, as one attack on Baillet suggested, two years after the first edition, "ordinary dreams excited by tobacco, beer and melancholy"),[25] Freud means exactly the opposite: dreams from above, he says "are fomulations of ideas which could have been created just as well in a waking state as during the state of sleep, and which have derived their content only in certain parts from mental states at a comparatively deep level. That is why these dreams offer for the most part a content which has an abstract, poetic or symbolic form" ("SD," p. 203). In 1923, six years earlier, Freud had also written on dreams from above; they correspond, he wrote then, "to thoughts or intentions of the day before which have contrived during the night to obtain reinforcement from repressed material that is debarred from the ego. When this is so, analysis as a rule disregards this unconscious ally and succeeds in inserting the latent dream-thoughts into the texture of waking thought."[26] Surely this is meant, from Freud's point of view, to serve as an excellent description of Descartes and the production of his dreams, especially in relation to the day of ecstasy which precedes them. The dream from above is from a deep level of the mind—but accessible, because it could have been created just as well in the waking state. "We cannot understand the dream," Freud continues in his response to Leroy, "but the dreamer—or patient—can translate it immediately and without difficulty, given that the content of the dream is very close to his conscious thoughts. There then remain certain parts . . . which belong to the unconscious and which are in many respects the most interesting" ("SD," p. 203). It is significant that Freud begins, in the same terms as Baillet, by proclaiming Descartes' dreams to be essentially *conscious:* the dreams of the philosopher of consciousness, in other words, match his waking thought. The above here is not heaven, of course ("this term must be understood in a psychological, not in a mystical, sense," says Freud of the "dreams from above"), but rather the outside, conscious, waking world. Freud's topographic model of the mind recapitulates this understanding of "above" (north, so to speak) and "below." "This way of judging 'dreams from above,' " writes Freud "is the one to be followed in the case of Descartes' dreams" ("SD," p. 203). The insistence on the same terminology as Baillet is here admitted, for Freud uses the same phrase with an inverted sense: a dream from above has come, with psychoanalysis,

24. Baillet, *La Vie,* 1:81.

25. See *Nouveaux mémoires pour servir à l'histoire du cartésianisme* par M. G. de l'A. (1692), pp. 43–44. Adam and Tannery note that the author is Gilles de l'Aunay, that is, Pierre-Daniel Huet, bishop of Avranches (see *Oeuvres de Descartes,* 10:185).

26. Freud, "Remarks on the Theory and Practice of Dream-Interpretation as a Whole" *Standard Edition,* 19:111. It should be noted that the unconscious portion of "dreams from above" is "disregarded" by analysis.

from consciousness. If the "below," as Jean Starobinski has shown, is modelled on the hell of the ancients—the Infernal Regions, as Virgil says—it is also the place of the profound, of what is worth taking note of.[27] Freud in reading Descartes' dreams achieves an inversion of the map of values—heaven (north) is of little interest; but hell is teeming with meaning and significance. The implication, then, is that Descartes, like his dreams, is shallow, as is any philosophy which privileges consciousness.

But as all dreams for Freud must have some element of the unconscious, there will be parts, it should be remembered, in a dream from "above" that will remain inexplicable, and those parts are from "below," from the unconscious. It will come as no surprise that the "parts" of Descartes' dreams which Freud finds inexplicable, and therefore from the unconscious, are the melon and the portraits. In the final four short paragraphs of his analysis, Freud makes four main points: (1) We should accept Descartes' own interpretation of these dreams, but "we have no path open to us which will take us any further." (2) The hindrances which prevent Descartes from moving in the first dream are "an internal conflict," the left side representing evil and sin, and the wind the evil genius. (3) Descartes would have known who all the figures in the dream were, but we cannot. (4) The melon is certainly not a symbol for the "'charms of solitude,'" but Descartes could probably have shed some light on it. "If it is correlated with his state of sin," says Freud, "this association might stand for a sexual picture which occupied the lonely young man's imagination." The final sentence of the letter to Leroy reads: "On the question of the portraits Descartes throws no light" ("SD," p. 204).

Freud has spent a mere one and a half pages explicating (so to speak) the most famous dreams in philosophy. And while his lack of interest in these may be relegated to his proclaimed distaste for philosophy in general, I think we must be suspicious of the whole business. Let us take Freud's own texts for a moment, to read these same dreams which this Freud tells us are simply unreadable. ("We have no path," he claimed, using the same metaphor of the path as Descartes, "open to us which will take us any further.") In part, of course, we have already been doing this. My reading of the dreams—the suggestions concerning Ausonius, Galileo, Mersenne, and so on—impose Freud's own dream analysis theory upon the dream texts of Descartes. Moreover, Descartes himself analyzes his dreams, and Freud says that he does a credible job: "the philosopher interprets them himself and, in accordance with all the rules for the interpretation of dreams, we must accept his explanation, but it should be added that we have no path open to us which will take us any further"

27. See Jean Starobinski's "*Acheronta Movebo*" (pp. 273–86) in this volume. Starobinski makes the most compelling analysis I have seen for Freud's debt to Virgil.

("SD," p. 204). Yet Freud's own dream interpretation allows us to go a bit further still.

It will be recalled that Freud cannot, and will not, make anything of the melon or the little portraits. He seems befuddled by them. And yet in the second chapter of his dream book, in the section on the specimen dream, Freud says: "There is at least one spot in every dream at which it is unplumbable—a navel, as it were, that is its point of contact with the unknown"(*ID*, p. 111 n. 1). And in the seventh chapter he refers to "the dream's navel, the spot where it reaches down into the unknown" (*ID*, p. 525). Note that we are back to "above" and "below" terminology: every dream, even one from "above," has something in it from "below," and that is the navel. We could just leave it at that, and call the melon and the portraits the blind spots in Descartes' dreams. But we have already done a bit more than that with both. In any case, the blind spot is the dream's own censorship—from "below."

Certainly, in considering the little portraits, Freud drops the matter very quickly. But we can consider the fact, for example, that Baillet's French version refers to the portraits as being "de taille douce." *Tailler* is also a verb used to describe the cutting of glass, and it is used frequently by Baillet in this context as well. Descartes worked on optics as early as 1613 in Paris. He drew elaborate charts of the eye, of perspective, and refraction. He worked on lenses (like Galileo, as we have noted). There would be a natural association here for Freud—one which he passes over. In the botanical monograph dream, a book lies before Freud, and he is turning over a folded colored plate. Bound in each copy there is a dried specimen of the plant, "as though it had been taken from a herbarium" (*ID*, p. 169). The botanical monograph dream is strangely like the third dream of Descartes—a book lies before the dreamer, and in it there is a plate, illustrating the contents. The dream suggests an entire method of thought (much as Descartes' dreams imitate the heuristic moves of his own *méthode*). More important, however, Freud associates the plant with the coca plant, the subject of one of his monographs which, like Descartes' work, was illustrated by his own hand. The monograph had to do with the uses and properties of cocaine. But at the crucial moment of his research, in 1884, Freud went to Hamburg to see his fiancée. It is she whom he later blamed when, during his absence, his friend Karl Koller rubbed some cocaine in the eye of a dog and discovered an ophthalmic anesthesia.[28] This discovery brought Koller instant fame. Meanwhile, Freud's studious monograph, "Über Koka," from the same year, fell into oblivion. Originality, in other words, and its concomitant fame—coming first—had eluded him. Now here is another monograph,

---

28. Ernest Jones dubs this Freud's second chance at a fame which eluded him, the first having been the use of gold chloride to stain nervous tissue. See Jones, *The Life and Work of Sigmund Freud*, 3 vols. (New York, 1953–57), 1:78–79.

entitled *The Interpretation of Dreams*—the basis of which is Freud's own dreams, dreams which demonstrate the method. Freud describes the dreams and then interprets them—exactly like Descartes. The botanical monograph dream, with the dream of Irma's injection, are specimen dreams marking out this method, echoing Descartes.

When Freud sets about analyzing his botanical monograph dream, he associates rather quickly to the coca plant and his lost chance at certain fame ("I had myself indicated this application [Koller's discovery of cocaine as an anesthetic] but I had not been thorough enough to pursue the matter further" [*ID*, p. 170]). From there he lapses into "a kind of day-dream." If he ever gets glaucoma, he imagines the possible collegial awkwardness which might ensue when Dr. Freud became the patient Freud. He would keep his identity a secret, he decides: "The operating surgeon, who would have no idea of my identity, would boast once again of how easily such operations could be performed since the introduction of cocaine; and I should not give the slightest hint that I myself had had a share in the discovery" (*ID*, p. 170). Then Freud remembers suddenly, at the end of this daydream, that his father "had in fact been attacked by glaucoma" and during the operation, Freud's friend Dr. Leopold Königstein had been the surgeon, and Koller in charge of the cocaine anesthesia. The latter had commented that "this case had brought together all of the three men who had had a share in the introduction of cocaine" (*ID*, p. 171). Koller's egalitarian view puts the three scientists—himself, Königstein, and Freud—all into the same position of fame with respect to the use of cocaine in ophthalmic surgery. In fact, however, what emerges is Freud's frustration over not having been recognized more fully for his "share in the discovery" (the same word we encountered in Freud's description of his work in psychoanalysis). The botanical monograph dream is the dream of a rivalry with a peer over optics ("Once, I recalled, I really *had* written something in the nature of a *monograph on a plant,* namely a dissertation on the *coca-plant* [Freud, 1884], which had drawn Karl Koller's attention to the anaesthetic properties of cocaine" [*ID*, p. 170]). It is a rivalry, moreover, which Descartes' dreams mirror at two levels: first, by suggesting the other rivalry between Descartes and Galileo (with Mersenne and his melon serving as mediator); and second, a rivalry Freud feels perhaps with Descartes himself, whose "Olympica" founded "modern philosophy" with no questions asked about originality.[29] I suggest that *The Interpretation of Dreams* is meant to be the monograph

29. There is a third mirroring here, one of which Freud is unaware: Descartes' increasing fear that his work is being "stolen"—in particular by Beeckman whom, in 1630, Descartes accuses of plagiarizing from his *Treatise on Music.* Perhaps Descartes' worries about his claims to originality were justified, since it is frequently noted that the *méthode* was not invented by him at all, but by Pierre de la Ramée. See Philippe Desan, *Naissance de la méthode: Machiavelle, la Ramée, Bodin, Montaigne, Descartes* (Paris, 1987).

that succeeds where "Über Koka" had failed. But Descartes succeeded the first time.

Freud's obsession with originality has been thoroughly documented. It is with this obsession in mind that I suggest that Descartes' copperplates, so resonant in sound and significance to Freud's colored plates, are a mystery to Freud; and this mystery, coupled with the subsequent indifference on Freud's part to the dreams of the French philosopher, are the first clue that something is afoot. The reader of Freud jumps to associate Descartes' text to Freud's. Only Freud remains in the dark and can, in his own words, "throw no light."

The first dream by Descartes is also open to a Freudian interpretation which Freud himself bypasses. Indeed, it might be seen as a "typical" dream called "embarrassing dreams of being naked" in the fifth chapter of the dream book. Dreams of being naked are dreams of exhibition, Freud tells us. Baillet, let us note, says that throughout the day of 10 November, Descartes rendered his mind naked: "son imagination lui présentât son esprit tout nud." And such dreams, says Freud, are associated with difficulty in walking: "one *does* feel shame and embarrassment and tries to escape or hide, and is then overcome by a strange inhibition which prevents one from moving and makes one feel incapable of altering one's distressing situation" (*ID*, p. 242). Here Freud mentions a dream of his own in which he suddenly is unable to move (up a flight of stairs). He adds that onlookers rarely notice the dreamer's difficulty in dreams of this sort, though they have no such problems in locomotion. Here again, then, Freud might have contributed to the Descartes dream sequence. Moreover, it is in the description of this type of dream that Freud makes the connection between typical dreams and creative writing: "It sometimes happens that the sharp eye of a creative writer has an analytic realization of the process of transformation of which he is habitually no more than the tool. If so, he may follow the process in a reverse direction and so trace back the imaginative writing to a dream" (*ID*, p. 246). Does not this last sentence describe *both* Descartes and Freud? Is Freud perhaps afraid that his new theory will, unlike Descartes', prove to be a fraud? Is that why, in this same section on this type of dream, he mentions the fable of the emperor's new clothes? Revealing the nakedness of the mind can lead sometimes to nothing at all, as in the case of the cocaine papers. The primary text for Descartes' written work is his own dreams—so, too, for Freud. Descartes dreams his consecutive dreams and ushers in a new system of thought—so, Freud hopes, will he. It is Freud's fear of failure to be original which may well explain his "boredom" with Descartes. A double rivalry, as I have already suggested.

And there is another detail which Freud might have noted—an association, once again, which might have linked the Descartes dreams to Freud's own work. In "The Dream and the Primal Scene," he tells us that the Wolf-Man suffered from malaria as a young boy, having an attack every day "at a particular hour." This factor, says Freud in a note, is metamorphosed in the patient's dreams while he is in treatment; the malaria will be replaced by a violent wind in the Wolf-Man's dreams.[30] Freud realizes that this is a pun for the mal-aria (evil wind). This *ventus malus* is the same vocabulary Descartes used to describe his dream. But, as we have noted, Descartes' dream pulls together the wind with spirit (both good and bad)—a combination which, as we have said, is traditional in ancient Greek and Hebrew. The God-spirit connection is linked with creation; in Genesis, it is the wind and spirit of God hovering over the waters which begin the moment of creation. In the same passage in which Hegel discusses Descartes' transparency of being and thought, he distinguishes between two Enlightenments: one calls "being" a predicateless Absolute (spirit or God), and the other calls it matter, or Nature. Both, he notes, are unconscious and conscious and are in fact the same Notion.[31] Paul Ricoeur has noted that the problem of consciousness is at least as problematic as that of the unconscious.[32] Perhaps Freud's problem with Descartes is that the French philosopher, echoed by Hegel, says that the secret of the *tota simul* is that the mind is one, and that there can be no distinction, ultimately, between conscious and unconscious mind. As Freud believed his greatest discovery to have been, in fact, the unconscious, his originality (not to mention system of thought) is seriously impugned if he, in turn, takes the discovery of Descartes' dreams seriously: that consciousness and unconsciousness, like spirit or God and the manifestations thereof, are indistinguishable. This is part of the secret of Descartes' dreams—in direct conflict with the philosophy Freud builds on the secret of his own dreams.

If the insistence on originality has replaced here the desire for "truth" (let us remember that it is Freud who says that there is not much proof that man is even comfortable with the idea of truth)—if this is the case, it is a historical as much as a personal insistence. Freud's plant in the botanical monograph dream is also a common symbol (beginning with the eighteenth century) for original genius. The plant contains the seed, which, like the genius (no longer evil), impounds its own substance. Freud's obsession with originality, his later fear that his ideas would be plagiarized by his associates, is the result of his greatest desire: fame. If not with cocaine, then with dreams. This is not yet the "phantom" of Descartes' dreams, although Descartes would share those fears, eventually, in ways that bring him far closer to Freud than the latter would ever know.

When Freud writes to Leroy that, ultimately, the reading of Descartes' dreams "turned out to be easier than I anticipated" (SD," p. 203), he is

---

30. Freud, "The Dream and the Primal Scene," *Standard Edition*, 17:37 n. 1.

31. Hegel, *Phenomenology of Spirit*, pp. 351–52.

32. Paul Ricoeur, *The Conflict of Interpretations: Essays in Hermeneutics*, ed. Don Ihde (Evanston, Ill., 1974), p. 99.

admitting to an ease which should not, by now, surprise us, since it is his own method which teaches us that what is *too* evident usually signifies denial. The denial here, as I have argued, is of the possibility that the unconscious, hence Freud's originality, may not exist. And the reading of Descartes' dreams as dreams "from above" (echoing Baillet's "d'enhaut"), and as *conscious* dreams, born of waking moments, is like an unwilled acquiescence (what I have called an epistemological imitative fallacy) to *both* Descartes' seamless mind and Baillet's reading. Fortunately, there is still the melon—that cord leading to the unknown, which Freud hopes he can call the unconscious. The birth imagery of the navel is not unrelated to Freud's problem with originality. By insisting that every dream has a navel, and thus an unconscious, Freud is giving birth, in each dream, to his discovery. Thus genius remains *original*—but also, therefore, fallible, individual, and imminently vulnerable to the whims of fate (Koller) and the hands of thieves (Tausk, Jung, and others).[33]

In short, it is Freud's method of approaching the dream text which first teaches us to gloss, in part, the dreams from which Freud turns away. And it is this same "method" which helps to trace Freud's fear of failure, which in this case results in a blindness to a text—a text which perhaps too successfully reveals an easy move from dream to method, and from there to fame. And above all, it is a text which joins literature (the *corpus poetarum*) with science, to create an original, established philosophy.

Appendix

Dream #1

Several phantoms presented themselves and frightened Descartes. Walking through the streets, he had to turn to the left side to advance to where he wanted to go, because he felt a great feebleness on the right side, on which he couldn't support himself. Ashamed of walking this way, he tried to straighten himself, but an impetuous wind carried him in a sort of whirlwind and whirled him about three or four times on his left foot. He thought he would fall at each step, until having seen an open college

---

33. The plagiarized text is given the feminized pose: that which is kidnapped and, Helen-like, forced into another's camp. It is Descartes, further, who likens science to a woman, just as it is Freud who gives the unconscious feminine attributes. Both are "mysterious" and need to be "conquered" (Descartes) or "discovered" and thus claimed (Freud). For Freud, the thieves began (as they did for Descartes) to take from him as well—or so he feared. For the Freud, Tausk, and Lou Andreas-Salomé triangle of competition, see Paul Roazen, *Brother Animal: The Story of Freud and Tausk* (New York, 1969). For the second triangle of Freud, Tausk, and Deutsch, and the ensuing disaster, see Neil Hertz, "Freud and the Sandman," in *Textual Strategies: Perspectives in Post-Structuralist Criticism*, ed. Josué V. Harari (Ithaca, N.Y., 1979), pp. 296–321.

on the road, he entered to find a retreat and a remedy for his sickness. He wished to reach it with the thought first of prayer, but having passed a man he knew without greeting him, he tried to retrace his steps to do so, but was pushed violently by the wind against the Church. In the middle of the college court, he saw another person who called him courteously by name, and told him that if he was looking for Monsieur N., he had something to give him. Descartes imagined it was a melon which had been brought from a foreign country. What surprised him more was to see that those who were gathered around this person stood firm on their feet, while he always remained bent and unsteady. The wind meanwhile subsided. He then awoke, and felt a real pain, which made him fear that some evil genius had wished to seduce him. He had been sleeping on his left side, and turned to the right, praying God to save him from misfortune and punishment of his sins.

Dream #2

He had fallen asleep after meditating for two hours on the goods and evils of this world. Then he dreams that he hears a sharp and piercing noise which he took for a peal of thunder. The fright awoke him, and he perceived many sparks of fire scattered in the room. This had often happened to him before. He would awake in the middle of the night his eyes quite glittering. But this time he desired philosophical reasons, and he drew conclusions favorable to his mind.

Dream #3

This dream was not accompanied by feelings of anxiety. Descartes finds a book on the table, opens it, discovers it's a Dictionary, and is delighted with it. Then, that very instant, he finds another book under his hand, and doesn't know where it had come from. He ascertains it is an anthology of poems of different authors entitled CORPUS POETARUM. He was curious to read something, and at the beginning of the book, happened upon the verse: *Quod vitae sectabor iter?* At the same time he saw a man he didn't know but who presented him with a verse beginning *Est et Non,* which he praised. Descartes told him he knew what it was, and that it was one of the Idylls of Ausonius found in the big collection of poets on the table. He wished to show it himself to this man, and began to leaf through the book whose order and arrangement he had boasted he knew perfectly. While he was looking for the place, the man asked him where he had obtained the book, and Descartes answered that he was unable to tell him how he had it; but that a moment before he had held still another which had disappeared, without his knowing who had brought it or taken it back from him. He hadn't finished when he saw the book appear once more at the other end of the table. But he discovered that this Dictionary was not complete as it had been when he saw it the first time. However, in perusing the Anthology of Poets, he came upon the poems of Ausonius; but not finding the piece which began with *Est et Non,* he told the man he knew another one by the same poet which was still more beautiful than the former, and which began *Quod vitae sectabor iter?* The person asked him to show it to him, and Descartes set about looking for it, whereupon he found several small portraits engraved in copper-plate; this made him say that the book was very beautiful, but that it was not of the same printing as the one he had known. There he was when the books and the man disappeared, and faded from his imagination, without nevertheless re-awakening him.

What was singular in the circumstances of the dream, continues the account, was that "Descartes, wondering whether what he had just seen was a dream or vision, not only decided that it was a dream, but he rendered its interpretation even before he awoke. He judged that the Dictionary represented all the sciences gathered together; and that the Anthology of Poems, entitled CORPUS POETARUM, indicated particularly, and in a distinct fashion, Philosophy and Wisdom joined together. For he believed one shouldn't be much surprised to see that the poets, even those who fool their time away, have many maxims which are deeper, more sensible and better expressed than those which are found in the writings of philosophers. He attributed this wonder to the divinity of Enthusiasm and the force of Imagination, which emitted the seeds of wisdom (which are found in the minds of all men, like the sparks of fire in flint-stones) with much more ease and brilliance even than Reason can among the philosophers. Descartes, continuing to interpret the dream in his sleep, thought that the verse on the uncertainty of the way of life which one must choose, which begins with *Quod vitae sectabor iter,* marked the sound advice of a wise person, or even of Moral Theology.

"Thereupon, uncertain whether he was seeing or imagining, he awoke without emotion, and his eyes open, continued to interpret his dream along the same line. By the poets gathered in the anthology he understood Revelation and Enthusiasm, which he hoped would still favor him. By the piece of verse *Est et Non,* which is the Yes and No of Pythagoras, he understood Truth and Falsehood in human knowledge and the secular sciences. Seeing that his work in all these fields was succeeding so well, he was bold enough to persuade himself that it was the Spirit of Truth which had wished to open for him (by this dream) the treasures of all the sciences. There was left for him only to explain the little portraits in copper-plate, which he had found in the second book. He didn't try to explain this any more after an Italian painter visited him the next day.

"This last dream, which was altogether very pleasant and agreeable, indicated to him the future and what must happen to him for the rest of his life. But he took the two preceding ones as threatening warnings concerning his past life, which may not have been as innocent before God as before men. And he believed that it was the reason for the terror and fright with which these two dreams had been accompanied. The melon, which was offered him in the first dream, signified, he said, the charms of solitude, but available through purely human attractions. The wind which pushed him towards the Church of the college, when he felt bad on the right side, was nothing but the evil Genius which tried to throw him by force into a place he had voluntarily planned to go."

The Struggle of Psychiatry with Psychoanalysis: Who Won?

Sander L. Gilman

1. The Historical Background

What if Wittgenstein and Popper were right after all? What if psychoanalysis is not "scientific," not scientific by any contemporary definition—including Adolf Grünbaum's—but what if it works all the same?[1] What if psychoanalysis is all right in practice, but the theory isn't scientific? Indeed, what if "science" is defined ideologically rather than philosophically? If we so redefine "science," it is not to dismiss psychoanalysis but to understand its origin and impact, to follow the ideological dialectic between the history of psychiatry, its developing as a medical "science," and the evolving self-definition of psychoanalysis which parallels this history.

We know that Freud divided psychoanalysis into three quite discrete areas—first, a theory, a "scientific structure"; second, a method of inquiry, a means of exploring and ordering information; and last, but certainly not least, a mode of treatment. Let us, for the moment, follow the actual course of history, at least the course of a history which can be described by sorting out the interrelationship between psychoanalysis and psychiatry, and assume that we can heuristically view the mode of treatment as

1. The debate about the scientific status of psychoanalysis is summarized in Adolf Grünbaum, *The Foundations of Psychoanalysis: A Philosophical Critique* (Berkeley and Los Angeles, 1984). A brief historical overview of the nature of psychotherapeutic treatment is given by Sol L. Garfield, "Psychotherapy: A 40-Year Appraisal," *American Psychologist* 36 (Feb. 1981): 174–83.

relatively independent of the other two aspects of psychoanalysis. What if the very claims for a "scientific" basis for psychoanalytic treatment and by extension the role of the psychoanalyst as promulgated by Freud and his early followers were rooted in an ideologically charged historical interpretation of the positivistic nature of science and the definition of the social role of the scientist? This may seem an odd premise to begin an essay on the mutual influence of psychoanalysis and psychiatry, but it is no stranger than the actual historical practice.

Psychoanalysis originated not in the psychiatric clinic but in the laboratories of neurology in Vienna and Paris.[2] Its point of origin was not nineteenth-century psychiatry but rather nineteenth-century neurology. That origin points to a major difference between the traditional practice of nineteenth-century psychiatry and modern clinical psychiatry in our post-positivistic age. Psychiatry in nineteenth-century Europe, in Vienna as well as in Paris, was an adjunct to the world of the asylum. Indeed, the second great battle (after Pinel's restructuring of the asylum) which nineteenth-century psychiatry waged was the creation of the "alienist" as a new medical speciality. The alienist was the medical doctor in administrative charge of the asylum, rather than a medical adjunct to the lay asylum director as had earlier, in the age of "moral treatment," been the practice.

The medicalization of psychiatry was, by the closing decades of the nineteenth century, successful. Its success, however, was due to political factors.[3] In Britain, a series of parliamentary commissions began, in the first decade of the century, to examine the abuses of the asylum, abuses

---

2. The historical background is outlined by Peter Amacher, *Freud's Neurological Education and Its Influence on Psychoanalytic Theory* (New York, 1965); Kenneth Levin, *Freud's Early Psychology of the Neurosis: A Historical Perspective* (Pittsburgh, Pa., 1978); and polemically in Frank J. Sulloway, *Freud, Biologist of the Mind: Beyond the Psychoanalytic Legend* (New York, 1979).

3. On the history of psychiatry as a mode of control, see Michel Foucault, *Histoire de la folie à l'âge classique* (Paris, 1972), and, more recently, Andrew Scull, ed., *Madhouses, Mad-Doctors, and Madmen: The Social History of Psychiatry in the Victorian Era* (Philadelphia, Pa., 1981).

Sander L. Gilman is professor of humane studies in the departments of German literature and Near Eastern studies, Cornell University, and professor of psychiatry (history) at the Cornell Medical College. He is the author of numerous books on intellectual and literary history. His most recent study is *Jewish Self-Hatred* (1986). Forthcoming is his study *Oscar Wilde's London* and the English edition of his *Conversations with Nietzsche*.

which seemed to provide a rationale for the medicalization of the asylum. This view was not based on the actual benefit which medicine had to offer the mentally ill; rather, it was an attempt to place the asylum within the growing sphere of medicine as science. But it also continued the separation of psychiatry as a mode of treatment undertaken in asylums, rather than in general hospitals. Moral treatment, coming as it did out of a religious (the Tukes and Quaker) tradition or a more radical, revolutionary tradition (Pinel and the "freeing" of the insane), was seen as scientifically "old-fashioned" and/or politically "dangerous." This development of the asylum out of the early nineteenth-century "reformed" British asylums with their lay directors relied on a new scientistic definition of the nature of psychiatry. It ran on a parallel but clearly different track to the development of the general medical hospital. "Reform" was simply not enough; medicalization was needed. For "madness" came to be seen as "mental illness" in what was understood as a natural extension of the general model of somatic pathology. The new science of psychiatry had been imbued with the status of science, but it was placed in its own ghetto, the asylum, which still isolated it from all of the other medical specialities being practiced in the general hospital.

Psychiatry was a rather unique case in other ways, too. For in accepting the power of the state to control directly the actions of a group labeled as "different" and "diseased," psychiatrists straddled the worlds of politics and science, much like the police doctors, whose area of control, public health, was the inspection of prostitutes. While they laid claim to the status of the world of science through the introduction of the medical model of madness, they were still perceived in their older, nonscientific function as the administrators of institutions of control. This function lowered the prestige of the alienists. It was the search for a higher status within medicine, and thus within the academy, which drove the psychiatrist to lay claim to the status implicit in the world of the anatomically based areas of medicine. But it was also the relatively lower status of psychiatry which enabled individuals viewed as marginal, such as Jews, to enter this new medical speciality.

The German and Austrian situation (if one can generalize over a wide range of experiences and a large number of national variations) was likewise the result of a gradual professionalization of medicine and an extension of this medicalization into those areas of health care delivery, from the running of lying-in hospitals to the direction of the asylums, which were not traditionally seen as part of "medicine."[4] This made itself especially evident in the creation in the mid-nineteenth century of the huge centralized state asylum at Bielefeld with its professional staff. But the central focus of all of these movements is the medicalization of the

---

4. On the history of the psychiatric hospital see Dieter Jetter, *Grundzüge der Geschichte des Irrenhauses* (Darmstadt, 1981).

office of asylum director and the concomitant rise in the status of this role. Psychiatry in Germany and Austria was as much the administration of the asylum as the treatment of the insane. Neurology, on the other hand, was often seen as a "pure" medical science, using the positivistic model of late nineteenth-century science, and was seen as quite independent of any "applied" function (at least to the degree that psychiatry had claimed for itself).

After the mid-nineteenth century, however, both neurology and psychiatry shared a set of scientific presumptions which were heavily laced with nineteenth-century racist ideology. Their basis was, indeed, first articulated in the academic forum by Kant in his essay of 1764 on the nature of illness of the head.[5] There he mocks the view that mental illness could have its roots in the emotions, seeing mental illness as inherently somatic. What Kant undertook was to apply to the area of mental illness the rising status of the new French biology and its attempt to explain all aspects of human nature (such as racial difference) through the biological model. It was an attempt to move the understanding of mental illness out of what Kant perceived to be the moralizing tendency of religion which had labeled madness the result of the stigma of sinfulness. Madness was a disease and, like all diseases in the age of Jenner, was understood to be somatic. (It was not the wrath of God which caused illness, but the failure of the corporeal machine.) But it is vital to understand that inherent in views such as those espoused by Kant are the racist premises of eighteenth-century French biology and anthropology: the great chain of being, with its implicit hierarchy of the various races, as well as the polygenetic origin of the races.[6] Kant, in his own anthropology, commented that the Jews are a unique group in the West, marked by their own sign—for him the corruption of their discourse—which sets them apart from all other groups.[7]

Kant's view was clearly in the avant-garde of the eighteenth century. But the general view after the mid-nineteenth century was, following Wilhelm Griesinger's standard textbook of 1845, that "mind illness was brain illness," and much attention was given to the description and localization of neurological pathologies.[8] Between Kant and Griesinger, however, lay an epoch which stressed the independent existence of mental illness, illness rooted in the mechanics of the emotions and their repression.

5. See Immanuel Kant, *Werke*, ed. Wilhelm Weischedel, 6 vols. (Wiesbaden, 1956–64), 1:887–906.
6. See William Bynum, "Time's Noblest Offspring: The Problem of Man in British Natural Historical Sciences" (Diss., Cambridge University, 1974).
7. See Kant, *Werke*, 6:517–18.
8. On the general background of this debate see Henri Ellenberger, *The Discovery of the Unconscious: The History and Evolution of Dynamic Psychiatry* (New York, 1970), and U. H. Peters, "Die Situation der deutschen Psychiatrie bei Beginn der psychiatrischen Emigrationsbewegung 1933," in *Zusammenhang: Festschrift für Marielene Putscher*, ed. Otto Baur and Otto Glandien (Cologne, 1984), pp. 837–64.

J. G. Langermann in his 1797 dissertation on mental illness cast these views into their most representative form.[9] Langermann not only presented a theory of the origin of mental illness that dismissed the origin of psychopathologies as anomalies of the brain but also stressed the origin of psychopathology in the "spirit." He separated the mind-body dichotomy completely. But even more important, Langermann presented a case study of a "psychological" cure. Langermann was not alone. Later "romantic" psychiatrists such as Ideler, Heinroth, Carus, Kieser, and the widely translated Belgian asylum director Guislain stressed the centrality of psychological mechanisms in the manifestation of mental illness.

Such a view was dynamic in that it denied the primacy of human biology in shaping the human psyche and assumed a certain flexibility of human emotions. It was also implicitly racist. Indeed, the most widely read popularization of this view, Christian Heinrich Spiess' *Biographies of the Mentally Ill* (1795–96) had as one of its centerpieces the tale of the "beautiful Jewess" Esther L —— and her collapse into madness.[10] Spiess' views are typical of the strain of seeing mental illness as the result of psychological rather than physical disease. Spiess uses this case as his exemplary case of "love madness," erotomania, stressing above all the sexual nature of the Jew and the relationship of this psychological weakness to psychopathology. Thus both biological and romantic psychopathology were strongly formed by contemporaneous attitudes toward race.

The domination of the biological model over the psychological was in point of fact the presumptive success of the "scientific" over the "religious," or at least that is how the nineteenth century perceived it. The position which late nineteenth-century clinical psychiatry took was not merely in line with the sense of the status of medicine as it existed after mid-century but also in opposition to what Emil Kraepelin as late as 1918 felt compelled to dismiss as such "natural-philosophical speculation." Kraepelin's views, however, were not aimed at the "romantic" psychiatrists of the early nineteenth century, but at the resurrection of their position in the works of Sigmund Freud.[11]

2. The Nature of Medical Science in Freud's Vienna and Freud's Early Understanding of the Medical Practice

Sigmund Freud's early work in the laboratories of Theodor Meynert centered about the neurological description of primitive vertebrates, with

9. See J. G. Langermann, *De methodo cognoscendi curandique animi morbos stabilienda* (Diss., Jena, 1797).

10. See Christian Heinrich Spiess, *Biographien der Wahnsinnigen*, ed. Wolfgang Promies (Cologne, 1966).

11. Emil Kraepelin, "Hundert Jahr Psychiatrie," *Zeitschrift für Neurologie und Psychiatrie* 38 (1919): 161–275.

the hope that such analysis would lead to an understanding of the mechanisms and structures which are also present in human neurological development. His work was aimed at a purely mechanistic description of the nature of human psychology. When he came into contact with Jean Martin Charcot in Paris, he maintained his attitude toward the nature and value of such a scientific undertaking, an undertaking which was "pure" science. For Meynert and Charcot shared the patriarchal status of the new scientific medicine following Claude Bernard's lead. Or so the legend created by Freud is supposed to be read.[12] As I have shown elsewhere, the tradition of French, as well as German, anthropological psychiatry labeled Jews at high risk for specific forms of mental illness.[13] But neurology, the origin of modern psychoanalytic thought, was itself not free from such perversions. And it was in Freud's relationship with one individual, the Berlin ear, nose, and throat specialist, Wilhelm Fliess, that the racist overtones of "scientific" medicine were articulated and distanced.

In Freud's correspondence with Fliess, the question of the nature of the scientific undertaking of psychiatry and neurology and the definition of the medical practitioner was drawn into question.[14] Traditionally Fliess is represented as a marginal figure in the history of medicine. He is seen as the mute sounding board for Freud's views. Everyone (up to but not including Peter Swales, who is now writing Fliess' biography) has wondered how Freud, as bright and insightful as he evidently was, could have gotten himself associated with this Berlin quack. It has been accepted that Fliess was a quack—he put forth absolutely mad views such as the intimate relationship between the nasal passages and the genitalia as well as the idea that male as well as female physiology reflected rigid periodic cycles. But quackery implies a misappropriation of the status of scientific medicine, and it is the implication of this misappropriation which can help us understand Freud's gradual redefinition of the science of medicine.

Fliess actually acted on his theories, undertaking surgical procedures on the nose to relieve sexual problems. His surgical ineptitude almost killed Freud's patient Emma Eckstein. He left a wad of surgical dressing

---

12. Sulloway, in *Freud, Biologist of the Mind*, claims that Freud's perception of anti-Semitism and the marginality of his own views were "myths." If, indeed, Sulloway is right, and there is little doubt about the force of his argument and the materials he has mustered to prove it, we must ask the next evident question: Why did Freud perceive the world in the manner in which he reported? It is the reconstruction of the fantasies about the world rather than the assumption that there are "realities" in history to be "discovered" that is the central undertaking, especially of the historian of psychoanalysis.

13. See my essay "Jews and Mental Illness: Medical Metaphors, Anti-Semitism, and the Jewish Response," *Journal of the History of the Behavioral Sciences* 20 (April 1984): 150–59.

14. See Hannah S. Decker, *Freud in Germany: Revolution and Reaction in Science, 1893–1907* (New York, 1977).

in the cavity which caused massive bleeding and infection. Since Fliess had operated on Freud's nose during the same stay in Vienna during which he undertook the Eckstein operation, his action, as Max Schur stated when he first revealed this material, must have negatively influenced Freud's understanding of the implications of science both in the ineptitude it revealed and because Freud had placed Fliess on an intellectual plane that clearly paralleled the level which he himself wished to obtain.[15] Fliess' assumed role as a "surgeon," the highest of the medical specialities, was only disguised by his label as a "nose" doctor. His actions were those of medical practitioners whose status was clearly higher than that permitted him by the society in which he lived. This denial was based on Fliess' racial identity.

And it is no accident that all of Fliess' patients, Freud included, were Jewish. The isolation still felt by the Jewish health care practitioner formed both Freud and Fliess. Both saw in the social status of medicine a chance to establish themselves in a society which rejected Jews but acclaimed academic physicians. Freud and Fliess both sought out specialities which were open to Jews. But they conceptually restructured these areas to reflect the higher sense of status of other medical specialities.[16] Sexual questions were dealt with by the psychiatrist in the role of forensic specialist on deviant behavior as well as by the syphilologist, who, as a dermatologist, occupied the lowest rung in Viennese medicine. Indeed, when Ferdinand Hebra assumed the chair in dermatology (a field nicknamed *Judenhaut*) in Vienna, he was able to recruit only Jewish assistants! And psychiatry, with its transitional status between administration and practice, had an equivalently heavy and early Jewish representation. Thus Freud and Fliess sought out two areas, psychopathology and sexuality, where Jews were permitted to function on the level of the academician. Their meetings, which they dubbed "congresses," were mock academic events. And their desire was to move the study of psycho- and sexual pathologies into a new area—that of neurology.

Freud and Fliess both needed the status of the higher academic specialities. Both sought this status in the area of neurology and addressed their need for status through their attempt to ask traditional (in Viennese medicine) "Jewish" questions about sexuality and psychopathology through the higher status subspeciality of neurology. For Fliess, it was the movement from a concentration on the ear, nose, and throat to the interconnection of all human experience through the nervous system. Now Fliess was

15. See Max Schur, "Some Additional 'Day Residues' of the Specimen Dream of Psychoanalysis," in *Psychoanalysis, a General Psychology: Essays in Honor of Heinz Hartmann,* ed. Rudolph M. Löwenstein et al. (New York, 1966), pp. 45–85.

16. See Monika Richarz, *Der Eintrittcher Juden in die akademische Berufe* (Tübingen, 1974), pp. 28–43, and Erna Lesky, *Die Wiener medizinische Schule im 19. Jahrhundert* (Graz, 1978).

clearly marginal to the Berlin medical community, as was Freud to that of Vienna. But being "marginal" means relating in a direct manner to the center. Both Freud and Fliess oriented themselves to the center of German medicine; both sought after (and Freud obtained) the status of the medical academic. Both functioned in relationship to a discourse, that of medicine, that was critical of marginality—and that defined marginality in racial terms!

Fliess' theories, based on the best of late nineteenth-century endocrinological and neurological theory, appear to us as more than slightly mad.[17] But they fulfilled a function for Fliess, as well as for Freud, in creating a sense of the new pathway which medicine, stripped of its overt racist overtones, could take. Let us look at two of Fliess' "mad" ideas—the relationship between the nose and the genitalia as well as his "proof" of male periodicity—in the light of the science of medicine, with all its racist overtones in late nineteenth-century Germany and Austria. It is precisely the implications of even the higher medical specialities, such as neurology, which colored Freud and Fliess' sense of the status of medicine and the medical practitioner.

The older popular idea that the nasal cavities were anatomically interrelated with the genitalia had a renewal with the study of human embryology during the nineteenth century. As early as G. Valentin's 1835 handbook of human development, the chronological parallels in the development of soft-tissue areas and cavities of the fetus had been noted.[18] By the time of the publication of the standard atlas of human embryological development by Wilhelm His in 1885, the assumption of such parallels was at the center of European embryology.[19] But the history of embryology, and His' very creation of "standard developmental stages," is rooted in the ideology of recapitulation. Nineteenth-century biologists believed that they could see in the development of the human fetus the "highest" form of life, the repetition of all of the evolutionary stages. Central to this biological reworking of the "great chain of being" was the innate superiority of the human as the end of the teleological development of evolution. Biology placed humanity at the epitome of this development and saw in Ernst Haeckel's commonplace that "ontogeny recapitulates phylogeny" the statement of human superiority.[20] But in

---

17. See the introduction by Jeffrey Moussaieff Masson to his edition of *The Complete Letters of Sigmund Freud to Wilhelm Fliess, 1887–1904* (Cambridge, Mass., 1985), pp. 1–14; all further references to this work, abbreviated *FF*, will be included in the text. See also Peter Heller, "A Quarrel over Bisexuality," in *The Turn of the Century: German Literature and Art, 1890–1915*, ed. Gerald Chapple and Hans H. Schulte (Bonn, 1978), pp. 87–116.

18. See G. Valentin, *Handbuch der Entwickelungsgeschichte des Menschen* (Berlin, 1835).

19. See Wilhelm His, *Anatomie menschlicher Embryonen*, 3 vols. (Leipzig, 1880–85).

20. See Ernst Mayr, *The Growth of Biological Thought: Diversity, Evolution, and Inheritance* (Cambridge, Mass.: 1982).

late nineteenth-century Germany some humans are better than other humans. And it is the implied sense of the hierarchy which is present in German embryology.

Hierarchy in late nineteenth-century German and Austrian science implied the hidden analogy to the science of race—and the key group which defined this hierarchy were the Jews. Christianity saw in the Jews a stage through which modern humans had progressed. Hegel labeled the Jews as an atavistic structure in Western history. For, once having played a role in history, like other ancient peoples, they should have vanished. Their presence in the society of the West was a sign of how much further modern humans had come. If indeed "ontogeny recapitulates phylogeny," then the Jew was at a lower rung on the hierarchy of the human races. This view was so powerful that it was shared even by Friedrich Ratzel, the originator of modern geographical anthropology, when he looked at the Jews of Western Europe.[21]

But embryology also proved that the development of the nasal passages and the incipient genitalia was very early in the development of the fetus. Fliess, by making this association overt, showed that the "head," as the source of the rational, and the "genitalia," as the source of the irrational, were related on an atavistic level and that the manipulation of one could affect the other. The presumption of a primitive relationship between sexuality and the nose is not only bad embryology but bad medicine.

It points, however, to a necessary preoccupation of two *Jewish* scientists of *fin-de-siècle* Europe with the significance of this relationship between the "nose" and the "genitalia." For Fliess and Freud it served as a sign of universal development rather than as a specific sign of an "inferior" racial identity. The association between the Jewish nose and the circumcised penis was made in the crudest and most revolting manner during the 1880s. In the streets of Berlin and Vienna, in penny-papers or on the newly installed *Litfassäulen,* or advertising columns, caricatures of Jews could be seen.[22] These extraordinary caricatures stressed one central aspect of the physiognomy of the Jewish male, his nose, which represented that hidden sign of his sexual difference, his circumcised penis. For the Jews' sign of sexual difference, their sexual selectiveness, as an indicator of their identity was, as Friedrich Nietzsche strikingly observed in *Beyond Good and Evil*, the focus of the Germans' fear concerning the superficiality of their recently created national identity.[23] This fear was represented in caricatures by the elongated nose. (The traditional folkloric association

21. See Jacob Katz, *From Prejudice to Destruction: Anti-Semitism, 1700–1933* (Cambridge, Mass., 1980).

22. See Judith Vogt, *Historien om et Image: Antisemitisme og Antizionisme i Karikaturer* (Copenhagen, 1978).

23. See Friedrich Nietzsche, *Beyond Good and Evil*, trans. Marianne Cowan (Chicago, 1955), pp. 184–88.

between the size of the nose and that of the male genitalia was made a pathological sign.[24]) When Fliess attempted to alter the pathology of the genitalia by operating on the nose (in this age before plastic surgery), he was drawing on an accepted sense of the implication of human development joined to the association of the nose and the genitalia in the German biology of race.

This association of the nose and the genitalia was not merely in the popular mind. The central sign of male periodicity for Fliess (and for Freud) is male menstruation. And its representation, according to Freud in his letter of 20 July 1897 to Fliess, is an "occasional bloody nasal secretion" (*FF*, p. 256). Later, in his letter of 15 October 1897, Freud traces the implications of male menstruation for himself as well as (one assumes) for Fliess:

> My self-analysis is in fact the most essential thing I have at present and promises to become of the greatest value to me if it reaches its end. In the middle of it, it suddenly ceased for three days, during which I had the feeling of being tied up inside (which patients complain of so much), and I was really disconsolate until I found that these same three days (twenty-eight days ago) were the bearers of identical somatic phenomena. Actually only two bad days with a remission in between. From this one should draw the conclusion that the female period is not conducive to work. Punctually on the fourth day, it started again. Naturally, the pause also had another determinant—the resistance to something surprisingly new. Since then I have been once again intensely preoccupied [with it], mentally fresh, though afflicted with all sorts of minor disturbances that come from the content of the analysis. [*FF*, p. 270]

The editor of the new edition of the letters, Jeffrey Masson, comments on Fliess' observations on male menstruation that it is "highly unlikely that these communications to Freud played any role in Freud's research at the time" (*FF*, p. 199). Quite to the contrary—had Masson researched a bit into the history of the concept of male menstruation he would have found a lively nineteenth-century medical literature on this topic, by writers such as F. A. Forel and W. D. Halliburton, as well as a fascination with this question in regard to the problem of hermaphroditism as a sign of bisexuality.[25] With the rise of modern sexology at the close of the nineteenth century, especially in the writings of Magnus Hirschfeld, male

---

24. See Hanns Bächtold-Stäubli, ed., *Handwörterbuch des deutschen Aberglaubens*, vol. 6 (Berlin and Leipzig, 1934–35), "Nase," pp. 970–79.

25. See, for example, F. A. Forel, "Cas de menstruation chez un homme," *Bulletin de la Société médicale de la Suisse romande* (Lausanne) (1869): 53–61, and W. D. Halliburton, "A Peculiar Case," *Weekly Medical Review and Journal of Obstetrics* (St. Louis) (1885): 392.

menstruation came to hold a very special place in the "proofs" for the continuum between male and female sexuality.[26] The hermaphrodite, the male who menstruated, became one of the central focuses of Hirschfeld's work. But all of this new "science" which used the existence of male menstruation still drew on the image of the marginality of those males who menstruated and thus pointed toward a much more ancient tradition.

The idea of male menstruation is part of a Christian tradition of seeing the Jew as inherently, biologically different. Thomas de Cantimpré, the thirteenth-century anatomist, presented the first "scientific" statement of this phenomenon (calling upon St. Augustine as his authority).[27] Male Jews menstruated as a mark of the "Father's curse," their pathological difference. This image of the Jewish male as female was introduced to link the Jew with the corrupt nature of the woman (both marked as different by the same sign) and to stress the intransigence of the Jews. Thomas de Cantimpré recounts the nature of the Jews' attempt to cure themselves. They are told by one of their prophets that they would be rid of this curse by *Christiano sanguine*, the blood of a Christian, when in fact it was *Christi sanguine*, the blood of Christ in the sacrament, which was required. Thus the libel of the blood guilt, the charge that Jews sacrifice Christian children to obtain their blood, is the result of the intransigence of the Jews in their rejection of the truth of Christianity and is intimately tied to the sign of Jewish male menstruation. The persistence of Jewish male menstruation among Jewish males is thus not only a sign of the initial "curse of the Father" but of the inherent inability of the Jews to hear the truth of the Son. For it is the intrinsic "deafness" of the Jews which does not let them hear the truth which will cure them. The belief in Jewish male menstruation continued through the seventeenth century. Heinrich Kornmann repeated it in Germany in 1614 as did Thomas Calvert in England in 1649.[28]

Franco da Piacenza, a Jewish convert to Christianity, repeated this view in his catalogue of "Jewish maladies," published in 1630 and translated into German by 1634.[29] He claimed that the males (as well as the females) of the tribe of Simeon menstruated four days a year! These charges continued throughout the age of Enlightenment in slightly altered form. In F. L. de la Fontaine's survey of the health of the Polish Jews, published

26. See Magnus Hirschfeld, *Sexualpathologie*, 2 vols. (Bonn, 1917–18), 2:1–92.

27. See Thomas de Cantimpré, *Miraculorum et exemplorum memorabilium sui temporis libro duo* (Duaci, 1605), pp. 305–6.

28. See Heinrich Kornmann, *Opera curiosa I: Miracula vivorum* (1614; Frankfurt, 1694), pp. 128–29; Thomas Calvert, *The Blessed Jew of Marocco; or, A Blackmoor Made White Being a Demonstration of the True Messias out of the Law and Prophets by Rabbi Samuel* (York, 1649), pp. 20–21.

29. On Franco da Piacenza, see Leon Poliakov, *The History of Anti-Semitism*, 3 vols., vol. 1 trans. Richard Howard (New York, 1965–75), 1:143n.

in 1792, their sexual pathology is stressed.[30] Jews show their inherent difference through their damaged sexuality, and the sign of that is, in the popular mind, the fact that their males menstruate. Freud's contemporary, the arch-racist Theodor Fritsch—whose *Antisemite's Catechism,* published in 1887, was the encyclopedia of German anti-Semitism—saw the sexuality of the Jew as inherently different from that of the German: "The Jew has a different sexuality than the Teuton; he will and cannot understand it. And if he attempts to understand it, then the destruction of the German soul can result."[31] The hidden sign, the link between the homosexual, the woman, and the Jew is the menstruation of the Jewish male.[32]

Freud and Fliess attempt to move this sign from being a sign of difference to one of universality. Just as Franco da Piacenza tried to remove himself from the "curse of Eve" by claiming that only ancient Jews (and those of one of the "Lost Ten Tribes" at that) menstruated— not of course himself and his contemporaries—so, too, do Freud and Fliess distance this charge from the Jews by making it universal. Thus the public sign of Jewish identity (from the standpoint of the anti-Semitic society in which they live) is the nose that "menstruates." But its significance for Freud and Fliess, who are desperately trying to escape classification as "Jews" in the racial sense and therefore as inferior and different, is as a universal sign, a sign of the universal law of male periodicity which links all human beings, males and females.

The implicit charge of pathological bisexuality had traditionally been lodged against the Jews. (Jews are like women, among other ways, because they both menstruate as a sign of their pathological difference.) Freud and Fliess turn this into a universal sign of human nature in a successful form of resistance to the racist substructure of European medicine. Fliess is not simply a quack; his "quackery" is accepted by Freud since it provides an alternative to the pathological image of the Jew in conventional medicine.

30. See F. L. de la Fontaine, *Chirurgisch-Medicinische Abhandlungen verschiedenen Inhalts Polen betreffend* (Breslau, 1792). See also J. A. Elie de la Poterie, *Questio medica. An viris lex eadem quä mulieribus, periodicas evacuationes pati?* (Diss., Paris, 1764).

31. Theodor Fritsch, *Handbuch der Judenfrage* (Leipzig, 1935), p. 409 (with a further discourse on psychoanalysis as a sign of Jewish degeneracy); my translation.

32. See E. P. Eckholm, *The Picture of Health: Environmental Sources of Disease* (New York, 1977). The irony is that the image of male menstruation among the Jews probably has a pathological origin. Even today in parts of Africa "male menstruation," in the form of urethral bleeding, seems to be an indicator of "sexual maturation." What actually happens is that, for reasons not completely understood, a parasite, *Schistosoma haematoboum,* which lives in the veins surrounding the bladder, becomes active during the early teenage years. One can imagine that Jews infected with schistosomiasis, giving the appearance of menstruation, would have reified the sense of difference which the Northern European, not prone to this snail-born parasite, would have sensed. On the symbolic value of this manifestation, see Herbert Ian Hogbin, *The Island of Menstruating Men; Religion in Wogeo, New Guinea* (Scranton, Pa., 1970).

The basic nature of the medical sciences during the late nineteenth century was racist. And this was true whether the speciality was a "Jewish" one, such as syphilology, or a "non-Jewish" one, such as surgery. Freud's attempt to distance the racism of medicine through his identification with Fliess' neurological theories was an attempt to use the status of science to overcome the stigma of race. Freud could not nor did he wish to abandon the status which he needed to define himself as a full member of his own community. But using the model of medicine and accepting the role of the medical practitioner, whether in psychiatry or neurology, meant that he had to deal with their racist attitudes toward the Jews.[33]

3. The Changing Concept of the Practitioner

Sigmund Freud was forced to decide between a series of poisoned alternatives: psychiatry (like dermatology/syphilology) had implicit police functions and a relatively low status; neurology, like psychiatry, was damaged by the racist implications. But, of course, psychiatry and sexology (in the guise of syphilology) were medical specialities open to Jews, as was neurology, but only with great difficulty and as long as it remained on the level of laboratory science rather than clinical practice. What takes place in the early history of psychoanalysis is that the desire of the psychoanalyst for the higher status of specific medical specialities competes with the innate understanding that medicine condemns (in labeling as pathological) those groups which it perceives as marginal. Thus medicine is initially poisoned for the Jewish physician, whose marginality is linked to racial identity and is thus labeled as part of a group at risk. Jews can be patients, but can they be doctors? But it is also poisoned for the psychoanalyst in the pre-World War I period, who took this definition of marginality as part of the new definition of the psychotherapist. This sense of marginality is rooted in this Jewish identity of the early psychoanalysts.

Freud's desire to recruit non-Jewish psychoanalysts, such as C. G. Jung and L. Andreas-Salomé, was based in his need to overcome the sense of marginality implicit in the parallel position of the Jew and the

---

33. On the implications of the attitudes of Christian Vienna toward the new "Jewish" science of psychoanalysis, see Dennis B. Klein, *Jewish Origins of the Psychoanalytic Movement* (New York, 1981). Freud's ambiguous quest for status in science was paralleled by his fascination with Christianity. Just as the society he lived in never permitted him to become a full-fledged academic, at least in his own eyes, it also tantalized him with the promise of acceptance based on conversion. As with the fascination of science, Freud remained on the outside in terms of his relationship to structures of power, such as the Church, but was clearly fascinated by them. See Paul C. Vitz, "Sigmund Freud's Attraction to Christianity: Biographical Evidence," *Psychoanalysis and Contemporary Thought* 6 (1983): 73–83.

psychoanalyst in the intellectual world of *fin-de-siècle* Viennese medicine.[34] However, the psychoanalyst, whether Jew or non-Jew, was to the medical profession as the Jew was to society at large—a frightening outsider. Thus Freud's "myths" (to use Frank Sulloway's highly suspect term) about isolation and anti-Semitism had a real basis in the perception of reality shared by nineteenth-century Jewish medical practitioners. In Freud's history of the psychoanalytic movement, there is a tendency to perceive the opposition to the equal access of Jews (and therefore psychoanalysts) in medicine as absolute. It is this sense of the monolithic nature of the medical profession (whether true in detail or not) which shaped Freud's relationship to medicine and medicine's perception of psychoanalysis.

What Freud came to understand by the 1920s was that the status given to him as a medical doctor was not sufficient to counter the hesitancy and animosity directed at him as an outsider—both as a Jew (with the increase of public anti-Semitism in Vienna and Freud's own increased visibility) and as a psychoanalyst. During World War I he began to dismiss the various conceptual categories beginning with those of anthropology which had given psychiatry its status in the nineteenth century.[35] This was not difficult, for by this period the presence of anthropology in psychiatry was viewed as slightly old-fashioned as well as decidedly "French," two categories which, in *fin-de-siècle* Vienna, with its stress on the modern and the Teutonic, were quite easily dismissed. He assigned to the anthropologist a negative role as the creator of the idea of degeneration. (In this, of course, he was right—Morel had introduced this concept into psychiatry as a means of labeling entire groups perceived as marginal. Among those groups were the Jews.)

But Freud also began to doubt whether the status that medicine had grudgingly granted to psychoanalysis was a positive factor, especially since he saw in psychiatry much of the state control which he feared elsewhere. Psychoanalysis was to be its own master. Thus in 1926, in a court case for quackery brought against Theodor Reik, one of Freud's most orthodox supporters, the question of the relationship of psychoanalysis to the status of medicine was raised for the first time within the structures of power which Freud had always associated with medicine. Reik, whose doctorate was in German and French literature, had been accused of practicing medicine without a license. Freud, and a number of his supporters in the Viennese Psychoanalytic Society, undertook Reik's defense with the argument that it was not necessary to be a medical practitioner in order to be a psychoanalyst.

34. See the discussion in Robert S. Steele, *Freud and Jung: Conflicts of Interpretation* (London, 1982).

35. See the discussion of this influence in my essay "Sexology, Psychoanalysis, and Degeneration: From a Theory of Race to a Race to Theory," in *Degeneration: The Dark Side of Progress,* ed. J. Edward Chamberlin and Sander L. Gilman (New York, 1985), pp. 72–96.

While the charges against Reik were eventually dropped, Freud used that occasion, in a memoir written in support of Reik, to examine the relationship between the expanding status of psychoanalysis and the more evident racism of medicine. He states his position quite directly: "Doctors have no historical claim to the sole position of analysis."[36] He continues by defining (or actually redefining) what a quack is by dismissing the need for state control ("possessing a state diploma to prove he is a doctor") and stressing the "knowledge and capacities necessary" to undertake treatment. The shadow of Fliess stretches over this view of the primacy of "knowledge" over certification. "Knowledge" is, however, not to be understood as the knowledge of the "science" of medicine. For it is precisely this type of "knowledge" which Freud dismisses, rejecting the "doctor" as the ideal practitioner, just as he had rejected the anthropologist:

> His [the doctor's] interest is not aroused in the mental side of vital phenomena; medicine is not concerned with the study of the higher intellectual functions, which lies in the sphere of another faculty. Only psychiatry is supposed to deal with the disturbances of mental functions; but we know in what manner and with what aims it does so. It looks for the somatic determinants of mental disorders and treats them like other causes of illness. [*LA,* p. 230]

Psychiatry is but medicine; medicine is but biological science; and (we can add) biological science is racist.

But Freud could not cavalierly abandon the status of science which he had so painstakingly acquired. He continued his argument with the (in recent years) oft-quoted passage: "In view of the intimate connection between the things that we distinguish as physical and mental, we may look forward to a day when paths of knowledge and, let us hope, of influence will be opened up, leading from organic biology and chemistry to the field of neurotic phenomena" (*LA,* p. 231). This future time also will mark the period when purified science no longer needs to label the marginal as diseased. In his microautobiography *cum* minihistory of the psychoanalytic movement which he appends as the 1927 postscript to the publication of his essay on lay analysis, Freud outlines this sense of marginality within science without giving actual voice to its racist implications:

> In my youth I felt an overpowering need to understand something of the riddles of the world in which we live and perhaps even to

36. Freud, "The Question of Lay Analysis: Conversations with an Impartial Person," *The Standard Edition of the Complete Psychological Works of Sigmund Freud,* trans. James Strachey, 24 vols. (London, 1953–74), 20:229 and see 20:177–258. All further references to this work, abbreviated *LA,* will be included in the text. On the debate in the United States see Norman S. Greenfield and Gene M. Abroms, "The Role and Status of the Non-Medical Psychotherapist in the United States," *Human Context* 5 (1973): 657–58.

contribute something to their solution. The most hopeful means of achieving this end seemed to be to enrol myself in the medical faculty; but even after that I experimented—unsuccessfully—with zoology and chemistry, till at last, under the influence of Brücke, who carried more weight with me than any one else in my whole life, I settled down to physiology, though in those days it was too narrowly restricted to histology. By that time I had already passed all my medical examinations; but I took no interest in anything to do with medicine till the teacher whom I so deeply respected warned me that in view of my impoverished material circumstances I could not possibly take up a theoretical career. Thus I passed from the histology of the nervous system to neuropathology and then, prompted by fresh influences, I began to be concerned with the neuroses. I scarcely think, however, that my lack of a genuine medical temperament has done much damage to my patients. [*LA*, pp. 253–54]

Implicit in Freud's statement is the fact that Jews could acquire the status of the academy within the laboratory sciences in Vienna, while they were much more limited in their ability to acquire academic appointments in the medical faculty. While a private practice was possible, such a private practice did not give the individual status unless it was at least tangentially connected with the university, which was, of course, merely an extension of the "royal and imperial" state of Austro-Hungary.

Freud's postscript to his critique of the medicalization of psychoanalysis concludes with an eye cast toward the American scene. He condemns the American psychoanalytic community's rejection of lay analysts (spear-headed by A. A. Brill) while acknowledging that "local conditions" may alter the reputation of the lay analyst, as was the case with Fliess in Berlin. Nevertheless, Freud maintains his newly articulated position, rejecting the medicalization of psychoanalysis. The status of psychoanalysis in Vienna by 1926 had been grounded in public as well as academic opinion.[37] Freud had been granted his academic position at the University of Vienna, and he had acquired a series of major academic disciples, among them Eugen Bleuler. Training institutes had sprung up throughout Europe—all of them created after the pattern of academic institutions. Freud saw that psychoanalysis no longer depended on the status of medicine. Indeed, the inability of the "brain mythologists" of the 1890s to localize the anatomical lesions purported to lead to most forms of mental illness had brought their work into some disrepute by the 1920s. (The more recent work by Kurt Goldstein on aphasia avoids any discussion

37. See the debate between Josef Gicklhorn and Renée Gicklhorn, *Sigmund Freuds akademische Laufbahn im Lichte der Dokumente* (Vienna, 1960), and Kurt R. Eissler, *Sigmund Freud und die Wiener Universität: Uber die Pseudo-Wissenschaftlichkeit der jüngsten Wiener Freud-Biographik* (Bern, 1966).

of mental processes other than strictly observable ones, such as the disruption of speech and movement.) Freud no longer needed the status of medicine, even though he still did not feel himself free to abandon its protection completely.

In 1933 Reik fled the Nazis from his position in the psychoanalytic institute in Berlin, first to Den Haag and then, in 1938, to New York. In that year, the question of lay analysis was again raised before the American Psychoanalytic Society's "council on professional training." A "majority resolution" was proposed "against the future training of laymen for the therapeutic use of psychoanalysis" which definitively banned the training of lay analysts except for "non-therapeutic purposes" such as "research and investigation in such nonmedical fields as anthropology, sociology, criminology, psychology, and education, etc."[38] (This excluded, among others, Reik from ever becoming a full-fledged member of the American Psychoanalytic Association.)

From that moment, what had been a general policy became a specific rule which exists today. But this was not sufficient. In February 1939 Sandor Rado proposed to the same committee a "numerus clausus" on the admission of analytic candidates to the American Psychoanalytic Association. The extraordinary move of limiting the number of qualified medical practitioners admitted to candidacy, following the exclusion of the nonmedical practitioners, bears examination. It documents the high status of the "new" science of psychoanalysis in the medical profession. For the three fellowships at the Boston institute in 1938, there were seventy-five inquiries and twenty-five actual applications from qualified applicants. But who were the individuals whom Rado wished to exclude—and why?

The minutes of the 26 February 1939 meeting, chaired by Franz Alexander, the director of the Chicago training institute, summarized Rado's proposal: "Advisability of a date as a limitation of registration for students in each institute each year. For frank attention to the problem of social and financial deterioration of any professional medical group. Necessitates a limitation of students on social, intellectual and economic grounds." Bertram Lewin saw this as a problem specifically in the New York Psychoanalytic Institute: "They [the students in New York] work under exceptional economic pressure. They are primarily interested in earning a living and not in academic or scientific work. They hold meetings like county medical politicians."[39] This is an extraordinary statement given the influx of Jewish, Viennese-trained psychotherapists in the United States. Lewin stresses the image of the psychoanalyst as scientist, but as

38. All of the material cited is from the archives of the American Psychoanalytic Society, now housed in the the Archives of Psychiatry, Cornell Medical College. See also Hendrik M. Ruitenbeek, *Freud and America* (New York, 1966).
39. Ibid.

a scientist in a mode both attractive to as well as clearly rejected by Freud. For inherent in this image, as stated by Freud in his postscript, is the image of the scientist as a well-to-do individual undertaking science as an extension of an haute-bourgeois identity. The image of the analyst as money-grubbing practitioner is thus contrasted with that of the pure scientist, pure in a number of senses of the word—pure as unsullied by filthy lucre, pure in devotion to an abstract science.

But Lewin picked up the thread of racism present in Freud's rejection of science. It was Theodor Billroth, one of Freud's teachers, who put the case against the admission of Jews to the Viennese medical faculty most directly (and most publicly), in his survey of medical education in the German-speaking countries:

> Young men, mostly Jews, come to Vienna from Galicia and Hun-gary, who have absolutely nothing, and who have conceived the insane idea that they can earn money in Vienna by teaching, through small jobs at the stock exchange, by peddling matches, or by taking employment as post office or telegraph clerks in Vienna or elsewhere, and at the same time study medicine. These people, who present to anyone not acquainted with Viennese conditions a most puzzling problem, who are not seldom inherently queer, but whose numbers are fortunately diminishing year by year, could hardly exist anywhere else. . . . So this outcast [the Jewish student] in the Viennese world must first of all look for pupils, but he finds that the lesson hours conflict with the lectures. Still, he must live before he can study; the private lessons that he is to give cannot be postponed; he must accept them, and therefore cannot attend his classes.[40]

The image of the student as Jew and its extension, the urban psychoanalytic candidate as Jew, is thus part of the idea of the Jew as incapable of *Bildung,* the type of culture represented by the abstraction of science in nineteenth- and early twentieth-century Vienna. For Lewin, it was the Eastern Jew who filled the conceptual category of the "money-grubbing Jew" in European anti-Semitic rhetoric. In a rejection of this image, status is associated with the pure idea of science, an idea that in many ways, as we have shown, for the Jews involved is corrupted by racism.

During the succeeding decades psychoanalysis is transferred from the anti-Semitism of European science to the United States, where the racism of science had another, more accessible object, the black. The status of the Jewish psychoanalyst was tied to the status of European science, and Freud's attempt to loosen these bonds ran counter to the needs of the exiled or emigrant psychoanalysts to call upon the status of

---

40. Theodor Billroth, *The Medical Sciences in the German Universities: A Study in the History of Civilization,* trans. William H. Welch (New York, 1924), pp. 106, 108.

European science to establish themselves within the closed world of American medicine. The specter of racism which had haunted psychoanalysis because of its questionable reliance on the status of Viennese medicine undermined the status of the psychoanalyst. In terms of the perspective of the European, especially the German and Austrian of the 1930s and 1940s, the psychoanalyst no longer had the status of medical practitioner; rather, the very term *psychoanalyst* became a sign of quackery.

In the United States the case was quite different. Jewish medical practitioners, once they were certified to practice in the United States, entered into a world where medicine not only had high status, but where continental medicine had even higher status. And one of the medical specialities most representative of continental medicine was psychoanalysis. The psychoanalyst was free, at least momentarily, from the blemish of race, but of course, as we have seen, that blemish remained within their sense of themselves and their profession. The high status of medicine in the United States was still tied to the biological definition of medicine and an acceptance of the medical model in defining medical practice. Psychoanalysis furthered this attitude in part during the 1940s and 1950s with its enthusiasm for "general medicine" in the form of psychosomatics. As Robert Michels cogently observed: "In fact, for a time, one of the appeals of psychoanalysis to psychiatry was that it seemed to offer a chance for psychiatry to join the mainstream of medicine. Surprising though this may seem today [1981], psychoanalytic ideas concerning psychosomatic illness marked the first legitimatization of the return of the alienist-psychiatrist to the general hospital and the medical community—in many ways playing the same sociological role in the 1940s that neurobiology and psychopharmacology played in the seventies."[41] With the introduction of psychotropic drugs in the 1960s, the centuries-old division between the definition of psychiatry as the treatment of the brain versus its definition as the treatment of the mind reappeared, and at that point the question of the status of psychoanalysis became ever more tenuous.

Even with the perceived decline in the status of psychoanalysis in the 1970s and 1980s, the debate about who was to be given the title of psychoanalyst continued. The American Psychoanalytic Society put a series of committees in place—on professional standards, on the feasibility and desirability of the training of lay analysts. And this debate marked another turning point in the relationship between the now firmly entrenched biological psychiatrist and the ever more isolated psychoanalyst. The status of "medicine" during the 1970s and 1980s had become the status of the biological model of medicine. One marker of this sense of dissolution and separation was Michels' address, referred to above, to

41. Robert Michels, "Psychoanalysis and Psychiatry—The End of the Affair," *Academy Forum* 25 (1981): 7–8.

the fiftieth anniversary celebration of the Washington Psychoanalytic Institute in December 1980. Michels, the Chair of the Department of Psychiatry at the Cornell Medical College, spoke on "Psychoanalysis and Psychiatry—the End of the Affair" and saw the pressure for lay analysts as the potential watershed that marked the dissolution of the relationship between psychiatry and psychoanalysis. Contemporary psychoanalysis (represented by Klein, Schafer, Ricoeur, and Lacan) has consciously moved away from the older, "biologically rooted" psychoanalytic model toward "the study of language, symbols, and meaning." Michels thus sees the movement away from psychiatry as a parallel movement toward the humanities and the social sciences, replacing the older model of the *Naturwissenschaften* with the antithetical model of the *Geisteswissenschaften*. It is understood as a movement from science to its antithesis. And this movement takes place even though "psychoanalysis continues to be the dominant paradigm organizing the way that psychiatrists think about patients and treatment." Michels sees this "end of the affair" as moving both fields "to a more open, less monogamous, but more honest, relationship, and I believe a far more promising future as a result."[42] The separation of practice from theory has become absolute. Freud saw the need to distance himself from the corruption inherent in the medical model, with its image of domination (and the racist implications of the model of control). But the risk which he took was to distance himself, at least tenuously, from the status of medicine. The debates that this position caused centered around the newly undermined position of psychotherapy and the need, at least within American medicine (Freud's bête noire), to undermine it. To address the question of who is or is not to be considered a psychoanalyst would be to write a history of modern American psychoanalysis. Innumerable committees set up by the American Psychoanalytic Association as well as study groups set up by the various institutes of psychoanalysis chronicled the growing sense of defensiveness brought about by the redefinition of the status of psychoanalysis in the age of the re-Kraepelinization of American psychiatry, the age of DSM-III.

The objections which grew out of the altered sense of status present before World War II have not been accepted by the profession, but with quite different motivations. As late as 1985 the debate about who a psychotherapist is rages within the psychiatric and psychoanalytic communities. But the imperatives of status are now quite different. For within the psychoanalytic institutes the lack of M.D.s to train reveals the diminished attraction of psychoanalysis for the medical practitioner. The institutes are now turning to other areas, such as social work, for their potential students. But the opposition is loud and shrill. A letter written to the *New York Times* on 19 May 1985 by Seymour C. Post, Associate Clinical

---

42. Ibid., pp. 8–10.

Professor of Psychiatry at Columbia's College of Physicians and Surgeons, bemoans the coming age of the "barefoot psychotherapist." He objects to the introduction of "lay psychotherapy" into psychiatry, which "threatens to denude the country of its only wholly qualified line of defense against mental and emotional illness: the physician trained both in biological and psychodynamic psychiatry." For Post, the villains are clear—the professionals, but especially the psychoanalysts: "And Freud was the first psychiatrist, but not the last, to train a member of his family (his daughter, Anna) to do psychotherapy or psychoanalysis. Conflict of interest makes it difficult to speak frankly. Absence of criticism has emboldened lay therapists."[43]

We have now come full circle—medicine, represented by clinical psychiatry, first accepted psychoanalysis to purge itself of the last vestiges of the stigma of political control and thus moved it back into the general hospital. Rejected by Freud because of its inherent racism, of its need to marginalize the mentally ill, medicine continued to draw on the status of the new science of psychoanalysis, to the degree that psychoanalytically oriented psychotherapy became the norm even for those practitioners who rejected psychoanalysis. With the introduction of psychotropic drugs in the 1960s, medicine began to loosen itself from the theory of psychoanalysis, while maintaining the model of treatment. Psychoanalysis wished to rid itself of medicine and its pretensions. But psychoanalysis (like osteopathy), now firmly established within the status of Western medicine, worked to preserve its sense of centrality by retaining a pre-Freudian definition of the appropriate (or competent) psychotherapist. Thus the question of whether Freud's theories are scientific may well rest on a definition of *science* quite different from that debated on by the philosophers of science—it may well rest on the sociology of status (and its relationship to definitions of centrality and marginality) within the greater culture.

43. *New York Times,* 19 May 1985, p. 20E.

Reading the Mother Tongue:
Psychoanalytic Feminist Criticism

Jane Gallop

In the early seventies, American feminist literary criticism had little patience for psychoanalytic interpretation, dismissing it along with other forms of what Mary Ellmann called "phallic criticism."[1] Not that psychoanalytic literary criticism was a specific target of feminist critics, but Freud and his science were viewed by feminism in general as prime perpetrators of patriarchy. If we take Kate Millett's *Sexual Politics*[2] as the first book of modern feminist criticism, let us remark that she devotes ample space and energy to attacking Freud, not of course as the forerunner of any school of literary criticism, but as a master discourse of our, which is to say masculinist, culture. But, although Freud may generally have been a target for feminism, feminist literary critics of the early seventies expended more of their energy in the attack on New Criticism. The era was, after all, hardly a heyday for American psychoanalytic criticism; formalist modes of reading enjoyed a hegemony in the literary academy in contrast with which psychoanalytic interpretation was a rather weak arm of patriarchy.

Since then, there have been two changes in this picture. In the last decade, psychoanalytic criticism has grown in prestige and influence, and a phenomenon we can call psychoanalytic feminist criticism has arisen.[3]

1. See Mary Ellmann, *Thinking About Women* (New York, 1968), pp. 27–54.
2. See Kate Millett, *Sexual Politics* (Garden City, N.Y., 1970).
3. This paper was originally written to be read at a 1985 MLA Convention Forum entitled "Psychoanalytic Criticism: Its Place and Potential." The forum was sponsored by the Division for Psychological Approaches to Literature and included four ancillary workshops exploring the meaning, impact, and future of this recent growth in psychoanalytic criti-

I would venture that two major factors have contributed to this boom in American psychoanalytic criticism. First, the rise of feminist criticism, in its revolt against formalism, has rehabilitated thematic and psychological criticism, the traditional mainstays of psychoanalytic interpretation. Because feminism has assured the link between psychosexuality and the socio-historical realm, psychoanalysis is now linked to major political and cultural questions. Glistening on the horizon of sociopolitical connection, feminism promises to save psychoanalysis from its ahistorical and apolitical doldrums.

The second factor that makes psychoanalytic reading a growth industry in the United States is certainly more widely recognized: it is the impact of French post-structuralist thought on the American literary academy. There is, of course, the direct influence of Lacanian psychoanalysis which promotes language to a principal role in the psychoanalytic drama and so naturally offers fertile ground for crossing psychoanalytic and literary concerns. Yet I think, in fact, the wider effect in this country has come from Derridean deconstruction. Although deconstruction is not strictly psychoanalytic, Freud's prominent place in Derridean associative networks promises a criticism that is, finally, respectably textual and still, in some recognizable way, Freudian. Although this second, foreign factor in the growth of American psychoanalytic criticism seems far away from the realm of homespun feminist criticism, I would contend that there is a powerful if indirect connection between the two. I would speculate that the phenomenal spread of deconstruction in American departments of English is in actuality a response to the growth of feminist criticism. At a moment when it was no longer possible to ignore feminist criticism's challenge to the critical establishment, deconstruction appeared offering a perspective that was not in opposition to but rather beyond feminism, offering to sublate feminism into something supposedly "more radical."

Thus, feminist criticism has, both directly and indirectly, given new viability to psychoanalytic criticism. Central to this viability has been the

cism. I would like to thank Claire Kahane and David Willbern for their invitation which led me to write the present paper. The central panel, chaired by Willbern, included Peter Brooks, Murray Schwartz, Cary Nelson, and myself. The workshop on psychoanalysis and feminism, chaired by Kahane, included Marianne Hirsch, Judith Kegan Gardiner, and Jerry Aline Flieger and provided excellent examples of psychoanalytic feminist criticism. I would particularly draw attention to Hirsch's paper—"Why Didn't I Recognize My Mother (or, Why Didn't My Mother Recognize Me?): Psychoanalytic Theories and Maternal Silence"—where the focus and concerns intersect with those of the present paper.

Jane Gallop, professor of humanities at Rice University, is the author of *Intersections: A Reading of Sade with Bataille, Blanchot, and Klossowski* (1981), *The Daughter's Seduction: Feminism and Psychoanalysis* (1982), and *Reading Lacan* (1985). She wrote the present essay while awaiting the birth of her first child.

burgeoning new field of psychoanalytic feminist criticism. Again, I see two major factors accounting for this growth. One is actually another effect of French post-structuralism—likewise stemming from Lacan and Derrida but, significantly, passing through those women thinkers we Americans have come to call the "French feminists."[4] Through writers like Luce Irigaray, Hélène Cixous, and Julia Kristeva, we have seen a way of thinking that appears to be at once feminist and psychoanalytic, and also highly literary. The second factor has been the enormous impact made by Nancy Chodorow's study of mothering.[5] Chodorow has taken an object-relations view centered on the pre-Oedipal relation to the early mother and set in a feminist framework cognizant of the sociohistorical determinants of the institution of mothering. This particular mix of mother-centered psychoanalysis and American social scientific feminism has proven especially suggestive for feminist literary critics.

Psychoanalytic feminist criticism thus provides the vehicle which allows two heretofore unlikely couples to meet. In this vehicle, we not only find feminism joining hands with psychoanalysis but, behind that more obvious couple in what constitutes a theoretical double date, we might possibly glimpse the coming together of post-structuralism and American feminist social science, a pair that has rarely been known to speak.

A historic year for American psychoanalytic criticism, 1985 saw the appearance of a major monument in the field: the first anthology of psychoanalytic feminist criticism, *The (M)other Tongue*, edited by Shirley Nelson Garner, Claire Kahane, and Madelon Sprengnether.[6] The coupling of psychoanalysis and feminism is clearly conducive to good reading, writing, and thinking. The anthology is excellent: a collection of first-rate pieces of feminist interpretation. As an attempt to survey this field, I would like to do a reading of this monument, at the very least of the inscription on its face.

The heroine in this book is surely the mother. The story progresses from "father-based" Oedipal structures to "mother-based" pre-Oedipal models and finally to an insistence that even in pre-Oedipal theories we attend not only to the child but to the mother.[7] At the beginning of the

4. For an introduction to the French feminists, see *New French Feminisms: An Anthology*, ed. Elaine Marks and Isabelle de Courtivron (Amherst, Mass., 1980).

5. See Nancy Chodorow, *The Reproduction of Mothering: Psychoanalysis and the Sociology of Gender* (Berkeley and Los Angeles, 1978); all further references to this work, abbreviated *RM*, will be included in the text.

6. See *The (M)other Tongue: Essays in Feminist Psychoanalytic Interpretation*, ed. Shirley Nelson Garner, Claire Kahane, and Madelon Sprengnether (Ithaca, N.Y., 1985); all further references to this work will be included in the text.

7. The phrases "father-based" and "mother-based" come from the preface to *The (M)other Tongue*, pp. 9–10.

book, in a critical survey of Freud's Oedipal scripts for girls, the mother is silent, ignored, invisible; by the end, in Susan Suleiman's strong statement, the mother is coming into her own, coming to writing. Our heroine would seem to be the ideal figure to bless the marriage of psychoanalysis and feminism. A powerful figure in familiosexual configurations of subjectivity, the mother is, of course, also a woman.

When I read this paper aloud, I said that the title of the anthology was "The Mother Tongue," but that in fact was *telling* not *reading* the title, for the title is, above all, a piece of writing not easily transcribed into oral language. Since the second word is actually written "(M)other," the title is both "The Mother Tongue" and "The Other Tongue," or perhaps not quite both but neither. Not quite the mother tongue nor quite the other tongue. The title itself is no longer quite in *our* mother tongue (plain English), although it is not in any other. It brings out the other in the mother.

The play on mother and other reminds us that in psychoanalytic theory the mother is the subject's first other, the other in opposition to which the self constitutes itself. Or rather, as becomes clear in object-relations theory and particularly in Chodorow, the mother is the site of something which is both other and not quite other, of the other as self and the self as other.[8] Thus the monstrous word—"Mother-other"—in its fluid, double identity could be said to body forth the borderline status of the powerful, early mother, so central to psychoanalytic feminist theory.

Yet the title of the book is not "The (M)other" but "The (M)other Tongue." The book would appear to be not just about Mother but about language. The title phrase is nowhere glossed, or even used in the book, at least not with the *M* in parentheses. But we do find the simpler phrase, "The Mother Tongue" (without parentheses). In fact, the editors' introduction concludes on that more familiar phrase: "Feminists working from a number of critical approaches are concluding that it is time to learn, to begin to speak our mother tongue" (p. 29).

Although not marked or marred in any way by unseemly, unpronounceable punctuation, the phrase "mother tongue" in this sentence clearly does not mean what it usually means in *our* mother tongue, in the idiomatic English we know so well. If it is only now time "to learn, to *begin* to speak" this language, then this is not what we usually refer to as our native language. It may look familiar on the page, but this is not the same old mother tongue, but precisely an other mother tongue.

However "other" we can imagine his tongue to be, in this unmarked version it still looks like the idiomatic phrase. No mark forces the reader to see the otherness in this "mother tongue." This lack of marking may be part of a larger tendency, in this concluding sentence, to cover over an alterity that is, elsewhere, carefully noted. In this last sentence of the

---

8. I owe the phrases "other as self" and "self as other" to a related use by Naomi Schor, "*Eugénie Grandet:* Mirrors and Melancholia," in *The (M)other Tongue*, p. 218 n. 2.

introduction, "feminists working from a number of critical approaches are" jointly, in a plural, inclusive verb, "concluding." In the "mother tongue," we are not divided. Yet the triumphant conclusion forgets a difference articulated earlier in the introduction between two "critical approaches," between the Chodorovians and the post-structuralists.

In the vicinity of the "mother" there is perhaps a tendency to cover over difference. Something about the figure of the mother seems to bless marriage and frown upon separation. From object-relations theory we learn that, for the infant, differentiation *is* differentiation *from the mother.* Imagining that the mother demands symbiosis, the infant experiences the drive toward separation as a guilty betrayal of the mother. Guilty to see the mother as other, to see the other in the mother; guilty thus to differentiate within the oceanic symbiosis. According to Chodorow, this atmosphere particularly characterizes the daughter's relation to the mother, long past infancy, and finally carries over into adult relations between women. This special feminine lack of rigid separation has been celebrated by feminists, but let us not forget the corollary uneasiness that attends the drive toward differentiation, never wholly absent from this complex. I would speculate that the tendency within feminist criticism to glorify the figure of the mother might often occur along with a concomitant pressure to cover over differences between feminists.[9] "Feminists working from a number of critical approaches are concluding that it is time . . . to speak our mother tongue." In "the mother" we are not divided.

The conclusion of the editors' introduction quoted above, with its lack of marked alterity, might be read as a happy ending. Given generic conventions, comedy concludes with the resolution of previous differences in a festive joining of all parties. But earlier in the narrative when the pressure of triumphant conclusion does not yet weigh so heavily, the differences between critical approaches can be delineated. In rehearsing the history of psychoanalytic feminism, the introduction finds that the French feminists have, like their American sisters, "turned to the preoedipal relation." The editors then carefully add: "Although this shift to the mother has brought some degree of rapprochement between this line of French feminist concern and Anglo-American theory, the French detour though Lacan results in a difference. The insertion of the question of langauge introduces the notion of a form of expressivity outside the dominant discourse" (pp. 22–23).

"The mother" brings us some rapprochement, a lessening of difference; but "the question of language," "the mother *tongue*" comprises difference. The question of the mother tongue inserts itself in the very reading of this passage. The word "rapprochement" can be found in an

9. For a similar discussion of the relation of pre-Oedipal psychology to feminism, see Jane Flax, "The Conflict between Nurturance and Autonomy in Mother-Daughter Relationships and within Feminism," *Feminist Studies* 4 (June 1978): 171–91.

English dictionary, yet it is still pronounced in such a manner as not to let us forget that it is a French import. Not quite the mother nor quite the other tongue, it brings out the other in the mother. The French and English versions of the word remain close, so that "rapprochement" itself may be said to function as a point of rapprochement between the two languages. The appearance of this word in the text wishfully enacts a closing of the difference between the French and the Anglo-Americans.[10] The book itself represents a wish to close up that gap, to be able to speak the mother tongue and the other tongue simultaneously, hence the title. But however ardent that wish, it is also true that the relation between the mother tongue and the other tongue involves us with real material difference so that the book's title cannot simply be pronounced.

Chodorow is everywhere in this book, appearing in three-quarters of the essays and providing its theoretical framework and coherence. But Chodorow's theory, however useful for feminism and psychoanalysis, remains, as the editors point out (p. 20), solidly within the traditional American paradigm for social science and has nothing to say about "the question of language," a question that remains crucial for literary critics, for us feminists reading texts.

Yet this book also partakes of the "difference" of the "French detour":[11] "the insertion of the question of language [which] introduces the notion of a form of expressivity outside the dominant discourse." The title of the book is an attempt to write beyond dominant discourse. The play of its parenthesis, using the material of the language to reflect on the language, resembles the stylistic devices of post-structuralist writers such as Derrida and Irigaray as well as American feminists such as Mary Daly. The feminists and the post-structuralists are trying to find a mode of expressivity which is not already shackled by the ideological weight of standard language, the dominant discourse. Standard language might be called the mother tongue, so the attempt to write outside the dominant discourse could be construed as a try for the other rather than the mother tongue. But as the title of our anthology makes us see, "the other" is already inscribed *in* "the mother tongue." These feminist and post-structuralist attempts at new expressivity do not really go outside the dominant discourse but

---

10. In this context let us remark the phrase "Anglo-American." It is not at all obvious that English and American feminists share a theory. For example, British psychoanalytic feminists tend to be Lacanian. Of course one could say that object-relations theory is an English movement. But then Chodorow has not been very influential in Britain. Perhaps the phrase stems rather from the fact that the English and Americans more or less share a "mother tongue." The contrast between the French and the Anglo-Americans is thus a difference between two language groups.

11. For a similar appearance of the concept of the "French detour," see Jane Gallop, *The Daughter's Seduction: Feminism and Psychoanalysis* (Ithaca, N.Y., 1982), pp. 139–40. In her essay "Enforcing Oedipus: Freud and Dora" in *The (M)other Tongue*, Sprengnether makes reference to this passage from *The Daughter's Seduction* (p. 61 n. 15).

rather bring out what deconstructionists such as Barbara Johnson have called "the difference within."[12] We are not looking for a new language, a radical outside, but for "the other within," the alterity that has always lain silent, unmarked and invisible within the mother tongue.

Another name—a more specifically feminist name—for dominant discourse is "patriarchal discourse," and that phrase appears at the beginning of the book's preface where the editors write: "Oedipally organized narrative . . . that is based on the determining role of the father and of patriarchal discourse tells a different story from preoedipal narrative, which locates the source of movement and conflict in the figure of the mother" (p. 10).

The Oedipal is associated with the father; the pre-Oedipal with the mother. Psychoanalytic feminists valorize the pre-Oedipal because the mother is a woman and she is suppressed in Oedipally organized narrative. But there is a fifth term that intrudes upon the two couples. Whereas the pre-Oedipal finds its source uniquely in "the figure of the mother," the Oedipal is based not just on the father but also on "patriarchal discourse." The use of that phrase here bespeaks "the French detour through Lacan" where the Oedipal father, the third term that intrudes upon the dyad, is the symbolic father, representing the order of language and law. As the editors will later say, "the French detour through Lacan results in a difference." From the very beginning of the book, "the insertion of the question of language introduces" a disruption into psychoanalytic feminism's tendency to polarize into mother vs. father, pre-Oedipal vs. Oedipal. Words like "narrative" and "story" in the sentence from the preface remind us that we are still very much in the realm of literary criticism. And no "story," however primal, however familial, psychoanalytic, or basic to our culture can forgo the question of discourse. If, like the Oedipal, the pre-Oedipal is "narrative," then it must be transmitted in some sort of discourse. Patriarchal discourse determines Oedipal narrative, but what sort of language would be associated with the pre-Oedipal?

One answer provided in this book is what Naomi Schor calls "the myth of a sort of prelapsarian preoedipus": the pre-Oedipal is an Edenic world of immediacy before the advent of language (p. 223).[13] Such an answer retains the purity of the polar opposition between the golden pre-Oedipal and the fallen Oedipal, but in that case—rather than the new fertile topos for literary criticism announced by the book—the pre-Oedipal would be beyond narrative, beyond the reach of the literary critic.

12. See, for example, Barbara Johnson, *The Critical Difference: Essays in the Contemporary Rhetoric of Reading* (Baltimore, 1981), p. 4.
13. For examples in *The (M)other Tongue* of this myth at work, see Dianne Hunter, "Hysteria, Psychoanalysis, and Feminism: The Case of Anna O.," pp. 98–99, and Jim Swan, "Difference and Silence: John Milton and the Question of Gender," p. 168.

Another answer, certainly the most prominent in the anthology, is of course "the mother tongue" itself, which sounds like it would be the language spoken by the figure who dominates the pre-Oedipal. In the introduction, the editors write: "At this juncture ... the tendency of Anglo-American psychoanalytic feminism to focus on the drama of the preoedipal relationship between mother and daughter intersects with French feminist dreams of another mode of discourse, another side of language whose authority is the mother" (p. 24). A mode of language where mother not father is authority—matriarchal discourse—is not an object of focus but a dream, that is to say, in psychoanalytic terms, the fulfillment of a wish. *Another* mode, *another* side: the mother tongue as other tongue, a dream devoutly to be wished.

Anglo-Americans focus; French dream. On one side, "the drama of the preoedipal relationship"; across, "another mode of discourse." The only term repeated on both sides: "mother." Hitching the "expressivity outside the dominant discourse" to the mother seems to promise a lessening of difference, a rapprochement on various fronts. This "juncture," this "intersection": paths that seemed to run parallel on either side of a gap are crossing. In "mother," we are not divided.

If "French feminist dreams" come down to the mother tongue, then perhaps we can ignore the differences between "focus" and "dream," "drama" and "language." For those terms represent other differences between Anglo-American and French "critical approaches." To focus (telescope or microscope) is the classic mode of empiricist scientific investigation. The drama of the pre-Oedipal is treated as a classic object of positivist study. That it is then, figuratively, a "drama" renders the pre-Oedipal relationship (figuratively) literary and preps it for use in analogical operations on literary works.

On the other side, to dream is to become, oneself, the classic object of psychoanalytic study, the dreamer's psyche. If Freud invented psychoanalysis through interpreting his own dreams, then psychoanalysis may be the locus of an uncanny self-knowledge where subject and object are neither identical nor different, where the subject and object of knowledge are aspects of "the same person" separated by the opaque materiality of the dream. Such study no longer partakes of the positivist objectivity of the focusing lens, but rather inevitably implicates the subject's desires and defenses in the investigation.[14]

In *The Interpretation of Dreams,* Freud provides us with a method of interpretation that involves attention to marginal specificity, to details we overlook when we reduce a story to its central drama. That aspect of Freud's work has influenced a different sort of literary criticism, one indebted to psychoanalysis for its interpretive methods rather than its

14. For exemplary instances of critical self-implication in *The (M)other Tongue,* see Schor, *"Eugénie Grandet,"* pp. 236–37 and Kahane, "The Gothic Mirror," p. 340.

dramatic analogies. This sort of dream-reading is more typical of psychoanalytic criticism deriving from French post-structuralism.

Focus on narrative structure ("drama" and "relationship") in the anthology has led us to the "figure of the mother," central to the book. But this other sort of psychoanalytic reading might be applied to our dream of the mother tongue. For example, the word "patriarchal" is actually spelled five different ways in this book: aside from its standard spelling, we can read "partriarchial" (p. 16), "patriarchial" (p. 22), "partiarchal" (p. 105), and "partriarchal" (p. 264 n. 11). Presumably these are typographical errors, yet no other word in the book is so frequently misspelled, as if some unconscious (editors'? typist's? typesetter's?) was insistently trying to alter patriarchal discourse in one way or another, trying to speak something other than patriarchal.[15] This is not a language "whose authority is the mother," not matriarchal, but other than patriarchal. This is clearly no one's mother tongue, but it may be the other tongue, perhaps what Lacan calls the discourse of the Other, that speaks in and through the mother tongue.[16]

The mother tongue, the language we learn at our mother's breast, *is* patriarchal language. That is where we learned the language which feminism has taught us to see as full of masculinist bias. In trying to move beyond the father, the mother looks like an alternative, but if we are trying to move beyond patriarchy, the mother is not outside. As Chodorow—among others[17]—has shown us, the institution of motherhood is a cornerstone of patriarchy. Although the father may be absent from the pre-Oedipal, patriarchy constitutes the very structure of the mother-child dyad.[18] The early mother may appear to be outside patriarchy, but that very idea of the mother (and the woman) as outside of culture, society, and politics is an essential ideological component of patriarchy.

There is a drive in this book to speak outside of patriarchal discourse. But to the extent that drive fixes on "the figure of the mother" and/or glorifies the pre-Oedipal, the book risks losing its title to diacritical marks

15. In *The Psychopathology of Everyday Life,* Freud opens the possibility of treating mistakes by copyists and compositors as psychologically motivated, that is, interpretable; see Freud, *The Standard Edition of the Complete Psychological Works of Sigmund Freud,* ed. and trans. James Strachey, 24 vols. (London, 1953–74), 6:129.

16. According to Jacques Lacan, "the unconscious is the discourse of the Other." See Lacan, *Ecrits* (Paris, 1966), pp. 265, 379, 469, 549, 628, 632–34, 654, 814–15, 830, and 839.

17. See, principally, Dorothy Dinnerstein, *The Mermaid and the Minotaur: Sexual Arrangements and Human Malaise* (New York, 1976), and Adrienne Rich, *Of Woman Born: Motherhood as Experience and Institution* (New York, 1976).

18. Schor makes the same point in *The (M)other Tongue:* "What Eugénie begins to understand is that even as she enjoyed the shelter of the symbiotic mother-daughter relationship, even then she lived under the sway of the Symbolic, the order in which she was inscribed before her birth" (*"Eugénie Grandet,"* p. 227).

and settling for a mother tongue which is not recognizably an other tongue.

In their preface, the editors of the anthology write: "It is clear that fascination by the preoedipal period and a corresponding focus on the figure of the mother in theories of human development have had a profound impact on the discipline of psychoanalysis and on the feminist interpretation of literature" (p. 10). "The discipline of psychoanalysis" and "the feminist interpretation of literature" are two widely separated realms, with apparently little in common. The opposition here is not only between Freudian and feminist ways of thinking but also between a quasi-medical practice of healing and a mode of literary interpretation. And yet these widely divergent domains are simply conjoined under the aegis of the pre-Oedipal period and the figure of the mother. Perhaps, since the pre-Oedipal is the realm of fusion and indifferentiation, its "impact" might include a preference for merger over distinction.

Or rather I should say, not the impact of the pre-Oedipal, but the impact of the "fascination by the preoedipal." Coppélia Kahn, in her contribution to the anthology, speaks of the "charmed preoedipal dyad" (p. 74). From the preface, we might infer that the pre-Oedipal period is not only a magical moment for infant and early mother but exercises a charm over those who contemplate it, who study and theorize. "Fascinate": "1. To be an object of intense interest to; attract irresistibly. 2. To hold motionless; to spellbind or mesmerize. 3. *Obsolete.* To bewitch; cast under a spell. [Latin *fascināre,* to enchant, bewitch, from *fascinus,* a bewitching, amulet in the shape of a phallus.]"[19] The pre-Oedipal fascinates, attracts us irresistibly and holds us motionless, and in place of the phallic amulet, we are bewitched by the figure of the mother. The maternal having replaced the phallic, the early seventies' opposition between psychoanalysis and feminism can give way to a charmed union.

But, in fact, all charms, dreams, and wishes aside, what is the status of this marriage blessed by the mother? How mutual is the fascination?

The editors' introduction to *The (M)other Tongue* is comprised of two sections: its last four pages briefly summarize the articles to be found in the book; but the bulk of the introduction is a history of the encounters between psychoanalysis and feminism. The last paragraph of that history begins: "So far we have traced the ways in which feminism has reacted to psychoanalysis. . . . But there may be another story here, that of the response of psychoanalysis to feminism" (p. 25). For ten pages they have traced feminism's response to psychoanalysis, and now with but one paragraph left, they are just beginning to imagine the other side ("there *may be* another story"). This relationship seems far too one-sided; psychoanalytic feminism is simply the influence of psychoanalysis on feminism.

19. *The American Heritage Dictionary of the English Language,* new college ed., s.v. "fascinate."

One party has done all the talking; the other all the listening. Not a very good model for a marriage.

In the psychoanalytic context, however, we know of another relationship in which the one who does all the listening is not necessarily in the subordinate position, in which knowledge and authority in certain ways derive from the one who does all the listening. Perhaps, after all, psychoanalysis has been doing all its talking in relation to the knowledge it presumes feminism (or women) to have. That may be why feminism has been so willing to listen. But that other story, the influence of feminism on psychoanalysis, remains to be told.

That story would have to begin with what the other story has left out, what psychoanalysis for all its talking could not say. For if feminism, in its listening posture, is in the place of the analyst, then when we speak we will intervene in response to some marked gap in the story of the one who does all the talking. In the last paragraph of the historical introduction, the editors start to imagine that story: "Psychoanalysis, whether it posits in the beginning maternal presence or absence, has yet to develop a story of the mother as other than the object of the infant's desire or the matrix from which he or she develops an infant subjectivity" (p. 25). "Whether it posits in the beginning maternal presence or absence": that is, whether we are dealing with object-relations theory or Lacanian theory. Finally, even these two opposing schools of psychoanalysis are united in their common lack. In Lacanian models she is the prohibited object of desire; in object-relations she is the mirror where the infant can find his or her subjectivity. In either case her only role is to complement the infant's subjectivity; in neither story is she ever a subject. It is not mother that is lacking from psychoanalytic accounts, but precisely mother as other ("Psychoanalysis . . . has yet to develop a story of the mother as other").

In *The Reproduction of Mothering,* Chodorow begins to notice this blind spot in psychoanalysis, but she too quickly attributes it to the gender of the theorists: "male theorists . . . ignore the mother's involvements outside her relationship to her infant and her possible interest in mitigating its intensity. Instead, they contrast the infant's moves toward differentiation and separation to the mother's attempts to retain symbiosis" (*RM,* p. 87). Since the subject of both sentences is "male theorists," we might infer that now that women are theorizing they will not make the same mistake. Such a supposition about female theorists is equivalent to the assumption that the mother is outside patriarchy.

Susan Suleiman's essay in *The (M)other Tongue* begins with an account of the same syndrome in psychoanalytic theory ("It is as if, for psychoanalysis, the only self worth worrying about in the mother-child relationship were that of the child" [p. 356]). Although explicitly following Chodorow's lead, Suleiman's examples (from Helene Deutsch, Melanie Klein, Alice Balint, and Karen Horney) expose this bias not (merely) in the fathers but in the mothers of psychoanalytic theory. Toward the end of her exposé of the mother's position in psychoanalysis—entitled "The Psychoanalytic Projection"—Suleiman remarks in a footnote: "It will certainly be noticed that almost all of the analysts I have been quoting are women" (p. 356 n. 8).

Only remarking this in a footnote, Suleiman makes no serious or prolonged attempt to understand why these women might perpetrate such patriarchal bias. It might be argued that, although women, these theorists are not, strictly speaking, feminists, or at least are not in a position to benefit from the work done in the contemporary field of psychoanalytic feminism. It might also be argued that they are all practicing analysts and therefore have an investment in the discipline of psychoanalysis that a literary critic, for example, need not share. Yet I think the problem might be more pervasive, that the maternal figure may move many of us to wish for an embrace that obliterates otherness. And those of us who are attracted to psychoanalytic theory may be particularly susceptible to the mother's charming figure, the dream of the mother without otherness.

I want to cite just one example of the bias against maternal alterity in contemporary psychoanalytic feminist criticism. My example comes not from this anthology but from an article by Ronnie Scharfman published in the 1981 issue of *Yale French Studies* entitled *Feminist Readings*. That volume shares many traits with *The (M)other Tongue:* in particular, a lot of psychoanalytic feminist theory and an attempt to bring together American and French feminisms.[20] Scharfman's text is an example of a feminist literary application of object-relations theory as it has come down through Chodorow. Scharfman writes: "Winnicott . . . asks what a baby sees upon looking at the mother's face. . . . 'Ordinarily, what the baby sees is himself or herself.'" Again drawing on Winnicott, Scharfman describes an "unsuccessful mirroring bond": "When a mother reflects her own mood or the 'rigidity of her own defenses,' rather than her child's, what the baby sees is the mother's face, and the 'mother's face is not then a mirror.' The consequences are tragic."[21] Scharfman does not critique Winnicott's position but simply produces a very agile literary application of it. Tragedy here remains the consequence of seeing the mother's subjectivity, seeing the mother as other.

20. I have done a reading of this volume which explores many of the same themes as the present paper, "The Monster in the Mirror: The Feminist Critic's Psychoanalysis," which will be published in an anthology on psychoanalysis and feminism, edited by Richard Feldstein and Judith Roof.

21. Ronnie Scharfman, "Mirroring and Mothering in Simone Schwartz-Bart's *Pluie et vent sur Télumée Miracle* and Jean Rhys' *Wide Sargasso Sea*," *Yale French Studies* 62 (1981): 91, 99. Scharfman is quoting from D. W. Winnicott, "Mirror-role of Mother and Family in Child Development," *Playing and Reality* (New York, 1971), pp. 111–18.

By focusing on the women theorists, Suleiman goes beyond Chodorow to show us a problem that stems not from the theorists' gender but from a bias in psychoanalytic theory itself: "Psychoanalysis is nothing if not a theory of childhood. We should not be surprised if it locates . . . every . . . aspect of adult personality in the child the adult once was, and often continues to be" (p. 358). Psychoanalysis is "a theory of childhood," that is, not merely about childhood, but a childhood theory, theorized from the child's point of view. That is its great strength: it has given us access to what is denied by any psychology that assumes that the child simply becomes an adult, rational, civilized. But the child's particular blind spot is an inability to have any realistic notion of the mother as an other subjectivity.[22]

Chodorow, drawing on Alice Balint's work, focuses on this aspect of the relation to the mother, pointing to its continuation in adults and its determining role in ideology. In *The Reproduction of Mothering* she writes that "people continue not to recognize their mother's interests while developing capacities for 'altruistic love' in the process of growing up. They support their egoism, moreover, by idealizing mothers and by the creation of social ideology" (*RM*, p. 81). The child the adult continues to be cannot tolerate the mother's otherness. And that child is the source of psychoanalytic theory. If one of the major goals of feminism has been to put a stop to women's self-sacrifice, their exploitation through the ideology of maternal altruism, then it must counter every adult child's wish for the mother to be the perfect selfless mirror. That is where psychoanalysis and feminism may find themselves on opposite sides, one taking the child's wishes into account, the other defending the mother's side of the story.

Pointing us toward this opposition between psychoanalysis and feminism, Suleiman's essay stands out from the rest of the texts in the anthology, representing so to speak the internal alterity, the other within *The (M)other Tongue*. She goes beyond "the figure of the mother"—object for the infant's psyche—in search of the mother's subjectivity. In fact, Suleiman's text is not an example of psychoanalytic feminism but rather a feminist reading of psychoanalysis, which ultimately rejects psychoanalysis. Her essay is the last one in the anthology. Thus by the time we reach the end of the first anthology of psychoanalytic feminist criticism, we have in some way gone beyond the boundaries of the new field into a critique of its very possibility. That such an essay should be included and positioned last suggests that perhaps such a move is finally inevitable. If this collection is the first to celebrate the alliance of feminism and psychoanalysis, then

---

22. According to Chodorow, "Alice Balint argues that the essence of 'love for the mother' is that it is not under the sway of the reality principle" (*RM*, p. 79). Chodorow's source here is Alice Balint, "Love for the Mother and Mother Love," in *Primary Love and Psycho-Analtyic Technique*, ed. Michael Balint (New York, 1965), pp. 91–108.

it also bears within it a sense of the limitations of such an alliance. *The (M)other Tongue* would be very different if it did not end with Suleiman's text. Since it does, we are, in some ways, forced to rethink what has come before.

Earlier, in looking at the editors' introduction, I said that *The (M)other Tongue* seemed to follow the generic code for comedy, culminating in a procession of couples marching hand in hand (psychoanalysis with feminism, Anglo-American theory with French feminism, the discipline of psychoanalysis with the feminist interpretation of literature). But an editors' introduction is always a secondary revision (in the psychoanalytic sense of the term[23]) of the unruly material of an anthology. Ending with Suleiman's text, *The (M)other Tongue* actually concludes not with marriage but divorce.

And the accusations we hear typify the contemporary subgenre of the feminist divorce tale. Psychoanalysis does not allow mother her selfhood, makes her an object of service, and expects her to sacrifice herself to her partner's fantasies about her.[24] If "the figure of the mother" blesses the marriage of psychoanalysis and feminism, the mother as other presides over their divorce.

The anthology thus indeed leads us from the mother (fantasy figure and ideological construction) to the (m)other . . . But what of the (m)other tongue? In this book, it seems that the question of language is always tied to that other tongue, French, and to those "French feminists." As we have also seen, the other tongue, the "expressivity outside the dominant discourse," is usually construed as a mother tongue. On this question, Suleiman's essay is no exception. She discusses a less well-known French woman writer, Chantal Chawaf, who "has tied the practice of feminine writing to the biological fact of motherhood" (p. 370). Like other women of the French school, Chawaf is trying to practice *écriture féminine* (feminine writing), but more explicitly than with the other practitioners, her "expressivity outside" would be a mother tongue. ("Chawaf has stated in interviews and in commentaries on her work that for her motherhood is the only access to literary creation" [p. 370].)

Yet even here in this exemplary instance of a mother tongue, we can find the intrusion of an other tongue. Suleiman is discussing in particular a novel by Chawaf entitled *Maternité* (French cognate for "maternity"). When she quotes from the novel (p. 370), the footnote reads: "42. Chantal Chawaf, *Manternité* (Paris, 1979), 20." In the text, the title

---

23. "Secondary revision" is the "rearrangement of a dream so as to present it in the form of a relatively consistent and comprehensible scenario." This definition is taken from J. Laplanche and J.-B. Pontalis, *The Language of Psycho-analysis*, trans. Donald Nicholson-Smith (London, 1973), p. 412.

24. The phrase "object of service" is taken from the editors' introduction to *The (M)other Tongue*, p. 19.

reads correctly, *Maternité,* but there at the bottom of the page we find an alien within the mother tongue. Perhaps the monstrous word "man-ternité" includes the English word "man" in the French word, producing a composite that is in no one's mother tongue, that can only be read in two languages at once, that cannot simply be pronounced.[25] Not quite the mother tongue nor quite the other tongue; that errant *n* brings out the other in the mother.

In the classic psychoanalytic story, the "man" comes to disrupt the charmed pre-Oedipal dyad. As Janet Adelman puts it in another footnote in the anthology, this Oedipal intrusion of the man is but a late form, a repetition of an otherness already there in the early mother: "For the infant, the mother's separateness constitutes the first betrayal; insofar as she is not merely his, she is promiscuously other. I suspect that this sense of otherness itself as promiscuous betrayal antedates the more specific oedipal jealousies and is retrospectively sexualized by them" (p. 134 n. 17). Those of us under the fascination of the pre-Oedipal often see the man's entry as the fall from Eden. In a Lacanian version of that story, the man's intrusion saves us from symbiotic fusion, from the mother's engulfment. Adelman (and Chodorow and Suleiman) remind us however that both the positive and the negative valuations of the pre-Oedipal equally ignore the fact that the pre-Oedipal mother is already other.

The disruptive appearance of the word "man" within maternity may also remind us that maternity may not be simply a form of feminine writing. The masculine is inscribed in motherhood; patriarchal discourse structures the institution and the experience of motherhood as we know it. In any case, whether suppressed wish for separation or unauthorized critique, the *n* in Suleiman's footnote continues the legacy of the title's parentheses, interrupting the mother tongue by an other tongue.

Although there may be a wish to link French feminine writing with the pre-Oedipal, at the specific point in the editors' introduction where they remark that the question of language results in a difference, they make it clear that the other tongue is not pre-Oedipal. "The insertion of the question of language introduces a notion of a form of expressivity outside the dominant discourse . . . an *'écriture féminine.'* . . . Such French feminists as Cixous and Irigaray seek to formulate a female poetics that would allow mother and daughter, once locked in a symbiotic fusion and plenitude, to become women and subjects, in and through language" (p. 23). Symbiotic fusion and plenitude lock women in, pre-Oedipal fascination holds them motionless.[26] The question of language must be inserted as the wedge to break the hold of the figure of the mother. *Ecriture féminine*

25. In the month following my writing of the present essay, I find myself regularly making a certain typo: "materity" for "maternity." It is as if I felt there was an *n* that did not belong in "maternity."

26. Kahane uses the same image of being "locked into a symbiotic relation" in her essay in *The (M)other Tongue,* pp. 336, 337.

must not be arrested by the plenitude of the mother tongue, but must try to be always and also an other tongue.

The other tongue is hard to pronounce, but those of us who have learned critical interpretation from psychoanalysis and from feminism are learning how to read it. At its best, psychoanalytic feminist criticism is teaching us not how to speak the mother tongue, not *only* how to see the mother as other and not mirror, but how to read the other within the mother tongue.

Psychoanalysis and Marxism

Ernesto Laclau

Translated by Amy G. Reiter-McIntosh

To think the relationships which exist between Marxism and psychoanalysis obliges one to reflect upon the intersections between two theoretical fields, each composed independently of the other and whose possible forms of mutual reference do not merge into any obvious system of translation. For example, it is impossible to affirm—though it has often been done—that psychoanalysis *adds* a theory of subjectivity to the field of historical materialism, given that the latter has been constituted, by and large, as a negation of the validity and the pertinence of any theory of subjectivity (although certainly not of the category of "subject"). Thus, no simple model of supplement or articulation is of the slightest use. The problem is rather that of finding an *index of comparison* between two different theoretical fields, but that, in turn, implies the construction of a new field, within which the comparison would make sense.

This new field is one which may be characterized as "post-Marxist" and is the result of a multitude of theoretico-political interventions whose cumulative effect in relation to the categories of classical Marxism is similar to what Heidegger called a "de-struction of the history of ontology." For Heidegger, this "de-struction" did not signify the purely negative operation of rejecting a tradition, but exactly the opposite: it is by means of a radical questioning which is situated beyond this tradition—but which is only possible in relation to it—that the originary meaning of the categories of this tradition (which have long since become stale and trivialized) may be recovered. In this sense, effecting a "de-struction" of the history of Marxism implies going beyond the deceptive evidence of concepts such as "class," "capital," and so on, and re-creating the meaning of the originary synthesis that such concepts aspired to establish, the total system of theoretical alternatives in regard to which they represented only limited options, and the ambiguities inherent in their constitution itself—the "hymen" in the Derridean sense—which, although violently repressed, rise up here and there in diverse discursive surfaces. It is the systematic and genealogical outline of these nuclei of ambiguity which initially allows for a destruction of the history of Marxism and which constitutes post-Marxism as the field of our current political reflection. But it is precisely in these surfaces of discursive ambiguity that it is possible to detect the presence of logics of the political which allows for the establishment of a *true* dialogue, without complacent metaphorization, between Marxism and psychoanalytic theory. I would like to highlight two points, which I consider fundamental, concerning these discursive surfaces.

1) Marxism has so often been presented as a prolongation and a culmination of the Enlightenment—and therefore as one of the pinnacles of modernity—that any attempt at deconstructing its categories must begin by focusing on two decisive points where Marxism *breaks* with the tradition of the Enlightenment. These points are: (a) the affirmation of the central character of negativity—struggle and antagonism—in the structure of any collective identity; and (b) the affirmation of the opaqueness of the social—the ideological nature of collective representations—which establishes a permanent gap between the real and the manifest senses of individual and social group actions. It is easy to see how it is possible, from these two points, to establish a dialogue with psychoanalysis. The second point may be linked to the action of the unconscious and to the plurality of "systems" established in the various Freudian topographies. The first, by establishing the non-immanent and ever-threatened character of any collective identity (resulting from the negativity inherent to antagonism), allows the consideration of class struggle as a dialectic of identifications composed around a real/impossible kernel.

However, let us not proceed too quickly. This reading of Marxism, which sees within it not the pinnacle of modernity but rather one of its first crises, is only possible if one is unaware of at least—in an optimistic calculation—half of Marx's work. (The same could be said about Hegel.) Marxism is not only a discourse of negativity and the opaqueness of the

Ernesto Laclau is a lecturer in the Department of Government and director of the Graduate Program in Ideology and Discourse Analysis at the University of Essex. He is the author of *Politics and Ideology in Marxist Theory* (1977) and, with Chantal Mouffe, *Hegemony and Socialist Strategy: Towards a Radical Democratic Politics* (1985). **Amy G. Reiter-McIntosh** is a lecturer and Ph.D. candidate at the University of Chicago.

social, it is also an attempt—perfectly compatible with the Enlightenment—to limit and master them. The negativity and opaqueness of the social only exist in "human prehistory," which will be definitely surpassed by communism conceived as homogeneous and transparent society. It is from this mastery of totality that the moment of negativity loses its constitutive and foundational character: it shone for just a brief moment in theoretical discourse, only to dissolve an instant later into the full positivity which reabsorbed it—positivity of history and society as totalizations of their partial processes, the positivity of the subject—the social classes—as agents of history. It would be absurd to deny that this dimension of mastery/transparency/rationalism is present in Marxism. Even more: this is the dimension which reaffirms itself increasingly from the *Anti-Dühring* to Stalin.

2) Consequently, if we want to trace the genealogy of post-Marxism, we cannot stop at the dichotomy of positivity/negativity, opaqueness/transparency. We must also highlight the radical inconsistency of these two dimensions. It is necessary to detect the surface where rationalist logic meets its limits—in other words, to detect those nuclei of ambiguity, those hymens where the *arbitrariness* and the *contingency* of any logic of closure is shown. Now, in the discursive field of historical Marxism, we find a privileged zone of deconstructive effects which dissolve the rationality, positivity, and transparency of Marxist categories: this is the ensemble of phenomena linked to what is known as "unequal and combined development."

Let us consider the problem in its simplest terms. "Unequal and combined development" exists when a synchronic articulation occurs between stages which Marxist theory considers as successive (for example, the articulation between democratic tasks and the socialist leadership of those tasks). The key term to describe this articulation is "hegemony." In fact, the concept of hegemony as it was developed in the Marxist tradition, from Plekhanov and Axelrod to Gramsci, is that of a dislocation of a "strategy" which is irreducible to a full presence that encloses, of a self-sufficient totality, the differential ensemble of its terms. Hegemony exists when that which would have been a rational succession of stages is interrupted by a *contingency* that cannot be subsumed under the logical categories of Marxist theory: in other words, it exists when the (democratic) tasks, which in a "normal" development would have corresponded to a class (the bourgeoisie), must pass, given the weakness of the latter, to another class (in this case, the working class). A moment of reflection suffices to realize that what is explicitly thought in this relationship—the actors of the hegemonic relationship (the social classes), the class nature of the hegemonized task—is that which, strictly speaking, is absent to the extent that normal development has been dislocated; while that which is actually present—the relationship of dislocation—is *named* but not *thought*. Therefore, hegemony is in reality a hinge, given that on the one hand it sutures the relationship between two elements (the task and the agent); but, on the other hand, since this suture is produced in the field of a primary and insurmountable relationship of dislocation, we can only attribute a character of inscription to it, not one of necessary articulation. In other words, the hegemonic relationship can be thought only by assuming the category of *lack* as a point of departure. We can clearly see the pertinence of some central concepts of Lacanian theory. The hegemonic subject is the subject of the signifier, which is, in this sense, a subject without a signified; and it is only from this logic of the signifier that the hegemonic relationship as such may be conceived. But in this case, the categories of negativity and opaqueness, which we presented as characteristic of that first crisis of modernity represented by the Hegelian/ Marxist moment, are not reabsorbed as a partial moment by any rationalist transparency. They are constitutive. Thus, there is no *Aufhebung*. This is precisely the point where the logic of the unconscious, as the logic of the signifier, reveals itself as an essentially political logic (insofar as politics, from Machiavelli onward, have primarily been the thought of dislocation); and where the social, ultimately irreducible to the status of full presence, also reveals itself as political. The political thus acquires the status of an ontology of the social.

Therefore, the "de-struction" of the history of Marxism is not a speculative operation—an epistemological operation, if you will—given that it presupposes no duality of subject/object, but rather the generalization of the logic of the signifier to the ensemble of its theoretical categories. Consequently, these categories are neither *removed* nor *reabsorbed* by a higher rationality but *shown* in their contingency and historicity. For the same reason, this generalization is not a speculative/abstract process, but a practical/discursive one. It is the generalization of the phenomena of the "unequal and combined development" of the imperialist age into any social identity which, as in the Heideggerian image of the broken hammer, transforms the *dislocation* into a horizon from which all identity may be thought and constituted (these two terms being exactly synonymous).

This indicates the direction and the way in which a possible confluence of (post-)Marxism and psychoanalysis is conceivable, neither as the addition of a supplement to the former by the latter nor as the introduction of a new causal element—the unconscious instead of economy—but as the coincidence of the two, around the logic of the signifier as a logic of unevenness and dislocation, a coincidence grounded on the fact that the latter is the logic which presides over the possibility/impossibility of the constitution of *any* identity.

The Idea of a Psychoanalytic Literary Criticism

Peter Brooks

Psychoanalytic literary criticism has always been something of an embarrassment. One resists labeling as a "psychoanalytic critic" because the kind of criticism evoked by the term mostly deserves the bad name it largely has made for itself. Thus I have been worrying about the status of some of my own uses of psychoanalysis in the study of narrative, in my attempt to find dynamic models that might move us beyond the static formalism of structuralist and semiotic narratology. And in general, I think we need to worry about the legitimacy and force that psychoanalysis may claim when imported into the study of literary texts. If versions of psychoanalytic criticism have been with us at least since 1908, when Freud published his essay on "Creative Writers and Day-dreaming," and if the enterprise has recently been renewed in subtle ways by post-structuralist versions of reading, a malaise persists, a sense that whatever the promises of their union, literature and psychoanalysis remain mismatched bedfellows—or perhaps I should say playmates.

The first problem, and the most basic, may be that psychoanalysis in literary study has over and over again mistaken the *object* of analysis, with the result that whatever insights it has produced tell us precious little about the structure and rhetoric of literary texts. Traditional psychoanalytic ciriticism tends to fall into three general categories, depending on the object of analysis: the author, the reader, or the fictive persons of the text. The first of these constituted the classical locus of psychoanalytic interest. It is now apparently the most discredited, though also perhaps the most difficult to extirpate, since if the disappearance of the author

This essay was presented as a lecture at the Centre for Literary Studies of the Hebrew University of Jerusalem, at the kind invitation of Professors Shlomith Rimmon-Kenan and Sanford Budick.

has been repeatedly announced, authorial mutants ceaselessly reappear, as, for instance, in Harold Bloom's *psychomachia* of literary history. Like the author, the fictive character has been deconstructed into an effect of textual codes, a kind of thematic mirage, and the psychoanalytic study of the putative unconscious of characters in fiction has also fallen into disrepute. Here again, however, the impulse resurfaces, for instance in some of the moves of a feminist criticism that needs to show how the represented female psyche (particularly of course as created by women authors) refuses and problematizes the dominant concepts of male psychological doctrine. Feminist criticism has in fact largely contributed to a new variant of the psychoanalytic study of fictive characters, a variant one might label the "situational-thematic": studies of Oedipal triangles in fiction, their permutations and evolution, of the roles of mothers and daughters, of situations of nurture and bonding, and so forth. It is work often full of interest, but nonetheless methodologically disquieting in its use of Freudian analytic tools in a wholly thematic way, as if the identification and labeling of human relations in a psychoanalytic vocabulary were the task of criticism. The third traditional field of psychoanalytic literary study, the reader, continues to flourish in ever-renewed versions, since the role of the reader in the creation of textual meaning is very much on our minds at present, and since the psychoanalytic study of readers' responses willingly brackets the impossible notion of author in favor of the acceptable and also verifiable notion of reader. The psychoanalytic study of the reader may concern real readers (as in Norman Holland's *Five Readers Reading*) or the reader as psychological everyman (as in Simon O. Lesser's *Fiction and the Unconscious*). But like the other traditional psychoanalytic approaches, it displaces the object of analysis from the text to some person, some other psychodynamic structure—a displacement I wish to avoid since, as I hope to make clear as I go along, I think psychoanalytic criticism can and should be textual and rhetorical.

If the displacement of the object of analysis has been a major failing of psychoanalytic literary criticism, it has erred also in its inability to rid itself of the underlying conviction that it is inherently explanatory. The problem with "literature and psychoanalysis," as Shoshana Felman has pointed out more effectively than any other critic, lies in that "and."[1]

1. See Shoshana Felman, "To Open the Question," *Yale French Studies* 55/56 (1977): 5–10.

Peter Brooks is the Tripp Professor of the Humanities at Yale University, where he is also director of the Whitney Humanities Center and chairman of the French department. His most recent book is *Reading for the Plot: Design and Intention in Narrative*, which has recently been reissued in paperback. His work in progress concerns psychoanalysis and storytelling.

The conjunction has almost always implied a relation of privilege of one term to the other, a use of psychoanalysis as a conceptual system in terms of which to analyze and explain literature, rather than an encounter and confrontation between the two. The reference to psychoanalysis has traditionally been used to close rather than open the argument, and the text. This is not surprising, since the recourse to psychoanalysis usually claims as its very *raison d'être* the capacity to explain and justify in the terms of a system and a discourse more penetrating and productive of insight than literary critical psychology as usual, which of course harbors its own, largely unanalyzed, assumptions. As Lesser states the case, "no 'common-sense' psychology yet employed in criticism has been helpful"; whereas psychoanalysis provides a way to explore "the deepest levels of meaning of the greatest fiction."[2]

Why should we reject such a claim? Even if psychoanalysis is far from being a "science" with the formal power of linguistics, for instance, surely some of its hypotheses are so well established and so universally illustrated that we can use them with as much impunity as such linguistic concepts as "shifters" or "the double articulation." Yet the recourse to linguistic and to psychoanalytic concepts implies a false symmetry: linguistics may be universalistic, but its tools and concepts are "cool" and their overextension easily recognized as trivial, whereas psychoanalysis is imperialistic, almost of necessity. Freud works from the premise that all that appears is a sign, that all signs are subject to interpretation, and that they ultimately tell stories that contain the same dramatis personae and the same narrative functions for all of us. It is no wonder that Freud called himself a "conquistador": he extends remarkably the empire of signs and their significant decipherment, encompassing all of human behavior and symbolic action. Thus any "psychoanalytic explanation" in another discipline always runs the risk of appearing to claim the last word, the final hermeneutical power. If there is one thing that post-structuralist criticism has most usefully taught us, it is the suspicion of this last word in the interpretive process and history, the refusal of any privileged position in analysis.

But if we refuse to grant psychoanalysis any position of privilege in criticism, if we refuse to consider it to be explanatory, what do we have left? What is the status of a de-authorized psychoanalytic discourse within literary-critical discourse, and what is its object? If we don't accord explanatory force to psychoanalysis, what is the point of using it at all? Why do we continue to read so many critical essays laced with the conceptual vocabulary of psychoanalysis? What is *at stake* in the current uses of psychoanalysis?

I want to begin this inquiry with the flat-footed (and unfashionable) assertion that I believe that the persistence, against all the odds, of psy-

2. Simon O. Lesser, *Fiction and the Unconscious* (Boston, 1957), pp. 297, 15.

choanalytic perspectives in literary study must ultimately derive from our conviction that the materials on which psychoanalysts and literary critics exercise their powers of analysis are in some basic sense the same: that the structure of literature *is* in some sense the structure of mind— not a specific mind, but what the translators of the *Standard Edition* call "the mental apparatus," which is more accurately the dynamic organization of the psyche, a process of structuration. We continue to dream of a convergence of psychoanalysis and literary criticism because we sense that there ought to be, that there must be, some correspondence between literary and psychic process, that aesthetic structure and form, including literary tropes, must somehow coincide with the psychic structures and operations they both evoke and appeal to. Yet here we encounter the truth of the comment made by Jack Spector in his book, *The Aesthetics of Freud:* "Neither Freud nor his followers . . . have ever shown concretely how specific formal techniques correspond to the processes of the unconscious."[3]

Part of the attraction of psychoanalytic criticism has always been its promise of a movement *beyond* formalism, to that desired place where literature and life converge, and where literary criticism becomes the discourse of something anthropologically important. I very much subscribe to this urge, but I think that it is fair to say that in the case of psychoanalysis, paradoxically, we can go beyond formalism only by becoming more formalistic. Geoffrey Hartman wrote a number of years ago—in *Beyond Formalism,* in fact—that the trouble with Anglo-American formalism was that it wasn't formalist enough.[4] One can in general indict Anglo-American New Criticism for being too quick to leap from the level of formal explication to that of moral and psychological interpretation, neglecting the trajectory through linguistics and poetics that needs to stand between. This has certainly been true in traditional psychoanalytic criticism, which has regularly short-circuited the difficult and necessary issues in poetics. The more recent—rhetorical and deconstructive—kind understands the formalist imperative, but I fear that it may too often remain content with formal operations, simply bracketing the human realm from which psychoanalysis derives. Given its project and its strategies, such rhetorical/ deconstructive criticism usually stays within the linguistic realm. It is not willing to make the crossover between rhetoric and reference that interests me—and that ought to be the *raison d'être* for the recourse to psychoanalysis in the first place.

One way to try to move out from the impasse I discern—or have perhaps myself constructed—might be through a return to what Freud

3. Jack J. Spector, *The Aesthetics of Freud: A Study in Psychoanalysis and Art* (New York, 1973), p. 118.
4. Geoffrey Hartman, *Beyond Formalism: Literary Essays 1958–1970* (New Haven, Conn., 1970), p. 42.

has to say about literary form, most notoriously in the brief essay, "Creative Writers and Day-dreaming." We would probably all agree that Freud speaks most pertinently to literary critics when he is not explicitly addressing art: the most impressive essays in psychoanalytic criticism have drawn more on *The Interpretation of Dreams,* the metapsychological essays, and *Beyond the Pleasure Principle,* for example, than on *Delusions and Dreams,* "The Moses of Michelangelo," or the essays on Leonardo and Dostoyevski. "Creative Writers and Day-dreaming" in fact gives an excessively simplistic view of art, of the kind that allows Ernst Kris, in his well-known *Psychoanalytic Explorations in Art,* to describe artistic activity as regression in the service of the ego.[5] Yet the essay may be suggestive in other ways.

Freud sets out to look for some common human activity that is "akin to creative writing," and finds it in daydreaming, or the creation of fantasies. Freud then stresses the active, temporal structure of fantasy, which

> hovers, as it were, between three times—the three moments of time which our ideation involves. Mental work is linked to some current impression, some provoking occasion in the present which has been able to arouse one of the subject's major wishes. From there it harks back to the memory of an earlier experience (usually an infantile one) in which this wish was fulfilled; and it now creates a situation relating to the future which represents a fulfilment of the wish. What it thus creates is a day-dream or phantasy, which carries about it traces of its origin from the occasion which provoked it and from the memory. Thus past, present and future are strung together, as it were, on the thread of the wish that runs through them.[6]

Freud will promptly commit the error of making the past evoked in the construction of fantasy that of the author, in order to study "the connections that exist between the life of the writer and his works" ("CW," p. 151)—an error in which most critics have followed his lead. For instance, it is this fantasy model, reworked in terms of D. W. Winnicott and object relations psychoanalysis, that essentially shapes the thesis of one of the most interesting recent studies in literature and psychoanalysis, Meredith Skura's *The Literary Use of the Psychoanalytic Process;* Skura, too, ultimately makes the past referred to in fantasy a personal past, that of author or reader, or both.[7] Yet the fantasy model could instead be suggestive for

5. See Ernst Kris, *Psychoanalytic Explorations in Art* (New York, 1952).

6. Sigmund Freud, "Creative Writers and Day-dreaming," *The Standard Edition of the Complete Psychological Works of Sigmund Freud,* ed. and trans. James Strachey, 24 vols. (London, 1953–74), 9:147–48; all further references to this essay, abbreviated "CW," will be included in the text.

7. See Meredith Anne Skura, *The Literary Use of the Psychoanalaytic Process* (New Haven, Conn., 1981).

talking about the relations of textual past, present, and projected future in the plot of a novel, for example, or in the rhyme scheme of a sonnet, or simply in the play of verb tenses in any text. I would want to extrapolate from this passage an understanding of how fantasy provides a dynamic model of intratextual temporal relations and of their organization according to the plot of wish, or desire. We might thus gain a certain understanding of the interplay of *form* and *desire*.

Freud is again of great interest in the final paragraph of the essay—one could make a fruitful study of Freud's final paragraphs, which so often produce a flood of new insights that can't quite be dealt with—where he asks how the writer creates pleasure through the communication of his fantasies, whereas those of most people would repel or bore us. Herein, says Freud, lies the poet's "innermost secret," his "essential *ars poetica*" ("CW," p. 153). Freud sees two components of the artistic achievement here: "The writer softens the character of his egoistic day-dreams by altering and disguising it, and he bribes us by the purely formal—that is, aesthetic—yield of pleasure which he offers us in the presentation of his phantasies. We give the name of an *incentive bonus*, or a *fore-pleasure*, to a yield of pleasure such as this, which is offered to us so as to make possible the release of still greater pleasure arising from deeper psychical sources. In my opinion, all the aesthetic pleasure which a creative writer affords us has the character of a fore-pleasure of this kind" ("CW," p. 153). I am deliberately leaving aside the end of this paragraph, where Freud suggests that the writer in this manner enables us "thenceforward to enjoy our own day-dreams without self-reproach or shame," since this hypothesis brings us back to the *person* of the reader, whereas I wish to remain on the plane of form associated with "fore-pleasure."

The equation of the effects of literary form with forepleasure in this well-known passage is perhaps less trivial than it at first appears. If *Lust* and *Unlust* don't take us very far in the analysis of literary texture, *Vorlust*—forepleasure—tropes on pleasure and thus seems more promising. Forepleasure is indeed a curious concept, suggesting a whole rhetoric of advance toward and retreat from the goal or the end, a formal zone of play (I take it that forepleasure somehow implicates foreplay) that is both harnessed to the end and yet autonomous, capable of deviations and recursive movements. When we begin to unpack the components of forepleasure, we may find a whole erotics of form, which is perhaps what we most need if we are to make formalism serve an understanding of the human functions of literature. Forepleasure would include the notion of both delay and advance in the textual dynamic, the creation of that "dilatory space" which Roland Barthes, in *S/Z*, claimed to be the essence of the textual middle. We seek to advance through this space toward the discharge of the end, yet all the while we are perversely delaying, returning backward in order to put off the promised end and perhaps to assure its greater significance.

Forepleasure implies the possibility of fetishism, the interesting threat of being waylaid by some element along the way to the "proper" end, taking some displaced substitute or simulacrum for the thing itself—a mystification in which most literature deals, sometimes eventually to expose the displacement or substitution as a form of false consciousness, sometimes to expose the end itself as the false lure. It includes as well the possibilities of exhibitionism and voyeurism, which surely are central to literary texts and their reading. In the notion of forepleasure there lurks in fact all manner of perversity, and ultimately the possibility of the polymorphous perverse, the possibility of a text that would delay, displace, and deviate terminal discharge to an extent that it became nonexistent—as, perhaps, in the textual practice of the "writable text" (*texte scriptible*) prized by Barthes, in Samuel Beckett, for instance, or Philippe Sollers. But we find as good an illustration of effective perversity in the text of Henry James, and in the principle (well known to the New Critics) that the best poems accommodate a maximum of ironic texture within their frail structures, a postponement and ambiguation of overt statement. In fact, the work of textuality may insure that all literature is, by its very nature, essentially perverse.

What is most important to me is the sense that the notion of fore-pleasure as it is advanced by Freud implies the possibility of a formalist aesthetic—one that can be extended to the properly rhetorical field—that speaks to the erotic, which is to say the dynamic, dimensions of form: form as something that is not inert but part of a process that unfolds and develops as texts are activated through the reading process. A neo-formalist psychoanalytic criticism could do worse than undertake the study of the various forms of the "fore" in forepleasure, developing a tropology of the perversities through which we turn back, turn around, the simple consumption of texts, making their reading a worthy object of analysis. Such a study would be, as Freud suggests, about "bribing," or perhaps about *teasing* in all its forms, from puns to metaphors, ultimately—given the basic temporal structure of fantasy and of the literary text—about what we might call "clock-teasing," which is perhaps the way we create the illusion of creating a space of meaning within the process of ongoing temporality.

A more formalist psychoanalytic criticism, then, would be attuned to form as our situation, our siting, within the symbolic order, the order within which we constitute meaning and ourselves as endowed with meaning. This kind of psychoanalytic criticism would, of course, pay the greatest attention to the rhetorical aspect of psychic operations as presented by psychoanalysis and would call upon the rhetorical and semiotic re-interpretation of Freud advanced by Emile Benveniste, Jacques Lacan, and others. Yet it might be objected that this more obviously rhetorical version does not automatically solve the problem of how to use the crossover between psychic operations and tropes. The status of the *and* linking psychoanalysis and literary text may still remain at issue: what does one want to *claim* in showing that the structure of a metaphor in Victor Hugo is equivalent to the structure of a symptom? What is alleged to be the place and the force of the occulted name of the father that may be written in metaphor as symptom, symptom as metaphor?[8] Is there, more subtly now, a claim of explanation advanced in the crossover? Or is an ingenious piece of intertextuality all that takes place?

Something, I think, that lies between the two. My views on these questions have been clarified by an acute and challenging review of my book, *Reading for the Plot*, that appeared in *TLS*. In it, Terence Cave asks what he calls "the embarrassing question . . . what is the Freudian model worth?" In his discussion of a possible answer to this question, Cave notes that "Brooks's argument for a Freudian poetics doesn't appear to depend on an imperialist move which would simply annex a would-be science of the psyche and release it from its claim to tell the truth. He talks repeatedly as if the value of the Freudian model is precisely that it does, in some sense, give access to the way human desires really operate."[9] I think this is accurate, and I am happy to be exonerated from the charge of imperialism in the reverse—the imperialism that would come from the incursion of literary criticism into psychoanalysis in search of mere metaphors, which has sometimes been the case with post-structuralist annexations of psychoanalytic concepts. I certainly do want to grant at least a temporary privilege to psychoanalysis in literary study, in that the trajectory through psychoanalysis forces us to confront the human stakes of literary form, while I think also that these stakes need to be considered *in* the text, as activated in its reading. As I suggested earlier, I believe that we constitute ourselves as human subjects in part through our fictions and therefore that the study of human fiction-making and the study of psychic process are convergent activities and superimposable forms of analysis. To say more precisely in what sense psychoanalysis can lead us to models for literary study that generate new insight, we might best look toward a concept that lies at the very heart of Freudian analytic practice, the concept of the transference as it is constituted between analysand and analyst. Here we may find the most useful elaboration of the fantasy model of the text. Let me, then, briefly explore the transference, in order to indicate one possible way of conceiving the relations of psychoanalysis to literary discourse.

The transference, as I understand it, is a realm of the *as-if*, where affects from the past become invested in the present, notably in the

8. I allude here to an example used by Jacques Lacan in "L'Instance de la lettre," *Ecrits* (Paris, 1966), pp. 506–9.

9. Terence Cave, "The Prime and Precious Thing," review of *Reading for the Plot* by Peter Brooks, *Times Literary Supplement*, 4 January 1985, p. 14; all further references to this review, abbreviated "PPT," will be included in the text.

dynamics of the analysand-analyst relation, and the neurosis under treatment becomes a transference-neurosis, a present representation of the past. As Freud puts it in the Dora case history, the transference gives us "new impressions or reprints" and "revised editions" of old texts.[10] One can call the transference textual because it is a semiotic and fictional medium where the compulsions of unconscious desire and its scenarios of infantile fulfillment become symbolically present in the communicative situation of analysis. Within the transference, recall of the past most often takes place as its unconscious repetition, an acting out of past events as if they were present: repetition is a way of remembering brought into play when recollection in the intellectual sense is blocked by repression and resistance. Repetition is both an obstacle to analysis, since the analysand must eventually be led to renunciation of the attempt to reproduce the past, and the principal dynamic of the cure, since only by way of its symbolic enactment in the present can the history of past desire, its objects and scenarios of fulfillment, be made known, become manifest in the present discourse. The analyst (I paraphrase Freud here) must treat the analysand's words and symbolic acts as an actual force, active in the present, while attempting to translate them back into the terms of the past.[11] That is, the analyst must work with the analysand to fit his emotional impulses into their proper place in his life history, to restore the links between ideas and events that have fallen away, to reconnect isolated memories, and to draw conclusions from interconnections and patterns. The analyst must help the analysand construct a narrative discourse whose syntax and rhetoric are more plausible, more convincing, more adequate to give an account of the story of the past than those that are originally presented, in symptomatic form, by the analysand.

Freud writes in one of his key essays on the transference, "Remembering, Repeating and Working-Through":

> The transference thus creates an intermediate region [*Zwischenreich*] between illness and real life through which the transition from the one to the other is made. The new condition has taken over all the features of the illness; but it represents an artificial illness which is at every point accessible to our intervention. It is a piece of real experience, but one which has been made possible by especially favourable conditions, and it is of a provisional nature.[12]

Freud's description of this intermediate region—this *Zwischenreich*—that is both artificial and a piece of real experience makes it sound very much

---

10. Freud, "Fragment of an Analysis of a Case of Hysteria," *Standard Edition*, 7:116.

11. On these points, see Freud, "The Dynamics of Transference" (1912), *Standard Edition*, 12:97–108; and "Remembering, Repeating and Working-Through" (1914), *Standard Edition*, 12:145–56.

12. Freud, "Remembering, Repeating and Working-Through," *Standard Edition*, 12:154.

like the literary text. He who intervenes in it is the analyst or reader, first of all in the sense that the simple presence of this other brings to the analysand's discourse what Lacan calls "the dimension of dialogue."[13] Texts are always implicitly or even explicitly addressed to someone. The "I" that speaks in a lyric ever postulates a "thou." Indeed, as Benveniste has shown, "I" and "thou" are linguistically interdependent, both signifiers without signifieds, and with referents that constantly change as each speaker in turn assumes the "I" in relation to the interlocutor, who from "I" becomes "thou."[14] This situation is frequently dramatized in narrative texts, in what we call "framed tales," which stage the presence of a listener or narratee whose reactions to what is told are often what is most important in the narrative. Such is the case of Balzac's *Sarrasine*, which has become a classic point of reference since Roland Barthes in *S/Z* made it a model for the workings of the "narrative contract," and also Mary Shelley's *Frankenstein*, where the narratee of each embedded narrative is supposed to act upon what he has been told. In other cases, the simple presence of the narratee, even when silent, "dialogizes" the speech of the narrator, as Mikhail Bakhtin has so thoroughly demonstrated in the case of the Dostoyevskian monologue. A good example of dialogized monologue is Albert Camus' *La Chute*, where Jean-Baptiste Clamence's abject confession includes within it the unnamed and silent narratee's responses, with the eventual result of implicating the narratee within a discourse he would no doubt rather not listen to. Even in texts which have no explicit narrator or narratee, where the narrative is apparently "impersonal," there is necessarily a discourse which solicits a response, be it only by the play of personal pronouns and the conjugation of verbs.

The narratee, the addressee, the "you" of these texts is always in some measure a surrogate for the reader, who must define his own interpretation in response to the implied judgment, and the discursive implication, of the explicit or implicit textual "you." Contemporary reader-response criticism has often made excessive claims for the role of the reader—to the point of abolishing the semiotic constraint that the text exercises upon reading—but it has usefully shown us that the reader necessarily collaborates and competes in the creation of textual meaning. To return to Freud's term, we "intervene" in a text by our very act of reading, in our (counter)transferential desire to master the text, as also in the desire to be mastered by it. When we are what we call literary critics, our interventions—our efforts to rewrite and retransmit—may

13. Jacques Lacan, "Intervention sur le transfert," *Ecrits*, p. 216. I note that Murray Schwartz argues, briefly but evocatively, the relevance of the transference to literary interpretation. See Schwartz, "Critic, Define Thyself," in *Psychoanalysis and the Question of the Text, Selected Papers from the English Institute, 1976–77*, n.s. 2, ed. Geoffrey Hartman (Baltimore, 1978), pp. 1–17.

14. Emile Benveniste, "De la subjectivité dans le langage," *Problèmes de linguistique générale* (Paris, 1966), pp. 258–66.

closely resemble the psychoanalyst's, with all the attendant perils of transference and countertransference.

However self-absorbed and self-referential they may appear, lyric and narrative discourses are always proffered for a purpose: to establish a claim on the listener's attention, to make an appeal to complicity, perhaps to judgment, and inevitably to interpretation and retransmission. In the transferential situation of reading, as in the psychoanalytic transference, the reader must grasp not only what is said, but always what the discourse intends, its implications, how it would work on him. He must—in Lacanian terms—refuse the text's demand in order to listen to its desire. In narrative, for instance, the reader must reconstruct and understand not only story events but also the relation of this story to the narrative discourse that conveys it in a certain manner, discourse that itself constitutes an interpretation which demands further interpretation. As Freud writes in "Remembering, Repeating and Working-Through," it occurs that the analysand "does not listen to the precise wording of his obsessional ideas."[15] Narrators may be similar to the analysand in this respect, most obviously in such modernist and postmodernist narratives as those of Conrad, Gide, Faulkner, and Sarraute, but also in many more traditional novels, especially in the eighteenth century—in the work of Diderot and Sterne, for instance—and even at the very origins of the genre, in the *Lazarillo de Tormes,* a novel which both reveals and conceals its story. A certain suspicion inhabits the relation of narrative discourse to its story, and our role as readers calls for a suspicious hearing, a rewriting of the narrative text in a sort of agonistic dialogue with the words we are given to work with. Freud repeatedly describes the relations of analyst and analysand in the transference as one of struggle—struggle for the mastery of resistances and the lifting of repressions—which continually evokes a realm of the demonic. With reader and text, the struggle must eventually put into question any assumed position of mastery or privilege, which is why we must reread, speak again, retransmit.

The advantage of such a transferential model, it seems to me, is that it illuminates the difficult and productive encounter of the speaker and the listener, the text and the reader, and how their exchange takes place in an "artificial" space—a symbolic and semiotic medium—that is nonetheless the place of real investments of desire from both sides of the dialogue. The transference actualizes the past in symbolic form so that it can be repeated, replayed, worked through to another outcome. The result is, in the ideal case, to bring us back to actuality, that is, to a revised version of our stories. As Freud writes in the last sentence of another important essay, "The Dynamics of Transference": "For when all is said and done, it is impossible to destroy anyone *in absentia* or *in effigie.*"[16]

15. Freud, "Remembering, Repeating and Working-Through," *Standard Edition,* 12:152.
16. Freud, "The Dynamics of Transference," *Standard Edition,* 12:108.

The statement appears paradoxical, in that it is precisely "in effigy"—in the symbolic mode—that the past and its ghosts may be destroyed, or laid to rest, in analysis. What Freud means, I think, is that the transference succeeds in making the past and its scenarios of desire live again through signs with such vivid reality that the reconstructions proposed by analytic work achieve the *effect* of the real. They do not change past history—they are powerless to do that—but they rewrite its present discourse. Disciplined and mastered, the transference ushers us forth into a changed reality. And such is no doubt the intention of any literary text.

In such a conception of the transference, we have a rhetorical elaboration of the fantasy model of the text adumbrated in "Creative Writers and Day-dreaming." The text is conceived as a semiotic and fictive medium constituted as the place of affective investments that represent a situation and a story as both symbolic (given the absence of situation and story except "in effigy") and "real" (given the making-present of situation and story through their repetition). The text conceived as transference should allow us to illuminate and work through that which is at issue in the situation of the speaker, or the story of the narrator, that is, what must be rethought, reordered, interpreted from his discourse. Transference and interpretation are in fact interdependent, and we cannot assign priority to one over the other. If it is evident that transference calls forth interpretation, it is equally true that it is the potential of interpretation on the part of "the subject supposed to know"—as Lacan characterizes the analyst—that sets the transference going.[17]

When, as analysand or as text, you call for interpretation from the analyst/reader, you put yourself into the transference. Through the re-thinkings, reorderings, reinterpretations of the reading process, the analyst/reader "intervenes" in the text, and these interventions must also be subject to his suspicious attention. A transferential model thus allows us to take as the object of analysis not author or reader, but reading, including, of course, the transferential-interpretive operations that belong to reading. Meaning in this view is not simply "in the text" nor wholly the fabrication of a reader (or a community of readers) but comes into being in the dialogic struggle and collaboration of the two, in the activation of textual possibilities in the process of reading. Such a view ultimately destabilizes the authority of reader/critic in relation to the text, since, caught up in the transference, he becomes analysand as well as analyst.

Yet here I once again encounter Cave, who finds my evocations of "transference" and "dialogue" in *Reading for the Plot* to be largely metaphorical. "It seems curious," writes Cave, "to speak of a once-and-for-all written narrative as the medium for transference for a reader who

---

17. On this point, I am indebted to an exposition of the transference according to Lacan presented by Jacques-Alain Miller at the conference, "Lacan's Legacy," held at the University of Massachusetts, Amherst, 14–16 June 1985.

has not supplied its materials. . . . How can there be a transference where there is no means by which the reader's language may be rephrased in coherent and manageable form by the text-as-analyst?" ("PPT," p. 14). Cave has reversed the basic model, which would see text as analysand and reader as analyst; but that is a reversal that can, I have suggested, take place in the process of reading and interpretation. What is more to the point, there happens to be an essay of Freud's that indirectly responds to some of Cave's questions: "Constructions in Analysis" (1937), an essay from late in Freud's career in which he explicitly addresses the roles played by analysand and analyst in the creation of a life story and its discursive meaning.

Near the start of this essay, Freud notes that since the analyst has neither experienced nor repressed any of the story in question, he cannot be called upon to remember it. "His task," writes Freud, "is to make out what has been forgotten from the traces which it has left behind or, more correctly, to *construct* it."[18] As Freud's essay proceeds, this construction becomes a radical activity. The analyst constructs a hypothetical piece of narrative and, writes Freud, "communicates it to the subject of analysis so that it may work on him; he then constructs a further piece out of the fresh material pouring in on him, deals with it in the same way and proceeds in this alternating fashion until the end." Confirmation that these constructions are correct does not take the form of a simple assent: a "yes" from the analysand has little value, says Freud, "unless it is followed by indirect confirmations, unless the patient . . . produces new memories which complete and extend the construction" ("CA," p. 262). As in reading, hypotheses of construal prove to be strong and valuable when they produce more text, when they create in the text previously unperceived networks of relation and significance, finding confirmation in the extension of the narrative and semantic web. The analytic work, the process of finding and making meaning, is necessarily a factor of listening and reading as well as telling. Freud indeed goes on to concede that there are moments when the analyst's construction does not lead to the analysand's recollection of repressed elements of his story but nonetheless produces in him "an assured conviction of the truth of the construction which achieves the same therapeutic result as a recaptured memory" ("CA," p. 66). Parts of the story thus seem to belong to the interpreter rather than to the person whose story it is, or was.

"Constructions in Analysis" as a whole gives a view of psychoanalytic interpretation and construction that notably resembles the active role of the reader in making sense of a text, finding hypotheses of interpretation that open up ever wider and more forceful semantic patterns, attempting always to reach the totality of the supreme because necessary fiction.

18. Freud, "Constructions in Analysis," *Standard Edition*, 23:258–59; all further references to this essay, abbreviated "CA," will be included in the text.

The reader may not have written the text, yet it does change and evolve as he works on it—as he rewrites it, as those readers we call literary critics necessarily do. And as the reader works on the text, it does "rephrase" his perceptions. I think any of us could find confirmation of such a truly transferential and dialogic relation of text and analysis in our own experience. And there are of course literary texts that inscribe and dramatize acts of reading, interpretation, and construction: for instance, Balzac's *Le Lys dans la vallée,* where Natalie de Manerville reads Félix de Vandenesse's long confession and tells him that he has misinterpreted his own desires. Benjamin Constant's *Adolphe* stages a similar case of retrospective reading that provokes an entire reconstruction of the story. The epistolary novel of course stages nothing else: *Les Liaisons dangereuses* is all about different models and levels of construction in the reading of messages, and the writing of messages with a view toward their interpretation. The novels of Conrad and Faulkner are similar to Laclos' masterpiece in that they offer multiple constructions of events that never are verifiable, that can be tested only by the force of conviction they produce for listeners and readers.

Interpretation and construction are themselves most often dramas of desire and power, both within literature and in the reading of literary texts. Hence I would claim that the model of the transference is a far more literal model of reading than Cave would allow. I find it significant that toward the end of "Constructions in Analysis," Freud turns to a discussion of delusions, similar to hallucinations, which are produced in the analysand by the analyst's constructions: delusions that evoke a "fragment of historical truth" that is out of place in the story. Freud writes at this point, in an astonishing sentence, "The delusions of patients appear to me to be the equivalents of the constructions which we build up in the course of an analytic treatment—attempts at explanation and cure" ("CA," p. 268). That is, not only does the patient, in any successful analysis, become his own analyst; the analyst also becomes the patient, espouses his delusional system, and works toward the construction of fictions that can never be verified other than by the force of the conviction that they convey. And this seems to me a fair representation of good criticism, which involves a willingness, a desire, to enter into the delusional systems of texts, to espouse their hallucinated vision, in an attempt to master and be mastered by their power of conviction.

One final point needs to be made, again in reference to Cave—a resourceful critic whom one can never finally lay to rest. It can be argued—and I have myself argued—that much of Freud's understanding of interpretation and the construction of meaning is grounded in literature, in those "poets and philosophers" he was the first to acknowledge as his precursors. "In which case" writes Cave, psychoanalysis "can't itself provide a grounding, since it is part of the system it attempts to master." Cave continues: "Its advantage (though a precious one) would only be that, in its doubling of narrative and analysis, story and plot, it provides a poetics appropriate to the history of modern fiction" ("PPT," p. 14). Cave here reverses the more traditional charge that psychoanalysis imperialistically claims to explain literature in order to make the more subtle (and contemporary) charge that psychoanalysis may be nothing *but* literature, and the relations of the two nothing more than a play of intertextuality, or even a tautology.

I am unwilling to concede so much. One can resist the notion that psychoanalysis "explains" literature and yet insist that the kind of intertextual relation it holds to literature is quite different from the intertextuality that obtains between two poems or novels, and that it illuminates in quite other ways. For the psychoanalytic intertext obliges the critic to make a transit through a systematic discourse elaborated to describe the dynamics of psychic process. The similarities and differences, in object and in intention, of this discourse from literary analysis creates a tension which is productive of perspective, of stereoptical effect. Psychoanalysis is not an arbitrarily chosen intertext for literary analysis, but rather a particularly insistent and demanding intertext, in that crossing the boundaries from one territory to the other both confirms and complicates our understanding of how mind reformulates the real, how it constructs the necessary fictions by which we dream, desire, interpret, indeed by which we constitute ourselves as human subjects. The detour through psychoanalysis forces the critic to respond to the erotics of form, that is, to an engagement with the psychic investments of rhetoric, the dramas of desire played out in tropes. Psychoanalysis matters to us as literary critics because it stands as a constant reminder that the attention to form, properly conceived, is not a sterile formalism, but rather one more attempt to draw the symbolic and fictional map of our place in existence.

Psychoanalysis and the Place of *Jouissance*

Stephen Melville

> La psychanalyse, à supposer, se trouve.
> Quand on croit la trouver, c'est elle, à supposer, qui se trouve.
> Quand elle trouve, à supposer, elle se trouve—quelque chose.
> —JACQUES DERRIDA

1

Jacques Lacan's explorations in the formalization of psychoanalysis grew simultaneously more prominent and more obscure over the course of his career, especially during the last decade or so of his teaching, and at least certain of his formalizations—the mapping of "The Four Discourses" most especially—have taken on the status of central tests for and markers of Lacanianism. Among the several divisions within American interest which were exemplified in a 1985 meeting on Lacan's legacy at the University of Massachusetts, Amherst, one of the most striking was between those claiming some kind of direct inheritance from Lacan, supporting themselves with what I am tempted to call an absolute reference to the mathemes of the four discourses (and showing as well a marked interest in the datability of Lacan's utterances), and those taking what one might loosely call a more literary interest in Lacan—and some part of that "literariness" is perhaps signaled in a resolute avoidance of Lacan's mathematical and symbolic excursions. This division was not without its tensions and minor dramas, most centered on Jacques-Alain Miller, very much the official inheritor of Lacan as he extended an uneasy welcome

Diagrams by Alfred Masters.

to Lacan's American audience—a welcome that combined talk about who was and was not "one of us" with a plea that his own remarks be taken not as "dogmatic" but simply "axiomatic."

I offer these preliminary observations in order to underline the ways in which psychoanalysis is troubled not only in its movement beyond itself into other places but in its relation to itself, to its own place. Psychoanalysis finds its object in *ein anderer Schauplatz*. It is in the name of its privileged access to this other place that psychoanalysis moves into other disciplines and appropriates their objects to its own. But such a movement depends first of all on the ability of this presumed science to secure itself; its own place is not directly given but must be achieved. For Lacan, the post-Freudian, primarily American history of the discipline more than adequately testified to the fragility of psychoanalytic self-relation or self-mastery, and he repeatedly described his enterprise as one of returning psychoanalysis to its place.

Psychoanalysis has, in the very nature of its object, an interest in and difficulty with the concept of place as well as an interest in and difficulty with the logic of place, topology. The Unconscious can thus seem to give rise to a certain prospect of mathesis or formalization; and such formalization, achieved, would offer a ground for the psychoanalytic claim to scientific knowledge relatively independent of empirical questions and approaching the condition of mathematics. This might then seem to have been Lacan's wager in organizing the researches of his *école* around works of theoretical elaboration rather than clinical study; certainly some such notion must underlie Miller's claim to be "axiomatic."[1]

In this paper I want to explore some of Lacan's formalizations as they are unfolded in the seminar *Encore*. (I will also draw some material from the interview transcript *Télévision* and Lacan's appearances at Yale University in 1975.)[2] I will in effect be looking at the place of place or

---

1. By and large the evidences of the Lacanian clinic are closed to us in consequence of Lacan's insistence on theoretical elaboration. But it should not go unremarked that much of the work of Lacan's school seems to have focused on areas traditionally recalcitrant to psychoanalytic treatment—alcoholism, retardation, and psychosis—and that such an emphasis is responsive to traditional empirically minded critiques of the limits of psychoanalysis.

2. It should perhaps be noted in this context that the project of a genuinely public presentation of Lacan's seminars seems to have been abandoned in favor of the more circumscribed circulation of texts through the Lacanian journal *Ornicar?*

Stephen Melville is assistant professor of English at Syracuse University. He is the author of *Philosophy Beside Itself: On Deconstruction and Modernism* (1986) and is currently completing a series of essays on postmodern art and criticism.

places in psychoanalysis—in particular, I will be looking at the place of *jouissance* in Lacan's psychoanalysis and at the places of what Lacan punningly calls *jouis-sens*. The joint problematic here might be called one of "enjoymeant," combining the logic of pleasure with the pleasure of logic. For Lacan, questions of *jouissance*, however punned, are questions of unity and selfhood, so in examining the reciprocal play of pleasure and sense I will be examining how Lacanian psychoanalysis secures itself in place. This last topic touches implicitly in *Encore* on questions of legacy and inheritance, so in the end I will also have something to say about the limits Lacan's formalizations would impose on our enjoyment of Freud. I should note in advance that *Encore*, Lacan's seminar of 1972–73, is an extraordinarily compact and involuted text, even by his standards, and of a corresponding richness, weaving sustained meditations on such figures as Georges Bataille, Roman Jakobson, Kierkegaard, and Aquinas with "mathemystical" digressions on sexuality, discourse, Borromean knots, and the like. The reading offered here is perforce schematic.

2

One of the earliest American responses to Lacan came from an understandably frustrated Angus Fletcher:

> Freud was really a very simple man. . . . He didn't try to float on the surface of words. What you're doing is like a spider; you're making a very delicate web without any human reality in it. For example, you were speaking of joy (*joie, jouissance*). In French one of the meanings of *jouir* is the orgasm—I think that is most important here—why not say so? All the talk I have heard here has been so abstract! . . . All this metaphysics is not necessary. The diagram was very interesting, but it doesn't seem to have any connection with the reality of our actions, with eating, sexual intercourse, and so on.[3]

3. Angus Fletcher in discussion following Jacques Lacan, "Of Structure as an Inmixing of an Otherness Prerequisite to Any Subject Whatever," in *The Human Sciences and the Languages of Man: The Structuralist Controversy*, ed. Richard Macksey and Eugenio Donato (Baltimore, 1970), p. 195. See Lacan, *Encore, 1972–73*, Le Seminaire, livre 20, ed. Jacques-Alain Miller (Paris, 1975), p. 86:

> S'il m'était permis d'en donner une image, je la prendrais aisément de ce qui dans la nature, paraît le plus se rapprocher de cette réduction aux dimensions de la surface qu'exige l'écrit, et dont déjà s'émerveillait Spinoza—ce travail de texte qui sort du ventre de l'araignée, sa toile. Fonction vraiment miraculeuse, à voir, de la surface même surgissant d'un point opaque de cet étrange être, se dessiner la trace de ces écrits, où saisir les limites, les points d'impasse, de sans-issue, qui montrent le réel accédant au symbolique.

Further references to *Encore*, abbreviated *E*, will be included in the text.

No response to Fletcher is reported in the transcript. In the years since there have been a number of attempts to make out the sense of *jouissance* for Lacan, and some texts relevant to the discussion have been translated, but there has been little sustained effort to show how the things Fletcher was asking about do indeed hang together.[4]

Fletcher was asking where the bedrock of psychoanalysis is. He was asking what Lacan makes of its brutest facts: orgasm, pleasure, discharge. And the answer is that for Lacan there are no such brute facts and energetics at the bottom of psychoanalysis; it is the image of a science possessed of such objects that led Freud away from his own discoveries, and it is the replacement of this image with that of linguistics—or "linguisterie" [*E*, p. 92]—that will lead us back.

If we are speaking of sex, the important thing is that we are in fact speaking of it—we may even speak just to say that it is natural but our need to say *that* already places it elsewhere, condemns it to "culture." It is a fact of human being that a difference between, for example, the "clitoral" and the "vaginal" will not rest within the anatomical or physiological but can come to bear a weight we call political.

So Lacan's fundamental proposition is that there is no immediate or instinctual sexual relationship in some first instance which would then become subject to degeneration or detour or other hurt. What is human is precisely the absence of such relationship, the need for it to be constructed from or upon what is instinctual—hunger, evacuation, reproduction. When psychoanalysis speaks of "component drives" it points at the way in which sexuality emerges on the occasion and surface of that which is instinctive.[5] For such a view, Freud's insistence on the phallus, on Oedipus, on the "masculinity" of the libido, are to be read as answering not to considerations of instinct or naturalness or biological destiny but to a logic proper to the emergence and deployment of human sexuality, the sexuality of beings that speak. Sexuality is a matter of logic and inscription. Referring to a version of the table of contraries he will put up on the seminar's blackboard, Lacan says,

> On the whole one takes up this [masculine] side by choice, women being free to do so if they choose. Everyone knows that

4. On *jouissance*, see Stephen Heath, "Difference," *Screen* 19 (Winter 1978–79): 51–112; Jane Gallop, "*Encore* Encore," *The Daughter's Seduction: Feminism and Psychoanalysis* (Ithaca, N.Y., 1982); and Juliet Mitchell's and Jacqueline Rose's introductions to Lacan and the *école freudienne*, *Feminine Sexuality*, ed. Mitchell and Rose, trans. Rose (New York, 1982); further references to this work, abbreviated *FS*, will be included in the text. This book includes a translation of two chapters from *Encore*, "God and the *Jouissance* of The Woman" and "A Love Letter."

The only treatment of the mathemes I know of in English is in Sherry Turkle, *Psychoanalytic Politics: Freud's French Revolution* (New York, 1978), chap. 7 and the epilogue.

5. On anaclisis in Freud and Freudian conceptuality see Jean Laplanche, *Life and Death in Psychoanalysis*, trans. Jeffrey Mehlman (Baltimore, 1976).

there are phallic women and that the phallic function does not prevent men from being homosexual. [*FS,* p. 143][6]

Lacan begins to expound his table "on the side where all x is a function of Φx, that is, on the side of the man":

(1) $\forall x$ Φx

A logician reads this: all x is Φ. Lacan reads: all x is a function of Φx. I translate: all x answers to the phallus. What we cannot substitute for in attempting the translation here is the "x"; if we were to do so, we might come up with something like this: everything we want to take as human being, as human meaning, as my meaning or being—all that I most deeply want to be and say—answers to the phallus. We are, that is, given over in our inmost being to a function of which we are not masters; our self is organized elsewhere; there is an inmixing of otherness. This might then lead us to write another proposition or pseudoproposition concealed within or behind the first and on which our meaning and being would then depend, through which we would recover ourselves from this otherness:

(2) $\exists x$ $\overline{\Phi x}$

The logician's reading says: there is an x that is not Φ. Our elaboration says: *that* is what I really am—beneath my surfaces and roles and socializations, beyond my sex and my childhood, away from everything that conspires to keep me from saying what I really am, *there,* in that x that does exist. Together the two propositions seem to capture something of the primordial and constitutive alienation that Lacan takes to characterize human being.

Logically the two assertions are convertible into two others without loss or change of meaning:

(2) $\exists x$ $\overline{\Phi x}$ $\overline{\exists x}$ $\overline{\Phi x}$ (3)

(1) $\forall x$ Φx $\overline{\forall x}$ Φx (4)

Proposition (3) reads: there is no x that is not Φ. Proposition (4) reads: not all x is Φ. The two together reproduce the same universe as the first pair, generating a law on the one hand (that everything is submitted to

6. But one does well to note the French here: "On s'y range, en somme, par choix— libre aux femmes de s'y placer si ça leur fait plaisir" (*E,* p. 67). This last qualification is hardly neutral, and Rose's rendering "if they so choose" papers over a potential abyss in Lacan's remarks on feminine sexuality: sexual identity may be "conventional," but if that convention in its turn depends on one's pleasure, everything seems to dissolve back into mere nature after all.

the phallus) and its more individuated contrary (something is exempt) on the other—"I is an other, but I'm still me somewhere . . . " The two systems are logically equivalent. Lacan, however, insists on scanning each proposition separately—he does not, that is, handle them logically. He would, for example, have us remark that the Law formulated in (1) is universally quantified (∀), whereas in (3) it is given existentially (∃) and then doubly negated. If we simply read the things aloud, we read them differently.

This table is intended to chart a universe of sexual difference, and it should come as no or small surprise that if one "chooses" to inscribe oneself as "woman," one is going to find herself caught up with propositions (3) and (4) rather than (1) and (2). Since there is no logical difference here and no room for any question of biological difference, what there is of sexual difference has to do with how one inscribes oneself or is inscribed within this system of contraries and equivalents. Lacan treats his propositions as, in effect, dialectically charged: the "bars" over the various elements are understood less as simple logical negations than as quasi-Hegelian determinate negations. These formulas are no more subject to properly logical handling than Lacan's apparent fractions are subject to properly arithmetic manipulation. These things are not the stuff of which syllogisms are made. I will eventually say something about what they are made of, but for the moment I want to dwell somewhat longer on what they are trying to say.

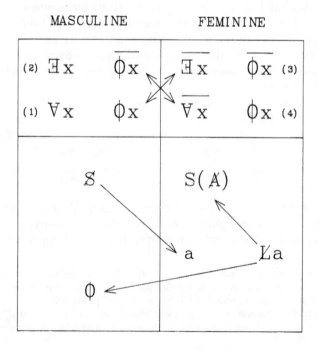

This is the full table as given by Lacan.[7] Some of the notation may be familiar: $ indicates, as elsewhere in Lacan, the subject in its radical inaccessibility; the *a* is, as always, the object of desire; and Φ is the phallus. The *a* is further specified in *Encore* as the *plus-de-jouir*, which might be rendered "the more-than-enjoyment-of" but might also be rendered as "the end" or "the no-more-of-pleasure"; the two possibilities conspire toward a reassertion of the object of desire as it holds itself—is constituted—beyond any possible satisfaction as well as beyond any conceivable coincidence of pleasure and utility. The place of the Other is marked by A, and the S indicates the signifier of that place, a place which is itself barred, uninhabitable, a hole or loss that can only be signified: S(A̶). L̶a is L̶a Femme, Woman.

The upper and lower parts of the table can be thought of as overlying one another so that $ answers to or covers the proposition (2) $\exists x \overline{\Phi x}$ just as Φ answers to (1) $\forall x \; \Phi x$. That is, the barred and impossible subject is the same exception to the phallic law that (4) $\overline{\forall x} \; \Phi x$ is to (3) $\overline{\exists x} \; \overline{\Phi x}$: in each couple the opposition is between the Law on the one hand and the claim to an exceptional reserve of subjectivity on the other. The opposite side of the table shows a similar set of duplications, S(A̶) echoing (3) $\overline{\exists x} \; \overline{\Phi x}$, and L̶a responding to (4) $\overline{\forall x} \; \Phi x$. Following out the full network of correspondences leads to an implicit equation of Φ and S(A̶) insofar as both are formulations of the Law. (In the better known Schema R this identity is marked in the lower right corner.)

If this attempt to read by symmetries is valid, it follows that $ and L̶a are the "same" in the way that Φ and S(A̶) are and that the various corresponding propositions are. In particular, both $ and L̶a are sites of the claim to radical subjectivity and exception to the Law. They differ in their grammar: the masculine position, $, is existentially quantified—"There is . . . " or, for our purposes, "I, really, am . . ."—while the position labeled feminine is universally quantified—"all . . . " Further, the first proposition is positive and direct: "I am (not this)," while the second is negative: "Not all are . . . " We could say then that the masculine position is one that thinks—poses—itself punctually and directly: "I am" (for example) "not a slave"; whereas the reserve of feminine subjectivity asserts itself only mediately, through a unity which it is not: "Not all women are slaves (and I am not all)." It is this "not-all," *pas-tout*, that Lacan takes to define woman.

The L̶a of L̶a Femme is then barred precisely because that which would be La Femme (unbarred) defines itself from the outset as *pas-tout*, not-all. As if to say: women cannot be thought except by thinking Woman;

7. See *FS*, p. 149; *E*, p. 73. I have added a bit to Lacan's diagram—numbers identifying various propositions, connections between logical equivalents in the upper part, and the labels "masculine" and "feminine."

but to think Woman ("as such") is to fail to think women, who are, precisely, not-Woman. The *pas-tout* can be appropriated as an essentialist notion—Luce Irigaray seems to do this—but Lacan's point seems both intended and most powerful as a grammatical remark, a means of diagnosing the ambiguities and contradictions that may arise within any discussion of gender.[8]

The logic of feminine inscription described by Lacan demands reference to an other, not as the object of desire, *a*, but as radically other, A, and even S($\cancel{A}$), the Other for which there is no other, a hole or whole that can only be signified:

> Nothing can be said of the woman. The woman relates to S($\cancel{A}$), which means that she is already doubled, and is not all, since on the other hand she can also relate to Φ. [*FS*, p. 152][9]

In a sense there is then nothing special about woman, which is why nothing can be said of her—we are all *né(e)s pas tout(e)s, hommelettes* all. But it is also the case that $\cancel{L}$a Femme, the subject to which a woman would lay claim, is submitted peculiarly to the Phallus and the Law, doubly and in division: the claim can never be punctual, is always already detoured.

In addressing here the way in which beings that speak, human beings, construct themselves as sexual in the absence of any immediate determination, in addressing the way in which such beings are engendered, Lacan is implicitly talking about how we come to our pleasure and, more particularly, about how a woman comes to hers. He is talking about *la jouissance de la femme, la jouissance de $\cancel{L}$a Femme.*

> There is a *jouissance* proper to her, to this "her" which does not exist and which signifies nothing. There is a *jouissance* proper to her and of which she herself may know nothing, except that she experiences it—that much she does know. She knows it of course when it happens.

Lacan goes on to disparage those

> petty considerations about clitoral orgasm or the *jouissance* designated as best one can, the other one precisely, which I am trying

8. See Luce Irigaray, *Ce Sexe qui n'est pas un* (Paris, 1977); see also Rose's introduction to *FS*, pp. 53–55.

9. "Rien ne peut se dire de la femme. La femme a rapport à S($\cancel{A}$) et c'est en cela déjà qu'elle se dédouble, qu'elle n'est pas toute, puisque, d'autre part, elle peut avoir rapport avec Φ" (*E*, p. 75). I have altered the symbols in the English translation to correspond to those in the original, which I use throughout this essay.

to get you to along the path of logic, since, to date, there is no other. [*FS*, pp. 145–46][10]

An Other Orgasm belongs, then, to the grammar of feminine pleasure—the grammar through which a sexuality that, as such, does not exist (that is, is not given in nature) is nonetheless deployed. If the physiologists and sexologists cannot find this Other Orgasm, there is no reason why they should; and if they do find it, they cannot know what they have found. No such discovery will make it central, other than other.

The masculine side of things is, on Lacan's account, no less divided in its pleasures—but the division is differently registered, as a certain Don Juanism, the pursuit, more or less, of another orgasm. The diagram we have been working from thus divides $\cancel{L}$a between Φ and S($\cancel{A}$) while the line of sexual difference divides $\cancel{S}$ from its object in a.[11] Shoshana Felman and Marie Balmary have in different ways recently explored the effects of this Don Juanism on the structure of psychoanalytic knowledge.[12]

For Lacan the question of orgasm is not answerable apart from the abstraction of his diagrams. What Fletcher called "the reality of our actions" Lacan knows only as the Real of our actions—and the Real is a register of psychoanalytic sense and not a brute fact on which one could take one's stand.[13] Faced with the desire that psychoanalysis should have some orgasmic bedrock, Lacan runs full tilt the other way:

> What was tried at the end of the last century, at the time of Freud, by all kinds of worthy people in the circle of Charcot and the rest, was an attempt to reduce the mystical to questions of fucking. If you look carefully, this is not what it is all about. Might not this *jouissance* which one experiences and knows nothing of, be that which puts us on the path of ex-istence? And why not interpret one face of the Other, the God face, as supported by feminine *jouissance*?
>
> In other words, it is not by chance that Kierkegaard discovered existence in a little tale of seduction. . . . This desire for a good at

---

10. " . . . parce que jusqu'à nouvel ordre, il n'y en a pas d'autre" (*E*, p. 69).

11. I take it that one is free to read this diagram as a pictogram of the sexual act as well.

12. See Shoshana Felman, *Le scandale du corps parlant: Don Juan avec Austin, ou, la séduction en deux langues* (Paris, 1980), and Marie Balmary, *Psychoanalyzing Psychoanalysis: Freud and the Hidden Fault of the Father,* trans. Ned Lukacher (Baltimore, 1982).

13. Lacan's interest in Borromean knots lies precisely in their ability to model the kind of mutual imbrication he sees holding between the three registers of the Imaginary, Symbolic, and Real; and the model in its turn makes clear the unavailability as ground of the Real.

one remove, a good not caused by a *petit a,* perhaps it was through the intermediary of Régine that he came to it. [*FS,* pp. 147–48][14]

3

If we have reached a point from which we can say that the feminine orgasm is somehow grounded through Kierkegaard in God, we are perhaps well enough prepared for the more orthodox Freudian insight that everything we take to be meaning reaches downward into sex. We are interested in this notion because we want to understand the status of the propositions to which Lacan has recourse in his account of feminine sexuality. If we have been examining orgasm, *jouissance,* the logic of pleasure, we want now to look at diagrams, mathemes, the spider in his web of words—*jouis-sens,* the pleasure of logic.

When Lacan offers his seminar the table of sexual difference, he warns that "after what I have just put up on the board for you, you might think that you know it all" (*FS,* p. 149). The burden of the warning seems to be that if we want psychoanalysis to know something for us, to give us something we can copy down and carry away, then what it will know is sex, and, knowing that, we will think we know it all. But sex is not where you think it is, and in the end you know nothing, psychoanalysis least of all. This is to say that we desire before we know, that we desire to know, and that our knowings are inscribed already within the psychoanalytic field in such a way that we know nothing until we have submitted our desire to know to analysis. So opens the structural trap proper to psychoanalysis: its claim to science and knowledge must be passed through its own critique of the desire of science.

We can put this either as a question of theory and epistemology or as a problem about the formation of the analyst. I am going to follow it here primarily as a theoretical matter with only an occasional glance at the question of training. I take it that the central issue for teaching and training must be whether the analyst is to be formed through the reception of a knowledge or through the acknowledgment of a desire. If we opt for the latter, we are left asking how that acknowledgment is to be accomplished except on the basis of a privileged knowledge derived from psychoanalysis.[15]

---

14. *E,* p. 71. Whatever the theological stakes here—and I don't doubt that for Lacan they are substantial—it should not go unremarked that the fiction appealed to here is epistolary, a matter of letters.

15. On the general topic of Lacan's teaching see Catherine Clement, *Vie et légendes de Jacques Lacan* (Paris, 1981); Stuart Schneiderman, *Jacques Lacan: The Death of an Intellectual Hero* (Cambridge, Mass., 1983); François Roustang, *Dire Mastery: Discipleship from Freud to Lacan,* trans. Ned Lukacher (Baltimore, 1982); Roustang, *Psychoanalysis Never Lets Go,* trans. Lukacher (Baltimore, 1983); and Turkle, *Psychoanalytic Politics.*

Both ways of setting the problem ultimately lead to the same task: psychoanalysis is called upon to provide itself with a theory of discourse as it is variously subtended by knowledge and desire. This is one of the projects of *Encore,* and Lacan has another chart to lay out his theory of discursive modes.[16] It looks like this:

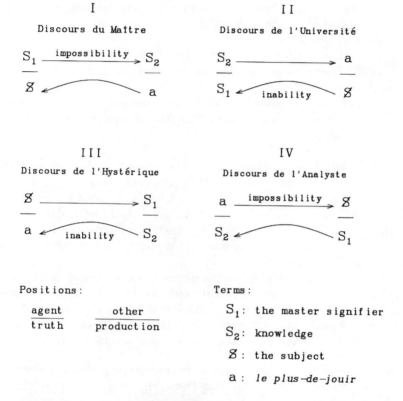

I

Discours du Maître

II

Discours de l'Université

III

Discours de l'Hystérique

IV

Discours de l'Analyste

Positions:

agent	other
truth	production

Terms:

S_1: the master signifier

S_2: knowledge

$\mathcal{S}$: the subject

a: *le plus-de-jouir*

Although the S/s notation may look familiar enough at first glance, a second glance will show that it is being used in neither linguistic nor arithmetic senses, however attenuated. The distinction of places and terms suggests that we are being given a species of grammatical template. I suggest that the abstract form reads something like this:

> The (impossibility of the) relation of speaker to receiver is supported by the (failure of the) production of truth.

The parentheses stake out two possible positions of negation: either the relation between speaker and receiver is impossible, or its possibility is

16. This table is adapted from *E,* p. 21. Mitchell and Rose offer a summary in a long note to their selection from *Encore;* see *FS,* pp. 160–61.

supported by a certain failure in the production of truth. On this basis we might attempt some translations:

> I. The impossibility of the master's communicating knowledge to the other is supported by the other's production of him or her self as inaccessible truth.
>
> II. The possibility of communicating knowledge to the other is supported by the inability of the subject to produce his or her master-signifier as truth.
>
> III. The subject's location of master-signification in the place of the other depends on the inability of knowledge to locate pleasure in the place of truth.
>
> IV. The impossibility of the analyst's attaining to the radical truth of the subject is supported by the master-signifier's production of knowledge in the place of truth.

I will not dwell on either the relative opacity of these translations or the equivocations grace of which they have been constructed (although we will see in the end that such equivocation, such need for voicing, is essential to Lacan's project). I want instead to look particularly closely at the last of them, since it is the discourse of the analyst to which Lacan devoted most of his energy and which thus offers the best case for testing and elaborating these translations.

We know, for example, that the discourse of the analyst is for Lacan the discourse of "the one-who-is-supposed-to-know" (*l'un supposé savoir*)— that is, of the one who is taken to have true knowledge, knowledge in the place of truth. Using the terms and places of the table, the analyst appears as $\frac{a}{S_2} \rightarrow$. And this analyst has as a goal producing in the patient a recognition of the relation between what insists opaquely and powerfully in his or her discourse and the knowledge it conceals or denies: $\rightarrow \frac{\$}{S_1}$ S_2 . It should be clear that we are now in the process of creating something that is in many respects a rewrite of (IV), but which could also be reduced to a simpler form:

$$\frac{a}{S_2} \rightarrow \frac{\$}{S_1}$$

This is the form in which it appears later in *Encore*.

As we play in and on such notations, they shift and throw different aspects of Lacanian theory and practice into the light. The difference between, for example, (IV) and its layered reconstruction ought to show something of what it means for—in the Lacanian catchphrase—the sender to receive his message from the receiver in inverted form. So the play

here between $\mathbb{S}$, S_1, and S_2 also ought to show us something of the radically and necessarily intersubjective dimensions of what we are perhaps more accustomed to seeing as a stack of signifiers displaying the metaphorical structure of repression, that is, $\underline{S'}$.[17]
$$\frac{S}{x}$$

Just as we can reduce (IV) to a simpler form, we can also expand it into greater complexity:

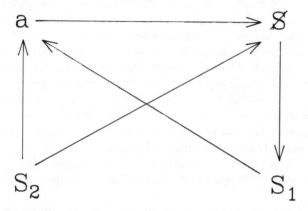

If this expansion is right (and it may not be: it is my derivation from some parallel algorithms in *Télévision* which I will consider shortly)—if this expansion is right, then we can recognize in the curved lines in Lacan's table of discursive modes (the supports for his bridge of discourse) a shorthand for a more complex interaction in which otherness is so inmixed that it only, as it were, averages into an interaction of two people facing one another.

I do not want to work through the other figures in the table in any detail here, but we do need to pause at least briefly over the discourse of the master. As I understand Lacan's table, the master is defined as the one who is capable of fully taking up into signification the radical truth of subjectivity. He is in this way an inversion of the hysteric in (III). If the patient is the one who is spoken by the Unconscious, the master is the one we place in the position of speaking the Unconscious—Lacan can be *heard* as *le maître*. The master is one who is heard, and is heard

---

17. This stack of signifiers can be made visible in Schema R by following Lacan's remarks in "On a Question Preliminary to Any Possible Treatment of Psychosis," *Ecrits: A Selection*, trans. Alan Sheridan (New York, 1977), p. 233 n. 18, which suggest that the schema is to be read as the flattening out of the figure that would be obtained by deforming the surface so that the lower right corner overlies the upper left. This figure would be a Moebius strip. It is worth noting that Lacan's psychoanalysis so mixes "self" and "other" that the mappings of "intersubjective discourse" and of "intrapsychic agencies" are just transformations of one another.

by the one who places knowledge in the place of the other and so makes of that other the producer of truth. The discourse of the master—as Lacan both argues and illustrates—represents a special risk for the teaching and practice of psychoanalysis. Insofar as the analyst represents himself—or allows himself to be represented—as the holder of the key to the subjectivity of the analysand (who then knows himself only from and as that other), the analyst ends as the master, shaping the patient's self in inevitable conformity with his own.

There is a complicity between the discourse of the university and that of the master. The glyph S_2/S_1 in the university figure offers the possibility of a transparent scientific knowledge that, in its turn, positions the bearer of that knowledge as the master $(S_1/\$)$. Lacan wanted in the long run to close off this dream of transparency, radically distinguishing the discourse of psychoanalysis from that of the university, in part to widen the gap between the analyst and the master. To mistake psychoanalysis for that kind of science is to mistake the analyst for that kind of knowing subject. It is in the face of this dream of science that Lacan will insist, frustratingly and problematically, that science is for him just "what is done with little letters"—nothing more or less. Lacan's fascination with the theory of the mathemes (if "theory" is the proper word) emerges here.

The table of discursive modes is complete only on the assumption that the terms are not freely substitutable through the places. That is, it is constructed by rotating a chain, a closed loop, through the system of places. This chain is S_1–S_2–a–$\$$–S_1 . . . This means that each of these discourses tends to turn into the other, or that all discourse tends to turn through the system without any subject being the master of it (including, of course and above all, he who would speak as master).[18] The entire system could be described as a charting of the vicissitudes of any attempt to find one's proper and fully meaningful name—one's final signifier, one's meaning, the end of one's desire, one's deepest self: a self that invariably turns back into one's signifier, at once escaping and imprisoning itself.

These structures are radically complex. They work at the level of intersubjectivity and are concerned with the manner in which the logic of intersubjectivity "speaks" those caught up in it. "I" cannot choose to be the master; perhaps more important, I cannot choose not to speak—not to be heard in any case—as the master. The circuit of these structures is a description of the Symbolic order and, like the meditation on Markov chains appended to the "Seminar on 'The Purloined Letter,'" it can can be read as intended to account for the way in which a destiny inevitably captures us, putting us always in our place.

18. Mitchell and Rose trace this chain back to the unpublished 1969–70 seminar *L'envers de la psychanalyse;* see *FS,* p. 160 n. 6.

4

We are left then with the matter of the little letters, the mathemes that have become the passwords of contemporary Lacanian orthodoxy. Much of the discussion after Lacan's 1975 lecture at Yale seems to have turned on Lacan's view of the nature of the psychoanalytic claim to scientific status, and the discussion seems to have been as frustrating to that audience or parts of it as his remarks at Johns Hopkins ten years earlier had been to some there. The definition on which he insisted is: "Science is that which holds itself in its relation to the real by virtue of the use of little letters."[19] He clung to this throughout the ensuing discussion, ending with the following exchange:

> DUPRÉ: But that's the problem. What is the exact status of the symbolism of the mathemes? Is it a universal symbolism or a . . .
> LACAN: It is a symbolism elaborated, always elaborated, by means of letters.
> HARTMAN: But *quid* of words? Even if analytic science contains mathemes, there is the question of practice and of the translation of such mathemes in analytic practice, which is verbal, isn't it?
> LACAN: There is nevertheless a world between the word and the letter.
> HARTMAN: But it is their link that you want to show . . .
> LACAN: Yes, and that amuses me. ["KS," pp. 30–31]

At issue here is the science Lacan would oppose to the mistaken Freudian dream of thermodynamics and with which he would return psychoanalysis to its place. There are, I think, two points to be remarked right away. The first is that Lacan's science is, here, a matter of pleasure, of *ce qui m'amuse* and, I would suggest, even of *jouissance.* What has to be said of the mathemes is not separable from what Lacan says elsewhere of the signifying chains that constitute the Unconscious:

> These chains are not of *sens* but of *jouis-sens,* to write as you please in conformity with the equivocation that composes the law of the signifier.[20]

Our problem is to engage this equivocation at the level at which the signifier, the little letter, pretends—both claims and feigns—to formalize psychoanalytic theory.

---

19. "Kanzer Seminar," *Scilicet* 6/7 (1976): 26. All further references to this work, abbreviated "KS," will be included in the text; all translations are mine.
20. Lacan, *Télévision* (Paris, 1974), p. 22; my translation.

The second point is implicit in what may well appear as the childishness with which Lacan approaches the whole business. There is something in the way he talks about the mathemes and his little letters that has all the naiveté of a child's imitation of the incomprehensible activity of the adults around him. Lacan knows this well enough.

> I tried to write a certain formula, that I expressed as well as I could, with a big S which represents the subject and which has to be barred ($), then a little sign (◊) and finally an (a). The whole put in parentheses. It is an attempt to imitate science. Because I think that science can begin only in that way. ["KS," p. 26][21]

If we look back at how we have handled the various little letters Lacan has sent us, it should be clear that they bear little relation to any normal project of scientific mathesis. Lacan rips off bits of this and that, giving us "notations" that have a certain validity within a highly restricted region. The manipulations to which they are submitted appear radically unprincipled, and their relevant features vary from the highly formal to the crudely pictorial. There is no ground for suspecting the existence of a systematic Lacanian algebra of some kind behind the various mathemes and charts. He is not dreaming that dream. He is dreaming a more dreamerly dream, in *ein anderer Schauplatz*, in which it is important precisely that these letters are ripped off, displaced, borrowed, imitative.

Lacan means his little letters to function as letters in the strictest of senses, as material supports for meanings or as pure signifiers.[22] In *Encore* he says—or writes—

> La formalisation mathématique est notre but, notre idéal. Pourquoi?—parce que seule elle est mathème, c'est-à-dire capable de transmettre intégralement. La formalisation mathématique, c'est de l'écrit, mais qui ne subsiste que si j'emploie à le présenter la langue dont j'use. C'est là qu'est l'objection—nullé formalisation de la langue n'est transmissible sans l'usage de la langue elle-même. C'est par mon dire que cette formalisation, idéal métalanguage, je la fais ex-sister. [*E*, p. 108]

21. This paper has left unexplored Lacan's application of the notion of *jouissance* to the jubilation of the mirror-stage infant in his anticipation of bodily unity; something of this sense is at work here.

22. The notion of the "pure signifier" is the impossible cornerstone of Lacanian theory, and the constellation of this notion with questions of feminine sexuality, psychosis, and the nature of psychoanalytic science seems to me fixed at least as early as the 1955–56 seminar, *Les psychoses*, 1955–56, Le Seminaire, vol. 3 (Paris, 1981). The "pure signifier" is the essential object of Jacques Derrida's critique in "Le facteur de la vérité" in *La carte postale: de Socrate à Freud et au-delà* (Paris, 1980), translated as "The Purveyor of Truth," *Yale French Studies* 52 (1975).

Mathematical formalization is our goal, our ideal. Why?—
because only it is mathemic, that is, capable of transmitting integrally.
Mathematical formalization is writing, but writing that subsists only
if I use and use up my language in presenting it. That is where
the objection arises—no formalization of language is transmissible
without the use of language itself. It is through my speech that I
make this formalization, this ideal metalanguage, come into existence. [My translation]

We have remarked that there is no logical difference between Lacan's
masculine and feminine fields of inscription; such of sexual difference
as there is insists in our reading of the logical negations that circumscribe
the table of contraries within which we live. *Encore* defines the Unconscious
as, above all, *ce qui lit,* that which reads, and we are now saying—and
Lacan is saying, in 1972–73, at a certain point in his career, in a context
in which transmission has come to matter, in which he means to post
these letters—that the little letters are, precisely, letters that must be
read. The claim seems then to be that such letters, being read, cannot
but reach their destinations. These little letters are "pure signifiers" capable
of meaning or transmitting everything precisely because in their purity
they mean nothing—apart from Lacan's voice. The flip side of this,
willingly avowed by Lacan at Yale, is that "we have no way of knowing
if the Unconscious exists outside of psychoanalysis" ("KS," p. 25) (and I
take it the ambiguities of this formulation are to be embraced).

Formalization matters to Lacan not because it offers a way for psychoanalysis to attain the condition of mathematics (or to attain the condition
of a certain ideal of mathematics) but precisely because psychoanalysis
is unable to do so: it inevitably falls back into, is dependent upon, mere
language and voice, tangled in the circuits of desire and the particularities
of the psychoanalytic object. The mathemes are a means of making visible
the "pure signifier" as that which organizes a "science" the objectivity of
which is disciplinary and hermeneutic, operating in a region apart from,
untouched by, and proofed against traditional discussions of the scientific
standing of psychoanalysis.

We thus enter a universe in which logic does not act as a guarantee
of truth; instead truth acts to guarantee the comprehensibility of logic
(a Heideggerian kind of universe, then), harnessing the letter into a
dialectic whose very openness is its best guarantee of closure. "La lettre,
ça se lit," Lacan writes—but this writing is already read, needs no reading
from us, and is enclosed in pure self-affection. Lacan's Unconscious,
even in its other place, reads itself with all the transparency of the *Phenomenology*'s Spirit, whose speculative logic *Encore* at once replicates and
inverts.

With this the prospect of metalanguage collapses, leaving in its stead
a problem of imitation and a vision of psychoanalysis as only infinitely

prospective and subjunctive science—*un discours qui ne serait pas du semblant,* as the title of an unpublished seminar has it. This may tempt us to a mathemic "neographism" of our own—*le discours analytique*—and this in its turn may lead us to recognize that Lacan's science is adequately described as *pas-tout,* its truth elusively and familiarly figured as woman, everywhere and nowhere, not-all. It is in the literal coincidence of *jouissance* and *jouis-sens* that psychoanalysis contains itself:

> Le but, c'est que la jouissance s'avoue, et justement en ceci qu'elle peut être inavouable. . . . la jouissance ne s'interpelle, ne s'évoque, ne se traque, ne s'élabore qu'à partir d'un semblant. [*E,* p. 85]

> The goal is that the *jouissance* avow itself and precisely in this— that it may be unavowable. . . . *Jouissance* is not called forth or evoked or hunted down or elaborated and celebrated except through a semblance. [My translation]

Early in *Encore* Lacan writes that

> ce qu'on appelle la jouissance sexuelle est marqué, dominé, par l'impossibilité d'établir comme tel, nulle part dans l'énonçable, ce seul Un qui nous intéresse, l'Un de la relation *rapport sexuel.* [*E,* p. 13]

> What we call *la jouissance sexuelle* is marked, dominated, by the impossibility of establishing as such, anywhere in the enunciable, that Unity which uniquely interests us, the Unity of the sexual relationship. [My translation]

We can—and must—read this now as a statement about what we are entitled to call *le jouis-sens scientifique* as well; and when Lacan goes on to write that the "signifier is the cause of *jouissance* . . . the signifier is what puts an end to *jouissance,*" we should see that these assertions are reversible (*E,* p. 27; my translation). *Jouissance/jouis-sens* names the limits of psychoanalysis and marks out that impasse of formalization in which psychoanalysis claims to find itself and its proper theoretical world.

> C'est là que le réel se distingue. Le réel ne saurait s'inscrire que d'une impasse de la formalisation. . . . Cette formalisation mathématique de la signifiance se fait au contraire du sens, j'allais presque dire à *contre-sens.* [*E,* p. 85]

> It is thus that the real is distinguished. The real cannot be inscribed except as an impasse of formalization. . . . This mathematical formalization of signification is accomplished against the grain of sense—I very nearly said à *contre-sens*—the wrong way, by misinterpretation, absurdly. [My translation]

Lacan elsewhere characterizes the Real as an impasse of the pleasure principle. Most commonly, however, he speaks of the Real in terms of its "fullness" and defines it as "that which always comes back to the same place."[23] What we have to see here is that this apparent invocation of place amounts in fact to the eradication of the notion of place itself ("There is no topology that does not have to be supported by some artifice"[24]). Psychoanalysis, *pas-tout*, finds itself in place everywhere, *partout*, and so claims to master itself without bound or limit—not so much out of as beyond all place.

5

I have said that this problematic of enjoymeant becomes explicit at a certain moment in Lacan's career and in relation to a certain interest.[25] One might note also that it emerges under a title—*Encore*—that seems to remark a certain perturbation within Lacan's project of return, as if it were no longer clear whether psychoanalysis en core and psychoanalysis encore, the thing and the return to it, converge or diverge. I suggest that what is happening is that Lacan is discovering himself to be read, exposed beyond the reach of his voice, his signifiers not waiting upon his *dire*. This is perhaps most explicit in his concern with Philippe Lacoue-Labarthe and Jean-Luc Nancy's *Le Titre de la lettre* (a text whose mere existence seems to threaten Lacan's carefully nurtured distinction between those who are and those who are not of his audience), barely veiled in his worries about the reading and readability of the Unconscious, and implicit in all the phrasings and worries that work to present *Encore* as

23. See Lacan, *The Four Fundamental Concepts of Psycho-analysis*, trans. Sheridan (New York, 1978) pp. 49, 167.

24. Lacan, *Four Fundamental Concepts*, p. 209; see also the useful translator's note, pp. 279–80.

25. It has been suggested to me that Lacan's interest in the mathemes was fueled by a highly ironized game between himself and the mathematical logician Georg Kreisel, opening up yet another region in which *les non-dupes errent*. This is certainly in line with my reading of the standing of these things, and I would suggest that the game is now being played out, stripped of its irony, in the claims of Jacques-Alain Miller. Readers less easily daunted than myself might want to look at Kreisel and Jean Louis Krivine, *Elements of Mathematical Logic (Model Theory)* (Amsterdam, 1967); Kreisel's evident foundationalist antipositivism, engagement with the "structuralist" work of Bourbaki, and friendship with Raymond Queneau are all likely to make him of interest to Lacan. One might note Kreisel's description of his work as a reformulation and analysis of "intuitive" or "informal" mathematics:

This reformulation is only a tool in the study of foundations; depending essentially, as does any description of an intuitively understood subject, on our conception of the objects described: it is only from this point of view, i.e., that of meaning, that the formal language expresses correctly the assertions of informal mathematics, since, from the point of view of external form, formal and informal language have (fortunately!) very little in common. [*Elements*, p. 160]

marking a certain ending.[26] In *Encore* Lacan is receiving not himself but his reception—his reception by Derrida most particularly. This reception mimes the circularity of the letter, exemplifying and contesting the impossible truth of Lacanian notions of communication (we need neither simply Lacan nor simply Derrida to understand this; we need their argument).

It is tempting to say that Lacan's reception cannot exist outside his movement of return, that he has himself no real property to pass on, having had but the usufruct, the enjoyment, the *jouissance* of Freud and of psychoanalysis. Here I am again reading *Encore,* in a certain sense and from a certain distance—the distance perhaps of reverie, perhaps of a certain floating attention. I am reading above all its opening pages, which tangle together considerations of the end of teaching, the end of analysis, and the law school setting in which Lacan speaks. I suppose I am taking this seminar as a will.[27] These opening pages offer the seminar's first use of the word *jouissance:* it is a legal use, and with it questions of inheritance, reception, and return are routed and rerouted by sexual difference. We might note, for example, that it is above all men who bequeath. (That is why we have the word "posthumous," born after the death of the father—it points to a difficulty in the structure of inheritance; although it may bear remarking the derivation from *post*—"after" and *humare*— "to bury" is a folk construct, the original form in fact being *posthumus,* the superlative of "post-".)

Kant points out in *The Metaphysical Elements of Justice* that "the rank of nobility is inherited by male descendants and is also acquired by their wives who are not nobly born. However, a woman born to the nobility does not convey her rank to a husband not nobly born; instead she herself returns to the class of common citizens (the people)."[28] This is one more version of *la jouissance de la femme* and a lesson in the enjoyment of women. *Encore*'s elaboration of *jouissance, la jouissance de la femme,* and the *jouissens* of psychoanalysis now seems a way of returning Lacan's psychoanalytic property to him, an elision of legacy in which woman may figure as aim but self is finally the goal—nothing is given away.[29]

The post-Kantian is, we might say, alien to Kant. He does not participate in it. It is left to his survivors. Hegel, later, numbering himself among his own survivors, receives his own legacy and makes an issue of the belatedness of his work ("Philosophy in any case always comes on the scene too late. . . . The owl of Minerva spreads its wings only with

26. Philippe Lacoue-Labarthe and Jean-Luc Nancy, *Le Titre de la lettre: une lecture de Lacan* (Paris, 1973). Lacan refers explicitly to this book in *E,* pp. 62–63.

27. My project thus arises in the wake of Derrida's reading of the Freudian legacy as it is inscribed in *Beyond the Pleasure Principle;* see "Spéculer—sur 'Freud' " in *La carte postale.*

28. Immanuel Kant, *The Metaphysical Elements of Justice,* trans. John Ladd (Indianapolis, 1965), p. 96.

29. On this distinction, see Lacan, *Four Fundamental Concepts,* pp. 174–86.

the falling of the dusk"[30]). He survives himself and makes that mean that he survives philosophy as well: we might call certain of his works posthumous. Thinking about Kant and Hegel we may be tempted to say that Kant, holding himself to the philosopher's business of argument, meant to move always toward philosophy. If he made any discovery about himself, it would have been that in his preliminaries he was in fact already there. Hegel, in contrast, wrote, and discovered himself in rereading, finding that in attempting to be there, in philosophy, he was already past it. Pre- and post-: philosophy somehow slips between, done by no one at no time, its place increasingly its problem.

Usufruct is all but inconceivable for Hegel as he constructs his *Philosophy of Right* on the far side of the Napoleonic divide. He can see in it only an "insanity of the personality" because, he writes, " 'mine' as applied to a single object would have to mean the direct presence in it of both my single exclusive will and also the single exclusive will of someone else."[31] The thought of usufruct seems to demand something like an unconscious, and family, property, and selfhood knot together in Hegel's text against such thoughts, pledging us to lucidity. It is in Hegel's wake, as Hegel's readers, that we are driven to think again about the enjoyment of science, the complexity of our disciplines and objectivities.

Modern philosophers, post-Hegelian philosophers, caught in this cleft, are obliged to their own reception. We—or they (reception confounds these terms)—divide their careers: the early Nietzsche and the late, Heidegger I and Heidegger II, the Wittgenstein of the *Tractatus* and the other Wittgenstein, the one who, like Heidegger II, may be no longer a philosopher if not yet a poet. Post-Heideggerian seems just to mean Heideggerian—but not the way post-Aristotelian means Aristotelian; the first has time inside it in a way the second does not (Heidegger, like Wittgenstein, like Nietzsche, participates in his own legacy, breaking with himself, mourning that self, that work).[32]

We might think to escape the closure of the system's interlocking circular syllogisms by writing our science on a Moebius strip. Writing so, we would think to name our post-Hegelian modernity, our slippage from ourselves; Lacan has without doubt been one of the great theorists of this complexity. The science he would capture in the space of *jouissance/jouis-sens* means to be adequate to this modernity.

It is perhaps a mark of Lacan's difference from philosophy (and of his ambition to it—his mode, then, of assuming its legacy) that he divides

30. G. W. F. Hegel, *Hegel's Philosophy of Right,* trans. T. M. Knox (Oxford, 1952), pp. 12–13.

31. Ibid., p. 50.

32. Inheritance, we might note, is a mode of translation (this is a point of Roman law as well as a fact of literary history), and we do not, for example, know what in "deconstruction" is to be taken as legacy and what as translation, or what the relations might be between legator and legatee, translator and translated, Heidegger and Derrida.

himself not as father and son, legator and legatee, but otherwise, as masculine and feminine, catching himself between legacy and return, and so recovering himself from his reception. This is a strange movement, folding filiation back into alliance and working to render Lacan essentially irreceivable.[33] The inevitable failure of this movement is at once obvious and elusive, inherent in the simple act of reading. This is perhaps why Lacan in his seminar seems so puzzled by the mixture of accuracy and critique in *Le Titre de la lettre*.

If this reverie, in its general cast and rhythm, seems loosely deconstructive, what should then be of interest is that the Derridian exists above all as a reading, a remarking, of the Lacanian—exists only as an exposure of its irrecuperable *readability*, its permanent openness to our placement and displacement. Our enjoyment of Lacan's letters always exceeds and wastes them, and in so doing re-marks them with the temporality they claimed to master, showing the Lacanian always unfolded into the post-Lacanian, the psychoanalytic always caught outside itself, in another place, unable to guarantee its self-enclosure, unable ever fully to fold its family back into itself. If there is a moral to this, it is, I suppose, first of all that Lacan's mathemes offer no support for an idea of psychoanalysis as an axiomatizable science and that to take them as such is only to mystify the more difficult and deeply problematic claims Lacan is making—claims whose radical inwardness render the apparently simpler question of empirical evidence and support profoundly obscure. More generally, the moral is that we have psychoanalysis in its place, haunting the margins of our knowledge, only for so long as we contest, displace, and replace it—finding it not everywhere but always somewhere.

33. A subsidiary question at work here is whether or not there are "phases" in Lacan. It seems to me that there are not—not in the senses I have been meditating. No doubt there are changes of emphasis and formulation, but the interlinking of questions of feminine sexuality, psychosis, and the nature of science with the doctrine of a "pure signifier" which I take to define Lacanian psychoanalysis is in place from early on and *Encore* elaborates on but does not revise these formulations. What is to be remarked about *Encore*—and may ground our sense of something like a turn in Lacan's work around 1970—is its awareness that it will be read, and its determination to overmaster that prospect.

Withholding the Missing Portion:
Psychoanalysis and Rhetoric

Stanley Fish

I was led to this paper by two moments in the proceedings of the 1958 Style in Language Conference; they are moments in which the topic of persuasion is allowed to surface and then is immediately suppressed. The first such moment coincides with the only substantive mention of Freud at the conference. Roger Brown is discussing the resistance of cognitive psychologists to psychoanalytic procedure in which, it is feared, "anything can mean anything."[1] Brown replies, in apparent defense of psychoanalysis, that one must take into account the fact that its results are often persuasive, and if they are persuasive there must be a good reason. The reason, he suspects, is that psychoanalytic evidence, while not falling obviously into the linear and logical forms with which we are familiar, must nevertheless be speaking to the criteria by which we determine validity, so that at a certain point it must be the case that the accumulation of evidence reaches a level which satisfies those criteria and at that point persuasion occurs. But while Brown's argument acknowledges persuasion, it does so by robbing it of any independent force. Persuasion ceases to be a scandal if it is the programmed consequence of a mechanical calculation. A persuasion so defined is thoroughly domesticated and ceases to be a threat to the formal projects of linguistics and cognitive psychology.

The first three parts of this essay appeared most recently in *The Linguistics of Writing: Arguments between Language and Literature*, ed. Nigel Fabb et al. (New York, 1987). A new fourth section appears for the first time here.

1. Roger Brown, "From the Viewpoint of Psychology: Opening Statement," in *Style in Language*, ed. Thomas A. Sebeok (Cambridge, Mass., 1960), p. 385. Much of what follows was worked out in a series of team-taught classes with Michael Fried. Although it is always

The second moment at which the conference defends itself against the threat of persuasion occurs at the very end, after the last paper, in a discussion between the participants, a discussion one finds, if one finds it at all, in exceedingly small print. There, hidden from view lest it infect the entire volume, is a brief consideration of rhetoric. The topic is introduced by I. A. Richards, who declares that the questions so often debated at the conference, the questions of value and meaning, are finally rhetorical; it is a matter, he says, of the context of discourse and, as Isocrates observes, good discourse is discourse that works. The response is literally terror. C. S. Osgood protests that if the rhetorical view is accepted then even advertising can be thought of as good discourse, in fact, as the best discourse; and W. K. Wimsatt adds that if rhetorical standards have any relevance, it is only with reference to productions like "the speeches of Hitler during the last war." Confronted with the choice of standing either with Hitler or with Wimsatt, Richards does the right thing, and in a supremely rhetorical moment withdraws from the defense of rhetoric. "Mr. Wimsatt and I," he says, "are not in disagreement."

I have two epigraphs for this essay. The first is from James Strachey's editor's introduction to his translation of Freud's *Complete Introductory Lectures*. Freud, he says, was "never rhetorical" and was entirely opposed to laying down his view in an authoritarian fashion.[2] The second is a report by the Wolf-Man of what he thought to himself shortly after he met Freud for the first time: "this man is a Jewish swindler, he wants to use me from behind and shit on my head." This paper is dedicated to the proposition that the Wolf-Man got it right.

1

" 'I dreamt that it was night and that I was lying in my bed. . . . Suddenly the window opened of its own accord, and I was terrified to see that some white wolves were sitting on the big walnut tree in front of the window.' "[3] Thus begins Freud's account of the most famous dream in the literature of psychoanalysis, the centerpiece of his most famous case. Freud tells us that although the patient recalled the dream at a "very early stage of the

---

difficult to determine who contributed what in such situations, I think it fair to say that anything unpersuasive or insufficiently nuanced is wholly mine.

2. Sigmund Freud, *The Complete Introductory Lectures on Psychoanalysis*, ed. and trans. James Strachey (New York, 1966), pp. 5–6; further references to this work, abbreviated *CIL*, will be included in the text.

3. *The Wolf-Man by the Wolf-Man*, ed. Muriel Gardiner (New York, 1971), p. 173; further references to this work will be included in the text.

Stanley Fish is professor of English and law at Duke University. His most recent book is *Doing What Comes Naturally: Essays in Practice and the Practice of Theory.*

analysis," its "interpretation was a task that dragged on over several years" without notable success (p. 177). The breakthrough, as it is reported, came in an instant and apparently without preparation. "One day the patient began to continue with the interpretation of the dream. He thought that the part of the dream which said . . . 'suddenly the window opened of its own accord' was not completely explained." Immediately and without explanation, the explanation came forth: " 'It must mean: "My eyes suddenly opened." I was asleep, . . . and suddenly woke up, and as I woke up I saw something: the tree with the wolves' " (p. 179). It is important to note that the patient does not say, "Now I remember," but rather, "It *must* mean." His is not an act of recollection but of construction. The question I would ask—and it is a question that will take us far—is simply what is the content of "must"? What compels him to this particular interpretation among all those he might have hit upon? To this Freud's answer is "nothing," at least nothing external to the patient's own efforts. For a long time, Freud tells us, his young charge "remained . . . entrenched behind an attitude of obliging apathy"; he refused, that is, to "take an independent share in the work" (p. 157). It was this "shrinking from a self-sufficient existence" (p. 157) that stood in the way of a progress that could be realized only if he were to come out from behind the fortress of his lethargy, and we are invited to assume that this is what finally happens when he declares "It must mean." Clearly Freud is here not only characterizing his patient; he is also providing us with a scenario of the analysis in which both his and the patient's roles are carefully specified: the analyst waits patiently for the patient to begin to work on his own and suddenly "one day" his patience is rewarded.

There is, however, another scenario embedded in this same paragraph, and it is considerably less benign. The sentence in which one finds the phrase "independent share in the work" reads as follows: "It required a long education to persuade and induce him to take an independent share in the work" (p. 157). The sentence is obviously divided against itself, one half proclaiming an independence which in the other half is compromised when it is identified as the product of persuasion and force. That independence is further compromised when Freud reveals the method by which it has been "induced." At the moment when he saw that the patient's attachment to him had become strong enough to counterbalance his resistance, Freud announced that "the treatment must be brought to an end at a particular fixed date, no matter how far it had advanced" (p. 157). As it is delivered, the announcement would seem to indicate that Freud doesn't care whether or not "advancement" will occur, but in fact it is a device for assuring advancement, and for assuring it in a form he will approve.[4] What Freud *says* is "do as you like, it makes no difference

---

4. Freud has been much criticized for this strategy. On this point see Patrick J. Mahony, *Cries of the Wolf Man* (New York, 1984), p. 34, and Robert J. Langs, "Misalliance in the Wolf-man Case," in *Freud and His Patients,* ed. Mark Kanzer and Jules Glenn (New York and London, 1980), pp. 375–80.

to me." What he *means* is, "if you do not do as I like and do it at the time I specify, you will lose the satisfaction of pleasing me to whom I know you to be attached by the strongest of bonds because I forged them." The coercion could not be more obvious, and Freud does not shrink from naming it as an exercise of "inexorable pressure"; yet in the very same sentence he contrives to detach the pressure from the result it produces: "Under the inexorable pressure of the fixed limit [the patient's] resistance . . . gave way, and now in a disproportionately short time the analysis produced all the material which made it possible to clear up his inhibitions and remove his symptoms" (p. 157). Here the analysis is presented as if it were independent of the constraints that father it. At the end of the sentence the clearing up of inhibitions and the removal of symptoms appear as effects without a cause, natural phenomena that simply emerge in the course of their own time—the time, presumably, when the patient suddenly, and of his own accord, exclaims, "It *must* mean."

It is a remarkable sequence, and one that is repeated in a variety of ways in the paragraphs that follow. The pattern is always the same: the claim of independence—for the analysis, for the patient's share, for the "materials"—is made in the context of an account that powerfully subverts it, and then it is made again. Each claim is a disclaimer on the part of the analyst of the control he is everywhere exercising; and his effort to deny his effort extends to a denial that he is exerting any influence on himself: "Readers may . . . rest assured that I myself am only reporting what I came upon as an independent experience, uninfluenced by my expectation" (p. 158). Here there are two claims, one more audacious than the other: the first is that his mental processes function independently of his psychic history (a claim directly at odds with the thesis of this very case); the second is that a similar independence can be achieved by those readers who rest in the assurances he offers. In other words, he counsels submission to himself as a way of being free, and he presents this counsel in the context of an argument for his own disinterestedness. Put yourself in my hands, he says, because my hands are not mine, but merely the instruments of truth.

Of course this is exactly what an analyst says (not always explicitly) at the beginning of a treatment. In effect the reader is being put on the couch where he is given the same double message Freud gives to his patient: be independent, rely entirely on me. In rapid succession Freud issues a series of confusing and contradictory directions. First he tells us, you must "eliminate" your "pre-existing convictions" and consider only the evidence. But within a few sentences we learn that there will be no evidence to consider. "Exhaustive verbatim reports," he declares, "would . . . be of no help at all," and, besides, such reports aren't available anyway since "the technique of the treatment makes it impossible to draw them up" (pp. 158–59). This leaves us at the mercy of what the analyst chooses to tell us, and it would seem that we are simply to exchange his "pre-existing convictions" for our own. But no. In a dazzling reversal the reader's independence is reaffirmed when it is revealed that one of his preexisting convictions will be retained, the conviction that psychoanalysis, as Freud practices it, is the true and only way. It is only for such readers, "already . . . convinced by their own clinical experiences" (p. 159), that Freud writes, and because they are convinced those readers will be proof against any attempt, on the part of Freud or anyone else, to convince them. The logic, to say the least, is suspect, but if one accepts it (and we are not given time to do anything else), one will also accept the amazing conclusion that this analysis is not published "in order to produce conviction."

The claim not to be producing conviction is of a piece with the other claims or disclaimers that fill the opening pages. Always they are disclaimers of influence and always their effect is to extend the influence they would disclaim. The inducing of independence undermines it; the denial of a strategy of conviction is itself a strategy of conviction. The text's overt assertions are continually in conflict with the actions it performs, as Freud proclaims the autonomy of a succession of children—the patient, the reader, the analysis—even as he contrives to control them.

The question that arises is one of motive. Why is Freud doing this? Is it simply a matter of a desire for personal power? The text suggests that he would reply in the negative and say that he was only defending the honor of psychoanalysis against what J. O. Wisdom has identified as the oldest charge against it, the charge that it "acts by suggestion," that what the analyst claims to uncover (in the archeological sense of which Freud was so fond) he actually creates by verbal and rhetorical means.[5]

---

5. J. O. Wisdom, "Testing an Interpretation within a Session," in *Freud: A Collection of Critical Essays*, ed. Richard Wollheim (Garden City, N.Y., 1974), p. 340. There is of course a huge literature focusing on the issues of evidence and testability. For representative positions, see the essays by Margaret A. Boden, Wesley C. Salmon, Clark Gylmour, Peter Alexander, and Theodore Mischel in the same collection. H. J. Eysenck articulates the general complaint of hard-core verificationists: "clinical work is often very productive of theories and hypotheses, but weak on proof and verification" (*Uses and Abuses of Psychology* [Harmondsworth, 1953], p. 229). Defenses typically take the form of arguing that verification is indeed available, albeit not always in the (impossibly strict) forms demanded by Freud's critics. Recently the debate has been given renewed life by the publication of Adolf Grunbaum's *The Foundations of Psychoanalysis: A Philosophical Critique* (Berkeley and Los Angeles, 1984). Although Grunbaum disagrees with Karl Popper's contention that psychoanalytic hypotheses are nonfalsifiable and therefore unscientific, he argues that psychoanalytic evidence, derived as it is from the clinical practice of free association, is unavoidably contaminated by "extraneous" influences such as the analyst's selection biases, the patient's sense of what the analyst wants to hear, the untrustworthiness of memory, and so on. For a recent review of the literature and the issues, see Marshall Edelson, *Hypothesis and Evidence in Psychoanalysis* (Chicago, 1984). The scientific question becomes a moral one in the work of Jeffrey Mousaieff Masson, who argues that Freud's rejection of the seduction theory in favor of fantasy was a turning away from the empirical reality of his patients' suffering, and was prompted by

Freud is vehement in his rejection of this accusation, declaring at one point that it is "unjust to attribute the results of analysis to the physician's imagination" (p. 231) and confessing at another that he finds it "impossible" even to argue with those who regard the findings of psychoanalysis as "artefacts" (p. 191). These and similar statements would seem to suggest that his motives are not personal but institutional; he speaks not for himself but on behalf of the integrity of a discipline. But since the discipline is one of which he is quite literally the father, his defense of its integrity involves him in the same contradiction that marks his relationship with the patient and the reader: no sooner has he insisted on the independence of psychoanalysis as a science than he feels compelled to specify, and to specify authoritatively, what the nature of that science is; and once he does that he is in the untenable position of insisting on the autonomy of something of which he is unable to let go. It is a position he can only escape by placing himself on an even ground with his opponents; but this is precisely what he cannot bring himself to do, and whenever their arguments surface he responds to them with the paternalism he so vigorously disavows. By rising to the institutional level, Freud only reinscribes the dilemma inherent in his role as analyst and author. He cannot be both liberator and master at the same time; and insofar as that is the task he assigns himself, he becomes the object of his own manipulation, demanding of himself, as he demands of the patient and the reader, that he be active and passive at the same time.

Freud's response to this double bind is to deny it by producing accounts of the analysis in which the actions he is unwilling to acknowledge are performed by others. The first such displacement occurs in the third paragraph of chapter 1, when he weighs the virtues and defects of competing methodologies. The two possibilities are (1) analyzing a childhood disorder when it first manifests itself in infancy, or (2) waiting until the patient is an "intellectually mature adult" (p. 155). Since Freud is at this very moment engaged in the second practice it is not surprising that he decides in favor of it, but he must find a way to defend it against the objection (which he anticipates) that because of the passage of time what results will be the product of interpretation. He replies by asserting that interpretation will play an even greater part if the child is examined

---

the general unwillingness of a patriarchal society to face the idea of sexual violence in the family (see *The Assault on Truth: Freud's Suppression of the Seduction Theory* [New York, 1984]). In short Freud ceased being a truth-seeker and became an apologist. Both Masson and the philosophical critics agree that psychoanalysis will have a serious claim on our attention only if its methods and conclusions rest on some objective foundation; but this is an assumption rejected by another group of analysts who see the "truth" of psychoanalysis as a narrative truth and invoke a standard not of correspondence with empirical facts but of coherence within a discursive structure. See Donald P. Spence, *Narrative Truth and Historical Truth: Meaning and Interpretation in Psychoanalysis* (New York, 1982), and the *International Forum for Psychoanalysis*, ed. Joseph Rippen, 1, no. 3–4 (1984).

directly because "too many words and thoughts have to be lent" to him. In contrast, when one analyzes an adult, these "limitations" do not obtain, although such analysis "necessitates our taking into account the distortion and refurbishing to which a person's own past is subjected when it is looked back upon" (p. 155). Once one begins to examine it, this is a curious contrast, since it is hard to tell the difference between "lending words" and "refurbishing." What makes the contrast work is the fact that the sentence shifts the burden of "refurbishing" onto the patient. It is a brilliant move which allows Freud to admit interpretation into the scene while identifying it as the work of another, leaving himself the (honorable) work of undoing its effects. In only a few brief sentences he has managed to twice distance himself from the charge of suggestion, first by pushing it off onto the practitioners of a rival method, and second by making it into a property of the illness of which his now innocent labors are to be the cure.

The strategy then is to foreground an accusation and to defend against it by turning it back on those who would make it; attribute to others what they would attribute unto you; allow the accusation to surface, but keep pushing it away. In another place it is pushed away before it appears because it is presented as an accusation not against Freud but against his patients, including, presumably, this one. The accusers are his opponents, Jung and Adler, who reject the thesis of infantile neurosis, regarding it as an elaborate rationalization that allows neurotics to avoid confronting their problems by projecting them onto a past for which they can then not be held responsible. "The supporters of this view," says Freud, "assume that the importance of childhood is only held up before our eyes in analysis on account of the inclination of neurotics for expressing their present interests in reminiscences and symbols from the remote past" (p. 192). To these arguments Freud responds with indignation, not on his own behalf, but on behalf of the class of neurotic patients who are impugned and defamed when their motives are reduced to the "self-assertive instinct" of a "will to power" (p. 167). But of course these are the very motives of which he has been accused, and it is difficult not to see in this ostentatious concern for the reputation of neurotics still another attempt to ward off the charges of manipulation and suggestion. He declares his patients innocent of a willfulness he cannot acknowledge in himself, and he constructs for both the familiar defense of passivity, telling a story in which both he and his patient are the passive instruments of forces over which they have no control. The difference is that in the case of the patient those forces live within him and have their source in the suppressed events of his infantile life, whereas in the case of the analyst, the forces to which he submits reside outside him and constitute a reality he does not influence but only registers. Logically these twin defenses contradict one another: one insists that the structures and patterns of psychic history cannot be escaped, the other claims to have escaped them, but the logical inconsistency is a rhetorical triumph as both the patient and the analyst are exonerated from the charge that they have fabricated what they report.

The triumph is complete when that same charge—the charge of rhetorical manipulation—is turned against the proponents of the opposing view. It is they, says Freud, who produce "twisted interpretations," which are, in fact, "high-handed attempts at re-interpretation," that is, blatant exercises of a "will to power" (pp. 155, 167). In this way Freud tars his adversaries with their own brush: after all it is they not he who make the argument for power, and Freud suggests that what they see in their patients is no more than a projection of their own personal and institutional desires, desires of which he is of course wholly innocent. But even as he thus distances himself from the scene of power, Freud is engaged in establishing (or reestablishing) his power by means that could not be more rhetorical. Whenever he speaks of his opponents he characterizes them in a very particular set of terms: they unthinkingly reject what is new, they resist the unmistakable evidence he brings forward, they cling obstinately to comfortable interpretations and refuse even to examine them. But these are also the terms in which he describes the behavior of infantile neurotics like his patient, whose illness is thereby validated when evidence of it is discovered in the actions of those who would dispute it. That is to say, patient and critic become interchangeable; the only difference is that while Freud's patients have placed themselves under his care and thereby taken the first step in achieving independence from their own resistances, the critics are precisely those who have broken with Freud—they are, in fact, his former pupils—and with their every word they move farther away from him and from the possibility of regaining their health. In the course of this argument the thesis of infantile neurosis is at once defended against its detractors and made into a weapon with which to club them, as the conditions of being an infantile neurotic and of being an opponent of Freud turn out to be one and the same.

It is a master stroke which accomplishes several things at once: whatever Freud's opponents might say about his handling of the present case is discredited in advance, because they are too much like its subject; and more important, Freud's reader is simultaneously introduced to the opinions of those opponents and inoculated against their effect; for the reader knows that should he hearken to these captious voices, he will identify himself as a neurotic child who "rejected what was new . . . and clung fast to what was old" (p. 221). In effect, the reader is given what appears to be a choice but is in fact an offer he can't refuse: you can either accept what I am about to tell you or you can look forward to being stigmatized as a resistant and recalcitrant infant. Either cast your lot with me or with those bad children who are so sick that they do not even recognize their illness.

2

Those of you who know the text already may have realized that to this point I have been dealing primarily with the very brief first chapter and the opening paragraph of chapter 2, some five pages out of more than one hundred. And yet, in a sense, most of the work—which is the work of denying that there has been or will be any work—has already been done, for although we have yet to hear a single detail either of the patient's history or of his therapy, we are already so much under Freud's influence that when the details do finally appear, they will fall into the place he has prepared for them. In the following pages Freud will repeatedly urge us, in effect, to take up our "independent share" in the work, but that independence has long since been taken from us. The judgment he will soon solicit is a judgment he already controls, and as he begins his narration proper, he increases that control by dictating the terms by which his efforts (or, as he would have it, nonefforts) will be judged. "I am unable," he says, "to give either a purely historical or a purely thematic account of my patient's story; I can write a history neither of the treatment nor of the illness, but I shall find myself obliged to combine the two methods of presentation" (p. 158). A "purely historical" account would be a narrative account tracing out relationships of cause and effect; and by declaring that he is unable to provide it, Freud releases himself from the requirement that in his explanations one thing be shown to follow from another. A "purely thematic" account would be one in which the coherence of events and details was a matter of their relationship to a single master theme; and by declaring that he is unable to provide it, Freud releases himself from the requirement that his explanations go together to form an unified whole. In effect, he neutralizes criticism of his conclusions before they are offered and is in the enviable position of being at once the architect and judge of his own performance.

The crowning (and typical) touch is the word "obliged" ("I shall find myself obliged"), for it allows him to present himself as operating under the severest of constraints just at the moment when he is fashioning the constraints under which and within which both his patient and his reader will labor. What obliges him, it turns out, is the nature of the unconscious, which he tells us is not a linear structure ruled by the law of contradiction but a geological accumulation of forms that never completely disappear and live side by side in an uneasy and unpredictable vacillation: "That there should be an instantaneous and clear-cut displacement of one phase by the next was not in the nature of things or of our patient; on the contrary, the preservation of all that had gone before and the co-existence of the most different sorts of currents were characteristic of him" (p. 204). This picture of the unconscious is offered as though it provided independent support of both his thesis and his procedure; but it *is* his thesis, and it is indistinguishable from the argument it authorizes. That is, the unconscious is not a concept but a rhetorical device, a placeholder which can be given whatever shape the polemical moment requires.[6] If someone were to object to his interpretation of a particular detail, he could point for confirmation to the nature of the unconscious, and if someone were to dispute the nature of the unconscious, he could point to the evidence of his interpretations. All the while he could speak of himself as being "obliged" by constraints that were at once independent *of* him and assured the independence *from* him of his patient and his reader. The rhetorical situation could not be more favorable. Freud can present himself as a disinterested researcher and at the same time work to extend his control until it finally includes everything: the details of the analysis, the behavior of the patient, and the performance of the reader. And he manages to do all of this before the story of the Wolf-Man has even begun to unfold.

I am aware that this is not the usual description of Freud's labors, which have recently been characterized by Peter Brooks as "heroic,"[7] a characterization first offered by Freud in 1938 as he cast a final retrospective look at his most famous case.[8] In Brooks' reading the Wolf-Man's case is a "radically modernist" text, a "structure of indeterminacy" and "un-decidability" which "perilously destabilizes belief in explanatory histories as exhaustive accounts whose authority derives from the force of closure" (*RP*, pp. 279, 275, 277). Freud's heroism, according to Brooks, consists precisely in resisting closure, in forgoing the satisfaction of crafting a "coherent, finished, enclosed, and authoritative narrative" (*RP*, p. 277).

This is an attractive thesis, but it has absolutely nothing to do with the text we have been reading, although, as we shall see, Brooks has reasons, and apparently good ones, for thinking as he does. Meanwhile we can note that Freud's own characterization of his narrative insists precisely on those qualities Brooks would deny to it: completeness, exhaustiveness, authority, and, above all, closure. The requirement that he expects his presentation to meet is forthrightly stated in a footnote as he begins to interpret the wolf dream: "It is always a strict law of dream-interpretation that an explanation must be found for every detail" (p. 186 n. 17). This is the vocabulary not of any "post-modernist narrative"

---

6. See Ernest Gellner, *The Psychoanalytic Movement* (London, 1985), p. 48: "The concept of the Unconscious is a means of devaluing all previous certainties. . . . It is not so much a hypothesis as a suspension of all other hypotheses." In other words, as a concept the unconscious validates *anything*, and this "suspension" of "all guidelines" is both its content and the operation (any operation at all) it makes possible.

7. Peter Brooks, *Reading for the Plot: Design and Intention in Narrative* (New York, 1984), p. 277; further references to this work, abbreviated *RP*, will be included in the text.

8. Freud, "Analysis Terminable and Interminable," *The Standard Edition of the Complete Psychological Works of Sigmund Freud*, ed. and trans. Strachey, 24 vols. (London, 1953–74), 23:217.

or "structure of indeterminacy," but of a more traditional and familiar genre—one of which we know Freud to have been very fond—the classic story of detection; a genre in which an absolutely omniscient author distributes clues to a master meaning of which he is fully cognizant and toward which the reader moves uncertainly, but always under the direction of a guide who builds the structure of the narrative and the structure of understanding at the same time. As Brooks notes, Freud assumes the stance of the detective in the second chapter, which is a quick survey of "the riddles for which the analysis had to find a solution. What was the origin of the sudden change in the boy's character? What was the significance of his phobia and of his perversities? How did he arrive at his obsessive piety? And how are all these phenomena interrelated?" (p. 163). These questions establish the agenda and anticipate the moment of pleasure and satisfaction, the moment when, with a click and a snap, everything falls into place and no detail is without an explanation, the moment when, as in so many of the stories of Arthur Conan Doyle, the detective reveals the solution and proclaims it to be elementary.

There is, however, a large difference between Freud's detective story and other instances of the genre: in the novels of Conan Doyle or Agatha Christie, author and reader are engaged in a contest in which they are armed with the same weapon, their ability to reason along lines of cause and effect; but these are precisely the lines that Freud has told us he will not pursue, and as a result the reader comes to his task with a double disability—not only must he look to Freud for the material on which his intelligence is to work; he must also be supplied with a way of making that material intelligible. And of course it will be Freud who supplies him, and who by supplying him will increase immeasurably the control he already exercises. Not only will he monitor the flow of information and point to the object that is to be understood; he will stipulate the form in which the act of understanding will be allowed to occur.

That is the business of chapter 3, "The Seduction and Its Immediate Consequences." The seduction in question is (or appears to be) the seduction of the Wolf-Man by his sister; but it is less important as an event than as a component in a structure of explanation that will serve as a model for the explanatory acts that will soon follow. The occasion is a succession of dreams "concerned with aggressive actions on the boy's part against his sister or against the governess and with energetic reproofs and punishments on account of them." For a while, Freud reports, a firm interpretation of these dreams seemed unavailable; but then "the explanation came at a single blow, when the patient suddenly called to mind the fact that, when he was still very small, . . . his sister had seduced him into sexual practices" (p. 164). What happens next is a bit of sleight of hand: first of all, the patient's recollection is not the explanation, which therefore does not come at a single blow (at least not at the single blow to which the reader's attention is directed). Rather the explanation emerges as the result of interpretive work done by Freud but never seen by us; the "single blow," in other words, occurs offstage and what we are presented with is its result, offered as if it were self-evident and self-generating. These dreams, Freud says, "were meant to efface the memory of an event which later on seemed offensive to the patient's masculine self-esteem, and they reached this end by putting an imaginary and desirable converse in the place of the historical truth" (p. 164). That is to say, the patient's masculine self-esteem was threatened by the fact that his sister, not he, was the aggressive seducer, and this threat is defended against in the dream material by reversing their respective positions. One critic has objected to this as one of Freud's "apparently arbitrary inversions,"[9] but it is far from arbitrary, for it is a precise and concise direction to both the patient and the reader, providing them with a method for dealing with the material they will soon meet and telling them in advance what will result when that method is applied. Freud says, in effect, if you want to know what something—a dream, a piece of neurotic behavior—means, simply reverse its apparent significance, and what you will find is an attempt to preserve masculine self-esteem against the threat of passivity and femininity. The real seduction in this chapter (which is accomplished at this moment and in a single blow) is the seduction not of the patient by his sister, but of both the patient and the reader by Freud who will now be able to produce interpretive conclusions in the confidence that they will be accepted as the conclusions of an inevitable and independent logic.

Moreover, in performing this act of seduction, Freud at once redoubles and reverses the behavior he explains: if the patient defends against his passivity by "weaving an imaginative composition" in which he is the aggressor, Freud defends against his own aggression by weaving an imaginative composition in which he is passive; and if it is the case, as Freud will later argue, that the patient is ambivalent and conflicted—at a level below consciousness he wants to be both passive and aggressive—it is no less the case with Freud who wants to be the father of everything that happens in the analysis and at the same time wants the analysis to unfold of its own accord. One is tempted to say then that the story Freud tells is doubled by the story of the telling or that his performance mirrors or enacts the content of the analysis; but in fact it is the other way around: the content of the analysis mirrors or enacts the drama of the performance, a drama that is already playing itself out long before it has anything outside itself to be "about," and playing itself out in the very terms that are here revealed supposedly for the first time, the terms of the preservation and concealing of masculine self-esteem and aggression. It is a commonplace of psychoanalysis that surface concerns are screens for concerns

9. Serge Viderman, *Le Céleste et le sublunaire: La Construction de l'espace analytique deux* (Paris, 1977), p. 287.

that are primarily sexual; what I am saying is that in the case of the Wolf-Man (where that commonplace was established historically) the concerns of infantile sexuality are screens for the surface concerns that Freud acknowledges but then apparently sets aside. What Freud presents as mere preliminary material—his prospective discussion of evidence, conviction, and independence—is finally the material that is being worked through even when the focus was ostensibly shifted elsewhere, to the patient and his infantile prehistory. The real story of the case is the story of persuasion, and we will be able to read it only when we tear our eyes away from the supposedly deeper story of the boy who had a dream.

Both stories receive their fullest telling in chapter 4, which begins as this paper begins: " *'I dreamt that it was night and that I was lying in my bed.'* " Here finally is the centerpiece of the case, withheld from the reader for three chapters, and now presented as the chief object of interpretation. But of course, it appears as an already-interpreted object, even before the first word has been said about it, since we know in advance that whatever configuration emerges need only be reversed for its "true" meaning to be revealed; and lest we forget what we have been taught, Freud reinforces the lesson with a pointed speculation. "We must naturally expect," he says, "to find that this material reproduces the unknown material of the scene in some distorted form, perhaps even distorted into its opposite" (p. 178). He then reports, as though it were not influenced by his expectations, the moment when the patient takes up his "independent share in the work." When in my dream the window suddenly opens of its own accord, " 'It must mean "my eyes suddenly opened." ' " Indeed it must, given the interpretive directions he has received, and it is hardly surprising to hear Freud's response: "No objection could be made to this" (p. 179). Indeed there could be no objection to a meaning he has virtually commanded, and in what follows the pretense that the work is independent is abandoned. "The point," he says, "could be developed further," and he immediately proceeds to develop it, not even bothering to indicate whether the development issues from him or from his patient:

> What, then, if the other factor emphasized by the dreamer were also distorted by means of a transposition or reversal? In that case instead of immobility (the wolves sat there motionless; . . .) the meaning would have to be: the most violent motion. . . . He suddenly woke up, and saw in front of him a scene of violent movement at which he looked with strained attention. [P. 179]

There remains only the final step of determining what the scene of violent motion precisely was, but before taking that step Freud pauses in a way that heightens its drama. "I have now reached the point," he says, "at which I must abandon the support I have hitherto had from the course of the analysis. I am afraid it will also be the point at which the reader's belief will abandon me" (pp. 180–81). Presumably it is because of gestures like this one that Brooks is moved to characterize Freud's text as open and nonauthoritative, but I trust that *my* reader will immediately see this as the gesture of someone who is so confident in his authority that he can increase it by (apparently) questioning it. The tone here is playful as Freud amuses himself by raising as spectres two dangers he has already avoided. The first is the danger that might follow were he to abandon the support of the analysis; but that danger cannot be real since what he calls the "course of the analysis" has been entirely determined by him. If he now "abandons" it to strike out on his own, he merely exchanges one rhetorically established support for another. No matter what step he takes next, the support under his feet will be as firm as it ever was. Nor can we take seriously the fear that he will be abandoned by the reader's belief, since that belief—our belief—rather than being independent of his will is by now the child of his will, accepting as evidence only what he certifies. Abandon him? To abandon him at this point would be to abandon the constraints and desires that make us, as readers, what we are. By raising the possibility, Freud only tightens the bonds by which we are attached to him and makes us all the more eager to receive the key revelation at his hands. I give it to you now: "What sprang into activity that night out of the chaos of the dreamer's unconscious memory-traces was the picture of copulation between his parents, copulation in circumstances which were not entirely usual and were especially favourable for observation" (p. 181). The credibility of this revelation is not a function of its probability—we have had many demonstrations of how improbable it is that any such event ever took place—but of its explanatory power. It satisfies the need Freud has created in us to understand, and by understanding to become his partner in the construction of the story. As at so many places in the text, what Freud presents here for our judgment is quite literally irresistible; for resistance would require an independence we have already surrendered. In return for that independence we are given the opportunity to nod in agreement—to say, "It *must* mean"—as Freud, newly constructed primal scene in hand, solves every puzzle the case had seemed to offer. In rapid order he accounts for the patient's fear of wolves, his fantasies of beating and being beaten, his simultaneous identification with and rejection of his father, and his marked castration anxiety:

> His anxiety was a repudiation of the wish for sexual satisfaction from his father—the trend which had put the dream into his head. The form taken by the anxiety, the fear of "being eaten by the wolf", was only the . . . transposition of the wish to be copulated with by his father. . . . His last sexual aim, the passive attitude towards his father, succumbed to repression, and fear of his father appeared in its place in the shape of the wolf phobia.

> And the driving force of this repression? ... it can only have
> been his narcissistic genital libido, which ... was fighting against
> a satisfaction whose attainment seemed to involve the renunciation
> of that organ. [Pp. 189–90]

What we have here is a picture of someone who alternates between passive and aggressive behavior, now assuming the dominant position of the male aggressor, now submitting in feminine fashion to forces that overwhelm him. This we are told is the secret content of the patient's behavior, expressed indirectly in his symptoms and fantasies, and brought triumphantly by Freud to the light of day. But if it is a secret, the drama of its disclosing serves to deflect our attention from a secret deeper still, the secret that has (paradoxically) been on display since the opening paragraphs—the secret that the true story of domination and submission is the story of Freud's performance here and now, the story of a master rhetorician who hides from others and from himself the true nature of his activities. Once more Freud contrives to keep that secret by publishing it, by discovering at the heart of the *patient's* fantasy the very conflicts that he himself has been acting out in his relationships with the patient, the analysis, the reader, and his critics. In all of these relationships he is driven by the obsessions he uncovers, by the continual need to control, to convince, and to seduce in endless vacillation with the equally powerful need to disclaim any traces of influence and to present himself as the passive conduit of forces that exist independently of him. He simply cannot help himself, and even when his double story is fully told, he has recourse to a mechanism that opens it again, not, as Brooks would have it, in order to delay or defeat closure, but in order to *repeat* it, and thereby to be master again.

3

The mechanism is the announcement that he has omitted a detail from the reconstruction of the primal scene. "Lastly," Freud tells us, the boy "interrupted his parents' intercourse in a manner which will be discussed later" (p. 182). This is the missing portion referred to in my title, and by calling attention to it, Freud produces a desire for its restoration, a desire he then periodically inflames by reminding us of the deficiency in our understanding and promising to supply it. "I have hinted," he says in chapter 5, "that my description of the 'primal scene' has remained incomplete because I have reserved for a later moment my account of the way in which the child interrupted his parents' intercourse. I must now add that this method of interruption is the same in every case" (p. 203). Again he leaves us without the crucial piece of information, and by suggesting that it is even more valuable than we had thought—it is a key not only to this case but to all cases—he intensifies our need for it. Moreover, in a manner entirely characteristic, he then shifts that need onto the patient who is described in the following chapter as "longing for some one who should give him the last pieces of information that were still missing upon the riddle of sexual intercourse" (p. 213). The displacement is transparent: it is of course we who are longing for a piece of information to be given us by a father with whom we will then join. Once again the drama of Freud's rhetorical mastery is at once foregrounded and concealed when it appears, only thinly disguised, as an event in his patient's history.

This technique of open concealment reaches a virtuoso level of performance when, in a gesture of excessive candor, Freud reveals that there is a subject he has "intentionally . . . left on one side" (p. 214). He then introduces as a *new* topic of discussion a term that names the very behavior he has been engaging in all the while, anal eroticism. Of course as he presents it, it is an aspect only of the patient's behavior, easily discernible, says Freud, in his inability to evacuate spontaneously without the aid of enemas, his habit of "making a mess in his bed," whenever he was forced to share a bedroom with a despised governess, his great fear of dysentery, his fierce piety which alternated with fantasies of Christ defecating, and above all his attitude toward money with which he was sometimes exceedingly liberal and at other times miserly in the extreme. All of this Freud relates to the management of "excretory pleasure," which he says plays "an extraordinarily important part . . . in building up sexual life and mental activity" (p. 215). Of course he offers his observation with no intention of including himself or his own "mental activity" within its scope. It is an observation about *others*, evidence (if it is evidence at all) only of his perspicuity. "At last," he tells us, "I recognized the importance of the intestinal trouble for my purposes," but as we shall see, he says this without any recognition whatsoever of what his real purposes are. His announced purpose is to find a way of overcoming the patient's resistance. For a long time, the analysis was blocked by the Wolf-Man's doubt. He remained skeptical of the efficacy of psychoanalysis, and it seemed that "there was no way of convincing him" until

> I promised the patient a complete recovery of his intestinal activity, and by means of this promise made his incredulity manifest. I then had the satisfaction of seeing his doubt dwindle away, as in the course of the work his bowel began, like a hysterically affected organ, to "join in the conversation," and in a few weeks' time recovered its normal functions after their long impairment. [P. 218]

One might describe this remarkable passage as an allegory of persuasion were it not so transparently literal. One persuades, in this account, by emptying the other of his "pre-existing convictions." The patient's doubts, or to speak more affirmatively, his beliefs, are quite literally eliminated; the fragmentary portions that comprise his convictions pass out through his bowel, and he is left an empty vessel, ready to be filled up with whatever new convictions the rhetorician brings forward. (It is no accident that the German word "Klaren" means both to explain and to defecate: one must be emptied out before one can be filled up.) The bowel that is said to "join in the conversation" is in fact the medium of the analyst's ventriloquism; it speaks, but the words are his. So is the satisfaction, as Freud explicitly acknowledges ("I then had the satisfaction"); the managing of "excretory pleasure," the mainspring of the patient's psychic life, is taken over by the analyst, who gives up nothing while forcing the other to give up everything. And even as Freud reveals and revels in his strategy, he conceals it, telling the story of persuasion to a reader who is himself that story's object, and who, no less than the patient, is falling totally under the control of the teller.

All of these stories come together at the moment when the missing portion is finally put into place. "I have already hinted," says Freud (in fact he has already already hinted) "that one portion of the content of the primal scene has been kept back." In the original German the sentence is continued in a relative clause whose literal translation is "which I am now able to offer as a supplement." Strachey makes the clause into an independent unit and renders it "I am now in a position to produce this missing portion" (p. 222). It would seem that this is one of those departures from the text for which the translator has been so often taken to task; but in fact Strachey is here being more literal than Freud himself. Rather than departing from the text, he eliminates its coyness and brings us closer to the nature of the act the prose performs, an act to which Strachey alerts us by the insistent physicality of the words "position" and "produce." Just what that position and production are becomes dazzlingly clear when the secret is finally out in the open: "The child . . . interrupted his parents' intercourse by passing a stool" (p. 222). We commit no fallacy of imitative form by pointing out what hardly needs pointing out, that Freud enacts precisely what he reports;[10] the position he is in is the squatting position of defecation, and it is he who, at a crucial juncture and to dramatic effect, passes a stool that he has long held back. What is even more remarkable is that immediately after engaging in this behavior, Freud produces (almost as another piece of stool) an analysis of it. In anal-erotic behavior, he tells us, a person sacrifices or makes a gift of "a portion of his own body which is ready to part with, but only for the sake of some one he loves" (p. 223). That love, however, is a form of

---

10. On this point see Mahony, *Cries of the Wolf Man*, p. 90: "In effect, the analyst and patient were locked in a quid pro quo of anal retention and release extending from the clinical setting to the pages of the deferred expository narrative."

possession or mastery, for in this pregenital phase, the "contrast between 'masculine' and 'feminine' plays no part" and "its place is taken by the contrast between 'active' and 'passive.' " "What appears to us as masculine in the activities of this phase . . . turns out to be an expression of an instinct for mastery" (*CIL,* p. 327). In other words, one who is fixed in the anal phase experiences pleasure as control, a control he achieves by the calculated withholding and releasing of feces. What the anal erotic seeks is to capture and absorb the other by the stimulation and gratifying of desire; what he seeks, in short, is power, and he gains it at the moment when his excretions become the focus and even the content of the other's attention. However accurate this is as an account of anal eroticism, it is a perfect account of the act of persuasion, which is, I would argue, the primal act for which the anal erotic is only a metaphor. It is persuasion that Freud has been practicing in this case on a massive scale, and the "instinct for mastery" of which persuasion is the expression, finds its fulfillment here when the reader accepts from Freud that piece of deferred information which completes the structure of his own understanding. Once that acceptance has been made, the reader belongs to Freud as much as any lover belongs to the beloved. By giving up a portion of himself Freud is not diminished but enlarged, since what he gets back is the surrender of the reader's will which now becomes an extension of his own. The reader, on his part, receives a moment of pleasure—the pleasure of seeing the pieces of the puzzle finally fitting together—but Freud reserves to himself the much greater pleasure of total mastery. It is a pleasure that is intensely erotic, full of the "sexual excitement" (p. 223) that is said to mark the *patient's* passing of a stool; it is a pleasure that is anal, phallic, and even oral, affording the multiple satisfactions of domination, penetration, and engulfment. It is, in a word, the pleasure of persuasion.

In what remains of his performance Freud savors that pleasure and adds to it by placing it in apparent jeopardy. I refer to the well-known fact that in the four years between the writing and the publishing of this case history Freud added two bracketed passages in which he calls into question precisely what he has been arguing for, the reality of the primal scene. He first wonders if "perhaps what the child observed was not copulation between his parents but copulation between animals, which he then displaced on to his parents" (p. 201). He later considers the possibility that primal scene fantasies may have their source in a "phylogenetic heritage"; when a child's own experience fails him, he "fills in the gaps in individual truth with prehistoric truth; he replaces occurrences in his own life by occurrences in the life of his ancestors" (pp. 238, 239). Brooks finds these speculations "daring" and (as I have already said) "heroic," since in his view they show Freud willing to open up what his text would seem to have closed. But in fact the only thing these later interpolations open up is the opportunity to perform closure once again,

and to perform it in conditions that have the appearance of being particularly difficult. What Brooks sees as a breaching of Freud's authority
is a confident exercise of that authority which now feels its strength to
such an extent that it can allow itself to be challenged with impunity.
The challenge comes in the form of alternative accounts of the primal
scene's origin, but the question of origin is beside the point once the
scene has been made real for both the patient and the reader. This, after
all, is the work of the analysis, not to uncover the empirical foundations
of the scene but to establish it as an integral part first of the patient's
psychic life and then of the reader's understanding of that life. As Freud
himself puts it, what is important is the "profound conviction of the
reality of these . . . scenes" (p. 195), and once that conviction has been
secured, it can tolerate any number of speculations without being shaken.
Freud is betting that it has in fact been secured; he is betting that he has
been persuasive and that at one level at least the question of the primal
scene has been closed. He now closes it again, after having ostentatiously
opened it, by saying that although he would "be glad to know whether
the primal scene in my present patient's case was a phantasy or a real
experience; . . . the answer to this question is not in fact a matter of very
great importance" (p. 238). That is why he raises it—so that it can be
dismissed as irrelevant by a conviction that now supports itself and is
unembarrassed by inquiries into its possible origins. Once that conviction
is firmly established it can be cited as confirmation of itself and invoked
as a sufficient response to any challenge, including the challenges Freud
calls up only so that they can be dramatically defeated.

He does this for the last time in chapter 8 when he declares, "I will
make a final attempt at re-interpreting the . . . findings of this analysis
in accordance with the scheme of my opponents" (p. 243). One might
characterize this as a demonstration of openness were it not so obviously
a demonstration of control. Freud is seizing an occasion to perform a
rhetorical feat whose value lies (to borrow a phrase from gymnastics) in
its degree of difficulty. (This is an old rhetorical tradition that goes back
at least far as the exercises of Seneca.) First he imagines what Jung and
Adler would say if they were presented with the materials he has now
marshaled. He imagines them as "bad" readers, readers who are uncon-
vinced, and he rehearses their likely objections. No doubt they would
regard the primal scene as the invention of a neurotic who was seeking
to rationalize his "flight from the world" and who was "driven to embark
on this long backward course either because he had come up against
some task . . . which he was too lazy to perform, or because he had every
reason to be aware of his own inferiority and thought he could best
protect himself . . . by elaborating such contrivances as these" (pp. 243,
244). What Freud is staging here is a moment of scrupulosity very much
like some earlier moments when he presses interpretive suggestions on
a resistant patient and then points to the patient's resistance as a proof

of the independence of the analysis. Here it is we who are (once more) in the position of the patient as Freud urges on us an interpretive direction and waits for us to reject it "of our own accord"; but of course at this late stage, any rejection we might perform would be dictated not by an independent judgment, but by a judgment Freud has in large measure shaped. Even so, he is unwilling to run the risk (really no risk at all) that we might respond in some errant way, and accordingly he responds for us:

> All this would be very nice, if only the unlucky wretch had not had a dream when he was no more than four years old, which signalized the beginning of his neurosis . . . and the interpretation of which necessitates the assumption of this primal scene. All the alleviations which the theories of Jung and Adler seek to afford us come to grief, alas, upon such paltry but unimpeachable facts as these. [P. 244]

Everything happens so fast in this sequence that we may not notice that the "unimpeachable fact" which anchors it is the *assumption* of the primal scene. In most arguments assumptions are what must be proven out, but in this argument the assumption is offered as proof; what supports it is not any independent fact, but the polemical fact that without the assumption the story Freud has so laboriously constructed falls apart. The necessity Freud invokes is a discursive necessity, the necessity of a founding moment in the absence of which an explanation could not be "found for every detail." In effect Freud says to us, "look, we've worked incredibly hard to put something together; are we now going to entertain doubts about the very assumption that enabled us to succeed?" The primal scene is important because it allows the story of its own discovery to unfold. In that story—the story, basically, of the analysis—the wolf dream comes first and initiates a search for its origin; that search then leads to the "uncovering" of the primal scene, and although it is the last thing to be put in place, it immediately becomes the anchor and the explanation of everything that precedes it.

This is precisely what Freud predicts will happen when early on he describes what it will feel like to look back on a successful analyst. The analyst will recall (as he now recalls)

> how gradually the construction of [the] phantasy . . . came about, and, . . . how independently of the physician's incentive many points in its development proceeded; how, after a certain phase of the treatment, everything seemed to converge upon it, and how later, . . . the most various and remarkable results radiated out from it; how not only the large problems but the smallest peculiarities in the history of the case were cleared up by this single assumption [P. 196]

In other words, the assumption of the primal scene proves itself by its effects, by its ability to bring order to an apparently heterogeneous mass of fragments and impressions; once order has been brought, there is nothing it does not comprehend, and therefore no vantage point from which it can be meaningfully challenged. Should a challenge be mounted, it can be met as Freud meets it here, with ridicule and incredulity. The investment of work and the yield of that work—certainty, conviction, knowledge—are simply too great to risk losing and comprise a resistance stronger even than the resistance that had to be overcome before they could be accomplished. What Freud is relying on here is not something newly or additionally persuasive, but on the fact that persuasion has occurred, and that having occurred, we will be unwilling and indeed unable to undo it.

It is the definition of a rhetorical object that it is entirely constructed and stands without external support; it is, we are accustomed to say, removed from reality; but we could just as well say that it becomes reality, that insofar as it has been installed at the center of a structure of conviction it acquires the status of that which goes without saying and that against which nothing can be said. It then becomes possible to argue both for and from it at the same time; or, rather, it becomes possible to not argue at all, but merely to point to something that now stands as irrefutable evidence of itself, as something perspicuous, autonomous, and independent, as something that need not be defended or even presented, as something *beyond rhetoric*. That is what Freud does here when the imagined objections to the primal scene are met simply by invoking it as a self-evident and indisputable authority. One might say then that at the conclusion of the case history the primal scene emerges triumphant as both the end of the story and its self-authenticating origin; but what is really triumphant is not this particular scene, which after all might well have assumed a quite different shape if the analysis had taken the slightest of turns, but the discursive power of which and by which it has been constructed. The true content of the primal scene is the story of its making. At bottom the primal scene is the scene of persuasion.[11]

11. To say that the primal scene is always a scene of persuasion is to say that it is a scene of closure; a scene marked by the achievement of a seamless coherence in which an explanation has been found for every detail; an explanation whose authority inheres precisely in its power to be wholly convincing, to secure belief. This is not to say that Freud's text cannot be opened, only that it is not his intention to open it. That is certainly the intention of Lacan, Brooks, Jacques Derrida, Ned Lukacher, Neil Hertz, and all the other "oppositional" readers who have recently been so busy. It is their project to interrogate the text from an angle that brings to the surface what its operations necessarily exclude, but the undoubted success of that project says nothing about the Freudian text; it says only that if one submits the text to an interpretive pressure different from the interpretive pressure that produced it in the first place, it will become a different text. There is no natural bar to such an exercise (no text in and of itself) which can be repeated ad infinitum, but to repeat it is

4

Of course this is not something that Freud knows, or, rather, if he knows it, it is a knowledge that he must compartmentalize lest it paralyze him and render his performance impossible. As we have seen, this compartmentalization often takes the form of displacement, as, time and again, the motives of power and manipulation, seduction and domination, are foregrounded but shifted onto others—the patient, Freud's critics, neurotic children, captious readers. Although the text is filled with accounts of its own workings, they are always disguised as accounts of the workings of other agents; and in this way the truth about itself is at once revealed and concealed. It is concealed not only from those who are the objects of the text's designs, but from the designer, from Freud himself, who displays a marvelous ability to hide from his right hand what his left hand is doing. Perhaps his most virtuoso moment in this "art" occurs late in the case history when the patient is reported as engaging in some "curious behavior." At times, Freud tells us, "he used to threaten me with eating me up and . . . with all kinds of other ill-treatment" (p. 248). Now by the rule of interpretation he himself has laid down, this moment should yield immediately to the principle of reversal and produce the following reading: the aggression the patient threatens is in fact the aggression he fears; it is he who is in danger of being eaten up and it is I who am the devourer. But this is a reading of the situation that Freud cannot bear to contemplate, and he substitutes for it a lame alternative—"all of which was merely an expression of affection" (p. 248). It is an edifying spectacle: the patient, aware at some level that he is being engulfed by the analyst, protests by simulating the analyst's behavior; the analyst in turn looks into a mirror and refuses to recognize what he sees. He is still refusing some years later when he meets the Wolf-Man again and is told by him that "after the end of the treatment he had been seized with a longing to tear himself free from my influence" (p. 262 n. 61). Here one would think is an explicit gloss on the "curious behavior" he had earlier displayed, but Freud makes no connection between the two moments and treats the Wolf-Man's later remark merely as a piece of transference, something left over from the case, a loose end. And what does one do with loose ends, with related but peripheral bits of information? Why, one puts them in a footnote, and that is exactly what Freud does in 1923, once again managing to hide in plain sight

---

to prove nothing except that it can be done; once it is done in the service of a thesis *about* the text it becomes a form of closure itself. Either Brooks and his party are demonstrating something about language—that it is infinitely capable of being appropriated—or he is asserting that something is true of *this* text. If he is doing the first I have no quarrel with him, although at this late date I find the point uninteresting; if he is doing the second I think that he is just wrong.

the truth he cannot confront. Interestingly enough, it is a truth the patient intuited even before the analysis began; after meeting Freud for the first time he recorded these thoughts: "A Jewish swindler; he wants to use me from behind and shit on my head."

Does this mean that the patient is more aware than the physician? Not at all, for he no less than Freud is caught up in the dialectic of independence and control, knowing at some level what has happened to him but committed at another level to denying it. In his own memoirs that denial emerges as a boast: "in my analysis with Freud I felt myself less as a patient than as a co-worker, the younger comrade of an experienced explorer setting out to study a new, recently discovered land" (p. 140). Here is the voice of someone who believes himself to have taken up his "independent share in the work" and who has written himself into a story that is positively epic. But only a few pages later he tells a quite different story. As the analysis drew to its end, Freud raised the question of the transference and "spoke of the danger of the patient's feeling too close a tie to the therapist" (p. 149). The Wolf-Man then reports with an absolutely straight face that in order to obviate the danger Freud suggested that the patient give him a gift, and thereby lessen "his feeling of gratitude and his consequent dependence on the physician" (pp. 149–50). In other words the patient is being urged to leave something of himself behind (a piece of stool perhaps?) as a way of *breaking* a tie that threatened to become too close. It seems incredible that he did not see how this de-vice—this soliciting and proffering of a *memento amoris*—could serve only to strengthen a bond that would now not be broken even by a physical separation. It seems even more incredible that he would have chosen as a gift a "female Egyptian figure," which he tells us Freud placed on his desk in the position usually reserved for a photograph of a spouse or a lover. Twenty years later, looking through a magazine, the Wolf-Man spies a picture of Freud at his desk and sees that the figure is still there. It is the first thing he notices in the picture—" 'My' Egyptian immediately struck my eye"—and it is obvious that he interprets it as evidence of Freud's continuing love. He goes so far as to say of the figure that "it symbolized my analysis with Freud" and although he does not gloss the symbolism, its meaning is transparent: he remains forever in the feminine position of submission, a captive work of art displayed as a trophy in the workshop of the analyst. And indeed the sentence ends with a recollection that makes sense only as an unacknowledged acknowledgment of the truth about their relationship. He called me, says the Wolf-Man, " 'a piece of psychoanalysis' " (p. 150). The significance of being a piece of psy-choanalysis is made apparent when, in what seems to be a random fashion, the Wolf-Man manages in the next few paragraphs to work his way around to a mention of Jung, "whom Freud had always praised highly and whom he had formally designated as his successor." One can only imagine the pleasure with which he then reports that Jung had "broken away" from Freud and "was now going his own way" (p. 151). Going his own way is what the Wolf-Man, in one mood, very much wants to do, and it is what Freud supposedly wants for him; but what they really want is what they get, a lifelong union in the course of which both parties celebrate an independence neither desires. Jung achieves that independence—he breaks the tie—and the price he pays for it is the loss of everything the Wolf-Man cherishes: his inheritance, the Father's approval, his position in psychoanalysis, his place on the desk. It is the Wolf-Man who by failing to go his own way succeeds in becoming the perfect rhetorical artifact, a wholly made object who wears his maker's signature like a badge, and who in later years introduced himself by saying "I am the most famous case" and answered the telephone with these words: "Wolf-Man here."

The Wolf-Man in short is a piece of language, a textually produced entity whose origins go back no farther than Freud's words. This of course is what Freud can never admit; indeed as Ned Lukacher, following Jacques Lacan, has recently put it, it is necessary for Freud to forget "that affect works through and within language and that the object of analysis is therefore the logic of the signifier." At the heart of psychoanalysis and therefore at the heart of the primal scene, Lukacher continues, language must not be allowed in, for "had Freud acknowledged that the . . . force of suggestion worked through the rhythms of language, he would have been deprived of any means with which to defend against it."[12] The defense, as we have seen, is more language, words denying the forces of words, rhetoric disclaiming rhetorical intention. It is a spectacle one finds everywhere in Freud's work, but nowhere more nakedly than in the first of his Introductory Lectures. These lectures were delivered in the winter terms of 1915–16 and 1916–17, some two years after the case of the Wolf-Man was first written up and during the period when Freud was revising it for publication. There is thus a close connection between the two productions, and indeed a case can be made for regarding Lecture I as an explicit working out of what remains hidden and disguised in the longer essay.

Especially revealing is Freud's frank acknowledgment of the way he will deal with his audience. "Do not be annoyed," he says, "if I begin by treating you . . . as . . . neurotic patients" (*CIL,* p. 15). He then describes what such a treatment will be like; it will begin in the assumption that everything the members of the audience know and believe constitutes an obstacle to their understanding. "I will show you," he goes on, "how the whole trend of your previous education and all your habits of thought are inevitably bound to make you into opponents of psycho-analysis, and how much you would have to overcome *in yourselves* in order to get the

12. Ned Lukacher, *Primal Scenes: Literature, Philosophy, Psychoanalysis* (Ithaca, N.Y., 1986), p. 145.

better of this instinctive opposition" (*CIL*, pp. 15–16; my emphasis). The cast of characters is smaller here and the audience must play both its own part and the part of the obstinate critics. Rather than being asked to reject those critics, the listener is asked to reject himself as the necessary source of error and to replace his "habits of thought" with new ones fashioned for him by the words of the analyst. But, Freud cautions, those words will have their effect only if the ear is receptive, and the ear will be receptive only if the hearer turns away from his previous education and surrenders to the speaker. Everything will depend, he announces, "on how much credence you can give to your informant," that is, to me. Freud himself raises the objection that such credence would be supported only "by hearsay"—by words—and replies by asking his listeners to imagine themselves attending a lecture on history. The historian in making his case would refer you to documents, "to the reports given by ancient writers"; but, after all, Freud points out, those documents would prove only that "earlier generations already believed" in the reality of what the historian asserts; in the end you would still be relying on words and on your own belief "that the lecturer had no conceivable motive for assuring you of the reality of something he himself did not think real" (*CIL*, pp. 18, 19). The rhetorical basis of psychoanalysis (and of all knowledge) could hardly be made clearer, but Freud seems determined to drive the point home. In a remarkable paragraph the power of persuasive language is given a due that would seem extravagant to Quintilian or Cicero. "Nothing," he declares, "takes place in a psycho-analytic treatment but an interchange of words," and it is this fact that is always cited by detractors who doubt whether " 'anything can be done about . . . illness by mere talking' " (*CIL*, p. 17). This doubt about talk is met, as it must be, with another piece of talk, with the assertion that it is only by talk—by words— that anything can be done:

> Words were originally magic and to this day words have retained much of their ancient magical power. By words one person can make another blissfully happy or drive him to despair, by words the teacher conveys his knowledge to his pupils, by words the orator carries his audience with him and determines their judgements and decisions. Words provoke affects and are in general the means of . . . influence among men. [*CIL*, p. 17]

It is but a short step from this ringing statement to the conclusion that the basis of argument, and therefore of conviction, is always rhetorical even when a discourse claims to be disinterested and rational. Freud makes this point in the closing paragraphs. The subject is once again the opponents of psychoanalysis who find its doctrines "repulsive and morally reprehensible" but know that in order to be persuasive they must recast their objections "in intellectual terms." Freud reports that they always succeed, for "it is inherent in human nature . . . to consider a thing untrue if one does not like it" and "it is easy to find arguments against it" (*CIL*, p. 23). But of course those arguments will not be truly logical or factual for they will always "arise from emotional sources" which, after all, are the only sources that human nature knows.

What Freud says next, in the opening sentences of the final substantive paragraph, is, to say the least, surprising: "We, however, Ladies and Gentlemen, can claim that . . . we have had no tendentious aim in view. We have merely wished to give expression to a matter of fact which we believe we have established by our painstaking labours" (*CIL*, pp. 23–24). At the very least we would seem to have a disjunction between Freud's general account of human nature and the claims he makes for his own assertions. The general account says that all knowledge is ultimately rhetorical ("arise[s] from emotional sources"); the claim he makes for his own assertions is that they are not rhetorical but true. How are we to explain this apparent contradiction? As usual Freud himself gives the answer (although unwittingly) when he says of society in general that it "does not wish to be reminded of [the] precarious portion of its foundations" (*CIL*, p. 23). I would go even further and say that neither society nor any member of society *could* be reminded of that precariousness, for to be so reminded would be to achieve what psychoanalysis itself declares to be unattainable, a distance on one's own concerns and obsessions. The question is whether or not the knowledge (the knowledge rhetoric offers us) that our convictions are unsupported by anything external to themselves will operate to undermine those convictions, and my answer to the question is no.[13] Whenever we are asked to state what we take to be the case about this or that, we will always respond in the context of what seems to us at the time to be indisputably true, even if we know, as a general truth, that everything can be disputed. *One who has learned the lesson of rhetoricity does not thereby escape the condition it names.* The fact that Freud lays bare the rhetorical basis of all convictions does not protect him from the appeal and power of his own. There finally is no contradiction here, only a lack of relationship between a truth one might know about discourse in general—that it is ungrounded—and the particular truths to which one is temporally committed and concerning which one can have no doubts. Once more we come round to the deep point that the case of

13. For an elaboration of this point, see Stanley Fish, "Consequences," *Critical Inquiry* 11 (March 1985): 440–41. The issue here is whether or not, having realized that we are always and already in a situation, we are now in a better position to operate in the situations we occupy. Those who answer in the affirmative commit what I call antifoundationalist theory hope, the mistake of thinking that a general awareness of groundlessness leads one to question and distrust the (interpretive) grounds of one's discourse. This distrust could only be performed if one could move to some other (noninterpretive) grounds from the vantage point of which distrust could be experienced, but that move is precluded by the antifoundationalist insight itself.

the Wolf-Man allows us to make: the rhetorical and constructed nature of things does not compromise their reality but constitutes it, and constitutes it in a form that is as invulnerable to challenge as it is unavailable to verification. Like his patient, Freud can only know what he knows within the rhetoric that possesses him, and he cannot be criticized for clinging to that knowledge even when he himself could demonstrate that it is without an extradiscursive foundation. At times in this essay I have spoken as if Freud ought to have been aware that his argument had its sources in his deepest anxieties; but it now should be clear that this is an awareness he could not possibly achieve, since, by the arguments of psychoanalysis itself, every operation of the mind, including the operation we might want to call awareness, issues from those same anxieties. The thesis of psychoanalysis is that one cannot get to the side of the unconscious; the thesis of this essay is that one cannot get to the side of rhetoric. These two theses are one and the same.

The Intertextual Unconscious

Michael Riffaterre

Literature is open to psychoanalysis as is any other form of expression—this much is obvious. Less so is the relevancy of analysis to the specificity of literary texts, to what differentiates them from other linguistic utterances; in short, to the literariness of literature.

The analyst cannot avoid this problem of focus. If he did, he would treat verbal art as a document for purposes other than an understanding of its defining difference. He would simply be seeking one more set of clues to the workings of the human mind, as the sociologist or historian exploits literature to explore periods or societies through their reflection in its mirror.

The only approach to the proper focus must be consistent both with the analyst's method and with the natural reader's practice. The analyst requires free association on the part of the analysand, and he matches this free flow of information with an attention equally open to all that is said. It is only after a passive stage of "evenly-hovering attention," or, as the French nicely call it, *écoute flottante,* that he seizes upon clues to build a model of interpretation. These clues are revealed to him by anomalies such as parapraxes and repetitions or deviant representations, as well as formal coincidences between what he hears and the corpus of observations on linguistic behavior accumulated since Freud. The reader, on the other hand, is faced with a text that is strongly organized, over-determined by aesthetic, generic, and teleological constraints, and in which whatever survives of free association is marshaled toward certain effects. The reader himself is far from passive, since he starts reacting to the text as soon as his own way of thinking, and of conceiving representation, is either confirmed or challenged. The text tends therefore not to be interpreted for what it is, but for what is selected from it by the reader's individual reactions. A segmentation of the text into units of significance thus occurs, and it is the task of the critic to verify the validity of this process. In pursuing this goal he must restrict himself to a segmentation that can be proven as being dictated by textual features rather than by the reader's idiosyncrasies, by those elements the perception of which does not depend on the latter and that resist erasure when they are in conflict with such individual quirks. The analyst's advantage in identifying such features is that he is trained to recognize the above-mentioned anomalies and to explain them by repression and displacement, that is, by the traces left in the surface of the text by the conflict between its descriptive and narrative structures and the lexicon and grammar that we call the unconscious.

The problem with standard analysis, however, is that it privileges ungrammaticalities that have already been recorded and tagged and whose traits have been observed to characterize complexes, stages of mental development, or regressions from them. Even when this selection is entirely justified at one point of the text, extending its application to the context, or in some cases even to a corpus, cannot be justified unless by an aprioristic reduction of the text to its author, or even of the author to one of the categories delineated by psychoanalytical typology.

In the case of Marcel Proust, for instance, an author I have chosen because he would seem to have written for analysis and because his readership is post-Freudian, preconceived categories have yielded fascinating results. Unfortunately, these categories all fail signally to account for the whole corpus of *A la Recherche du temps perdu,* and if they come close, their efficacy peters out with *Le Temps retrouvé.* Much has been said, for instance, on the novel as an epic of the Oedipal conflict. On the one hand, however, because of its universality, the Oedipus complex is bound to obtain in all of literature in general. On the other hand, focusing on it has not yet been shown completely or satisfactorily to explain such striking traits of the novel as its obsession with snobbery, or, more generally, with aspects of society that are not very significant except in terms of their literary mimesis. Again, much has been said, and quite rightly, about anamnesis as the principal generator of Proustian fiction, and especially about the exemplary incident of the *madeleine,* no doubt because

Michael Riffaterre, University Professor at Columbia University and a senior fellow of the School of Criticism and Theory, is the editor of *Romanic Review.*

it is the first example in the novel of the narrator's struggle to rebuild the past by exploring the unconscious, and also because it is a source of affect unrivaled by subsequent experiments with involuntary memory. And yet one cannot help suspecting that the *madeleine* instance is also privileged because it fits, for obvious reasons, a preestablished analytical model, namely the oral stage of infantile development. What then of the other instances—the tinkling of the spoon against china at a party, the narrator's ankle twisting on an uneven paving stone, and the feel of starch on a napkin—all of which receive equal billing in *Le Temps retrouvé*, when anamnesis absorbs the whole narrative and leads to a partial rewriting and an encapsulated replay of the previous volumes.

Even were these analyses always as convincing as they are brilliant, they still could not explain the whole of Proustian architecture. Many aspects of it are left unaccounted for, elements that the natural reader is not prepared to see as less Proustian, as less typical, or even as lesser sources of reading pleasure.

A second objection is that no evidence is given that the reader can share in these analyses and, unaided, perceive those peculiarities of the text on whose exegesis they are constructed. It matters little that the reader cannot equal the analyst's skill, or that, given the premises, he could duplicate at least some of these critical feats. What does matter is that we have no proof that he could, alone, find the starting point; that what is being explained as literature is indeed characterized by literariness—that is, perceptible, enjoyable, and readable within fixed hermeneutic parameters by anyone capable of reading French.

A third objection is that we have no certainty that the initial reading is indeed passive, docile, open to the text; that it is not, on the contrary, oriented, manipulated in the light of psychoanalytical preconceptions.

These objections can be answered and psychoanalysis made automatically relevant to literature's literariness if any of its hermeneutic strategies can be applied to the whole of the text, if the scanning of the text does not go beyond the reader's limits, and if that reader does not impose on the text a segmentation borrowed from elsewhere, units of significance which have been defined before and outside of that text.

The safest way to avoid premature decisions regarding the validity of an interpretation and to substitute a text-dictated segmentation for one based on preconceived models, is for the analyst to rely on the reader's linguistic competence in his scanning of the text for signs pointing to the unconscious.

Identifying these signs does not require preternatural insights, because such signs in literature are words or phrases that cannot be understood with the sole help of their context and of our familiarity with grammar, lexical distribution, and the descriptive systems that subordinate the mimesis of reality to the mythologies and ideological commonplaces of our society. In other words, literary signs point to the unconscious inasmuch as they repress a meaning in the process of conveying one. This dual action of the sign is best described as intertextuality: the perception that our reading of a text or textual component (paragraph, sentence, phrase, or word) is complete or satisfactory only if it constrains us to refer to or to cancel out its homologue in the intertext. Recovery of the intertext does not in itself constitute a discovery of the unconscious, but it directs the analyst toward it, and the more such "bearings" are collected along the written line, the easier it is to pinpoint the location of the repressed. Intertextuality, in short, is tantamount to a mimesis of repression. I submit that the application of psychoanalysis to literature needs no more than a description of that mimesis, for the mimesis, rather than a represented object or referent (or even its signifier outside the text), is the starting point of reading and the sole guideline to interpretation. If this is true of all literary representations, it must also be true of the sign that represents the suppression of another, intertextual, referent.

To pick one simple example, asparagus is a pleasurable dish, to be sure, but one served so often at Proustian dinners that there is clearly an obsessional aspect. Our gourmet writer is not thinking of the dark green *purée* of mashed asparagus, but of the vegetable in its full-bodied shape, of its stems whose succulent tips are eaten, sucked directly or cut off, depending on how formally we perform table rituals. Then comes the postprandial scene: their rigid shafts are left beheaded, bathing in their vinaigrette. The text itself clearly suggests that something is going on in the narrator's head as he reminisces about his childhood and his visits to Aunt Léonie's kitchen:

> What most enraptured me were the asparagus, tinged with ultra-marine and pink . . . I felt that these celestial hues indicated the presence of exquisite creatures who had been pleased to assume vegetable form and who . . . allowed me to discern in this radiance of dawn . . . that precious quality which I should recognize again when, all night long after a dinner at which I had partaken of them, they played (lyrical and coarse in their jesting as the fairies in Shakespeare's *Dream*) at transforming my chamber pot into a vase of aromatic perfume.[1]

The mock-metamorphosis of *asperges* into fairies, portrayed as desirable females, reveals an appeal certainly as much sexual as culinary. Furthermore, whenever asparagus is served, the context proffers words that

---

1. Marcel Proust, *Remembrance of Things Past,* trans. C. K. Scott Moncrieff and Terence Kilmartin, 3 vols. (New York, 1981), 1:131. In a few instances I have reworded the translation for the sake of greater accuracy. The original French is from Proust, *A la Recherche du temps perdu,* ed. Pierre Clarac and André Ferré, 3 vols. (Paris: Bibliothèque de la Pléiade, 1956), 1:121. All further references to this work (the translation and the original in that order) will be included in the text.

admit of two interpretations, one contextual and one sexual. During a dinner at the Guermantes', the Duke voices outrage at the price of a still life, Elstir's *Bundle of Asparagus:* " 'There was nothing else in the picture, just a bundle of asparagus exactly like the ones you're eating now. But I must say I refused to swallow Mr. Elstir's asparagus. . . . Three hundred francs for a bundle of asparagus! . . . I thought it a bit stiff (Je l'ai trouvée roide)' " (2:520; 2:501).[2]

This symbolism has little to do with a natural similarity between two objects that may strike only the dirty-minded. But it certainly owes much to verbal propinquity: *asperge* is also slang for 'penis,' and, in slang again, *aller aux asperges*, 'to go for asparagus,' describes a prostitute on the move. As if this were not enough, the noun *asperge* is the exact homonym of a verb *(il) asperge*—to drench, or to water, as with a watering can: the very verb for an ejaculatory wetting.

It is clear that the proliferating double entendres are produced by the suppression of the vulgar acceptation. Slang here is the intertext of the proper use of the word. The concept of syllepsis aptly describes this special case of intertextuality. Syllepsis is a trope consisting in the simultaneous presence of two meanings for one word. I modify this definition thus: the meaning required by the context represses the one incompatible with that context. Repression, however, entails a compensation: it generates a syntagm or even a text in which the repressed meaning reappears in various guises (adjectives, paraphrases, or new syllepses as with the Duke's remark).

Note that the risqué meaning remains in limbo: the "true" reason for the Duke's particular wording of his annoyance has no place in the narrative. Devoid of diegetic motivation, the detail therefore becomes entirely descriptive, and since what it describes is unimportant anyway, the sylleptic censoring merely serves to create verisimilitude, a mimesis of small talk. Literary realism here results from the fact that symbolism is firmly kept unconscious.

Syllepsis need not be limited to the tracing of elementary symbolism. In fact the trope (in my revised definition) provides us with an effective means of adapting the concept of condensation (Freud's *Verdichtung*) to literary analysis. I shall try to demonstrate how a character in *A la Recherche du temps perdu*, Madame de Villeparisis, is created at the point of intersection

2. Later on at the same dinner, the table talk leads unaccountably to a complex variation of that suggestive stiffness, put one peg higher on a scale of successive hyperboles by quoting an authority—the "green asparagus grown in the open air, which, as has been so amusingly said by the exquisite writer who signs herself E. de Clermont-Tonnerre, 'have not the impressive rigidity of their sisters' " (2:522–23; 5:503–4). Much earlier, in the first volume of the Proustian opus, a hilarious discussion between Aunt Léonie and her cook had opposed *asperges* as big as her arm to the puny ones that the parish priest grew in *his* garden: "he never grows anything but wretched little twigs" (1:59; 1:55).

of several associational sequences, the significances of which are now combined and embodied in that noblewoman. Her very character is structured as a syllepsis, since most of the subtext centered upon her can be read as the expansion of one name into a complex portrayal, but also as a sentence. The intertext of that name splits one person into two and describes the relationship between the two. Furthermore, it is a lexical syllepsis of the *asperge* type that first attracts the reader's attention to the ambivalent symbolism of the condensation.

It is a well-established fact in Proustian criticism, and indeed it is evident to the most absentminded reader, that the narrator's mother is identified with, and for a time replaced by, his grandmother. The latter assumes the role of the former, thus defusing the Oedipal conflict and for a time freeing the narrator of the bondage of rivalry with his father.

When the grandmother is struck by the illness that will kill her, her descent toward the kingdom of the dead (Proust's own image) begins in a public toilet on the Champs-Elysées, where she suffers a stroke. This toilet is watched over by a female attendant, whose ugliness seems to proclaim that her true role is to keep the door to the other world. The text leaves no room for any other interpretation. A transfer of physical features takes place whereby the grandmother now assumes the symbolism of this unpalatable character. This has been convincingly interpreted as a death wish toward the mother and as her desecration at one remove.

Now the identification of the two characters, the mutual exchange of symbolic features between the grandmother and the toilet attendant, is made unavoidable by the fact that both are figurative *marquises*. The grandmother's abiding literary passion is the *Lettres* of Madame de Sévigné, and she constantly quotes and glosses this book for the narrator's benefit. This metonymic relationship is matched by a jocular, or perhaps mythological, metaphor on the toilet attendant's side: lowbrow witnesses assert that she is really a *marquise* who has known better times.

I would like to prove that the novel offers a third *marquise* who contains in herself the other two. The sequence of events centered on her is more a subtext than the development of her character, more a commentary on the avatars of the mother than the unfolding of a subplot.

This third *marquise* is none other than Madame de Villeparisis. The Duc de Guermantes is her nephew, Ambassador Norpois her lover. She is the most important of the secondary characters. In the narrative, her function is to introduce the narrator to the *Côté de Guermantes*, bridging the gap between his bourgeoisie and the charmed kingdom of the aristocracy. Her salon is the vantage point from which he sees in one glance the snobs he wishes to conquer, the comedy of mores he is later to describe, and the world of his fantasies. It is through Madame de Villeparisis, a former schoolmate of his grandmother, that the narrator gets to know all the most important characters of the novel: Charlus, his key to Sodom; Saint-Loup, his key to friendship and the model for his ideal of a gentleman; and Oriane de Guermantes, his key to love. The old *marquise* is a text unto herself; her life is like a novel within the novel. She is a *grande dame* who lost some of her social status because of her deportment as a young woman, but she regains a precarious position by turning her salon into a literary scene, and so filling a gap in the decidedly unintellectual world of the aristocracy. She is thus essential to the narrative economy of the novel.

But next to this diegetic function, Madame de Villeparisis has a symbolic one, embodying as she does the other two *marquises*. She unites in her person features characteristic of the grandmother and of the public toilet attendant, and more specifically those elements that are exchanged between the two. She also exemplifies traits that the grandmother borrows or usurps from the mother. As a character, she is marked by none of the ravages that everyday life and old age bring about, changes that play so important a role in the literary mimesis of life in any fiction, but in Proust's novel perhaps more egregiously so. She comes pre-aged, as it were, an immutable figure with a past, deriving her significance from the legacy of that checkered past. Her imperviousness to time makes her a text of today whose explanatory intertext is yesterday. Every recurrence of the Villeparisis subtext reactivates a system of signs and a grammar of their associations, each reactivation repeating the previous one intact. Each recurrence posits one more and obtrudes on the reader special rules of equivalence between the two mother substitutes, the good one (the grandmother) and the negativized one (the *chalet* hag). Furthermore, these equivalences are sufficiently visible in this composite portrait for the *marquise* subtext to function as a model, as a hermeneutic template for the related interpretation of the two other *marquises*. The model sketches atemporal guidelines for the reader's understanding of the mother in the Oedipal conflict. Madame de Villeparisis first appears as an alternate for the grandmother in her role as a mother substitute. She takes over the care of the narrator when we first encounter her, in Balbec, taking him on the rides he needs for his health. She polishes his aesthetic education, plying him with books and all sorts of goodies, just as before the grandmother had taught him to appreciate Madame de Sévigné. Back in Paris, she introduces him into Parisian society (and discreetly protects him from molestation by Baron Charlus). In short, entire fragments of narrative, sketchily undeveloped stories, can be read as ghost identifications of the *marquise* with the mother. Her mentions of his father remain unexplained at the narrative level, with the result that she appears to view the latter with the eyes of a wife:

> altering the scale of her vision, she saw this one man, so large among all the rest so small, like that Jupiter to whom Gustave Moreau, when he portrayed him by the side of a weak mortal (à

côté d'une faible mortelle), gave a superhuman stature. [1:754; 1:701]

Later on, and more revealingly still, the Duchess de Guermantes offers pastry and tea to the narrator at a party, duplicating the key symbol of the real mother giving him tea and the all-important *madeleine*, but in so doing the Duchess states that she is acting the part of the mistress of the house—our *marquise*, thus once more put *in loco parentis* (2:272; 2:263).

Conversely, the *marquise* appears as an alternate for the public toilet attendant in her role as a desecrated incestuous mother. The symbolic attributes of the attendant contaminate her as they did the grandmother, and announce the impending demise of the positive grandmother-mother. Although Madame de Villeparisis comes from a family whose nobility is older than that of the French kings, her scandalous past has forced her to adopt a title as bogus as the *chalet* lady's (2:304; 2:294).[3] Her self-effacement makes her dress as if she were an usher in a theater, an occupation whose status is on a par with that of a toilet attendant (1:266; 1:244). In her last appearance, her clothes look like a concierge's (3:645; 3:630).

An identification by name, equally gratuitous for both characters, underscores the presence of the unconscious at work: the narrator's maid believes that the attendant is really a marchioness of *Saint-Ferréol* (1:531; 1:492). The same name pops up out of nowhere in a conversation at Madame de Villeparisis' to allude to an authentic noblewoman of that name. Unaccountably another guest seems annoyed not to know her. He petulantly affects to believe that she is a fake: "'Really, my family are amazing . . . they know people no one ever heard of, people whose name is *more or less* Saint-Ferréol ([my italics]; qui s'appellent plus ou moins)'" (2:263; 2:255). But the clincher is a quip made by Charlus, a typically "mad" statement from that hysterical gentleman: because the narrator mistakes one style of furniture for another, the Baron sneers, "'One of these days you'll be mistaking Madame de Villeparisis's lap for the lavatory, and goodness knows what you'll do in it'" (2:576; 2:555).

It is through her physiognomy, however, that the third *marquise* at once proclaims the synonymy of the first two and unveils the narrator's Oedipal transgression: Madame de Villeparisis' rough and red complexion, and specifically the coarse grain of her cheeks, are described precisely in the same terms as the *mufle* (muzzle) of the lavatory Cerberus, and again in the same terms as the cheeks and complexion of the grandmother after her stroke. And those cheeks are precisely where the oral cathexis

---

3. See also 2:303; 2:294: "[assuming] an aristocratic name with impunity, as people do in novels." The detail is the more telling because it goes straight from the repression into a metalinguistic gloss of the text born of the release of that repression.

takes place—the grandmother's cheeks are kissed by the narrator as a babe suckles the mother's breast (1:718; 1:668–69). Finally, Madame de Villeparisis' face and the reasons for its appearance point to the encrypted interpretation of the grandmother's sudden resemblance to the attendant—a symbol of the mother's desecration. The attendant guards the door of the toilets, but her looks make one feel as if that door opened on a netherworld that is at once death and sewer—Mallarmé's *bouche sépulcrale d'égout.*

Madame de Villeparisis' physiognomy tells the story that motivates the symbol. It is described as the scar tissue left by the fire of vice and sin. The image is not too strong: she is alluded to as having been a "true Messalina" (2:202; 2:197).[4] Other fallen women are depicted as ruined statues whose plaster is scaling off (2:207; 2:202). (In fact, time and again the narrator will be irresistibly attracted by women whose vice, as the phrase goes, is inscribed on their faces.) A naive but well-read bystander who believes her to be a kept woman and cannot bring himself to say it directly cites a sixteenth-century satirist, a French Juvenal, whose portrayal of a procuress was until about World War I the standard intertextual screen for such allusions in polite circles (1:755; 1:703). And as if scandalous gossip from the distant past were not enough, the narrative is confirmed by the descriptive: Madame de Villeparisis' given name is that of the sinner of the Gospel—Madeleine—a word that in context packs together the mother as lover and as giver of the *madeleine,* genital and oral compulsions.

Should I be suspected of seeing too much in these equivalencies, and perhaps of being guided more by Freudian categories than by the text, another incidental, narratively gratuitous name will vindicate my finding the *marquise* in the mother. When the grandmother assumes the role of the mother during a summer vacation, in the narrator's eyes the trip to a sea resort is nevertheless a disguise for his mother's infidelity. He is being jilted in favor of his father: "For the first time I began to feel that it was possible that my mother might live another life, without me, otherwise than for me" (1:697; 1:648). This, however, is only plain narrative, open to an innocent reading. But it comes as no surprise that once again a name out of nowhere should open up the latent import of what would seem to be the melancholy of parting at a railway station. The mother seems already far away, with a new hat and a flimsy summer dress "making her different, someone who belonged already to the Villa Montretout" (1:700; 1:651). The name of the villa taken by the father

4. The daughter of a former lover of Madame de Villeparisis is desperately anxious to see her. Her father was ruined by the *marquise.* Says the daughter, "my consolation is to think that he loved the most beautiful woman of his time" (3:648–49; 3:634). What she sees is "a little hunchbacked, red-faced hideous woman." On her past, see 2:187–88, 191, and 3:296–97; 2:184, 187, and 3:294.

for the season is of course a touch of verisimilitude. It should be taken as no more than a realistic detail referring presumably to the very French patronymic of the villa's owner. But this sign from the semiotic system of summer rentals is also, sylleptically, a descriptive phrase, or perhaps a command, *Montretout*, "show it all" or "(she) shows it all"—voyeurism or exhibitionism. Either interpretation resuscitates the fantasy of unfaithfulness, of the mother's dissolute conduct.

The above analysis, an analysis performed by the text, remains incomplete if we cannot explain another "gratuitous" articulation of the equivalency system, the very sign of the equation. Why should the three versions of the mother be *marquises?* Again the sociolect provides the answer: *marquise* is slang for the madame of a bawdy house. This is the answer, and not just a tempting hypothesis: critics have long marveled at the astounding episode in which the narrator gives to the madame of a brothel pieces of furniture that had belonged to his Aunt Léonie, another undoubted hypostasis of the mother. Nor is the symbolism of the gesture left in doubt: the furniture is a sofa where as an adolescent he was sexually initiated, and giving it to the brothel, which could have been cause for remorse or embarrassment, becomes a pretext for necrophiliac fantasies: "all the virtues that pervaded my aunt's room . . . appeared to me tortured by the cruel contacts to which I had delivered them defenseless. Had I engineered the rape of a dead woman, I would not have suffered more" (1:622; 1:578). Dead or alive the mother remains the object of desire, and desire cannot be expressed, let alone fulfilled, except through desecration.

Syllepsis, as we have seen, affects only isolated words. A second category of the intertextual unconscious involves subtexts, fully developed narrative units that are embedded in the main narrative and sometimes scattered through it. Whereas a syllepsis straddles the text and an intertext outside of it (sometimes simply the sociolect itself), here the text-intertext pair is present in its entirety within the text—a case of intratextual intertextuality.

This play on prefixes is no paradox, but a reminder of the changing nature of narrative components according to the standpoint from which the reader looks at them. Any subtext, or, more broadly still, any unit of significance that can be identified as the narrative unfolds, any segment of that narrative that can be isolated without cognitive loss, may serve as an intertext to some further such unit, if the latter has features in common with the former. Such features make it possible or necessary for the reader to see the two units as different versions of the same episode or of the same description, or two variants of the same structure. Components of the second will thus acquire a meaning other than what they convey in context because they will be perceived as referring also or primarily to their homologues in the first. On the other hand, the meaning of such a homologue may be retrospectively modified by our rethinking it in the light of the second version, in which case the latter now functions as the intertext of the first.

The existence of such pairings or couplings contradicts the basic rule of any narrative that demands a progression from one point to the next, or at any rate, a change that may be in accordance with the time sequence or counter to it, or anticipate or reverse it occasionally with prolepsis or analepsis. The rule of change applies even when nothing changes despite the passage of time, since this "pathological" state of affairs cannot be perceived and interpreted except by opposition to expected change: hence aesthetic or ethical judgments making negative change a sign, for instance, of stagnation, boredom, or of glorious resistance to the ravages of time. The intertextual relationship I have just described does not even apply the rule of change negatively. Indeed it ignores or bypasses it entirely, offering a nonsequential and nonnarrative reading of the chain of events, or of selected links in that chain. Because of the intertextual cross-reference, each such reading is in fact a rereading, a revised interpretation of a preceding stretch of text, the starting point being wherever the reader first becomes aware of a connection or an alternative between two or more textual segments. Rereading or revising bespeaks an exploratory, inquisitive, questioning approach quite like psychoanalytical procedures—and no wonder, for it must be obvious that the writer rewrites or tries variations because he obeys a repetition compulsion.

This repetition is at first perceived only because it violates the narrative rule above. But what makes both perception and a single "proper" interpretation unavoidable is the fact that in each instance, readers realize that similarities obtain (despite the formal variation from one subtext to the other) and that the differences are not essential; that they are only variations in the codes chosen to encode the same message, differences that refer to the same core of meaning as verified by the intertext's pertinence being maintained despite the changes in the subtexts. Readers therefore recognize that these are so many variegated periphrases around the same unsaid, hidden, taboo significance.

My example is a series of screen images hiding phantasms of oral sexuality, but hiding them with periphrases whose every component points to where the phantasm lurks and comes equipped with guidelines for bringing its cause to light. We first notice a series of variants with a subtext about proper names. Needless to say, patronymics and given names are a favorite topic in the conversations the narrator attributes to his characters. Proust's readers are especially impressed and bothered by his endless disquisitions on the etymologies of place-names and of patronymics. Whatever the ultimate significance of that preoccupation may be, there is a striking similarity between the theme and the lexical intertextuality already discussed. The proper name as empty frame and the meaning with which etymology attempts to fill that frame are a variant of the syllepsis. Inasmuch as etymology usually unearths common nouns or telling phrases under the patronymics and toponyms, an intertextuality in which the intertext is the etymon functions like a psychoanalyst finding a decipherable meaning in scrambled images. In the following instance, the intertext is not a commonplace phrase, but the very identity of the bearer of a first name. The dialogue is a tender scene of young love, a budding flirtation between a precocious little girl, Gilberte, and the narrator all simmering with puberty:

> And then there was another day when she said to me: "You know, you may call me Gilberte. In any case, I'm going to call you by your first name. It's too silly not to." Yet she continued for a while to address me by the more formal *vous*, and when I drew her attention to this, she smiled and composing a sentence like those that are put into the grammar-books of foreign languages to teach us to make use of a new word, ended it with my Christian name.

The French says *petit nom*, as if the intimacy suggested by the use of the given names meant in fact a synecdochic substitution of a small but representative part of the body for the whole man or his manhood: *petit nom* like *petit homme*, or in familiar French, *petit bout d'homme*, *petit Poucet*, with a displacement from 'little tip,' or Tom Thumb, to penis.

> Recalling, some time later, what I had felt at the time, I identified the impression of having been held for a moment in her mouth, myself, naked (l'impression d'avoir été tenu un instant dans sa bouche, moi-même, nu), . . . and, when she used my surname . . . her lips . . . seemed to be stripping me, undressing me, like taking the skin off a piece of fruit of which one can swallow only the pulp. [1:437–38; 1:403]

Let us assume that the innocent atmosphere of young love prevents most readers from accepting the stark implication that this is a fellatio phantasm. At any rate, this denial of evidence will not stop them from connecting the scene with another early memory treasured by the child narrator. It seems harmless enough on the surface since it harks back to the pleasures of summers spent in Combray at Aunt Léonie's, the first mother substitute of the novel, although her role is not as fully developed as the grandmother's. An important member of his aunt's household is the scullery maid, the pregnant *fille de cuisine* who looks like the personification of Charity, as Giotto painted her in his frescoes of Vices and Virtues. Next to her, in a way that is patently so farfetched that the motivation for it must be elsewhere, the text introduces Giotto's allegory of Envy:

Invidia . . . should have had some look of envy on her face. But in
this fresco, . . . the symbol occupies so large a place and is represented with such realism, the snake hissing between the lips of
Envy is so huge, and so completely fills her wide-opened mouth,
that the muscles of her face are strained . . . like those of a child
blowing up a balloon and her attention—and ours too for that
matter—is so utterly concentrated on the activity of her lips as to
leave little time to spare for envious thoughts. [1:87–88; 1:81]

So bizarre an assumption that blowing and envy are mutually exclusive
can only be understood as an unconscious fusion of the two allegories,
together with a reversal of Envy. Thus is achieved at a level that is neither
narrative nor descriptive a composite character, not unlike the Villeparisis
hybrid, composed of spiritual Caritas and of carnal Amor. The hybrid
is an intertextual correction or addition to the original Caritas in order
to account for the fact that the allegory is now also a representation of
the scullion surprised by sin. To be sure, oral sex cannot lead to pregnancy.
But the child's phantasm, unable to use Envy (turned into Amor) as a
metaphor, makes do by using it as a metonymy: thus the repressed
memory that associated turgid penis and inflated belly, the cause and
effect, the before and after of a narrative derived from the descriptive
system of the word *sin*, is committed to writing. Observe that there is no
need to take literally the repressed memory I hypothesize here. Even
this minor risk is rendered unnecessary by the nature of the representation:
by superimposing the realistic narrative of a maid's interesting situation
and the Giotto ekphrasis, the text produces a metaphor that has the same
double function of hiding and revealing as the periphrasis in the subtext.

Readers are, incidentally, not free to avert their eyes. The connection
between the scullion and the act whose commission she can no longer
hide is repeated once more through a private allegory, an allusive game
the text plays *sotto voce*. The scullion's special duties in preparing food
for cooking are restricted in a way quite incompatible with the common
concept of the female factotum that she is in reality, but quite to the
point if we read *scullion* as a translation of *sex* into *servant* code: she is
supposed to devote all her attention to "skinning" ("plumer") asparagus
(1:86; 1:80). As for the intertextual link, it is made more visible by the
fact that it is Swann, Gilberte's father, who, by slyly pointing out a resemblance between the kitchen maid and Giotto's Caritas, provides the
narrative motivation for a periphrasis of orality.

Nor does intertextuality stop here. Two more passages will in turn
transform the Gilberte text into *their* intertext. But since metaphor and
comparison have already been used as variants of the hiding/revealing
periphrasis, the narrative will try the two solutions left for variation. The
first two were figurative and literal (the narrator's imagining that Gilberte's
mouth holds his nakedness is not a simile, but an *as if* imaginary yet

literal statement): only the fantastic and the metalinguistic remain. And so it comes to pass that the next variant is a nightmare of the narrator's, one thousand pages later, in *The Guermantes Way:* he dreams that he cannot move because he is all tied up, and he is full of shame because he is naked in the midst of a silent watchful circle of faceless "friends," and he cannot speak (*je sentais le son s'arrêter dans ma gorge*). As if that image of sexual enslavement, feared and yet yearned for just as Envy and Charity had become equivalent, were not enough, a simile spells it out and in so doing maintains the momentum of compulsive repetition: "this figure of sleep projected by my sleeping [the basic narrative translated into its descriptive amplification] looked like those big allegories that Swann had given me, in which Giotto painted Envy with a snake in her mouth" (2:148; 2:146).

As for the fourth variant of the deep throat intertextual system (and the last one, since it exhausts the paradigm of possible stylistic choices), it tops the series in spectacular fashion in three different ways. First, because of its very metalinguistic nature: it is the beyond of the text, the crossing of the border separating it from the realm of commentaries, the annexation of critical discourse, and the advent of modernism in the guise of self-reflexive fiction. Second, because of its exemplary or hyperbolic nature: the speaker is Albertine, the emotional focus of the novel, the main target of the narrator's desire, and she inflames that desire by playing with orality, but a dissociated, inaccessible one, before him. Third, because it represents a clausula: Albertine parodies the narrator and speaks her phantasm the way he would have written it. The text authors its author in turn, as it were. The passage is Albertine's rhapsody on ice creams, where the mistress emulates her lover's literary games, delivering herself of a prose poem made of images so bookish that even he would not have dared employ such forms in speech. Evidently this far-reaching metaphorization on so prosaic a subject represents the most extreme form of catachresis, the climax of the periphrastic detour around the orality intertext:

> "Oh dear, at the Ritz I'm afraid you'll find Vendôme Columns of ice, chocolate or raspberry ice cream, and then you'll need a lot of them so that may look like votive pillars or pylons erected along an avenue to the glory of Coolness. They make raspberry obelisks too, which will rise up here and there in the burning desert of my thirst and I shall make their pink granite melt deep down in my throat." . . . and here her deep laugh broke out, whether from satisfaction of speaking so well, or in self-mockery for using such contrived images, or, alas, from physical pleasure at feeling inside herself something so good, so cool, which gave her the equivalent of sexual pleasure (*qui lui causait l'équivalent d'une jouissance*). [3:125–26; 3:130]

It would be difficult to find a text written more visibly as art for art's sake, as a fragment of writing for specialists, as an exercise. Nor could it be clearer that by imitating her author the character closes the creative circle, returning to the subject the object of that subject's desire:

> True [quoth the narrator], I myself wouldn't speak like that, and yet, all the same, but for me *she* wouldn't speak like that. She has been profoundly influenced by me, and cannot help but love me, since she is my creation (elle ne peut donc pas ne pas m'aimer, elle est mon oeuvre). [3:125; 3:129]

By this closing of the circle of orality, the author becomes child to the textual figment born of his desire; playing Pygmalion to Albertine's Galatea, he puts himself back in the position of the suckling babe.

The preceding discussion does not claim to exhaust the various modes of the intertextual unconscious, nor do I believe that this approach plumbs the depths of that unconscious, but it has the advantage of being demonstrably within reach of ordinary readers. It thus fulfills what seems to me to be the most important criterion of literary analysis in general and of criticism in particular, namely that none of the tools of inquiry require a technical training in order to be employed. Only thus can we insure that the text we analyze is the same as the text we read and not some kind of supertext requiring a special lens.

By replacing purely psychoanalytical techniques with the tools of an analysis based on words, we assure relevancy, a pertinence defined by textual features themselves. While it is true that the interpretations thus obtained are accessible only through a detour outside the text, this detour never goes beyond language, and the absent referent is still clearly outlined by elements of the text that need the complementarity or the opposability of an intertext to be units of significance. While meaning is wholly present in the text, significance rests on the inseparability of a visible sign from its repressed intertextual homologue.

One last point merits a remark. The intertextual unconscious that the reader maps out by bringing to light, step by step, successive intertextual correspondents of what troubles him in the text may be seen as a vast hypogram coextensive to the text, but a fundamental difference separates the two verbal layers: while the text is narrative, the intertext is not. Cross-references from one subtext to another are equally valid whichever point we are starting from in exploring them, and the syllepsis works as well whether we read it from the text to the intertext or reread it from language to literary discourse. Temporality is nonexistent in that hypogram: the intertext, the verbal unconscious, lies outside of the time dimension no less than does the unconscious of psychoanalysis.

Psychoanalysis and Cinema: The Melodrama of the Unknown Woman

Stanley Cavell

When the man in Max Ophuls' film *Letter from an Unknown Woman* reaches the final words of the letter addressed to him by the, or by some, unknown woman, he is shown—according to well-established routines of montage—to be assaulted by a sequence of images from earlier moments in the film. This assault of images proves to be death-dealing. His response to finishing the reading of the letter is to stare out past it, as if calling up the film's images; and his response to the assault of the ensuing repeated images is to cover his eyes with the outstretched fingers of both hands in a melodramatic gesture of horror and exhaustion. Yet he sees nothing we have not seen, and the images themselves (as it were) are quite banal—his pulling the veil of the woman's hat up over her face, the two of them at the Prater amusement park in winter, her taking a candied apple, their dancing, his playing a waltz for her on the piano in an empty ballroom. *An apparently excessive response to apparently banal images*—it seems a characterization of a response to film generally, at least to certain kinds of film, perhaps above all to classical Hollywood films.

This essay is the basis of the Edith Weigert Lecture, delivered October 18, 1985, sponsored by the Forum on Psychiatry and the Humanities, Washington School of Psychiatry, Washington, D.C. It was first printed in its entirety in *Images in Our Souls: Cavell, Psychoanalysis, and Cinema,* ed. Joseph H. Smith and William Kerrigan (Baltimore, 1987), pp. 11–43. An excerpt from it appeared in the issue of *Critical Inquiry* from which the present volume is derived. In that excerpting, and now further in this reprinting of the entire essay, a number of revisions and additions have been introduced and two instances of switched names have been corrected. I am grateful to the editors at *Critical Inquiry* for their care and help, most specifically to Arnold Davidson and James Williams. The fall I delivered the Weigert Lecture I presented its material to a seminar for discussions that have profited me beyond the instances in which I know that they caused local modifications in the present form of this work.

But since Max Ophuls is a director, and this is a film, of major ambition, the implication may be that this man's response to the returning images of the film and of his past—his horror and exhaustion—somehow underlies our response to any film of this kind, perhaps to major film as such, or ought to. It seems a particular mode of horror that these hands would ward off, since we may equally think of the images looming at this man not as what he has seen but as what he has *not* seen, has refused to see. Then are we sure that we have seen what it is up to us to see? What motivates these images? Why does their knowledge constitute an assault? If *Letter from an Unknown Woman* were merely the high-class so-called woman's film, or tearjerker, it is commonly taken to be—as the bulk of the melodramas I will refer to here are taken to be—it and they could not justify and satisfy the imposition of such questions of criticism. The only proof that any of them can do so is, of course, to provide a convincing reading in which one or another of them does so. That is not what I want to attempt here, but instead to do less and more than that. Less, because the passages of reading I provide here concern only certain isolated moments of any film. But more, because I will adduce moments from two groups of films designed at once to suggest the range and detail of their relations as a whole and to sketch the intellectual palette that convincing readings will, for my taste, have to support. Here I am looking for a sense of the ground on which any reading I would be moved to offer will succeed or fail.

In accepting the assignment to give this year's Weigert lecture on the topic of psychoanalysis and cinema, I knew that I would want to use the occasion to take further the work represented in my book *Pursuits of Happiness*. That book defines a genre of film—a genre I name the comedy of remarriage—on the basis of what I call reading the individual members of a set of films, which is meant to prove them to constitute a genre, where proving this constitution turns in part on showing the group as a whole to enact, and, I hope, to illuminate, Freud's early vision (in *Three Essays on the Theory of Sexuality*) that "the finding of the object is in fact the refinding of it," together with a surprising conjunction of preoccupations in what can be called philosophy. In remarriage comedy, unlike classical comedy, happiness, such as it is, is arrived at not by a young pair's overcoming social obstacles to their love, but instead by a somewhat older pair's overcoming obstacles that are between, or within, themselves (facing divorce, being brought *back* together, and finding one another

---

Stanley Cavell, professor of philosophy at Harvard University, is the author of many works, including *Must We Mean What We Say?*, *The Senses of "Walden," The Claim of Reason,* and, most recently, *Themes Out of School.*

again). A remarkable sequence of consequences flows from this shift of emphasis, segments of which will be rehearsed in what follows.

Remarriage comedy, in effect enacting what Freud calls the diphasic character of human sexuality, displays the nostalgic structure of human experience. Since these films, being major achievements of the art of film, thus reveal some internal affinity of the phenomenon of nostalgia with the phenomenon of film, the popular nostalgia now associated with movies stands to be understood as a parody, or avoidance, of an inherent, treacherous property of the medium of film as such. The drama of the remarriage genre, the argument that brings into play the intellectual and emotional bravery of the beautiful, lucid pairs whose interactions or conversations form the interest of the genre—Irene Dunne and Cary Grant, Barbara Stanwyck and Henry Fonda, Katharine Hepburn and Spencer Tracy—turns on their efforts to transform an intimacy as between brother and sister into an erotic friendship capable of withstanding, and returning, the gaze of legitimate civilization. They conduct, in short, the argument of marriage. In *The Philadelphia Story* (directed by George Cukor in 1940) this ancient intimacy—here between Katharine Hepburn and Cary Grant—is called, twice, having grown up together. In *The Awful Truth* (directed by Leo McCarey in 1937) the woman (Irene Dunne) actually, climactically, enacts a role as her husband's sister (the husband is again Cary Grant), in which this high-minded society lady blatantly displays her capacity for low-down sexiness.

The transformation of incestuous knowledge into erotic exchange is a function of something I call the achievement of the daily, of the diurnal, the putting together of night and day (as classical comedy puts together the seasons of the year), a process of willing repetition whose concept is the domestic, or marriage, however surprising the images of marriage become in these films. "Repetition" is the title Kierkegaard gives to his thoughts about the faith required in achieving marriage; and repetition, or rather eternal recurrence, is the recipe Nietzsche discovered as the antidote for our otherwise fated future of nihilism, the thing Nietzsche calls "the revenge against time and its 'It was'"—a revenge itself constituting a last effort not to die of nostalgia. Nietzsche explicitly invokes the concept of marriage in his prophetic cry (in *Thus Spoke Zarathustra*) for this redemption or reconception of time. He says it is "high time" for this, and in German the literal translation of "high time" is *Hochzeit* (wedding); moreover, his symbol of eternal recurrence is the (wedding) ring. These ideas of repetition may be said to require of our lives the perpetual invention of the present from the past, out of the past. This seems to be the vision of Freud's *Beyond the Pleasure Principle*, in which death—I take it to be psychological death—comes either through the success of this invention, that is, the discovery of one's own death (hence, surely, of one's own life, say, of one's willingness to live), or else through the relapse of the psychological into the biological and beyond into the inorganic, which may be viewed as counter modes of repetition.

In writing *Pursuits of Happiness* I incurred a number of intellectual debts that I propose here not to settle but somewhat to identify and organize—in effect, to rewrite certain of my outstanding promissory notes. My initial business will be to confirm a prediction of *Pursuits of Happiness* to the effect that there must exist a genre of film, in particular some form of melodrama, adjacent to, or derived from, that of remarriage comedy, in which the themes and structure of the comedy are modified or negated in such a way as to reveal systematically the threats (of misunderstanding, of violence) that in each of the remarriage comedies dog its happiness. I am calling the new genre the melodrama of the unknown woman. My next main business will be to say how I cloak my debt to the writing of Freud, which means to say what I conceive certain relations of psychoanalysis and philosophy to consist in. My concluding piece of business, as a kind of extended epilogue, will be to produce a reading of the moment I invoked in opening these remarks, a man's melodramatic covering of his eyes, from the Ophuls film from which I have adapted the title of the new genre.

The prediction that some form of melodrama awaited definition was based on various moments from each of the comedies of remarriage. In the earliest of the definitive remarriage structures, *It Happened One Night* (directed by Frank Capra in 1934, with Clark Gable and Claudette Colbert), the pair work through episodes of poverty, theft, blackmail, and sordid images of marriage; in *The Awful Truth* the pair face distrust, jealousy, scandal, and the mindless rumoring of a prospective mother-in-law; in *His Girl Friday* (from 1940, directed by Howard Hawks, with Cary Grant and Rosalind Russell) the pair deal with political corruption, brutal moralism, and wasting cynicism; in *The Lady Eve* (from 1941, directed by Preston Sturges, with Fonda and Stanwyck), with duplicity and the intractableness of the past; in *The Philadelphia Story*, with pretentiousness, perverseness, alcoholism, and frigidity.

But it is in the last of the remarriage comedies, *Adam's Rib* (from 1949, directed by George Cukor, with Hepburn and Tracy), that melodrama threatens on several occasions almost to take the comedy over. The movie opens with a sequence, in effect a long prologue, in which a wife and mother tracks her husband to the apartment of another woman and shoots him. Played by the virtuoso Judy Holliday, the part is continuously hilarious, touching, and frightening, so that one never rests content with one's response to her. An early sequence of the film proper (so to speak) consists of the screening of a film-within-a-film, a home movie that depicts the principal pair's coming into possession of their country house in Connecticut, in which Spencer Tracy twice takes on comically the postures and grimaces of an expansive, classical villain, threatening, with a twirl of his imaginary mustache, to dispossess Katharine Hepburn of something more precious than country houses. These passing comic glimpses of the man's villainous powers recur more disturbingly toward the end of the film, when he in turn tracks his spouse and confronts her in what he might conceivably take to be a compromising situation, and for all the world threatens to shoot her and her companion (David Wayne). What he is threatening them with soon proves to be a pistol made of licorice, but not too soon for us to have confronted unmistakably a quality of violence in this character that is as genuine—such is the power of Spencer Tracy as an actor on film—as his tenderness and playfulness. I say in the chapter on *Adam's Rib* in *Pursuits of Happiness* that Tracy's character as qualified in this film declares one subject of the genre as a whole to be the idea of maleness itself as villainous, say sadistic. (Having made his legal point, Tracy turns the candy gun on himself, into his mouth, and proceeds to eat it—a gesture that creates its comic effect but that also smacks of madness and of a further capacity for violence and horror hardly less frightening on reflection than the simple capacity for shooting people in anger.) The suggestion I drew is that if the male gender as such, so far in the development of our culture, and in so beautifully developed a specimen of it as Spencer Tracy, is tainted with villainy, then the happiness in even these immensely privileged marriages exists only so far as the pair together locate and contain this taint—you may say domesticate it, make a home for it—as if the task of marriage is to overcome the villainy in marriage itself. Remarriage comedies show the task to be unending and the interest in the task to be unending.

The taint of villainy leaves a moral cloud, some will say a political one, over these films, a cloud that my book does not try, or wish, to disperse. It can be pictured by taking the intelligent, vivid women in these films to be descendants of Nora in Ibsen's *A Doll's House*, who leaves her husband and children in search of what she calls, something her husband has said she required, an education. She leaves saying that he is not the man to provide her with one, implying both that the education she requires is in the hands of men and that only a man capable of providing it, from whom it would be acceptable, could count for her as a husband. Thinking of the woman of remarriage comedy as lucky to have found such a man, remarriage comedy studies, among other matters, what has made him, inescapably bearing the masculine taint, acceptable. That she can, with him, have what the woman in *The Awful Truth* calls "some grand laughs" is indispensable, but not an answer; the question becomes how this happens with him.

This prompts two further questions, with which we are entered into the melodrama of unknownness. What of the women who have not found, and could not manage or relish a relationship with such a man, Nora's other, surely more numerous, descendants? And what, more particularly, of the women of the same era on film who are at least the spiritual equals of the women of remarriage comedy but whom no man can be thought to educate—I mean the women we might take as achieving the highest reaches of stardom, of female independence so far as film can manifest it—Greta Garbo and Marlene Dietrich and, at her best, Bette Davis?

The price of the woman's happiness in the genre of remarriage comedy is the absence of her mother (underscored by the attractive and signal presence, whenever he is present, of the woman's father) together with the strict absence of children for her, the denial of her as a mother—as if the woman has been abandoned, so far, to the world of men. Could remarriage comedies achieve their happiness in good faith if they denied the possibility of another path to education and feminine integrity? It would amount to denying that the happiness of these women indeed exacts a price, if of their own choice, affordable out of their own talents and tastes, suggesting instead that women without these talents and tastes are simply out of luck. Such an idea is false to the feeling shown by these women toward women unlike themselves—as, for example, Rosalind Russell's toward the outcast woman in *His Girl Friday,* or Irene Dunne's toward the nightclub singer whose identity she takes on in *The Awful Truth,* or Claudette Colbert's toward the mother who faints on the bus in *It Happened One Night.* It is as if these moments signal that such films do not stand in generic insulation from films in which another way of education and integrity is taken.

With one further feature of the way of education sought by Nora's comedic progeny, I can formulate the character I seek in a melodrama derived from the comedy of remarriage that concerns those spiritually equal women (equal in their imagination of happiness and their demand for it) among those I am calling Nora's other progeny.

The demand for education in the comedies presents itself as a matter of becoming created, as if the women's lives heretofore have been non-existent, as if they have haunted the world, as if their materialization will constitute a creation of the new woman and hence a creation, or a further step in the creation, of the human. This idea has various sources and plays various roles as the theory of remarriage develops in *Pursuits of Happiness.* Theologically, it alludes to the creation of the woman from Adam in *Genesis,* specifically its use by Protestant thinkers, impressive among them John Milton, to ratify marriage and to justify divorce. Cinematically, it emphasizes the role of the camera in transforming human figures of flesh and blood into psychic shadows of themselves, in particular in transforming the woman, of whose body more than is conventional is on some occasion found to be revealed (today such exposure would perhaps be pointless), so that Katharine Hepburn will be shown pointedly doing her own diving in *The Philadelphia Story,* or awkwardly crawling through the woods in a wet, clinging dress, or having her skirt torn off accidentally on purpose by the man in *Bringing Up Baby,* or being given a massage in *Adam's Rib.* The most famous of all such exposures, I guess, is that of Claudette Colbert showing some leg to hitch a ride in *It Happened One Night.* Dramatically, the idea of creation refers to a structure Northrop Frye calls Old Comedy—he is, however, thinking primarily of Shakespearean drama—in which the woman holds the key to the happy outcome of the plot and suffers something like death and resurrection: *All's Well That Ends Well* and *The Winter's Tale* would be signal examples. I take Hermione in *The Winter's Tale* to be the other primary source (along with Ibsen's Nora) of the woman in remarriage comedy, understanding that play as a whole, in the light of the film genre, as the greatest of the structures of remarriage. *The Winter's Tale* also proves (along with *A Doll's House*) to underlie the women of the derived melodrama of unknownness, since while Hermione's resurrection at the close of the play (which I interpret as a kind of marriage ceremony) is a function of Leontes' faith and love, it is before that a function of Paulina's constancy and effectiveness, and the ceremony provides Hermione not just with her husband again (to whom she does not at the end speak) but as well with her daughter again (to whom she does speak).

In remarriage comedy the transformation of the woman is accomplished in a mode of exchange or conversation that is surely among the glories of dialogue in the history of the art of talking pictures. The way these pairs talk together I propose as one perfect manifestation of what Milton calls that "meet and cheerful conversation" (by which he means talk as well as more than talk), which he, most emphatically among the Protestant thinkers so far as I have seen, took to constitute God's purpose in instituting sexual difference, hence marriage. But now if deriving a genre of melodrama from remarriage comedy requires, as I assume, the retaining of the woman's search for metamorphosis and existence, it nevertheless cannot take place through such ecstatic exchanges as earmark the comedies; which is to say that the woman of melodrama, as shown to us, will not find herself in what the comedies teach us marriage is, but accordingly in something less or conceivably more than that.

Then the sense of the character (or underlying myth) of film I was to look for in establishing a genre of melodrama may be formulated in the following way: a woman achieves existence (or fails to), or establishes her right to existence in the form of a metamorphosis (or fails to), apart from or beyond satisfaction by marriage (of a certain kind) and with the presence of her mother and of her children, where something in her language must be as traumatic in her case as the conversation of marriage is for her comedic sisters—perhaps it will be an aria of divorce, from husband, lover, mother, or child. (A vast, related matter, which I simply mention here, is that what is normally called adultery is not to be expected in these structures, since normally it plays no role in remarriage comedies—something that distinguishes them from Restoration comedy and from French farce. Thus, structures such as *Anna Karenina* and *Madame Bovary* are not members of what I am calling the melodrama of the unknown woman. In this genre it will not be the threat of social scandal that comes between a woman and a man, and no man could recover from participation in the special villainy that exercises the law to separate a woman irrevocably from her child.)

The films I begin from that seem to obey these intuitive requirements, together with guesses as to their salient roles within the genre, are, in summary, these seven or eight: *Blonde Venus*, with Marlene Dietrich, directed by Josef von Sternberg in 1932, which particularly emphasizes that the woman has nothing to learn from the men there are; *Stella Dallas*, directed by King Vidor in 1937, with Barbara Stanwyck and John Boles, which emphasizes the woman's business as a search for the mother, perhaps carrying a shame of the mother; *Showboat*, the Oscar Hammerstein–Jerome Kern operetta (literally a melodrama), directed by James Whale in 1936, which, as it were, mythically prepares Irene Dunne, because of the supporting or grounding presence in it of Helen Morgan and Paul Robeson, for her lead in *The Awful Truth*, thus establishing an inner connection between this comedy and this melodrama; *Random Harvest*, with Ronald Colman and Greer Garson, directed by Mervyn le Roy, in 1942, which most purely underscores the persistence of the feature in this genre of melodrama of the goal of remarriage itself; *Now Voyager*, also from 1942, which elaborates most completely the feature of metamorphosis as Bette Davis is transformed from Aunt Charlotte into the mysterious, magnetic Camille Vale, unforgettably helped by Paul Henreid and Claude Rains; *Mildred Pierce*, directed by Michael Curtiz in 1945, in which Joan Crawford emphasizes the theatricality in this melodrama, although one may decide that the feel of this feature in the film is too crazy to link it to the other members, so that it becomes rather a link to some further genre; *Gaslight*, directed by George Cukor in 1944, with Ingrid Bergman and Charles Boyer, which portrays in full length, no doubt with melodramatic or operatic exaggeration, precisely the villainous, mind-destroying mode of marriage that both the comedy and the derived melodrama of remarriage set themselves against; *Letter from an Unknown Woman*, 1948, which emphasizes, by failure, fantasies of metamorphosis and fantasies of perfect communication and of the transcendence of marriage. I add to the list Eric Rohmer's *The Marquise of O*, made in 1977 with startling faithfulness to the Heinrich von Kleist tale of 1805. The odd dates of origin and cinematic transcription are not the only respects in which Kleist's tale plays a special role in relation to the genre of unknownness. This tale most hideously expresses the villainy of the husband of the genre (he has, under the signs of impeccable honor, raped the woman he wants to marry while she is in a drugged sleep), while it also finds an ending of the most secure conjugal happiness, of the comedy of existence truly achieved, of any member of the genre. It is as if this tale undertakes all by itself to redeem the violence and ugliness that will cling to sexual hunger and satisfaction at their best—as if to prepare the soul for what Jean Laplanche, in his *Life and Death in Psychoanalysis,* calls the traumatic nature of human sexuality, thus harking all the way back to Breuer and Freud's *Studies on Hysteria.*[1]

This list of candidates for membership in this genre of melodrama that I propose to derive from remarriage comedy is bound to seem less perspicuous than the list of films from which I began in defining the comic genre. While the melodramas were all made in Hollywood and all within the same two decades as the comedies (except for *The Marquise of O*), they lack the overlapping of directors, actors and actresses, and of that critical sound—of high and embattled wit—that gives a sensuous coherence to the group of comedies. And, of course, individually the melodramas are less ingratiating and, perhaps partly for that reason, less famous, or rather less beloved, than the comedies. (This difference in coherence may go to show, after all, something Tolstoy did not exactly say, that only happy remarriages are alike.) But if I am right that the melodramas belong together as I say they do, that will serve to justify my concept of the genre, which is used not primarily to establish a classification of objects but to articulate, let me say, the arguments among them. This is a significant matter, which I pass here with two remarks: (1) The list of members is in principle never closed, membership always being determined experimentally, which is to say, in specific acts of criticism, on the basis of a work's participation in the genre's argument; (2) if the case for the genre is good enough, it ought itself to suggest some understanding of its films' relative unknownness, or lack of love.

But what is all this about unknownness? What does it mean to say that it motivates an argument? And what has the argument to do with nihilism and diurnal recurrence? And why is it particularly about a woman that the argument takes place? What is the mystery about her lack of creation? And why should melodrama be expected to "derive" from comedy? And what is it that makes the absence of a woman's mother a scene of comedy and the presence of her mother a scene of melodrama? And—perhaps above all—what kinds of questions are these? Philosophical? Psychoanalytic? Historical? Aesthetic? If, as I hope, one would like to answer "All of these!" then one will want to say how it is that the same questions can belong to various fields that typically, in our culture, refuse to listen to one another.

The questions express further regions of what I called the intellectual debts incurred in writing *Pursuits of Happiness,* ones I had the luxury

1. See Jean Laplanche, *Life and Death in Psychoanalysis,* trans. Jeffrey Mehlman (Baltimore, 1976).

then of mostly leaving implicit. The debt I have worked on most explicitly in the past several years concerns the ideas of the diurnal, and of eternal repetition, and of the uneventful, as interpretations of the ordinary or everyday.

The concept of the ordinary reaches back to the earliest of my debts in philosophy. The first essay I published that I still use—"Must We Mean What We Say?" (1958)—is a defense of so-called ordinary language philosophy as represented by the work a generation ago at Oxford of J. L. Austin and at Cambridge of the later Wittgenstein. Their work is commonly thought to represent an effort to refute philosophical skepticism, as expressed most famously in Descartes and in Hume, and an essential drive of my book *The Claim of Reason* (1979) is to show that, at least in the case of Wittgenstein, this is a fateful distortion, that Wittgenstein's teaching is on the contrary that skepticism is (not exactly true, but not exactly false either; it is) a standing threat to, or temptation of, the human mind, that our ordinary language and its representation of the world *can* be philosophically repudiated and that it is essential to our inheritance and mutual possession of language, as well as to what inspires philosophy, that this should be so. But *The Claim of Reason,* for all its length, does not say, any more than Austin and Wittgenstein do very much to say, what the ordinary is, why natural language is ordinary, beyond saying that ordinary or everyday language is exactly not a special philosophical langue and that any special philosophical language is answerable to the ordinary, and beyond suggesting that the ordinary is precisely what it is that skepticism attacks—as if the ordinary is best to be discovered, or say that in philosophy it is only discovered, in its loss. Toward the end of *The Claim of Reason,* the effort to overcome skepticism begins to present itself as the motivation of romanticism, especially its versions in Coleridge and Wordsworth and in their American inheritors Emerson and Thoreau. In recent years I have been following up the idea that what philosophy in Wittgenstein and Austin means by the ordinary or everyday is figured in what Wordsworth means by the rustic and common and what Emerson and Thoreau mean by the today, the common, the low, the near.[2]

But then *Pursuits of Happiness* can be seen as beginning to pay its philosophical debts even as it incurs them. I have linked its films' portrait of marriage, formed through the concepts of repetition and devotion, with what, in an essay that compares the projects of Emerson and of Thoreau with—on an opposite side of the American mind—those of Poe and of Hawthorne, I called their opposite efforts at the interpretation of domestication, call it marriage. From this further interpretation of the ordinary (the ordinary as the domestic) the thought arises that, as in the case of literature, the threat to the ordinary that philosophy names skep-

---

2. See Stanley Cavell, *Must We Mean What We Say?* (Cambridge, 1969) and *The Claim of Reason: Wittgenstein, Skepticism, Morality, and Tragedy* (New York, 1979).

ticism should show up in film's favorite threat to forms of marriage, namely, in forms of melodrama. This thought suggests that, since melodramas together with tragedy classically tell stories of revenge, philosophical skepticism will in return be readable as such a story, a kind of violence the human mind performs in response to its discovery of its limitation or exclusion, its rebuff by truth.

The problem of the existence of other minds is the formulation given in the Anglo-American tradition of philosophy to the skeptical question whether I can know of the existence (not, as primarily in Descartes and in Hume, of myself and of God and of the external world, but) of human creatures other than myself, know them to be, as it were, like myself, and not, as we are accustomed to asking recently with more or less seriousness, some species of automaton or alien. In *Pursuits of Happiness*, I say explicitly of only two of the comedies that they are studies of the problem of the existence of the other, but the overcoming of skeptical doubt can be found in all remarriage comedy: in *It Happened One Night* the famous blanket that empirically conceals the woman and thereby magnifies her metaphysical presence dramatizes the problem of unknownness as one of splitting the other, as between outside and inside, say between perception and imagination (and since the blanket is a figure for a film screen, film as such is opened up in the split); in *The Lady Eve* the man's not knowing the recurrence of the same woman is shown as the cause of his more or less comic, hence more or less forgivable, idiocy; in *The Awful Truth* the woman shows the all-knowing man what he does not know about her and helps him find words for it that take back the divorce; in *Adam's Rib* the famously sophisticated and devoted couple demonstrate in simple words and shows and in surrealistic ordinariness (they climb into bed with their hats on) that precisely what neither of them knows, and what their marriage is the happy struggle to formulate, is the difference between them; in *The Philadelphia Story* the man's idea of marriage, of the teaching that the woman has chosen to learn, is his willingness to know her as unknown (as he expresses it, "I'll risk it, will you?").[3]

Other of my intellectual debts remain fully outstanding, that to Freud's work before all. A beholdenness to Sigmund Freud's intervention in Western culture is hardly something for concealment, but I have until now left my commitment to it fairly implicit. This has been not merely out of intellectual terror at Freud's achievement but in service of an idea and in compensation for a dissatisfaction I might formulate as follows: psychoanalytic interpretations of the arts in American culture have, until

3. See Cavell, *Pursuits of Happiness: The Hollywood Comedy of Remarriage* (Cambridge, Mass., 1981).

quite recently, on the whole been content to permit the texts under analysis not to challenge the concepts of analysis being applied to them, and this seemed to me to do injustice both to psychoanalysis and to literature (the art that has attracted most psychoanalytic criticism). My response was to make a virtue of this defect by trying, in my readings of film as well as of literature and of philosophy, to recapitulate what I understood by Freud's saying that he had been preceded in his insights by the creative writers of his tradition; that is, I tried to arrive at a sense for each text I encountered (it was my private touchstone for when an interpretation had gone far enough to leave for the moment) that psychoanalysis had become called for, as if called for in the history of knowledge, as if each psychoanalytic reading were charged with rediscovering the reality of psychoanalysis. This still does not seem to me an irrelevant ambition, but it is also no longer a sufficient response in our altered environment. Some of the most interesting and useful criticism and literary theory currently being produced is decisively psychoanalytic in inspiration, an alteration initiated for us most prominently by the past two or so decades of work in Paris and represented in this country by—to pick examples from which I have profited in recent months—Neil Hertz on the Dora case, Shoshana Felman on Henry James' "The Turn of the Screw," and Eve Kosofsky Sedgwick on homophobia in *Our Mutual Friend.*[4] And now my problem has become that I am unsure whether I understand the constitution of the discourses in which this material is presented in relation to what I take philosophy to be, a constitution to which, such as it is, I am also committed. So some siting of this relation is no longer mine to postpone.

I content myself here with saying that Freud's lifelong series of dissociations of his work from the work of philosophy seems to me to protest too much and to have done harm whose extent is only now beginning to reveal itself. I call attention to one of those dissociations in which Freud's ambivalence on the matter bleeds through. It comes in chapter 4 of *The Interpretation of Dreams,* just as he has distinguished "the operations of two psychical forces (or we may describe them as currents

---

4. See Neil Hertz, "Dora's Secrets, Freud's Techniques," in *In Dora's Case: Freud-Hysteria-Feminism,* ed. Charles Bernheimer and Claire Kahane (New York, 1985), pp. 221–42; Shoshana Felman, "Turning the Screw of Interpretation," *Yale French Studies* 55/56 (1977): 94–207; and Eve Kosofsky Sedgwick, "Homophobia, Misogyny, and Capital: The Example of *Our Mutural Friend,*" *Raritan* 2 (Winter 1983): 126–51.

In this connection I want to reaffirm my continuing indebtedness to the work and friendship of Michael Fried. His extraordinary book, *Realism, Writing, Disfiguration: On Thomas Eakins and Stephen Crane* (Chicago, 1987), also more explicitly relates itself to Freudian concepts than his past writing has done. I cannot forbear noting specifically, for those who will appreciate the kind of confirmation or ratification one may derive from simultaneous or crossing discoveries in writing that one admires, the light thrown by Fried's breakthrough discussion of Stephen Crane on the passage from James' "The Beast in the Jungle" on which the present essay closes.

or systems)." Freud goes on to say: "These considerations may lead us to feel that the interpretation of dreams may enable us to draw conclusions as to the structure of our mental apparatus which we have hoped for in vain from philosophy."[5] Given that this feeling is followed up by Freud in the extraordinary chapter 7, which ends the book, a piece of theoretical speculation continuous with the early, posthumously published "Project for a Scientific Psychology," the ambiguity of the remark seems plain: it can be taken, and always is, so far as I know, to mean that our vain waiting for *philosophy* is now to be replaced by the positive work of something else, call it psychoanalysis (which may or may not be a "scientific" psychology); but the remark can equally be taken to mean that our *waiting* for philosophy is at last no longer vain, that philosophy has been fulfilled in the form of psychoanalysis. That this form may destroy earlier forms of philosophizing is no bar to conceiving of psychoanalysis as a philosophy. On the contrary, the two thinkers more indisputably recognized as philosophers who have opened for me what philosophy in our age may look like, such as could interest me—Wittgenstein in his *Philosophical Investigations* and Martin Heidegger in such a work as *What Is Called Thinking?*— have both written in declared opposition to philosophy as they received it. Heidegger has called philosophy the deepest enemy of thinking, and Wittgenstein has said that what he does replaces philosophy.

The idea of "replacing" here has its own ambiguity. It could mean what the logical positivists roughly meant, that philosophy, so far as it remains intelligible, is to become logic or science. Or it could mean what I take Wittgenstein to mean, that the impulse to philosophy and the consequences of it are to be achieved by replacing, or reconceiving, the ground or the place of the thus preserved activity of philosophizing. And something like this could be said to be what every original philosopher since at least Descartes and Bacon and Locke has illustrated. It is as if in Wittgenstein and in Heidegger the fate to philosophize and the fate to undo philosophizing are located as radical, twin features of the human as such. I am not choosing one sense of replacement over the other for Freud's relation to philosophy. On the contrary, my sense remains that the relation so far is ambiguous or ambivalent. Such matters are apt to be discussed nowadays in terms of Freud's preoccupation with what is called priority or originality—issues differently associated with the names of Harold Bloom and Jacques Derrida. So it may be worth my saying that Bloom strikes me as unduly leveling matters when he speaks of Freud's crisis in *Beyond the Pleasure Principle* as obeying the structure of

5. Sigmund Freud, *The Interpretation of Dreams, The Standard Edition of the Complete Psychological Works of Sigmund Freud*, ed. and trans. James Strachey, 24 vols. (London, 1953–74), 4:144, 145; further references to this work, abbreviated *ID*, will be included in the text.

a poet's demand, against his precursors, for equal immortality.[6] Freud's problem there was less to *establish* his originality or uniqueness than to determine whether the cost or curse of that *obvious* uniqueness might not itself be the loss of immortality. I find that I agree here with what I understand to be Derrida's view (of chapter 2 anyway) of *Beyond the Pleasure Principle*—that in it, and in anticipation of his own death, Freud is asking himself whether his achievement, uniquely among the sciences (or, for that matter, the arts) in being bound to the uniqueness of one man's name, is inheritable.[7] This is the question enacted by the scenes of Freud the father and grandfather circling the Fort/Da game of repetition and domination, looking so much like the inheritance of language itself, of selfhood itself. What is at stake is whether psychoanalysis is inheritable—you may say repeatable—as science is inheritable, our modern paradigm for the teachable. If psychoanalysis is not thus inheritable, it follows that it is not exactly a science. But the matter goes beyond this question. If psychoanalysis is not exactly (what we mean by) a science, then its intellectual achievement may be lost to humankind. But now if this expresses Freud's preoccupation in *Beyond the Pleasure Principle* and elsewhere, then this preoccupation links his work with philosophy, for it is in philosophy that the question of the loss of itself is internal to its faithfulness to itself.

This claim reveals me as one of those for whom the question whether philosophy exists sometimes seems the only question philosophy is bound to, that to cease caring what philosophy is and whether it exists—amid whatever tasks and in whatever forms philosophy may appear in a given historical moment—is to abandon philosophy, to cede it to logic or to science or to poetry or to politics or to religion. That the question of philosophy is the only business of philosophy is the teaching I take from the works of Wittgenstein and of Heidegger whose inheritance I have claimed. The question of inheritance, of continued existence, appears in their work as the question whether philosophy can be taught or, say, the question how thinking is learned, the form the question takes in *Beyond the Pleasure Principle*. It is perhaps primarily for this reason that my philosophical colleagues in the Anglo-American profession of philosophy still generally (of course there are exceptions) hold Wittgenstein or Heidegger at a distance, at varying distances from their conceptions of themselves.

What would be lost if philosophy, or psychoanalysis, were lost to us? One can take the question of philosophy as the question whether the

6. See Harold Bloom, "Freud's Concepts of Defense and the Poetic Will" [lecture to Forum on Psychiatry and the Humanities, 1980], in *The Literary Freud: Mechanisms of Defense and the Poetic Will*, ed. Joseph H. Smith (New Haven, Conn., 1980), pp. 1–28.

7. See Jacques Derrida, "Coming into One's Own," in *Psychoanalysis and the Question of the Text*, ed. Geoffrey H. Hartman (Baltimore, 1978). The translator, James Hulbert, warns that he has abridged a section from a much longer work in progress.

life of reason is (any longer) attractive and recognizable, or as the question whether by my life I can and do affirm my existence in a world among others, or whether I deny this, of myself, of others, and of the world. It is some such question that Nietzsche took as the issue of what he called nihilism, a matter in which he had taken decisive instruction from Ralph Waldo Emerson. I persist, as indicated, in calling the issue by its, or its ancestor's, older name of skepticism; as I persist in thinking that to lose knowledge of the human possibility of skepticism means to lose knowledge of the human, something whose possibility I envision in *The Claim of Reason,* extending a problematic of Wittgenstein's under the title of soul-blindness.

It is from a perspective of our culture as having entered on a path of radical skepticism (hence on a path to deny this path) from the time of, say, Descartes and Shakespeare—or say from the time of the fall of kings and the rise of the new science and the death of God—that I see, late in this history, the advent of psychoanalysis as the place, perhaps the last, in which the human psyche as such, the idea that there is a life of the mind, hence a death, receives its proof. It receives its proof of its existence in the only form in which that psyche can (any longer) believe it, namely, as essentially unknown to itself, say unconscious. As Freud puts it in the closing pages of *The Interpretation of Dreams:* "The unconscious is the true psychical reality" (*ID,* 5:613). This can seem a mere piece of rhetoric on Freud's part, arbitrarily underrating the reality of consciousness and promoting the unconscious out of something like a prejudice that promotes the reality of atomic particles over the reality of flesh and blood and its opposable things—and certainly on less, or no, compelling intellectual grounds. But when seen in its relation to, or as a displacement of, philosophy, Freud's assertion declares that for the mind to lose the psychoanalytic intuition of itself as unconscious would be for it to lose the last proof of its own existence. (One may feel here the need for a dialectical qualification or limitation; this loss of proof, hence of human existence, is specific to the historical-political development in which the individual requires such a proof before, as it were, his or her own eyes, a private proof. The question may then be open whether, in a further development, the proof might be otherwise possible, say performed before the answering heart of a community. But in that case, would such a proof be necessary? Would philosophy?)

How easy this intuition is to lose (the mind's [psychoanalytic] intuition of its existence as unconscious), how hard the place of this intuition is to find—the place of the proof of existence constituted in the origin of psychoanalysis as a fulfillment of philosophy—is emblematized by how obscure this or any relation of philosophy and psychoanalysis is to us, an obscurity our institutions of learning serve to enforce. (I do not just mean that psychoanalysis is not usually a university subject and only questionably should become one; I mean as well that philosophy is, or should become, only questionably such a subject.) The tale to be told here is as yet perhaps untellable, by us and for us in America—the tale of Freud's inheritance (inescapable for an ambitious student of German culture of Freud's time) of the outburst of thinking initiated by Kant and then developed continuously by Fichte, Schelling, Hegel, Schopenhauer, and Nietzsche. One possible opening passage of this story is from the same closing pages I just cited from *The Interpretation of Dreams:* "What I . . . describe is not the same as the unconscious of philosophers. . . . In its innermost nature it [that is, psychical reality, the unconscious] is as much unknown to us as the reality of the external world, and it is as incompletely presented by the data of consciousness as is the external world by the communication of our sense organs" (*ID*, 5:614, 613). Freud allows himself to dismiss what he calls "the unconscious of philosophers" (no doubt referring to what some philosophers have referred to with the *word* "unconscious") without allowing himself to recognize that his connecting in the same sentence the innermost nature of psychic reality and the innermost nature of external reality as equally, and hence apparently for the same reasons, unknown, is pure Kant, as Freud links the unknown ground of both inner and outer to a realm of an unconditioned thing-in-itself, which Kant virtually calls the It (he spells it "X").[8] Kant's linking of the inner and the outer sounds like this: "The conditions of the *possibility*

8. Immanuel Kant, *Critique of Pure Reason*, trans. Norman Kemp Smith (New York, 1950), A109. In a set of editorial notes prepared for my use, Joseph H. Smith, in responding to my claim that Freud here takes on Kant's views exactly at a point at which he wishes to distinguish the psychoanalytic idea of the unconscious from "the unconscious of the philosophers," finds that "it is inconceivable to me that Freud was unaware of being Kantian here." I am grateful, first of all, for the confirmation that the Kantian provenance of Freud's thought seems so patent. But further, as to whether Freud could in that case have been "unaware" of the provenance, I would like to propose the following: if Freud was aware of it, then his omitting of Kant's name just here, where he is explicitly dissociating himself from philosophy, is motivated, deliberate, showing an awareness that his claim to dissociation is from the beginning compromised, say ambivalent; but if, on the contrary, Freud was not aware of his Kantianism just here, say unconscious of it, then he was repressing this fact of his origin. Either of these possibilities, suppression or repression, I am regarding as fateful to the development of psychoanalysis as a field of investigation (supposing this more distinct from psychoanalysis as a therapy than it perhaps can be) and rather in support of my claim that Freud's self-interpretation of his relation to philosophy is suspicious and, contrary to what I know of its reception by later psychoanalysts, ought to be treated.

I cite one piece of positive evidence here to indicate Freud's ambivalent awareness of resistant understanding of the depth of his intellectual debt to Kant (one may press this evidence to the point of suppression or repression). Of the dozen or so references to Kant listed in the general index of the *Standard Edition*, one bears directly on whether Freud saw the Kantianism of his view of the proof and the place of the unconscious. At the end of the first section of "The Unconscious" Freud says this:

The psycho-analytic assumption of unconscious mental activity appears to us . . . as an extension of the corrections undertaken by Kant of our views on external perception. Just as Kant warned us not to overlook the fact that our perceptions are subjectively conditioned and must not be regarded as identical with what is perceived though

of experience in general are at the same time the *possibility of the objects of experience.*"⁹ Heidegger, in *What Is Called Thinking?*, quotes this passage from Kant and from it in effect rapidly derives the tradition of German so-called Idealism. He adduces some words of Schelling, in which the pivot of inner and outer sounds this way: "In the final and highest instance, there is no being other than willing. Willing is primal being and to [willing] alone belong all [primal being's] predicates: being unconditioned, eternity, independence of time, self-affirmation. All philosophy strives only to find this highest expression."¹⁰ The predicates of being unconditioned and of independence of time will remind us of Freud's predicates of the unconscious. Schelling's lectures in Berlin in 1841 were, as noted in Karl Löwith's *From Hegel to Nietzsche,* attended by Engels, Bakunin, Kierkegaard, and Burckhardt. And 1841 is also the year of Emerson's first volume of essays. His volume sounds, for example, this way: "Permanence is a word of degrees. Every thing is medial." "It is the highest power of divine moments that they abolish our contritions also . . . for these moments confer a sort of omnipresence and omnipotence, which asks nothing of duration, but sees that the energy of the mind is commensurate with the work to be done, without time. . . . I unsettle all things . . . I simply experiment."¹¹ Compared with the philosophical

---

unknowable, so psycho-analysis warns us not to equate perceptions by means of consciousness with the unconscious mental processes which are their object. Like the physical, the psychical is not necessarily in reality what it appears to us to be. [*Standard Edition*, 14:171]

This expression of indebtedness to Kant precisely discounts the debt, since Kant equally "warned us" not to equate the appearance of the psychic with the reality of it, the warning Freud arrogates to psychoanalysis as an "extension" of Kant's philosophical contribution to the study of knowledge. It is the *connection* of the study of inner and outer that my paper claims is "pure Kant."

Now Freud might have meant something further in his arrogation. He might have been compressing, in his discounting of the debt to Kant, a claim to the effect that Kant did not lay out the conditions of the appearance of the inner world with the systematicness with which he laid out the conditions of the appearance of the outer world, the world of objects; in short, that Kant lacked the tools with which to elicit a system of categories of the understanding for the psyche, or the subjective, comparable to the one he elicited for the external, or the objective, world. These tools, unlike those of Aristotle that Kant deployed, came into the possession of Western thought only with psychoanalysis. Something of this sort seems to me correct. But if Freud had claimed this explicitly, hence taken on the obligation to say whether, for example, his "categories" had the same status as Kant's, then the awareness would have been inevitable that his quarrel with philosophy was necessary, was philosophy. Unawareness of his inheritance of Kant would then indeed have been inconceivable.

9. Ibid., A158, B197.

10. See Martin Heidegger, *What Is Called Thinking?*, trans. J. Glenn Gray (New York, 1964). The quotation from Kant is on p. 243; that from Schelling on pp. 90–91.

11. Ralph Waldo Emerson, "Circles," *Essays: First Series,* vol. 2 of *The Collected Works of Ralph Waldo Emerson,* ed. Joseph Slater, Alfred R. Ferguson, and Jean Ferguson Carr (Cambridge, Mass., 1979), pp. 180, 187–88.

culture of Schelling's audience, Emerson's mostly had none; yet his philosophizing was more advanced than Schelling's, if Nietzsche's is (since
Emerson's transcendental realm is not fixed; the direction or height of
the will is in principle open). Heidegger claims for his quotation from
Schelling that it is the classic formulation of the appearance of metaphysics
in the modern era, an appearance that is essential "to understand[ing]
that—and how—Nietzsche from the very start thinks of revenge [the
basis of nihilism] and the deliverance from revenge in metaphysical terms,
that is, in the light of Being which determines all beings."[12] However
remote the fate of such a claim may seem to us here now, it will, if
nothing else, at any time stand between us and our desire, however
intermittent, yet persistent, for an exchange with contemporary French
thought; since Heidegger's interpretation of Nietzsche is one determinant
of the Paris of, say, Derrida's Plato and Rousseau and of Lacan's Freud.
(It may be pertinent to cite the effort in recent decades to bring Freud
within the orbit of German philosophizing, in particular within that of
Heidegger's thought, made by the existential-analytic movement [*Daseins-
analyse*]. This is no time to try to assess that effort, but I may just note
that my emphasis on Freud as, so to speak, an immediate heir of German
classical philosophy implies that establishing this relation to philosophy
does not require mediation [or absorption] by Heidegger. The point of
my emphasis is that Freud's is to be understood as an alternative inheritance,
a competing inheritance, to that of Heidegger. Otherwise Freud's own
break with philosophy, his [continued] subjection to it and its subjection
to him, will not get clear. Then Wittgenstein's is a third inheritance, or
path, from Kant.)[13]

In these paths of inheritance, Freud's distinction is to have broken
through to a practice in which the Idealist philosophy, the reigning
philosophy of German culture, becomes concrete (which is roughly what
Marx said socialism was to accomplish). In Freud's practice, one human
being represents to another all that that other has conceived of humanity
in his or her life, and moves with that other toward an expression of the
conditions which condition that utterly specific life. It is a vision and an

12. Heidegger, *What Is Called Thinking?*, p. 90.

13. After a conversation with Kurt Fischer, I realize that I should, even in this opening
sketch of the problem of inheriting philosophy, be more cautious, or specific, in speaking
of Freud's "inheritance" of classical German philosophy. I do not mean that an Austrian
student in the later nineteenth century would have had just the same philosophical education as a German student of the period; nor does my claim require that Freud read so
much as a page in one of Kant's works. It would have been enough for my (or Freud's)
purposes for him to have received his Kant from the quotations of Kant he would have
encountered in his reading of Schopenhauer. My focus, that is to say, in speaking here of
Freud's inheritance of the German outburst, is rather on who Freud is, on what becomes
of ideas in that mind, than on what, apart from a mind of that resourcefulness, German
philosophy is thought to be. I assume that more or less the same ought to be said of the
inheritance of German thought by that other Austrian student, Wittgenstein.

achievement quite worthy of the most heroic attributes Freud assigned himself. But psychoanalysis has not surmounted the obscurities of the philosophical problematic of representation and reality it inherits. Until it stops shrinking from philosophy (from its own past), it will continue to shrink before the derivative question, for example, whether the stories of its patients are fantasy merely or (also?) of reality; it will continue to waver between regarding the question as irrelevant to its work and as the essence of it.

It is hardly enough to appeal here to conviction in reality, because the most untutored enemy of the psychological, as eagerly as the most sophisticated enemy, will inform you that conviction is one thing, reality another. The matter is to express the intuition that fantasy shadows anything we can understand reality to be. As Wittgenstein more or less puts an analogous matter: the issue is not to explain how grammar and criteria allow us to relate language to the world but to determine what language relates the world to be. This is not well expressed as the priority of mind over reality or of self over world (as, among others, Bloom expresses it).[14] It is better put as the priority of grammar—the thing Kant calls conditions of possibility (of experience and of objects), the thing Wittgenstein calls possibilities of phenomena—over both what we call mind and what we call the world. If we call grammar the Logos, we will more readily sense the shadow of fantasy in this picture.

From the reassociation of psychoanalysis with philosophy in its appearance on the stage of skepticism, as the last discoverer of psychic reality (the latest discoverer, its discoverer late in the recession of that reality), I need just two leaps in order to get to the interpretation I envision of the moment I began with from *Letter from an Unknown Woman*. The two leaps I can represent as questions that together have haunted the thoughts I am reporting on here. The first is: Why (granted the fact) does psychic reality first present itself to psychoanalysis—or, why does psychoanalysis first realize itself—through the agency (that is, through the suffering) of women, as reported in the *Studies on Hysteria* and in the case of Dora, the earliest of the longer case histories? The second question is: How, if at all, is this circumstance related to the fact (again, granted the fact) that film—another invention of the last years of the nineteenth century, developing its first masterpieces within the first decades of the twentieth century—is from first to last more interested in the study of individual women than of individual men? Men are, one could say, of interest to it in crowds and in mutual conflict, but it is women that bequeath psychic depth to film's interests. (It is to my mind a question

14. See Bloom, "Freud's Concepts of Defense," p. 7. Bloom means here to be speaking for Freud; as do I.

whether certain apparently obvious exceptions [Chaplin, Keaton, Gary Cooper, for example] are exceptions to the contrast with the masculine.) My conviction in the significance of these questions is a function, not surprisingly, of my speculations concerning skepticism, two junctures of it especially. The one is a result of my study of Shakespeare's tragedies and romances as elaborations of the skeptical problematic; the other concerns the role of the human body in the skeptical so-called problem of other minds. I will say something about each of these junctures.

Since we are about to move into speculations concerning differences in the knowing of women from that of the knowing of men, I just note in passing that I am not leaping to but skipping over the immensely important matter of determining how it is that the question of sexual difference turns into a question of some property that men are said to have that women lack, or perhaps vice versa—a development that helps to keep us locked into a compulsive uncertainty about whether we wish to affirm or to deny difference between men and women. As *Adam's Rib* ends, Tracy and Hepburn are joking about this vulgar error of looking for a *thing* that differentiates men and women. (It is my claim that they are joking; it is commoner, I believe, to assume—or imagine, or think, or opine—that they are perpetuating this common error. Here is a neat touchstone for assessing the reception of these comedies; perhaps their endings form the neatest set of such touchstones.)

In Jacques Lacan's work, the idea of the phallus as signifier is not exactly a laughing matter. The reification, let me put it, of sexual difference is registered, in the case of knowledge, by finding the question of a difference in masculine and feminine knowing and then to turn it into a question of some fixed way women know that men do not know, and vice versa. Since in ordinary, nonmetaphysical exchanges we do not conceive there to be some fact one gender knows that the other does not know, any more than we conceive there to be some fact the skeptic knows that the ordinary human being does not know, the metaphysical exchanges concerning their differences are apt to veer toward irony, a sense of incessant false position, as if one cannot know what difference a world of difference makes. No one exactly denies that human knowledge is imperfect; but then how does that become the skeptic's outrageous removal of the world as such? No one exactly denies that there are differences between men and women; but then how does that become an entire history of outrage? It is from this region that one must expect an explanation for climactic passages of irony that characterize the melodrama of the unknown woman.

When in *Blonde Venus* Marlene Dietrich hands a derelict old woman the cash her husband has handed her, repeating to the woman, in raging mockery, the self-pitying words her husband had used to her in paying her back, to be quits with her, the money she had earlier given him to save his life, the meanness of the man's gesture is branded on his character.

When toward the end of *Letter from an Unknown Woman* the man calls out smoothly to the woman, whose visit he interprets as a willingness for another among his endless dalliances, having disappeared to get some champagne, "Are you lonely out there?" and she, whose voice-over tells that she came to offer her life to him, replies, mostly to the camera, that is, to us, "Yes. Very lonely," she has taken his charming words as her cue for general death.

The state of irony is the negation, hence the equivalent in general consequence, of the state of conversation in remarriage comedy. Some feminists imagine that women have always spoken their own language, undetected by men; others argue that women ought to develop a language of their own. The irony in the melodrama of unknownness develops the picture, or figuration, for what it means idiomatically to say that men and women, in denying one another, do not speak the same language. I am not the only male of my acquaintance who knows the victimization in this experience, of having conversation negated, say, by the male in others. The finest description known to me of ironic, systematic incomprehension is Emerson's, from "Self-Reliance":

> Well, most men have bound their eyes with one or another handkerchief, and attached themselves to some one of these communities of opinion. This conformity makes them not false in a few particulars, authors of a few lies, but false in all particulars. Their every truth is not quite true. Their two is not the real two [as in the idea of two genders? or of just two Testaments?], their four not the real four [as in the idea of four corners of the earth? or of just four Gospels?]: so that every word they say chagrins us, and we know not where to begin to set them right.[15]

The first of my concluding leaps or questions about the origination of psychoanalysis and of film in the sufferings of women concerns the most theoretically elaborated of the studies I have so far produced of Shakespeare, on *The Winter's Tale*. It has raised unforgettably for me, I might say traumatically, the possibility that philosophical skepticism is inflected, if not altogether determined, by gender, by whether one sets oneself aside as male or female. And if philosophical skepticism is thus inflected then, according to me, philosophy as such will be. The issue arises as follows: Leontes obeys the structure of the skeptical problematic in the first half of *The Winter's Tale* as perfectly as his forebear Othello had done, but in the later play jealousy, as an interpretation of skeptical, world-removing doubt, is a cover story not for the man's fear of female desire (as Othello's story is) but for his fear of female fecundity, represented in Leontes' doubt that his children are his. Leontes' story has figured in

15. Emerson, "Self-Reliance," *Essays: First Series, The Collected Works*, p. 32.

various talks of mine in the past two or three years, and more than once a woman has afterward said to me in effect: If what Cartesian skepticism requires is the doubt that my children are mine, count me out. It is not the only time the surmise has crossed my mind that philosophical skepticism, and a certain denial of its reality, is a male business; but from the dawning of *The Winter's Tale* on me the business seems to me to be playing a role I know I do not fathom in every philosophical move I make. (It is the kind of answer I can contribute to the question who or what Shakespeare is to say that it is commonly in texts associated with this name that the bearing of a philosophical issue, or rather the issue of modern philosophy, is established.)

From the gender asymmetry here it should not be taken to follow that women do not get into the way of skepticism, but only that the passion of doubt may not express a woman's sense of separation from others or that the object of doubt is not representable as a doubt as to whether your children are yours. The passion is perhaps another form of fanaticism, as in part Leontes' is. (*Letter from an Unknown Woman* suggests that the fanaticism is of what you might call love.) And the object of doubt might be representable as one directed not toward the question of one's children but toward the question of the father of one's children. (This is the pertinence of Kleist's *The Marquise of O*, the main reason in its content for what I called its specialness in relation to the melodrama of unknownness.) But how can one know and show that this other passion and this other object create equivalents or alternatives to masculine skepticism?

It is at this juncture of the skeptical development that psychoanalysis and cinema can be taken as asking of the woman: How is it that you escape doubt? What certainty encloses you, whatever your other insecurities, from just this torture? At an early point in my tracking of the skeptic, I found myself asking: Why does my search for certainty in knowing the existence of the other, in countering the skeptic's suspicion concerning other minds, come to turn upon whether I can know what the other *knows*? So the formulation of what we want from the woman as an access to her knowledge would record the skeptical provenance of the woman's presence at the origin of psychoanalytic and of cinematic discovery. But then we must allow the question: But *who* is it who wants to know? A natural answer will be: The man wants the knowledge. This answer cannot be wrong; it is the answer feminists may well give to Freud's handling of the case of the woman he called Dora. But the answer might be incomplete.

At this point two sources of material bearing on psychoanalysis and feminism warrant being brought prominently into play, which I can now barely name. The first is represented in two texts by Lacan entitled "God and the *Jouissance* of The Woman" and "A Love Letter," which when I came upon them twelve months ago struck me at several points as having uncanny pertinence to the considerations that arise here. When Lacan announces, "There is no such thing as The woman" (sometimes paraphrased or translated as "The woman does not exist")[16] I was bound to ask myself whether this crossed the intuition I have expressed as the task of the creation of the woman. I find that some of Lacan's followers react to the remark as obvious and as on the side of what women think about themselves, while others deny this reaction. I take it to heart that Lacan warns that more than one of his pupils have "got into a mess" ("G," p. 144) about the doctrines of his in which his view of the woman is embedded; clearly I do not feel that I can negotiate these doctrines apart from the painful positions I am unfolding here.

My hesitations over two further moments in Lacan's texts—moments whose apparent pertinence to what I am working on strikes me too strongly to ignore—are hesitations directed less to my intellectual difficulties with what is said than to the attitude with which it is said. When Lacan says, "I believe in the *jouissance* of the woman in so far as it is something more" ("G," p. 147), he is casting his view of women as a creed or credo ("I believe"), as an article of faith in the existence and the difference of the woman's satisfaction. So he may be taken as saying: What there is (any longer?) of God, or of the concept of the beyond, takes place in relation to the woman. It matters to me that I cannot assess the extent or direction (outward or inward) of Lacan's (mock?) heroism, or (mock) apostlehood here, since something like this belief is in effect what I say works itself out, with gruesome eloquence, in the case of Othello, who enacts Descartes' efforts to prove that he is not alone in the universe by placing a finite, feminine other in the position assigned by Descartes to God. Moreover, letting the brunt of conviction in existence, the desire of the skeptical state, be represented by the question of the woman's orgasm, is an interpretation of Leontes' representation of the state of skepticism by the question of the woman's child (following a familiar equation in Freud's thinking of the production of the child with the form of female sexual satisfaction, an equation present in Shakespeare's play). So skeptical grief would be represented for the man not directly by the question "Were her children caused by me?" but by the double question "Is her satisfaction real and is it caused by me?"

The other source of material (still within my first leap) that I can do little more than name here is the excellent recent collection of essays, subtitled *Freud-Hysteria-Feminism*, on the Dora case.[17] Here I lift up one consideration that speaks to both of the leaps or questions at hand: How does the problem of knowing the existence of the other come to present itself as knowing what the other knows? And: Who is it who wants to

---

16. Lacan and the *école freudienne*, "God and the *Jouissance* of The Woman," *Feminine Sexuality*, ed. Juliet Mitchell and Jacqueline Rose, trans. Rose (New York, 1982), p. 144; further references to this essay, abbreviated "G," will be included in the text.

17. See n. 4.

know of the woman's existence? The former seems—in the light of the Dora collection—a way of asking what the point is of the "talking cure" (the name of psychoanalytic therapy that Anna O., the woman whose case was reported by Breuer in *Studies on Hysteria*, was the first to use); and the answer to the latter seems routinely assumed to be Freud the man. The contributors to the volume are about equally divided between men and women, and it seems to me that while the men from time to time are amazed or appalled by Freud's assaults upon Dora's recitations, the women, while from time to time admiring, are uniformly impatient with Freud the man. The discussions are particularly laced with dirty talk, prompted generally by Freud's material and drawn particularly by a remark of Lacan's on the case in which, in an ostentatious show of civilization, he coolly questions the position of the partners in Freud's fantasy of Dora's fantasy of oral intercourse. It is in their repetition of Lacan's question, not now coolly but accusingly, that the women's impatience is clearest; it is a kind of structural impatience. To talk to Freud about his talking cure is to be caught up in the logic expressed by Lacan in the formula: "Speaking of love is in itself a *jouissance*."[18] Feeling the unfairness in thus being forced to talk love to Freud, a woman may well accuse him of ignorance in his designs upon Dora, upon her knowledge, not granting him the knowledge that his subject is the nature of ignorance of exactly what cannot be ignored. She may well be right.

The consideration I said I would lift from the discussions of Dora takes on the detail of Freud's choice of the fictitious name Dora in presenting his case. Freud traces his choice to the paradigm of a change of name his sister had required of, and chosen for, her maidservant. The women represented in this collection on the whole use this information to accuse Freud of treating the woman he called Dora like a servant, of thus taking revenge on her for having treated him in this way. It is an angry interpretation, which seeks to turn the tables on the particular brilliance Freud had shown in calling Dora's attention to her angry treatment of him in announcing her termination of treatment by giving him two weeks' notice. A less impatient interpretation would have turned Freud's act of naming around again, taking it not as, or not alone as, a wish to dominate a woman, but as a confession that he is thinking of himself in the case through an identification with his sister: as if the knowledge of the existence of a woman is to be made on the basis of already enlisting oneself on that side.

This takes me to the other of my concluding leaps or questions, now concerning not generally the genderedness of the skeptical problematic, but specifically concerning the role of the body in the problem of other

18. Lacan, "A Love Letter," *Feminine Sexuality*, p. 154.

minds. To counter the skeptical emphasis on knowing what the other doubts and knows, I have formulated my intuition that the philosophical recovery of the other depends on determining the sense that the human body is expressive of mind, for *this* seems to be what the skeptic of other minds directly denies, a denial prepared by the behaviorist sensibility in general. Wittgenstein is formulating what behaviorism shuns—and so doubtless inviting its shunning of him—in his marvelous remark: "The human body is the best picture of the human soul."[19] One can find some such idea expressed in the accents of other thinkers—for example, in Hegel's *Philosophy of Fine Art:* "The human shape [is] the sole sensuous phenomenon that is appropriate to mind";[20] or again in Emerson's essay "Behavior": "Nature tells every secret once. Yes, but in man she tells it all the time, by form, attitude, gesture, mien, face and parts of the face, and by the whole action of the machine."[21] Freud is expressing the idea in one of his reasonably measured, yet elated, Hamlet-like recognitions of his penetration of the secrets of humanity. In the middle of his writing of the Dora case he turns aside to say: "He that has eyes to see and ears to hear may convince himself that no mortal can keep a secret. If his lips are silent, he chatters with his finger-tips; betrayal oozes out of him at every pore."[22] Freud's twist on the philosophers here is registered in his idea of our expressions as betraying ourselves, giving ourselves (and meaning to give ourselves) away—as if, let us say, the inheritance of language, of the possibility of communication, inherently involves disappointment with it and (hence) subversion of it.

Expression as betrayal comes out particularly in Freud's phrase from his preceding paragraph, in which he describes one of what he calls Dora's "symptomatic acts" as a "pantomimic announcement" (specifically in this case an announcement of masturbation). Freud and Breuer had earlier spoken of the more general sense of human behavior as pantomimic—capable of playing or replaying the totality of the scenes of hidden life—in terms of the hysteric's "*capacity for conversion*," "a psychophysical aptitude for transposing very large sums of excitation into the somatic innervation,"[23] which is roughly to say, a capacity for modifying the body as such rather than allowing the excitation to transpose into consciousness or to discharge into practice. While this capacity is something possessed by every psychophysical being—that is, primarily human beings—a particular aptitude for it is required for a given sufferer to

19. Ludwig Wittgenstein, *Philosophical Investigations*, trans. G. E. M. Anscombe (London, 1963), p. 178.

20. G. W. F. Hegel, *The Introduction to Hegel's Philosophy of Fine Art*, trans. Bernard Bosanquet (London, 1886), p. 150.

21. Emerson, "Behavior," *Conduct of Life*, vol. 6 of *The Complete Works of Ralph Waldo Emerson*, ed. Edward Waldo Emerson (Boston, 1904), p. 169.

22. Freud, *Fragment of an Analysis of a Case of Hysteria, Standard Edition*, 7:77–78.

23. Freud, "The Neuro-Psychoses of Defence," *Standard Edition*, 3:50.

avail herself or himself of hysteria over other modes of symptom formation, as in obsessions or phobias. The aptitude demands, for example, what Freud calls "somatic compliance," together with high intelligence, a plastic imagination, and hallucinatory "absences," which Anna O. (in *Studies on Hysteria*) taught Breuer to think of as her "'private theatre.'"[24]

It seems to me that Freud describes the aptitude for hysterical conversion with special fascination—as if, for example, the alternative choice of obsession were, though no less difficult to fathom, psychologically rather undistinguished.[25] Breuer and Freud's most famous statement of the matter, in their "Preliminary Communication" of 1893, is: "Hysterics suffer mainly from reminiscences" (*SH*, 2:7), a statement to be taken in the light of the insistence that hysterical motor symptoms "can be shown to have an original or long-standing connection with traumas, and stand as symbols for them in the activities of the memory" (*SH*, 2:95). Hysterical symptoms are "mnemonic symbols," where this means that they bear some mimetic allegiance to their origins. Freud will say fifteen years later, in the "Rat Man" case, that "the leap from a mental process to a somatic innervation—hysterical conversion . . . can never be fully comprehensible to us,"[26] a claim I find suspicious coming from him, as though he wishes sometimes to appear to know less than he does, or feels he does, about the powers of women.

In place of an argument for this, I offer as an emblem for future argument the figure of the woman who on film may be understood to have raised "the psycho-physical aptitude for transposing . . . large sums of excitation into the somatic innervation" to its highest art; I mean Greta Garbo, I suppose the greatest, or the most fascinating, cinematic image on film of the unknown woman. (Perhaps I should reassure you of my intentions here by noting that Freud's sentence following the one I just repeated about the psychophysical aptitude in question begins: "This aptitude does not, in itself, exclude psychical health.")[27] It is as if Garbo has generalized this aptitude beyond human doubting—call this aptitude a talent for, and will to, communicate—generalized it to a point of absolute expressiveness, so that the sense of failure to know her, of her being beyond us (say visibly absent) is itself the proof of her existence. (The idea of absolute expressiveness locates the moment in the history of skepticism at which such a figure appears as the moment I characterize in *The Claim of Reason* as the anxiety of inexpressiveness.)

24. For the phrase, "private theatre," see Josef Breuer and Freud, *Studies on Hysteria, Standard Edition*, 2:22; further references to this work, abbreviated *SH*, will be included in the text.

25. See, for example, Freud, "The Neuro-Psychoses of Defence," *Standard Edition*, 3:51.

26. Freud, *Notes Upon a Case of Obsessional Neurosis, Standard Edition*, 10:157.

27. Freud, "The Neuro-Psychoses of Defence," *Standard Edition*, 3:50.

This talent and will for communication accordingly should call upon the argument of hysteria for terms in which to understand it. In Garbo's most famous postures in conjunction with a man, she looks away or beyond or through him, as if in an absence (a distance from him, from the present), hence as if to declare that this man, while the occasion of her passion, is surely not its cause. I find (thinking specifically of a widely reprinted photograph in which she has inflected her face from that of John Gilbert, her eyes slightly raised, seeing elsewhere) that I see her *jouissance* as remembering something, but, let me say, remembering it from the future, within a private theater, not dissociating herself from the present moment, but knowing it forever, in its transience, as finite, from her finitude, or separateness, as from the perspective of her death: as if she were herself transformed into a mnemonic symbol, a monument of memory. (This would make her the opposite of the femme fatale she is typically said—surely in defense against her knowledge—to be.) What the monument means to me is that a joyful passion for one's life contains the ability to mourn, the acceptance of transience, of the world as beyond one—say, one's other.

Such in my philosophy is the proof of human existence that, on its feminine side, as conceived in the appearance of psychoanalysis, it is the perfection of the motion picture camera to provide.

Here I come upon my epilogue, and a man's hands over his eyes, perhaps to ward off a woman's returning images. *Letter from an Unknown Woman* is the only film in our genre of melodrama that ends with the woman's apparent failure; but as in *Gaslight*, her failure perfectly shadows what the woman's success in this genre of human perplexity has to overcome: the failure here is of a woman's unknownness to prove her existence to a man, to become created by a man; a tale the outcome of which is not the transcendence of marriage but the collapse of a fantasy of remarriage (or of perpetual marriage), perhaps in favor of a further fantasy, of revenge, of which the one we see best is a screen; a tale in which the woman remains mute about her story, refusing it both to the man and to the world of woman; and a tale in which the characters' perspective of death is not to know forever the happiness of one's own life but finally to disown it, to live the death of another (as they have lived the other's life). (For some this will establish the necessity of psychology; for others, the necessity of politics; for others, the need of art.)

A reading of the film, in the context I have supplied here, might directly begin with the marks of these fantasies, of their negations of the reality, as it were, of remarriage as established in the genre that explores remarriage. For example, the woman in Ophuls' film is shown to be created through metamorphosis, not, however, by or with the man, but for him, privately—as her voice-over tells him (and us) posthumously:

> From that moment on I was in love with you. Quite consciously I began to prepare myself for you. I kept my clothes neater so that you wouldn't be ashamed of me. I took dancing lessons; I wanted to become more graceful, and learn good manners—for you. So that I would know more about you and your world, I went to the library and studied the lives of the great musicians.

What is causing this vortex of ironies, the fact of change or the privacy of it? The idea that woman's work is not to converse with men but to allure them is hardly news, and it is laid out for observation in Ophuls' work, in his participation in the world of fashion and glamour. That the intimacy of allure exactly defeats the intimacy of conversation is a way to put the cause of irony in the film, not alone its incessance in its closing sequences ("Are you lonely out there?") but also at the beginning of their reencounter, as the woman tracks the man back in Vienna until he notices her. He says, "I ought to introduce myself," and she interrupts with, "No. I know who you are"—a remark that could not be truer or more false.

Privacy and irony are in turn bound up in the film with the theme and structure of repetitions. Again this feature here negates its definitive occurrences in remarriage comedy, where repetitiveness is the field of inventiveness, improvisation, of the recurrence of time, open to the second chance; in (this) melodrama time is transient, closed, and repetition signals death—whether the repetition is of its camera movements (for example, the famous ironic repetition of the girl's waiting and watching on the stairs) or its words ("I'll see you in two weeks, two weeks") or its imagery (the woman's denial of chance and her weddedness to fate is given heavy symbolization in the film's endless iteration of iterated iron bars, which become less barriers against this woman's desire than the medium of it). Passing these essential matters, the moment I close with is also one of ironic repetition, and I ask of the woman's returning images: Why are they death-dealing?

Of course, they must make the man feel guilt and loss; but the question is why, for a man whose traffic has been the sentiments of remorse and loss, the feeling this time is fatal. Surely it has to do with the letter itself, beginning as from the region of death ("By the time you read this I may be dead") and ending in the theme of nostalgia ("If only ... if only ..."). And, of course, it has to do with the fact that there is a double letter, the depicted one that ends in a broken sentence, and the one that depicts this one, the one bearing the title *Letter from an Unknown Woman,* this film that ends soon but distinctly after, narrated from the beginning, it emerges, by the voice of a dead woman, ghost-written. The implication is somehow that it is the (ghost) woman who writes and sends the film. What can this mean? That the author of the film is a question for the film is suggested when the man says to his mute servant, who enters as the man has finished reading the letter, "You knew her," and the servant nods and writes a name on a page on the desk on which the letter lies, by the feeling that the servant is signing the letter, and hence the film. No doubt Ophuls is showing his hand here, breaching and so declaring, as it were, his muteness as a director, as if declaring that directing (perhaps composing of any kind) is constantly a work of breaching muteness (how fully, and how well timed, are further questions). But this cannot deny that it is a woman's letter he signs, assigns to himself as a writer, a letter explicitly breaching, hence revealing, muteness.

Moreover, the letter already contained a signature, on the letterhead of the religious order in whose hospital the unknown woman died, of someone styled "Sister-in-charge." Whether or not we are to assume that this is the same locale to which the unknown woman had gone to be delivered anonymously of her and the man's child, her connection with the religious order happens in front of our eyes, as she leaves the train platform after rushing to see the man off for a hastily remembered concert tour. Walking directly away from us, she gradually disappears into blackness at the center of the vacant screen, upon which, at what we might project as her vanishing point, there is a rematerialization, and the figure of the woman is replaced by, or transformed into, walking at the same pace toward us, what turns out as it comes into readable view to be a nun. So the woman is part of the world of religion, of a place apart inhabited, for all we see of it, solely by women, a world Ophuls accordingly also assigns himself, I mean his art, in signing the woman's letter. (Whether in claiming the mazed position of the feminine the actual director is manifesting sympathy with actual women or getting even with them; and whether in competing with the feminine other the director is silencing the woman's voice in order to steal it and sport its power as his (?) own; and whether positive [or negative] personal intentions could overtake the political opportunism [or political insight] of any such gesture; these are questions that I hope are open, for my own good.)

Granted that forces both lethal and vital are gathered here, and granted that the film is the medium of visible absence, I ask again how these forces, in the form of returning images, deal death. Since I mostly am not considering here the narrative conditions of the woman depicted as writing the letter, I leave aside the question whether the vengeance in this act is to be understood as endorsed or reversed in the director's countersigning of it. I concentrate now on the sheer fact that the images return as exact moments we and the man have witnessed, or perhaps imagined, together. The present instants are mechanically identical with the past, and this form of repetition elicits its own amalgam of the strange and the familiar. I take it as a repetition that Freud cites as causing the sense of the uncanny in his essay to which he gives that title. Then this is also a title Ophuls' film suggests for the aesthetic working of film as such, an idea of some vision of horror as its basis. Freud's essay includes a reading of E. T. A. Hoffmann's romantic tale "The Sand-Man," a tale that features a beautiful automaton, something not untypical of Hoffmann or more generally of the romantic tale of the fantastic. Freud begins his reading by denying, against a predecessor's reading, that the uncanniness of the tale is traceable to the point in the story of "uncertainty whether an object is living or inanimate."[28] Now that point is precisely recognizable as an issue of philosophical skepticism concerning our knowledge of the existence of other minds. But Freud insists that instead the uncanny in Hoffmann's tale is directly attached to the idea of being robbed of one's eyes, and hence, given his earlier findings, to the castration complex.

I find this flat denial of Freud's itself uncanny, oddly mechanical, since no denial is called for, no incompatible alternative is proposed: one would have expected Sigmund Freud in this context to invoke the castration complex precisely as a new explanation or interpretation of the particular uncertainty in question, to suggest it as Hoffmann's prepsychoanalytic insight that one does not see others as other, acknowledge their (animate) human existence, until the Oedipal drama is resolved under the threat of castration. (This is a step, I believe, that Lacan has taken; I do not know on what ground.) Instead Freud's, as it were, denial that the acknowledgment of the existence of others is at stake amounts, to my mind, to the denial that philosophy persists within psychoanalysis, that the psychoanalytic tracing of traumatically induced exchanges or meta-morphoses of objects of love and subjects of love into and out of one another remains rooted in philosophy.

And I think we can say that when the man covers his eyes—an ambiguous gesture, between avoiding the horror of knowing the existence of others and avoiding the horror of not knowing it, between avoiding the threat of castration that makes the knowledge accessible and avoiding the threat of outcastness should that threat fail—he is in that gesture both warding off his seeing something and warding off at the same time his being seen by something, which is to say, his own existence being known, being seen by the woman of the letter, by the mute director and his (her?) camera—say, seen by the power of art—and seen by us, which accordingly identifies us, the audience of film, as assigning ourselves the position, in its passiveness and its activeness, of the source of the letter and of the film; which is to say, the position of the feminine. Then it is the man's horror of us that horrifies us—the revelation, or avoidance, of ourselves in a certain way of being feminine, a way of being human, a mutual and reflexive state, let us say, of victimization. The implications of this structure as a response to film, to art, to others, for better and for worse, is accordingly a good question. I guess it is the question Freud raises in speaking, in "Analysis Terminable and Interminable," of the "repudiation of femininity"—which he named as the bedrock at which

28. Freud, "The 'Uncanny,' " *Standard Edition*, 17:230.

psychoanalytic activity is at an end. My thought is that film, in dramatizing Freud's finding, oddly opens the question for further thought—the question, call it, of the differential feminine and masculine economies of the active and the passive.[29]

29. Freud, "Analysis Terminable and Interminable," *Standard Edition*, 23:252. Emerson devotes the ninth paragraph of "Fate" to a fair intuition, or tuition, of the question:

> Jesus said, "When he looketh on her, he hath committed adultery." But he is an adulterer before he has yet looked on the woman, by the superfluity of animal and the defect of thought in his constitution. Who meets him, or who meets her, in the street, sees that they are ripe to be each other's victim. ["Fate," *Conduct of Life, The Complete Works*, p. 11]

Transcribing so as to isolate a couple of Emersonian master-tones, I read as follows: Our "constitution" is of course both our physiology or individuality, the thing that what agrees with us agrees with, and at the same time it is the thing we are in agreement on; it is the fate at which private and public cross. Who the "we" is who are subject to agreement is given in the slightly later paragraph that begins: "The population of the world is a conditional population; not the best, but the best that could live now." I have argued that the essay "Fate," with a focus on "limitation," takes a focus on "condition" in its register as meaning "talking together," setting out "terms" (of agreement). (It is part of Emerson's interpretation/ obedience to/mastery of/appropriation/substantiation/underwriting/undermining of Kant.) This merely identifies "the population of the world" as talkers (hence, no doubt, as hearers). Now grant that Emerson's address to this population—I mean his writing—is what he has from the beginning defined as his "constitution" (anyway since the seventh paragraph of "Self-Reliance": "The only right is what is after my constitution" ["Self-Reliance," *Essays: First Series, The Collected Works*, p. 30]); it is what he means to bring to his nation (but surely not he alone?), as its bedrock, or say stepping-stone. Then the question of "adultery" (which is, as the word says, some question of the "other"), the question of victimization, is to be seen, and assessed, in each case of the saying of a word, the citing of any term, in all our conditions. In writing, hence in reading, we have to see for ourselves what our relations are—whether we conform to the demands and the scandals of our readers, or of our authors, when we do not recognize them as our own. Emerson's picture of meeting ("him or her") "in the street" is perhaps one of meeting his reader not at some bedrock but on some false ground, so that their intimacy victimizes them both, or say adulterates their originalities.

Freud, at the end of "Analysis Terminable and Interminable," pictures the repudiation of femininity or passiveness as a biological fact, perhaps because he wishes to conceive that "for the psychical field, the biological field does in fact play the part of the underlying bedrock." But suppose the relation of victimization or passiveness Freud descried is, as in Emerson, one he senses between his writing and his readers, that is to say, his progeny. Then the bedrock at which psychoanalytic activity ends (whatever the fate of the biological in psychoanalytic theory) is the fate of psychoanalytic understanding in its own terms. Psychoanalytic understanding of the matter of victimization, as of any other matter (for example, that of psychoanalytic theory and practice), has to take place in relation to reading Freud, in subjecting oneself to *this* inheritance. Biology has not lifted this burden from him. If the inheritance is not to take place "in the street," as victimization, it must take place in the recognition of, in the reading of, our countertransference to Freud, as we expect him to, and rebuke him for failing to, read his countertransference to Dora. Are we then certain what Freud's "prior" transference to "us" is, who it is we think he thinks we are, what it is he wants of us? The idea of countertransference here is meant as a gloss on a moment in an earlier essay of mine ("Politics as Opposed to What?," *Critical Inquiry* 9 [Sept. 1982]: 157–78) in which I interpret reading as a process of interpreting one's

I leave you with a present of some words from the closing paragraphs of Henry James' "The Beast in the Jungle."

> The creature beneath the sod [the buried woman companion] *knew* of his rare experience, so that, strangely now, the place had lost for him its mere blankness of expression.... [T]his garden of death gave him the few square feet of earth on which he could still most live.... by clear right of the register that he could scan like an open page. The open page was the tomb of his friend.... He had before him in sharper incision than ever the open page of his story. The name on the table smote him ... and what it said to him, full in the face, was that *she* was what he had missed.... Everything fell together ...; leaving him most of all stupefied at the blindness he had cherished. The fate he had been marked for he had met with a vengeance ...; he had been the man of his time, *the* man, to whom nothing on earth was to have happened.... This horror of waking—*this* was knowledge.[30]

James' tale in theme and quality better measures Ophuls' film than the story of Stefan Zweig's from which its screenplay was, excellently, adapted. Such is the peculiar distribution of powers among the arts.

---

transference to (as opposed to one's projection onto) a text. That idea implies that the fantasy of a text's analyzing its reader is as much the guide of a certain ambition of reading—of philosophy as reading—as that of the reader's analyzing the text. In now specifying the transference in question as of the nature of countertransference (that is, as a response to an other's transference to me) I do not deny the reversal of direction implied in the idea of the text as my reader, but I rather specify that that direction already depends upon a further understanding of a text's relation to me, and that that further relation cannot be said either (or can be said both) to be prior to or/and posterior to any approach (or say attraction) to a text. How could I suppose that this is an issue for women more than for men? Recall that " 'A Child is Being Beaten' " (*Standard Edition*, 17:179–204) is a text which Freud ends by using his material to "test" the theories of two competing men, of Fliess and of Adler—which is to say, to beat them. Talk about theory and practice.

30. Henry James, "The Beast in the Jungle," vol. 11 of *The Complete Tales of Henry James*, ed. Leon Edel (Philadelphia, 1964), pp. 397–402.

Mystics, Prophets, Rhetorics: Religion and Psychoanalysis

David Tracy

1. Introduction: Impasse and Exodus

Perhaps we have finally reached the end of the more familiar discussions of Freud and religion. Surely we do not need another round of theologians showing the "ultimate concern" in the works of Freud. Nor do we really need psychoanalysts announcing, once again, that religions are finally, indeed totally, illusion. Orthodox religionists have long since noted the many obvious religious analogues in Freud's work: the founding of the orthodox church, the purges of the heretical "Gnostic" Jung and the "Anabaptist" Adler, the debates over the translations of the sacred texts and their proper modes of interpretation. Orthodox Freudian psychoanalysts have amply demonstrated the psychological realities embedded in many religious phenomena: the obsessional nature of some religious rituals, the overdetermined character of all religious symbols, and, even, at times, the original patricide in totemic and monotheistic religions alike. In each case, the list could easily be extended. But should it? Or might it not prove more fruitful to reflect on the clashing rhetorical strategies in this clash of claims? Each rhetorical strategy has now proved its usefulness and its limits. These limits are now clear to everyone except those religionists who cannot help finding religion anywhere a serious concern (that is, literally everywhere) and those psychoanalysts incapable of noticing anything in religion except neurosis. For both these latter analyses, everything is finally the same thing. The only rhetorical strategy approved is a myth of the eternal return of more of the same.

Behind these two exhausted rhetorical moves lie two exhausted rhetorics: on the one side, a rhetoric of "pure science" that is neither pure nor notably scientific; on the other side, a rhetoric of "pure religion" that makes all religions so pure, so loving, so nice that no recognizable historical expression of religion fits the portrait. Even the entry of philosophy can often increase the problem rather than, as promised, resolve it. For any philosophy which effectively denies the reality of the unconscious in favor of its usual claims for consciousness and pure reason can hardly help. Sometimes, the philosophies straightforwardly deny that the unconscious means anything other than the pre-conscious (Sartre and de Beauvoir). At other times, more fruitful strategies are forged as when philosophers admit the challenge of psychoanalysis and then see what philosophical analysis might have to say in return (Paul Ricoeur and Stanley Cavell).[1] This second kind of move does lead to a new mutual challenge of psychoanalysis and philosophy: at least when Ricoeur's Hegel (rather than Kant) or Cavell's Wittgenstein (rather than Russell) helps the post-Freudian philosopher speak back in the presence of, rather than by means of the denial of, the unconscious.

Theologians have an even more difficult task than the philosophers. They, too, are tempted to deny any connection between those two notoriously overdetermined phenomena: the unconscious and religion. They, too, may prefer to rush back to safer rhetorical ground—the endless Western debate on "theism" and "atheism." In arguments for or against the existence of God, after all, there is no unconscious and there often may as well be no historical religion either. On this question of God, all is determined, nothing is overdetermined. Here a consciousness free of any unconscious can have one last fling—proving or disproving "God." Has "God" become the one clear and distinct idea left? Alternatively, "God" may become, for many, the favorite candidate for the "transcendental signified"—briefly mentioned before everyone rushes on to more interesting candidates like the "subject." The problem in all this is that God, religiously construed, is not primarily the problem of consciousness but the question of the unconscious. Mystics (and Jacques Lacan) know this. Most philosophers, theologians, and psychoanalysts do not. This is what makes Lacan's reading of Freud theologically interesting. At last the question of God is not who can produce the best philosophical argument

---

1. See Paul Ricoeur, *Freud and Philosophy: An Essay in Interpretation*, trans. David Savage (New Haven, Conn., 1970); see also Stanley Cavell's article ("Psychoanalysis and Cinema: The Melodrama of the Unknown Woman," pp. 227–58) in this book.

David Tracy is the Thomas and Mary Greeley Distinguished Service Professor of theology at the Divinity School and a member of the Committee on the Analysis of Ideas and Methods at the University of Chicago. His most recent book is *Plurality and Ambiguity: Hermeneutics, Religion, Hope.*

on the implications of consciousness. Nor is the question who (Peter Gay or Hans Küng) can give the best explanation for the fact that Freud's atheism was chronologically pre-psychoanalytical.[2]

The first question is not even what is the referent of all this God-talk—or, for that matter, all this talk of the unconscious. Rather the Lacanian reading of Freud suggests a more interesting question: what is the rhetorical character of Lacan's reading of Freud if construed as like the clash of two familiar religious rhetorics, the prophetic and the mystical? This new question, to be sure, has its own problems. It can seem to assume that we are all clear on the conflicting psychoanalytic rhetorics of Freud and Lacan, which, despite some fine studies, we are not.[3] The question can also seem to assume that we are all clear on the rhetoric of religion, which, again despite some good studies, we are not.[4] Despite these difficulties, the new question does have one advantage: it allows all rhetorical analysts to suspend the question of the referent, if any, of all this religious God-talk and simply analyze the necessary emergence of "god-terms" in all rhetorics, whether explicitly religious ones like those of the classic prophets and mystics or classically secular ones like Freud's and Lacan's.

To clarify the question itself, the following steps seem appropriate: first, analyze the "rhetoric of religion" and the emergence of "god-terms" in all rhetorics via Kenneth Burke (the best rhetorical analysis of religion available to date);[5] second, complicate Burke's general rhetoric of religion by introducing the more specific and contrasting rhetorics of the two classic religious types—the prophet and the mystic; third, see whether the classic conflict between prophetic and mystical rhetorics may illuminate the analogous clash between the rhetorics of Freud and Lacan. On this reading, the question "Does Lacan read Freud accurately?" becomes uncannily similar to the familiar theological question: can a mystic read correctly the prophetic texts she or he claims to be interpreting? In neither case is the answer self-evident. But by recalling the conflicting rhetorics of prophet and mystic, we may find a new way to suggest what is really at stake in the rhetoric of psychoanalysis itself: that is, the conflicting rhetorics of Freud and Lacan.

2. Peter Gay, *A Godless Jew: Freud, Atheism, and the Making of Psychoanalysis* (New Haven, Conn., 1987); Hans Küng, *Freud and the Problem of God*, trans. Edward Quinn (New Haven, Conn., 1979).

3. Patrick J. Mahony, *Freud as a Writer* (New York, 1982); Samuel Weber, *The Legend of Freud* (Minneapolis, 1982).

4. Representative studies may be found in *The Literary Guide to the Bible*, ed. Robert Alter and Frank Kermode (Cambridge, Mass., 1987).

5. Kenneth Burke, *The Rhetoric of Religion* (Berkeley and Los Angeles, 1970).

2. The Rhetoric of Religion: Kenneth Burke

Burke has been well described as an "analytical and moralizing therapist of the human mess."[6] Burke, as a good rhetorician, is principally interested in changing fundamental attitudes. We can, he urges, transform our temptations to scientism, romanticism, absolutism, monomania, and so on into a fundamental attitude which, while contemplating generic necessities, can allow us to "dance with tears in our eyes." One can name this Burkean "fundamental attitude," as Burke does, his own "neo-Stoic" resignation. One can also understand it (as I tend to do) as tragicomic: that is, the "representative anecdote" for Burke is closer to the *Oresteia:* three tragedies followed by a satyr play. This, at least, is the rhetorical structure of *The Rhetoric of Religion.* And since that work rhetorically analyzes our most fundamental attitudes it can serve as a good clue to Burke's own ultimate vision as a tragicomic one. We can use Burke's rhetoric of persuasion on generic necessities in the same way we (most of us, I suspect) have learned to use other great "analytical and moralizing therapists of the human mess" (Aeschylus, Augustine, Calvin, Edwards, Freud, Marx, Nietzsche, and others). All these "masters of suspicion" do provide persuasive analyses of the unnerving presence of certain generic necessities in the human mess. More exactly, there are certain fundamental attitudes in human beings which are frightening (and deserve some good analysis and sometimes, as Freud knew, even moralizing).[7] There are good persuasive reasons why, in concrete cases (for example, Freud's Dora), such analyses do illuminate what the problem may be. For many of our "masters of suspicion" the analysis can quickly become a totalizing interpretation of the "human situation."

But exactly here Burke's own candidate for a generic necessity is illuminating: namely, the drive to perfection seemingly incumbent upon all language use of any terministic screen. This Burkean rhetorical tool does analytically illuminate the totalizing temptation in all positions, including the masters of suspicion and retrieval; the rhetoric of deliberation on a multiplicity of goods; the absolutisms endemic to religion; the scientism endemic to science; the imperialism endemic to rhetoric; and the monomania endemic to most insights—recall René Girard in *Violence and the Sacred* yielding to a kind of monomaniacal totalizing of a good insight.[8]

The heart of Burke's tragicomic vision claims that endemic to human beings (and best disclosed in their language) is a drive to perfection. This drive, when analyzed, discloses a remarkable ambiguity: our creativity is

6. In an unpublished paper by David Smigelskis for the Seminar in Rhetoric of the Committee on the Analysis of Ideas and Methods, University of Chicago (1984).

7. On this side of Freud, see Philip Rieff, *Freud: The Mind of the Moralist* (Chicago, 1979).

8. René Girard, *Violence and the Sacred,* trans. Patrick Gregory (Baltimore, 1977).

dependent on this drive (and it is the best thing about us). At the very same time, we are "rotten with perfection." We turn every insight, every creative activity, into a total system. (Art, science, and religion become romanticism, scientism, absolutism; technology becomes *Helhaven* on the moon.) What then, in this situation, can we do? We can analyze this entelechy (enter Burke's two rhetorical strategies, dramatism and logology).[9] We can accept our fate by accepting *this* generic necessity. We can cultivate a fundamental attitude that is tragicomic (Freud-Lacan?) and, by that cultivation, we can "purify war" by turning war into, not peace (impossible on this perspective), but conversation, perspective by incongruity, irony, or, as Burke prefers, "dancing with tears in our eyes."

If we are persuaded on the need for a rhetoric of persuasion on fundamental attitudes like Burke's, then our problem becomes a familiar one: how persuasive is Burke's account of this generic necessity (the drive to perfection) and how does it relate to alternative accounts of generic necessities (Augustine, Marx, Freud, Nietzsche, and others)? What is unfamiliar and significant about this new kind of Burkean rhetorical analysis of perfection, however, is that even if Burke's account of the drive to perfection is persuasive, he has also built into his choice what other accounts of the radical ambiguity of the "human mess" possess less clearly: that is, the very necessity and ambiguity of perfection as the key generic necessity leads one to be suspicious of the key itself. This aspect of Burke's rhetoric of persuasion is, I think, more subtle (and, therefore, more persuasive?) than many alternatives. His major competitor for this particular subtlety would seem to be Nietzsche—at least the "new Nietzsche," that honorary French thinker of *différance.* This is probably the reason why Burke is sometimes made an honorary member of the "new rhetoric": if Nietzsche can become French, why not Kenneth Burke?

The *Rhetoric of Religion* becomes the *non plus ultra* text of all Burke's rhetorics of persuasion on attitudes. Burke is interested in religions because he is interested in attitudes:

> The subject of religion falls under the head of *rhetoric* in the sense that rhetoric is the art of *persuasion,* and religious cosmogonies are designed, in the last analysis, as exceptionally thoroughgoing modes of persuasion. To persuade men towards certain acts, religions would form the kinds of attitude which prepare men for such acts. And in order to plead for such attitudes as persuasively as possible, the religious always ground their exhortations (to themselves and

9. For two studies of Burke, see Frank Lentricchia, *Criticism and Social Change* (Chicago, 1983); William H. Rueckert, *Kenneth Burke and the Drama of Human Relations* (Berkeley and Los Angeles, 1982). For the present analysis, besides *The Rhetoric of Religion,* the central texts of Burke would be: *The Philosophy of Literary Form: Studies in Symbolic Action* (New York, 1957); *A Grammar of Motives* (New York, 1945); *A Rhetoric of Motives* (Berkeley and Los Angeles, 1969).

others) in statements of the widest and deepest possible scope, concerning the authorship of men's motives.[10]

The first two sentences of this crucial passage seem a clear illustration of Burke's enterprise: if rhetoric has to do with a persuasion to action by changing attitudes, then study that phenomenon which changes attitudes most "thoroughly." This is also the key to Burke's shift from considering "poetic" language as the privileged instance of "language as symbolic action" to "religious" language as the privileged instance of "language as such as motive." Religions are more "thoroughgoing" than poetic speech or dramas. They will not simply cancel out what we learned under the rubric "dramatism" but (by their greater abstractness, generality, and thoroughness) they will move the analysis of rhetorical persuasion to more general, more thorough, fundamental attitudes.

Hence we need a new form of analysis of this "ultimate" rhetoric of persuasion: namely, a new rhetorical enterprise named logology. But here some confusion enters: that is, logology will be a rhetorical discipline that will study words-about-words and since words-about-words discloses a drive to perfection in all words, then we must study *words*-about-God (god-terms). Is that why we need a rhetoric of religion? Well, not quite—for it seems that it is not so much religion we need to study but "theology." Why? It cannot simply be that theology is more verbal than religion, although that is true and Burke mentions it. For Burke's earlier dramatism already taught us (did it not?) not to have a simple contrast between words and actions.

Something else is at stake—and something, as Burke likes to say, "complicated." My guess is this: religions help Burke to reflect principally on a radicalized, generalized rhetoric of persuasion to attitudes; theologies help Burke to reflect principally on radicalized, generalized analysis of generic necessities (namely, the drive to perfection in all language).

Only logology can move our concerns past all "privileged cases" (whether drama, poetry, or religion) to a study of words as such (words-about-words). But we should still search for some "privileged case" that can at least initiate our analysis. Choose, then, "words-about-God," god-terms. An analysis of "words-about-God" reveals a generic necessity to all words, language, namely, the drive to perfection. God-language (for radical monotheists, at least) is perfection-language—recall Charles Hartshorne on the logic of perfection in God-language.[11] But the "early" Burke already argued that the peculiarity of human beings is that as "symbolic animals," human beings are language-beings. They learn by learning negatives (the prophetic negatives "thou shalt not") in order to create once they learn that they cannot stop going to the end of the

---

10. Burke, *The Rhetoric of Religion,* p. v.
11. Charles Hartshorne, *Man's Vision of God and the Logic of Theism* (New York, 1941).

line—the line of the widest possible generalization, the most perfect language for the truly creative act—to god-terms. (God *as* "Pure Act"; Genesis as Pure Act, as origin determining the whole cycle of terms: creation-covenant-guilt-redemption which seem narrative-temporal but are synchronic-systemic.)[12]

We are driven to perfect our creations, our language. We are driven, wherever we begin, to god-terms. The basic necessity for the symbolic animal is to speak, to learn negatives, to create and *not* to stop. Perfection is our *telos*—which seems to mean, paradoxically, that end *is* origin. Once we acknowledge that non-*telos*—*telos* via rhetorical analysis of privileged god-terms—we learn a generic necessity (our necessary drive to perfection) that becomes a vision of "transcendence" informing our move back to history ("the cave"?). Our freedom, as true freedom is determined (re-enter Calvin, Spinoza, and Freud). Even "symbol" and "animality" (those two generic necessities of the "symbol-making animal") seem to meet as our creative, symbolic power of words drives us to a perfection-language which returns history to nature, freedom to necessity, and narratives like Augustine's *Confessions* and Genesis to an atemporal cycle of terms. End is origin.[13]

3. Prophetic Rhetoric and Mystical Rhetoric: Freud and Lacan

Burke's analysis shows, in rhetorical terms, the further meaning of Hegel's or Hartshorne's philosophical interpretations of God-language as perfection-language. A rhetorical analysis, moreover, has one advantage over more purely dialectical enterprises: it opens to an acknowledgment of the reality of the unconscious in the words we use and the god-terms we inevitably employ. The "rottenness of perfection" position of Burke suggests at best ambiguity and, at the limit, overdetermination in all our conscious "god-terms."

However, Burke's properly general analysis of the rhetoric of religion as a drive to perfection-language needs further specificity. For religious languages arrive in two basic forms: the rhetoric of the prophet and the rhetoric of the mystic.[14] First, the prophet: the prophet hears a word that is not his or her own. It is Other. It disrupts consciousness, actions, deliberations. It demands expression through the prophet. The prophet

12. See Burke's unusual analysis of Genesis here in *The Rhetoric of Religion*.
13. A Burkean conclusion remarkably similar to that of Mircea Eliade on cosmogonic myths: see Eliade, *The Myth of the Eternal Return* (Princeton, N.J., 1957) and *The Sacred and the Profane: The Nature of Religion* (New York, 1954).
14. The same contrast can be made through a distinction between "manifestation" and "proclamation": see Ricoeur, "Manifestation and Proclamation," *The Journal of the Blaisdell Institute* 12 (Winter 1978) or my own reformulation in *The Analogical Imagination: Christian Theology and the Culture of Pluralism* (New York, 1981).

is not his own person; something else speaks here. Only on behalf of that Other may the prophet presume to speak her or his warnings, interruptive proclamations, predictions, and promises. Driven by a perfection-language needing god-terms to disclose this Other who or which speaks through the prophet, she or he cannot but speak. The others ordinarily do not want to listen. If matters get bad enough (and they usually will, given the "human mess"), others may begin to listen: first to the puzzling words of the prophet; then to the disturbing words of the Other in those words; then to the word of that Other in themselves. Some listen, some come for help, some are healed. Their healing will rarely prove a full recovery but, like Peter Brown's Augustine[15] or Freud's Dora, more like a continuous convalescence. For consolation from all sorrow they must go elsewhere—to those who deny the Other. For the rhetoric of the prophet can only listen and help them hear the words of the Other in themselves.

Prophets have good reason to be discouraged about how few will listen. "Let him who has ears to hear, hear" is not a ringing assurance of success. Sometimes the prophets reflect their own fury at this Other who insists on speaking in them: witness the lamentations of Jeremiah and many of the letters of Freud. At other times this fury will disclose itself in the gaps, the fissures, the repressions of the prophet's own too-clear prose.[16] At still other times, the prophets (or their successors) will yield to more reflective moods. They will face the fact that people seem to demand, not a word of the Other, but a consolation that cannot be given. They will note that the prophetic word is also "rotten with perfection." Ecclesiastes, that oddest of biblical books, is, rhetorically, that kind of work; so is *Civilization and Its Discontents*.

Freud was not a conquistador. His rhetoric was that of a prophet. Through his words—as clear, definite, and, at the same time, self-interruptive as those of Amos—some Other spoke. Like all prophets, he would not let his prose indulge itself in what, for the prophet, must be viewed as the obscure and bizarre allegories of an apocalypticist nor the weird, uncanny obfuscations of the mystic. He needed words that allowed the unconscious to speak and words persuasive enough to entice others to listen to that Other. But only clear, everyday words rendered with classic humanist restraint could allow that Other to be heard in such manner that others might hear and be persuaded. Freud called his god-term *Logos*—not mystery, not Other, not law.[17] He called his discipline scientific. Science was for him, as for most in his period, the longed-for

---

15. Peter Brown, *Augustine of Hippo: A Biography* (Berkeley and Los Angeles, 1970).

16. For a good example here, see Françoise Meltzer, "The Uncanny Rendered Canny: Freud's Blind Spot in Meeting Hoffmann's 'Sandman,'" in *Introducing Psychoanalytic Theory*, ed. Sander L. Gilman (New York, 1982), pp. 218–39.

17. Sigmund Freud, *The Future of an Illusion* (New York, 1975).

language of perfection after other languages (art, religion, myth) had failed. He often wanted to believe that his rhetoric was purely scientific. Happily, it was also something else:[18] a rhetoric of corrigibility, clarity, and a search for evidence that does resemble science; a prose whose subtlety and restraint does resemble Goethe's; yet both that scientific and humanist prose was finally an interruptive one—constantly interrupted, even disrupted, by the voice of the Other. By trying to render that subversive reality of the unconscious into seemingly scientific and humanist prose, Freud's powerful prophetic rhetoric challenged the ordinary prose of science and humanism alike as surely as the classic prophets' rhetoric, however clear and definite, smashed against the iconic proses, the idols, of the people. The prose becomes more and more polyvalent as it turns upon others and itself through the strange stories it narrates so well and the even stranger fissures and lapses it harbors within its own definiteness.

Finally every word, including every word about words, becomes not merely ambiguous and polyvalent, as Burke sees, but overdetermined and disseminating—as Freud saw. The very material reality of these words of the Other invades all words—even the scientific words of Freud, the humanistic prose, the care and search for clarity and harmony. In that sense, Freud's persuasive prophetic rhetoric becomes, in his greatest texts, something like a kabbalistic palimpsest filled with words whose very materiality are the central clues to the revealing and concealing of the Other-in-words.[19]

Freud may have wished to produce a purely scientific body of work. In one sense, he did. But he also produced something more—a prophetic rhetoric of persuasion to the Other. He may have called his god *Logos* but he was no neo-Platonist. As a "godless Jew," he consciously ignored the prophets, the rabbis, and the kabbalists only to have their most typical rhetorical strategies emerge in his own German-Greek humanist prose. Even as a Greek, he was odd: he praised *Logos* as much as any Platonist in the first academy but often wandered out of Plato's academy to attend to the forbidden texts of Aeschylus and Sophocles. Like so many Greeks of the classical age, he also seemed to long for some other wisdom, some other god-term than *Logos*. As Herodotus makes clear, for the classical Greek imagination, Egypt became the land where an other wisdom—

18. A reinterpretation of Wittgenstein's remarks on Freud leads to a similar conclusion—as argued well in the dissertation-in-progress of Charles Elder (University of Chicago).

19. This textual resemblance is not dependent on historical influence. The latter claim seems far more dubious: for the claim itself, see David Bakan, *Sigmund Freud and the Jewish Mystical Tradition* (New York, 1965). For rhetorical analyses of the classical "Jewish" ways of reading texts, see Susan A. Handelman, *The Slayers of Moses: The Emergence of Rabbinic Interpretation in Modern Literary Theory* (Albany, N.Y., 1982) and Harold Bloom, *Kabbalah and Criticism* (New York, 1975).

the wisdom of the Other?—may lie. Thus did the great Greek-Jew Freud often travel in his imagination to Egypt. Even Moses must become an Egyptian. Then his "murder" by the Jews and his puzzling Exodus from the homeland of Egypt might finally be intelligible.[20] Even Plato and Pythagoras—with their god *Logos*—must have learned from Egypt.

Freud's god-term was not "God"—and surely not the radically monotheistic God of Ahkenaton and Moses. It was also not really *Logos*, nor was it the radically monotheistic science of the *philosophes* and the nineteenth-century scientists. His god-term was not even the Unconscious. Indeed, the discovery of the unconscious teaches once again the most ancient of Jewish commands: the god-term should remain unnameable; it is not to be named. All we have are the words of the Other: material words to be deciphered and even then only partially understood by this nonbelieving prophet and this nonobservant kabbalist. What Freud sometimes wanted—from his god-term *Logos*—was a stabilizing rhetoric of the topics. What he received—from the Other in the unconscious— was a radically destabilizing prophetic rhetoric of the tropes. Lacan spotted this secret of the prophet with all the self-confidence of a mystic assuming that only he could understand what the prophet really meant. For mystics, unlike prophets, have no hesitation in allowing the destabilizing discourse of the Other the fullest sway.

Mystical religious discourse is startlingly different from prophetic discourse. Both are driven by an impulse toward perfection in their words about the Word. Both seem driven by an Other who speaks. For the prophet, the Other is Word acknowledged in a word of proclamation ("Thus says the Lord") that disrupts the prophet's own consciousness and disseminates the ego.[21] For the prophet, that Word, as One, demands a new center of unity beyond the ego. For the prophet is not her or his own person. The prophet, as responsible to the *fascinans et tremendum* of the Word, must become a new, responsible self—responsible to others, to history, to the cosmos, because made a responsible self by the Other-as-Word.[22] Only by losing the self can a new self be gained. The Word, the god-term named God, must remain Other or else the other in the new, responsible self cannot speak. The great Western monotheistic traditions (Judaism, Christianity, Islam) live by and through this prophetic rhetoric on the one God and the newly unified, responsible, othered self.

For many Eastern mystical traditions this prophetic discourse on God and the self is a symptom of the deeper problem, not an expression of the solution. For the most radical of these traditions, the Ch'an and

20. Sigmund Freud, *Moses and Monotheism* (New York, 1967), esp. pp. 3–72.

21. For some studies here, see *Interpreting the Prophets*, ed. James Luther Mays and Paul J. Achtemeier (Philadelphia, 1987) and *The Literary Guide to the Bible*, ed. Alter and Kermode, pp. 165–234.

22. See H. Richard Niebuhr, *Radical Monotheism and Western Culture* (Lincoln, Nebr., 1960).

Zen forms of Mahayana Buddhism, the prophet clings to a double illusion: that there is an Other that is Other (and thereby to be worshipped and trusted as "God") and that there is a self at all. Only by letting go of this form of primary ignorance (advaita) can all clinging and ultimately all desire cease. There is no "God" and there is no "self." Since there is not even a real nirvana and a real samsara, we must also not cling to enlightenment itself. For nirvana and samsara are one—one (more exactly, "not two") in their emptiness—but not one in the union/encounter of the prophet and the covenanting God, not one in the radical identity of the Hindu Shankara's Brahman-beyond-God and Atman-beyond-the-self.

This most radical of Buddhist mystical rhetoric illustrates, by its very radicality, certain crucial features of all mystical traditions: even the usually marginalized strands of mysticism in the Western prophetic traditions, even that of Buddhism's greatest opponent—the Vedantic tradition of Hinduism—even that of the return of the Other in the "other-power" of Pure Land Buddhism. For all mystics want to say something more than the prophet is willing to say—and say it as what the prophet really meant or should have meant. Zen Buddhist rhetoric does have certain affinities with some Western rhetorics—but not, I believe, with either Freud or Lacan. Rather Zen Buddhist rhetoric is far more like Derrida's. Indeed Nagarjuna and Derrida,[23] with all their differences, are natural allies with their insistence on nonpresence, their attempts to undo dialectic dialectically, and their disclosures of the radical instability of all linguistic attempts to secure a determinate meaning. Even the "undeterminate" will not suffice: Derrida's différance is not a candidate for a new transcendental category; Nagarjuna's no-self is not a doctrine, for it neither exists nor does not exist; both discover the play of Nothingness behind the mere nihility of all tragic humanisms obsessed with a "self."

However, this kind of radical Zen and deconstructionist discourse does not really fit the kind of rhetoric in the destabilizing tropes of Lacan. For an analogy to Lacan, we must return to the Western monotheistic traditions and note a peculiar kind of apophatic mysticism emerging there. The rhetoric of the great Western love-mystics (Bernard of Clairvaux, Teresa of Avila, John of the Cross) may attract a Julia Kristeva with her post-Lacan and anti-Derrida semiotic rhetoric of a subject-in-process in transference love.[24] But all—literally all—that interests Lacan in Teresa of Avila is her jouissance and the excess and radical negations it discloses.[25]

---

23. See Robert Magliola, Derrida on the Mend (West Lafayette, Ind., 1984). This difference may also help to interpret the differences of Lacan and Derrida: on the latter, see Barbara Johnson, "The Frame of Reference: Poe, Lacan, Derrida," in The Critical Difference: Essays in the Contemporary Rhetoric of Reading, ed. Johnson (Baltimore, 1980).

24. Julia Kristeva, Tales of Love, trans. Leon S. Roudiez (New York, 1987).

25. Lacan and the école freudienne, "God and the Jouissance of The Woman," Feminine Sexuality, ed. Juliet Mitchell and Jacqueline Rose, trans. Rose (New York, 1982), pp. 137–49.

But that all is everything and the clue of the radically apophatic, but not Zen, rhetoric of Lacan.

Mystics in prophetic traditions (as all Western monotheisms are) always have problems. Unless they are very cautious in their marginalized place, some prophet (or more likely, some hierarch with prophetic pretensions) will accuse them of betrayal. Where is the God of the prophets in the Godhead-beyond-God of Meister Eckhart? Where are the energetics of Freud's unconscious in the linguistic Unconscious of Lacan? Where is the radically monotheistic God and the responsible self in the apophatic Jewish, Christian, and Muslim mystics? Where is Freud's god Logos and where is the ego in the uncontrollable prose and the unnerving tropes of Lacan? Have the Western apophatic mystics betrayed the prophets for neo-Platonism? Has Lacan betrayed Freud for Hegel and Heidegger?

At first, it may seem that monotheism is still honored by the mystics and a scientific Logos is honored by Lacan. For the mystic will try to reduce the world portrayed in the Bible to its most basic elements (God, world, soul) in order to observe their structural relationships. Mystics almost always have some basic grammar as their first move. Even Buddhists have the language of "dependent originations." Even Eckhart possesses a highly peculiar grammar of analogy.[26] Lacan will also pay his tribute to structural relationships (and, thereby, "science") as his first move. Indeed, he will insist that only Saussure's linguistics (unfortunately not available to Freud) can render scientific the discovery of the unconscious—an unconscious, of course, structured like a language. Every apophatic mystic in the monotheistic prophetic traditions will answer their critics in much the same way: unfortunately, the prophets who wrote our sacred texts did not have available to them a grammar of the structural relationships of God-world-soul; fortunately, this grammar is now available to interpret the text correctly.

If the grammatical-structuralist move is the only move that the mystic makes, then all may be well: as the love-mystics hoped, as religious metaphysicians like Aquinas insist, as the Jungians with their strangely morphological if not structuralist archetypes believe, as all structuralists, from Saussure to Levi-Strauss, find sufficient.

But what if a second move is made? What if the apophatic element in mystical discourse takes a radical turn? Then, as in Pseudo-Dionysius, John Erigena, and Eckhart, the basic structural elements themselves (God-world-soul) dissolve into one another as self-negating, self-dissolving. When Eckhart paradoxically prays, "I pray to God to save me from God," he is not speaking classical prophetic rhetoric of humble submission to the will of God. He is rather apophatically moving. But where? Perhaps,

---

26. On Eckhart, see *Meister Eckhart: The Essential Sermons, Commentaries, Treatises, and Defense*, ed. and trans. Edmund Colledge and Bernard McGinn (New York, 1981). See also John Caputo, *Heidegger and Aquinas: An Essay on Overcoming Metaphysics* (New York, 1982).

after all, into a radical mystical rhetoric of the Other, the "Godhead beyond" the prophets' God? When Eckhart proclaims a vision of "Leben ohne Warum" as a model for the self which is no-self he is far, indeed, from the responsible self of the prophets as well as far from the agapic-erotic self of the Christian love-mystics. When Lacan informs us that "the unconscious is structured like a language" only then to insist that there is no unitary sign since the signifiers and not the signifieds rule (S/s), we are far, indeed, from the "sign" of Saussure and the god *Logos* of the scientific side of Freud. We are somewhere else. Perhaps in the discourse of the Other? Perhaps in the apophatic excess of *jouissance*? Surely not in the ego.

Like Eckhart with his strange appeals to the more orthodox analogical rhetoric for God-language of his fellow Dominican, Thomas Aquinas, Lacan will also occasionally appeal to more orthodox views of the Other. Hence Lacan will appeal to the dialectical rhetoric of the Other in that strangest of orthodox Lutherans, Hegel, and the rhetorical poetics on "Language Speaks" in that oddest of post-Catholic Catholics, Heidegger.[27] In Lacan's rhetoric there speaks, it seems, not only the Unconscious but the Other of the two most significant Greek-Christians of modernity, the Protestant Hegel and the Catholic Heidegger. Both of them, after all, often read as gnomically as Eckhart (whom, not surprisingly, they both respected). Both of them also wanted an end to "theism" and "atheism" alike in favor of an Other who is finally allowed to speak. The orthodox psychoanalytic institutions may expel Lacan as firmly as the papal commission at Avignon condemned certain propositions of Eckhart. Yet both would continue to insist on their higher orthodoxy: for them, only the mystic understands what the prophet really meant for only the mystic knows both the basic structure of the whole and its radically de-structuring actuality.

But even the mystic may eventually find it necessary to adopt a prophetic rhetoric and proclaim the word of the Other. Otherwise, the others in their secure institutions will trivialize and reify the words of the Other once again. If necessary, prophetic actions may follow: leave the official institution, open a new one, close it, and start again is an all too familiar prophetic activity. The careers of Eckhart and Lacan are often as uncannily parallel as their apophatic rhetorics. Neither was interested in either "theism" or "atheism." That quarrel they left to those who did not understand the Other at all. They wanted *jouissance* and the uncanny tropes familiar in the authentic speech of the Other.

The question, "Does Lacan interpret Freud correctly?," therefore, bears remarkable resemblance to the question, "Does the apophatic mystic

27. On Lacan's relationships to Hegel and Heidegger, see the representative studies of William Richardson, Edward Casey, and Antoine Vergote in *Interpreting Lacan*, ed. Joseph H. Smith and William Kerrigan (New Haven, Conn., 1983), pp. 49–223.

Acheronta Movebo

Jean Starobinski

Translated by Françoise Meltzer

It is doubtless appropriate to read *The Interpretation of Dreams* according to the image of the journey which Sigmund Freud describes in a letter to Wilhelm Fliess:

> The whole thing is planned on the model of an imaginary walk. First comes the dark wood of the authorities (who cannot see the trees), where there is no clear view and it is easy to go astray. Then there is a cavernous defile through which I lead my readers—my specimen dream with its peculiarities, its details, its indiscretions and its bad jokes—and then, all at once, the high ground and the open prospect and the question: "Which way do you want to go?"[1]

This walk has nothing of the nonchalant about it. Rather, it is strewn with tests and trials, as is usually the case in the "myth of the hero" or of the "conquistador," which we know played a major role in Freud's thought and in that of his disciples. The progress, in epic poetry, moves toward a discovery, the founding of a city, by means of difficult stages and combats. Every "discourse" capable of attaining a goal distant from

---

This article is the revised and expanded version of an essay which appeared with the same title in *L'Ecrit du Temps* 11 (Paris, 1986). It is part of a preface to the Italian edition of the *Traumdeutung*, which will appear soon (Rizzoli, B.U.R.).

1. Sigmund Freud to Wilhelm Fliess, 6 Aug. 1899, Freud, *The Origins of Psychoanalysis: Letters to Wilhelm Fliess, Drafts and Notes, 1887–1902*, ed. Marie Bonaparte, Anna Freud, and Ernst Kris, trans. James Strachey (New York, 1954), p. 290.

its prolegomena finds its appropriate metaphor in the hero's progress, or in the voyage of initiation. Discursivity then becomes the intellectual equivalent of the epic's trajectory. At the time of its publication, Freud found his book insufficiently probing, and imperfect in its discursivity. He criticized himself for having failed to link properly his arguments (*Beweisführung*). Doubt was momentarily cast on the achievement of the main goal. . . . But such severity was not to persist.

But one can also read the work by discerning its framing devices. Several authors mentioned in the first chapter reappear at the work's conclusion. Such a return is far from fortuitous; it is the result of an extremely well-calculated strategy. Another framing system which has been noticed by many readers is the one, shortly before the end of the book, which returns to a line from Virgil that Freud had placed as an epigraph on the title page: *Flectere si nequeo superos, Acheronta movebo.* This line, because of its repetition at two crucial points in the book, traces its message in the form of an emblem. When it breaks in, it makes explicit that the dream mechanism is the return of the repressed:

> In waking life the suppressed material in the mind is prevented from finding expression and is cut off from internal perception *owing to the fact that the contradictions present in it are eliminated*—one side being disposed of in favour of the other; but during the night, under the sway of an impetus towards the construction of compromises, this suppressed material finds methods and means of forcing its way into consciousness.

> *Flectere si nequeo superos, Acheronta movebo.*[2]

The line from Virgil does not belong to the category of dreams to be interpreted. Rather, it is an interpretive illustration, an imaged equivalent of the theory that has just been introduced.

2. Freud, *The Interpretation of Dreams*, ed. and trans. Strachey (New York, 1965), p. 647; my emphasis. The Latin is translated in n. 1 on that page of Freud's text: "If I cannot bend the High Powers, I will move the Infernal Regions." All further references to this work, abbreviated *I*, will be included in the text. Another framing device is created by the theme of the prophetic dream, discussed at the outset of the first chapters and taken up again, with the ambivalence of denial and concession, in the final paragraph of the book.

Jean Starobinski, professor emeritus at the University of Geneva, has devoted studies to Montaigne, Diderot, Rousseau, Saussure, and modern French poets. As an M.D., he is familiar with psychoanalysis and participates in the editorial board of *La Nouvelle Revue de Psychanalyse* (Paris). Some of his recent research deals with the history of melancholia; his most recent books are *Montaigne in Motion* (1985) and *Rousseau* (forthcoming). He was awarded the Balzan Prize in 1984.

This moment in the text is important because it gives rise, in 1909, to an insertion immediately after the Latin line of verse. The added sentence, which became famous, is printed in italics; it also contains a Latin phrase. It is obviously a solemn statement. The subject of this sentence returns to the very title of the book: "*The interpretation of dreams is the Via regia which leads to the knowledge of the unconscious in psychic life*" (*I*, p. 647; translation modified). As is clear, here the theme of the progressing march—moreover on a "royal road"—comes to be a part of the framing device. We have come to the culminating point, from which all ground already covered is contemplated in retrospect as a triumphal march toward knowledge.

The line from Virgil was charged with such a considerable meaning in Freud's eyes that it asked for an impressive underlining. From a letter to Fliess of 4 December 1896, Freud, it is known, wanted already to keep this line in reserve for an epigraph to a chapter on symptom formation (see *I*, p. 647 n. 1). In another letter of 17 July 1899, the line is referred to as a "hint at repression."[3] In a note added to the 1925 edition, Freud declares that this line "is intended to picture [*andeuten . . . soll*] the efforts of the repressed instinctual impulses" (*I*, p. 647 n. 1). The line of verse then works in tandem with interpretation (*deuten*), but obliquely, through application, as indicated by the prefix *an-*. In fact, it is not the dream that it interprets, but Freud's theory as he articulated it. The line from Virgil's epic was available, predestined—perhaps predestined to serve as the model upon which Freud was to construct or fortify his theory of the repressed, and of the return of the repressed.

We know what passage from Virgil Freud had to analyze for his final high school examination. It was a passage which he had been lucky enough to read "for pleasure"[4] shortly before the exam: the beginning of the Nisus and Euryalus episode.[5] One might see, as an extension of this text, the tracing of Freud's friendship and heroic rivalry with Fleischl, with Fliess, and so on . . . We can surmise (with, it is true, insufficient proof) that Freud read the *Aeneid* in its entirety and that he remembered it, keeping the memory, more or less accurately, within him. In this regard it is unnecessary to speak of "cryptomnesia," as Freud did in reference to Börne's text on free writing.[6]

3. Freud, *Origins*, p. 286.

4. See Freud to Emil Fluss, 16 June 1873, *Letters of Sigmund Freud, 1873–1939*, ed. Ernst L. Freud, trans. Tania and James Stern (London, 1961), p. 21.

5. See Virgil, *Aeneid*, bk. 9, ll. 176–223; all further references to this work, abbreviated *A* and with book and line numbers, will be included in the text. References to the translation by Robert Fitzgerald (New York, 1980), abbreviated *F* and with book and line numbers, will also be incorporated in the text.

6. See Freud, "Zur Vorgeschichte der analytischen Technik," *Gesammelte Werke*, 18 vols. (Frankfurt-am-Main, 1961–68), 12:309–12.

Virgil, at first glance, does not seem to belong to that category of authors who, like Shakespeare or Goethe, furnished Freud with his most frequent literary references. Let us say that, with the exception of a limited number of quotations, Virgil must rather be regarded as an integral part of the Roman horizon, so important to Freud's personal imagination. Whether one considers the psychic obstacle which delayed the first voyage to Rome; the interest in Hannibal, the hero who endangered Roman power; the attraction, because of the Pompeian setting, of Wilhelm Jensen's *Gradiva,* proof is abundant. Suffice it to recall the way in which, at the beginning of *Civilization and Its Discontents,* Freud strives to give a pictorial equivalent for the "conservation of psychic images." Instead of conjuring up layers of ruins, of crumbled plaster, or of old reconstructions, Freud suggests the "fantasy" of a Rome in which all the monuments—even the most ancient—have remained intact:

> This would mean that in Rome the palaces of the Caesars and the Septizonium of Septimus Severus would still be rising to their old height on the Palatine and that the castle of S. Angelo would still be carrying on its battlements the beautiful statues which graced it until the siege by the Goths, and so on.[7]

It is known, moreover, that for Freud, Rome is a place which gives rise to ambivalence. Another line from the *Aeneid,* cited in *The Psychopathology of Everyday Life,*[8] attests to Freud's at least divided sympathies between the founding hero, Aeneas, and Dido, the abandoned woman. Dido is a Phoenician, which makes her a "Semite." At her death, Dido prophesies:

> Exoriare aliquis nostris ex ossibus ultor
> [A, 4:625]
>
> . . . Rise up from my bones, avenging spirit!
> [F, 4:869]

Anzieu properly emphasizes the importance of the journey to the Underworld in book 4 of the *Aeneid,* and of the Virgilian memories which abound inside Freud's consciousness in 1896:

> Like Aeneas, Freud has lost his father. And the mourning work, which makes him rediscover the image of the dead father in the deepest part of himself, no doubt did not fail to remind him that

7. Freud, *Civilization and Its Discontents, The Standard Edition of the Complete Psychological Works of Sigmund Freud,* ed. and trans. Strachey, 24 vols. (London, 1953–74), 21:70.
8. See Freud, *The Psychopathology of Everyday Life, Standard Edition,* 6:9.

it was in order to consult his father Anchises that Aeneas descended into Hades.[9]

In the progressing march of the epic, the descent toward the dead (unless, as in the *Odyssey*, there occurs the rise of the dead, moving up toward the hero who will interrogate them) constitutes a retrogression, or a regression, to use Freud's term. It also constitutes the condition for a more self-assured march toward a future goal, the true nature of which can only have been revealed by the voice of the paternal shade. The descent into Hades (the downward march, the catabasis) arrives at the forbidden threshold, in order to hear—and even to see—*that which will be* from the oracular mouths of *those who are no longer*. The reappearance of dead companions (Misenus, Palinurus, Deiphobus) permits the completion of the narration of previous events: it is analepsis. The words of Anchises unfold Roman history until the death of Marcellus: they form a prolepsis. From this double narrative dimension, Freud will give prominence to analepsis. In Virgil, analepsis retells the death of seafaring comrades; in Freud, who evokes dead colleagues, analepsis goes back to the earliest scenarios of the personal past. The work of analysis is anamnesic and may have been sustained by the model of Virgilian catabasis—on the condition that there be a fairly complete suppression of prophetic prolepsis, which a truly scientific procedure of psychic analysis refrains from accomplishing.

If Freud reread the sixth book of the *Aeneid* at the time of the editing of *The Interpretation of Dreams* and of the correspondence with Fliess, and even later, then we may suppose that many passages struck a chord in him. Anzieu mentions several such passages (incest punished by eternal torment, the waters of Lethe). Other passages might be added: just before the shade of Dido appears in the "fields of tears," inhabited by those who suffered from love, Virgil mentions "Caeneus, / A young man once, a woman now, and turned / Again by fate into the older form" (*F*, 6:603–5). Bisexuality is here represented as the central element of a destiny (but Freud was equally familiar with Ovid's *Metamorphoses* and the story of Tiresias). In the middle of the entryway which leads to the world below, "a shadowy giant elm / spreads ancient boughs, her ancient arms where dreams, / False dreams, the old tale goes, beneath each leaf / Cling and are numberless" (*F*, 6:386–89). The entrance by the place of dreams, like the exit by the ivory gate, through which "false dreams are sent . . . by the ghosts to the upper world" (*F*, 6:1214–15), tightly links the enigma of the dream to the quest for truth and promised glories . . . But I will go no further down this path which risks becoming a Freudian

9. Didier Anzieu, *L'auto-analyse de Freud et la decouverte de la psychanalyse*, 2 vols. (Paris, 1975), 1:590–91; on dreams of Rome, see pp. 250–88. See also Marthe Robert, *D'Oedipe à Moïse: Freud et la conscience juive* (Paris, 1974), p. 154.

interpretation of the Virgilian myth. As we have seen, the line twice cited in *The Interpretation of Dreams,* each time in a position of strength, is put forth as a condensed and figural interpretation of repression and symptom theory themselves. The quotation uses a cultural model in order to fully explicate the repression theory. It urges us to proceed along a Virgilian interpretation of Freudian knowledge, since the Freudian text itself establishes an isomorphism, or at least an occasional equivalence, between myth and psychological theory.

Flectere si nequeo . . . even if this had appeared in the epigraph alone, it would have easily allowed for an ironic biographical reading—the one precisely suggested by H. E. Ellenberger: "This motto can be interpreted as an allusion to the fate of the repressed drives, but also as referring to Freud's failure to obtain academic recognition and his revolutionizing the science of the mind."[10] Carl Schorske points out that the same line from Virgil was used as an epigraph by Ferdinand Lassalle in a pamphlet, and goes on to analyze its political significance in the context of Lassalle's work. But he adds that the threat addressed to "those above" is transferred by Freud "from the realm of politics to that of the psyche."[11]

The multivalence of Virgil's line cannot be overemphasized. For the modern reader, it is a dynamic model. Or it can be seen as an allegory which attests to the capacity of mythology to constitute a form which can in turn be inhabited by contents belonging to varying orders of reality. In its various modern applications, the epic text will acquire the value of an explanatory trope. But the trope, even while attesting to the similarity of one type of thought, after having helped psychoanalysis to represent itself, is then conversely susceptible to being absorbed into the field of psychoanalytic thought. The latter will claim (and how could this be refuted?) that the epic text is the bearer of a psychic movement which, like the dream that is recounted, assumes the "figurability" of unconscious thought.[12]

Virgil's line must be approached both from within its internal development and from the perspective of its contextual relations.

10. Henri F. Ellenberger, *The Discovery of the Unconscious: The History and Evolution of Dynamic Psychiatry* (New York, 1970), p. 452.

11. Carl E. Schorske, *Fin-de-siècle Vienna: Politics and Culture* (New York, 1979), p. 200. In a letter to Werner Achelis, Freud confirms acquiring the Virgilian "motto" from Lassalle. Lassalle had used it at the beginning of a political work on the war in Italy (see Freud to Achelis, 30 Jan. 1927, *Letters of Sigmund Freud,* p. 376). See also Walter Schönau, *Sigmund Freuds Prosa; Literarische Elemente seines Stils* (Stuttgart, 1969), esp. pp. 53–89. He makes interesting remarks on the different epigraphs Freud used, and on the fairly numerous commentaries which they inspired. Overall, it is the Freudian context which is considered, and not the context of the borrowings themselves. Of course, lines which have "resonance" stand out, become proverbial, and circulate widely. All the more reason to return to the original material.

12. "Le principal mérite de Freud est d'avoir 'pensé à la façon des mythes' " (Claude Lévi-Strauss, *La Potière jalouse* [Paris, 1985], p. 251).

It appears in the seventh book of the *Aeneid,* in Juno's furious speech, that enraged diatribe of sorrow. Enemy of Aeneas and of the Trojans, Juno has already imposed all of her destructive powers upon them. She has unleashed Aeolus and his savage winds; but the storm did not prevail. She favored Dido, who wanted to keep hold of the seafaring hero; but Aeneas tore himself away from that love to follow Jupiter's command and to take sail for Hesperia. The Trojans landed in Italy and hid themselves in the Tiber's bed (*in alveo*). Now marriage plans with the daughter of Latinus are announced; and the Fates promise the progeny of Aeneas a right of legitimate possession on the Italian soil. But Juno, the hostile pursuer, will not tire of putting new obstacles in the hero's path—Turnus and the Rutuli, to begin with . . . (I am purposely using Vladimir Propp's terminology in order to underline the functions of various characters, since the epic and the folktale can be submitted to the same morphological analysis.) The persecuting goddess insists that the ineluctable workings of the Fates be paid for by a bloodbath. But the reader of the *Aeneid* already knows from the epic's preamble that the Trojan project is successful, and knows too of the lineage that will make Rome the heiress of Troy. Jupiter assures Venus, mother and protector of the hero, that this will be so. The future has already been decided upon; the "empire without end" will be Rome's and, after centuries of war, "the Gates of War will . . . be shut" (*F,* 1:375, 394–95).

Juno, too, knows this. But she is loyal to her hatred. She will not be able to prevent what Jupiter *wants,* nor what he *knows* from the Fates, who are his superiors. She is herself warned of what Jupiter foresees, and of what he declares from the beginning of the poem: that Juno "will mend her ways" in the centuries to come, and that, in harmony with her husband, she will protect the "lords of the world, the toga-bearing Romans" (*F,* 1:378, 379). The line Freud quotes is the one in which Juno, in order to make trouble for the descendants of Venus, announces the advent of a *delaying* action. The lines which immediately follow are explicit:

> It will not be permitted me—so be it—
> To keep the man from rule in Italy;
> By changeless fate Lavinia waits, his bride.
> And yet to drag it out, to pile delay
> Upon delay in these great matters—that
> I can do.
>
> [*F,* 7:427–32]

The line cited by Freud assumes a failure ("I cannot bend those above") and proclaims that there will be recourse to a power from below—the Acheron—the delaying powers of which (through wars and massacres) will not, by the goddess' own admission, prevent the ultimate triumph of the hero. Warned of her final powerlessness, the goddess wants to exhaust all resources and assistance. She who could abandon nothing, "who nerved [herself] / To leave no risk unventured" (*F*, 7:420–21), she who could turn herself against all things in all things (*memet in omnia verti* [*A*, 7:309])—for her now to be vanquished by Aeneas is intolerable. If one considers that *verti* corresponds to the Greek *trepesthai*, one can say that Juno multiplies the *versions* or *tropes* of her hatred, but in vain. She must now resort to extremes. The sentence preceding the line cited by Freud also begins with a hypothesis: "Quod si mea numina non sunt / Magna satis, dubitem haud equidem implorare, quod usquam est (If my powers fall short, / I need not falter over asking help / Wherever help may lie [*F*, 7:423–25])." This is a peculiar euphemism which conceals, beneath the vagueness of a place "somewhere," the figure of the destructive Fury. She will be referred to by her proper name—"Allecto, / Grief's drear mistress" (*F*, 7:444–45)—only in the narrative which follows the goddess' words. Similarly, by designating the Acheron more precisely, Juno again uses a metonymic process (the place instead of its resident) as if to avoid pronouncing a name too terrible to utter. And when Juno, descended to earth, lifts Allecto up from the "infernal shadows," it is again without naming her, but by means of a periphrasis. That is how the goddess speaks to the one who will become the executor of her designs: she will call Allecto "Daughter of Night" (*virgo sata Nocte*). She designates her by her obscure origins, or attributes "a thousand names" to her and "a thousand ways of wounding" (*F*, 7:461, 462). The goddess employs every means for designating without naming. Saussure might perhaps have discovered the name of Allecto as a hypogram hidden in the now famous line:

> *Flectere si nequeo Superos, Acheronta movebo*
> LECT   O   A

But one can as easily read the phonemes of AENEAS here.

Sower of hatred, herself an object of hatred for her father Pluto and her two sisters the Furies, Allecto is a creature in which so much violence is centered that it makes her multiform and plural: "her myriad / Faces, ... her savage looks, her head / Alive and black with snakes" (*F*, 7:448–50). "Dripping venom deadly as the Gorgon's," she has concentrated within her an overabundance of hostile forces and is thus akin to the Medusa (*F*, 7:468). She detaches one of the serpents from her "gloomy tresses" (*F*, 7:476), and it slinks over the bosom of Amata, wife of Latinus, to slide all over her body. At first, the snake's venom which flows in Amata's veins acts as an infection (*F*, 7:490) which she however does not feel (*necdum percepit*). But the effect of the poison does not remain imperceptible; it grows with a craving for vengeance. And now the delirium of the Bacchantes takes up the other women with Amata. Virgil describes the whirlwind and shouting which characteristically overtake all those possessed by the Dionysiac frenzy (in which late nineteenth-century readers thought they recognized the breakdown of major hysteria) . . . Allecto then appears to Turnus in a dream, in the guise of an old priestess. She informs him that the Trojans are going to carry off Lavinia, whom Latinus and Amata had promised him in marriage. Turnus, still in his dream, speaks mockingly of Allecto, who "hurl[s] a torch and plant[s] it / Below the man's chest, smoking with hellish light" (*F*, 7:629–30), and reveals herself to him in the entire extent of her horror. Drenched in sweat, Turnus awakens terrified. Once again, but more brutally, Allecto has burned her way into a human breast. I only mention these developments in the narrative to emphasize the sequence of active beings or powers: Juno, Allecto, the serpent, the venom, and Amata in the first series; Juno, Allecto, the old priestess, then the torches and Turnus in the second. The vengeful work of Juno, in both cases, unfolds through a succession of intermediary agents, culminating in an exterior flame which will finally propagate an external violence: war. War is the result which Juno's hatred wished to provoke, but which she indirectly determines by the numerous secondary causes which relay, translate, and transmit her furor. In the first book, she had turned to air and water, to hurricane and storm. In her last attempt (book 7), she appeals to two other elements: to the power of deepest earth and of fire; to Pluto's daughter, carrier of torches.

Flectere si nequeo Superos, Acheronta movebo.

Virgil's line is organized in the form of a free chiasm: (a) verbal syntagm (*flectere si nequeo*), (b) "mythic" complement (*Superos*), (*b*) "mythic" complement (*Acheronta*), (*a*) verb (*movebo*). The two parts of the chiasm allow for inverted structures. The first inverts the conjunction (*si*) and one part of the verbal syntagm. Following Latin usage, the infinitive of action (*flectere*) precedes the present tense of powerlessness (*nequeo*) which governs it. The second part of the chiasm inverts, according to the grammatical rule, the verb (*movebo*) and the object (*Acheronta*). The chiasm and its inversions are like the figuration of the unrealistic but desired "bending." And the contiguity of *Superos Acheronta* marks the subversion of the order which maintains heaven and hell at a distance from each other. The chiasmatic arrangement, moreover, emphasizes and accentuates a double antithesis: the opposition between the altitude at which "those above" reside, and the subterranean abyss where the Acheron's whirlpool boils with mud (see *F*, 6:404–7). The second opposition is between the present tense of impotence (*nequeo*) and the future tense of putting into action (*movebo*). The progression of the line is extraordinary. The first three feet and the beginning of the fourth, in which impotence becomes total with the inflexibility of "those above," make all the more striking the rapid dynamic of movement announced in seven syllables by a verb and its object. But what a verb, and what an object! The verb produces a displacement, from what is impossible (in the form of a hypothetical concession), to the act projected into the future, extracting from below that opaque mass that gouges into the very depths themselves. "I shall lift up the Acheron"—this does not only mean, as I first suggested, a metonymy designating the Fury Allecto by her legendary habitat. The "literal" sense must also be taken into account, the act of moving must be understood to mean moving the mythic river itself, in its entirety. Juno subverts the very order of the world when she changes the course of the river, whose first letter A to its final a make it seem to arch back into itself (even though, as Virgil knew, the river actually spilled into the Cocytus). Once Allecto has completed her evil rounds, Juno sends her back to Hades. Allecto rushes into the Underworld through "an abyss that opens jaws of death / Where Acheron burst through" (*F*, 7:781–82). Even though the valley of the Amsanctus is a natural site, everything seems to indicate that Juno has succeeded in her act: the Acheron has been displaced, as if lifted up.

It should be added that in the *Aeneid*, several other references to the Acheron are tightly associated with dreams and with paternal figures (and such an association is perhaps not lost on Freud, beginning with his high school education). As we have seen (at the opening of book 6), the great tree whose leaves shelter dreams (*somnia*) is located at the start of the road leading to the Acheron. Early in book 7, King Latinus goes into the deep forest to consult the oracles of Faunus, his divine father:

> Here a priest brought gifts,
> Here in the stillness of the night he lay
> On skins taken from sheep of sacrifice
> And courted slumber. Many visions came
> Before his eyes and strangely on the air;
> He heard their different voices, and took part
> In colloquies of gods, in undergloom
> Addressing the grim powers of Acheron.
> [*F*, 7:113–20]

The voice of the dead father tells Latinus, ritually stretched out on the skins of sacrificed lambs, that he will have a "foreign son-in-law." Such "incubation" in the forest is determined by the anticipation of the prophetic dream—a conception which Freud calls "pre-scientific" in the first chapter of his book, but which he will leave an open-ended question until the final paragraph.

A mythical character, then, one of the great figures of Olympus, speaks in the first person in Virgil's verse. Given the application Freud makes of this in his own conception of the dream or of the symptom, *who* then could speak in the same way inside his own text? Most probably it is that "dream-thought" which thinks from inside the conscious subject. A neuter subject, like the one in the sentence immediately preceding the citation. I will attempt a literal translation: "That which has been psychically pushed down (*das seelisch Unterdrückte*) and which, in waking life, has been prevented from achieving expression by the antagonistic presence of contradictions, and has been cut off from internal perception—all of this will, in nocturnal life and under the aegis of compromise formations, find the ways and the means to penetrate forcefully into consciousness." Virgil's line, through an emblematic remythologization, allows for interpreting what Freud describes as an impersonal process as a personal discourse. Juno says, "I cannot, *nequeo*." And we read in Freud, "That which has been prevented . . . that which has been excised." *Nequeo*, that verb of incapacity, is still an active verb. But Freud uses a subject which is grammatically both neuter and passive (*das Unterdrückte*) and conjugated in the passive (*welches . . . gehindert . . . und abgeschnitten wurde*). But let us note that the passive is limited to the subject of the clause and to the relative clause which clarifies it (we might say that it is limited to a nominal syntagm). When the main clause appears, Freud shifts to a doubly active verb: *find . . . in order to penetrate . . .*

The parallelism with the *movebo* of the Latin text becomes striking once the transposition from the third person into the first has been accepted. There is nothing particularly astonishing about the announcement of a future deed (*movebo*) from the mouth of a divinity. But in Freud's phrase, what is surprising is that the neuter-passive ("that-which-has-been-pushed-down," the repressed, *das Unterdrückte*) should suddenly become, grammatically, an active subject which *finds* and *penetrates*. What had been the object of the repression becomes, on the clausal axis, the active subject engaged in a search and in movement. We cannot fail to perceive the animistic character of those terms. But one discovers that such an animization was already secretly at work, since the neuter thing, having been *repressed*, is, in Freud's words, rendered unable to *express itself*. (The German terms oppose each other as well, through their prefixes. They refer to the pressure exerted, one downward, the other outward: *unter*-drücken, *Aus*-druck. A simple thing, a mere object, is not "expressed.") In this sentence, the neuter is nothing other than the chain of driving forces (*Triebkräfte*) mentioned earlier in the text. In the logic of Freud's sentence, the word *Ausdruck* corresponds to the *flectere* of the Latin sentence. As to "those above," the inflexible ones, they too are present in Freud's sentence in the form of the implicit power pushing downward, repressing, opposing. This power, as Freud has also told us previously, is the censure exerted by the "secondary system." The intrapsychical conflict, then, as it is described by Freud, is perfectly suited to be allegorized as a type of conflict between divine *characters*. We know that the beginning of chapter 7 had already sketched out a quantitative model of this conflict. Freud's sentence is located *halfway* between the line from Virgil which follows and the quantitative models which had served to establish the existence of the two systems, primary and secondary. In any case, let us note that even though the secondary system is superimposed *upon* the primary one, Freud refuses all spatial schematizations. The "processes," the systems, have no localization. The temporal connections are considered more important: the system called secondary is posterior to the organization of the one called primary. The repressing force is an aftereffect. (But in mythology, too, "those above" belong to a later generation, having established their reign by repressing the Titan upheaval, and so on.)

The Acheron is a river. And in Freudian psychology, in the *Outline of Psycho-Analysis* as in the seventh chapter of *The Interpretation of Dreams,* the predominant metaphorical system is that of the flow of "quantities," of the "current" of excitation, of the "breakthroughs," of the "drive" opposed to resistance, of the "progressive path" and of the "regressive path," and so on. (To this, of course, can be added metaphors of a different order: refraction, virtual images, translations, traces, associations.) The image of flux was perceived as adequate, and this is no doubt one of the major reasons that Virgil's line found its way into Freud's text. It was an image which stimulated the intuition of a resemblance. These homologies can be pursued to include the concept of investment, or the later notion of the libido, it too "fluidicized." But such substantial and dynamic homologies, once established, leave the question with which we started unanswered: why did Freud think that the line from Virgil would act as a complement to the interpretation of his own thought, a complement to be offered to the "cultured reader"? In what way may it have played a role in the development of Freud's thought?

We must turn our attention to the final verb, *movebo,* "I will put in motion." Here there is the formulation of an intention, the source of movement and of displacement . . . But is it enough to leave it at that? What can be more general than movement? From antiquity onward, are not dreams already described as moving images? Freud was aware of this, and in his first chapter he cites a sentence from Cicero: "Maximeque reliquiae rerum earum *moventur* in animis et agitantur de quibus vigilantes aut cogitavimus aut egimus" (*I*, p. 43; my emphasis). Cicero's *reliquiae* will become Freud's *Tagesreste.*

For Virgil, to move is also to unfold. In the first book, Jupiter, before revealing the future to Venus, makes an announcement: "*Volvens fatorum arcana movebo*" (*A,* 1:262) ("now let me speak of him [Aeneas], / . . . Unfolding secret fated things to come—" [*F,* 1:352, 354]). We have seen that what Juno puts into motion when she makes Allecto emerge from the depths of the Acheron is a series of acts accomplished by a series of agents. Thus begins a long narrative chain, the result being the adversaries which grow in number to confront Aeneas and his small tribe of conquerors. Juno impels movement with a series of delaying tactics: she indirectly kindles the enemy's wrath, and she lays traps everywhere. The hero, having surmounted so many trials, will be all the more glorious for them. He and his kinsmen will have paid abundantly enough to have earned, in time, the empire to be given to their descendants. It is an unavoidable fact that Juno and the adversity she creates are the midwives of the narrative itself. Without them, there would be no epic; and the poet would have been able to sing neither of the "arms" nor of "the man."

First in the theory, then in the cure, what distinguishes Freud from his predecessors is the narrativization of the psychological events considered necessary to an understanding of a "case," and to the "recollection of meaning" (Ricoeur). Such a narrativization, in practice, is produced by deferred action only, once the fragments of the analysis, which are obtained in a jumbled order, are put end to end and form a satisfactory sequence. It is a narrativization which in theory multiplies the obstacles between a masked hero, whose name is Desire, and the gratification—more often than not substitutive—with which he must content himself. As he goes down his road, having failed to arrive by a direct route, he will have to change faces or masks. And he will have to make strange alliances, foil traps laid out before him, avoid imprisonment in the dungeons of perversion . . . The dreamwork, until secondary revision, will follow such a path, all the while inscribing an earlier story as well—that of the birth of desire. And to this will be added (since the dream lives on in the waking words addressed to the analyst) a post-history: that of the transference. Freud, to be sure, refuses all allegorization. Each individual has his own story, even if psychology admits to general truths concerning sexual stages or to "instincts and their vicissitudes." In *The Interpretation of Dreams* and, more precisely, in the sentence preceding the line from Virgil, the narrativization is proclaimed in the clearest way possible: "under the sway of an impetus towards the construction of compromises, this suppressed material finds *methods and means of forcing its way* into consciousness" (*I*, p. 647; my emphasis). In Virgil, these "methods" and "means" comprised Allecto's path from the depths of the Acheron; the serpent she detached from her hair and threw into Amata's breast; the poison which coursed through the queen's veins and the madness to which it drove her . . .

There can never be such a long story when what dominates is the short-acting causality of the reflex arc or organic excitation. Most doctors around 1900 did not see beyond such weak tales of interaction and, even if they could recognize desire and the unconscious without much difficulty, they thought that these were capable of finding rapid gratification. With Freud, the "story" is lengthened, even though he did not reject the reflex arc as a point of departure. It is the "story" which can take account of the subject's biography. And it is by means of the pathways of myth, and through the behavior of Oedipus, Hamlet, Juno, and perhaps even Allecto, that psychoanalysis has developed the story of the soul, and its own story.

*   *   *

The Virgilian *movere* condenses, in a particularly opportune fashion, the double sense of *movement* which Freudian thought both assumes and presupposes. It is at once a physical movement and a dramatic plot. It is the play of an energy flow and of a destiny. To use the language of psychoanalysis itself, we might say that, in a manner which first appears provocative, *The Interpretation of Dreams* brought about for twentieth-century man the conjunction (first "gratifying" and then conforming to his desires) of a double language: that of science and that of a cultural heritage; that of the rational superego and that of "archaic" affectivity. We might say, somewhat schematically, that what is at issue is a bivalent language. Or, if I may myself use a notion which Fliess gave to Freud, a bisexed language.

In a well-known passage from one of the *Studies in Hysteria*, Freud had asserted:

> It still strikes me myself as strange that the case histories I write should read like short stories and that, as one might say, they lack the serious stamp of science. I must console myself with the reflection that the nature of the subject is evidently responsible for this, rather than any preference of my own. The fact is that local diagnosis and electrical reactions lead nowhere in the study of hysteria, whereas a detailed description of mental processes such as we are accustomed to find in the works of imaginative writers enables me, with the use of a few psychological formulas, to obtain at least some kind of insight into the course of that affection.[13]

---

13. Freud, *Studies in Hysteria, Standard Edition*, 2:160–61. The writings of the Swiss novelist C. F. Meyer have an important place in Freud's letters to Fliess. Some of Meyer's texts inspire in Freud an attentive psychological interpretation.

Index